KIERKEGAARD AS A CHRISTIAN THINKER

C. Stephen Evans and Paul Martens
General Editors

The KIERKEGAARD AS A CHRISTIAN THINKER series seeks to promote and enrich an understanding of Søren Kierkegaard as a Christian thinker who, despite his many critiques of Christendom, self-consciously worked within the Christian tradition and in the service of Christianity. Volumes in the series may approach Kierkegaard's relationship to Christianity historically or topically, philosophically or theologically. Some will attempt to illuminate Kierkegaard's thought by examining his works through the lens of Christian faith; others will use Kierkegaard's Christian insights to address contemporary problems and competing non-Christian perspectives.

That Søren Kierkegaard profoundly influenced nineteenth- and twentieth-century theology and philosophy is not in doubt. The direction, extent, and value of his influence, however, have always been hotly contested. For example, in the early decades of the twentieth century, Swiss theologians Karl Barth and Emil Brunner and German theologian Dietrich Bonhoeffer all acknowledged deep debts to Kierkegaard, debts that would echo through the theological debates of the entire century. In spite of this, by the middle of the twentieth century, Kierkegaard was also hailed (or cursed) as a father of existentialism and nihilism because of his appropriation by Heidegger, Sartre, and others. At the same time, however, he was beginning to become the reveille for a return to true Christianity in North America through the translating efforts of Walter Lowrie and David Swenson. At the beginning of the twenty-first century, Kierkegaard's legacy is once again being seriously and rigorously debated.

While acknowledging and affirming the postmodern appreciation of elements of Kierkegaard's thought (such as irony, indirect communication, and pseudonymity), this series aims to engage Kierkegaard as a Christian thinker who self-consciously worked as a Christian in the service of Christianity. And, as the current discussion crosses the traditional boundaries of philosophy and theology, this series will necessarily do the same. What these volumes all share, however, is the task of articulating Kierkegaard's continuities with, challenges to, and resources for Christianity today. It is our hope that, in this way, this series will deepen and enrich the manifold contemporary debates concerning Kierkegaard and his legacy.

KIERKEGAARD'S CONCEPT OF FAITH

Merold Westphal

WILLIAM B. EERDMANS PUBLISHING COMPANY
GRAND RAPIDS, MICHIGAN / CAMBRIDGE, U.K.

Published 2014 by

Wm. B. Eerdmans Publishing Co.

2140 Oak Industrial Drive N.E., Grand Rapids, Michigan 49505 /

P.O. Box 163, Cambridge CB3 9PU U.K.

www.eerdmans.com

Printed in the United States of America

20 19 18 17 16 15 14   7 6 5 4 3 2 1

Library of Congress Cataloging-in-Publication Data

Westphal, Merold.

Kierkegaard's concept of faith / Merold Westphal.

pages   cm. — (Kierkegaard as a Christian thinker)

ISBN 978-0-8028-6806-0 (pbk.: alk. paper)

1. Kierkegaard, Søren, 1813-1855. 2. Faith.   I. Title.

BX4827.K5W47   2014

234´.23 — dc23

2014008817

Unless otherwise noted, Scripture quotations are from the New Revised Standard Version of the Bible, copyright © 1989 by the Division of Christian Education of the National Council of the Churches of Christ in the U.S.A., and used by permission.

Contents

v

CONTENTS

Foreword

The publication of any new book by Merold Westphal is an event worth celebrating. For several decades Westphal has been one of the foremost philosophers writing about Kierkegaard, Hegel, and philosophy of religion in general, as well as about such contemporary continental figures as Heidegger and Levinas. We think *Kierkegaard's Concept of Faith* is especially noteworthy, however, and we are delighted it will appear in the KIERKEGAARD AS A CHRISTIAN THINKER series.

The book initially distinguishes itself as clearly the product of a lifetime of reading and study of Kierkegaard. Westphal not only grasps the nuances of Kierkegaard's complex and diverse authorship, but also knows the secondary literature well. The erudition the book embodies is worn lightly, however. The book is written so clearly that it could well serve as an introduction to Kierkegaard's thought for a thoughtful reader, especially for one who wishes to take Kierkegaard's Christian faith seriously. Westphal begins with one of Kierkegaard's earliest and best-known pseudonymous books, *Fear and Trembling,* and then moves to the important "middle" works attributed to the pseudonym Johannes Climacus, before concluding with some close readings of the later writings of the "super-Christian" character of anti-Climacus. The reader thus is initiated into several of the most representative and important writings from Kierkegaard's entire corpus. This allows for a clear overview of both the continuities and the developments in Kierkegaard's authorship.

A second element that distinguishes this book is the commitment Westphal shows to the important Kierkegaardian maxim that truth must be edifying. Westphal does not merely give us an academic treatise on faith, an "objective" portrait drawn from a detached standpoint. Rather, the book is edifying from beginning to end. Or at least it can be and will be edifying for the right kind of reader, precisely the kind of reader Kierkegaard himself hoped for.

Only a scholar who has really mastered a corpus of writings can write so clearly about them as Westphal has here done with Kierkegaard. And only a scholar who himself provides a model of committed, Christian scholarship can write a book that manages to be both "rigorous" and "edifying," as anti-Climacus says Christian scholarship should be in the Preface to *The Sickness unto Death*.

Merold Westphal was a teacher of one of us, and both of us have profited hugely from his writings on Kierkegaard and on so much else. We do not agree with every claim made in the book, and Westphal would surely be disappointed if we did. But we can say, with gratitude and affection, that this is the kind of book we aspire to be able to write ourselves.

C. STEPHEN EVANS
PAUL MARTENS

Sigla

BA   *The Book on Adler,* trans. Howard V. Hong and Edna H. Hong. Princeton: Princeton University Press, 1998.

CA   *The Concept of Anxiety,* trans. Howard V. Hong and Edna H. Hong. Princeton: Princeton University Press, 1980.

CD   *Christian Discourses* and *The Crisis and a Crisis in the Life of an Actress,* trans. Howard V. Hong and Edna H. Hong. Princeton: Princeton University Press, 1997.

CI   *The Concept of Irony, together with "Notes on Schelling's Berlin Lectures,"* trans. Howard V. Hong and Edna H. Hong. Princeton: Princeton University Press, 1989.

COR   *The Corsair Affair,* trans. Howard V. Hong and Edna H. Hong. Princeton: Princeton University Press, 1982.

CUP   *Concluding Unscientific Postscript to "Philosophical Fragments,"* 2 vols., trans. Howard V. Hong and Edna H. Hong. Princeton: Princeton University Press, 1992.

EO 1   *Either/Or,* Part One, trans. Howard V. Hong and Edna H. Hong. Princeton: Princeton University Press, 1987.

EO 2   *Either/Or,* Part Two, trans. Howard V. Hong and Edna H. Hong. Princeton: Princeton University Press, 1987.

EUD   *Eighteen Upbuilding Discourses,* trans. Howard V. Hong and Edna H. Hong. Princeton: Princeton University Press, 1990.

FT   *Fear and Trembling* and *Repetition,* trans. Howard V. Hong and Edna H. Hong. Princeton: Princeton University Press, 1983.

JP   *Søren Kierkegaard's Journals and Papers,* 7 vols., trans. Howard V. Hong and Edna H. Hong. Princeton: Princeton University Press, 1967-78.

PC   *Practice in Christianity,* trans. Howard V. Hong and Edna H. Hong. Princeton: Princeton University Press, 1991.

PF   *Philosophical Fragments* and *Johannes Climacus,* trans. Howard V. Hong and Edna H. Hong. Princeton: Princeton University Press, 1985.

PV   *The Point of View,* trans. Howard V. Hong and Edna H. Hong. Princeton: Princeton University Press, 1998.

SUD   *The Sickness unto Death,* trans. Howard V. Hong and Edna H. Hong. Princeton: Princeton University Press, 1980.

TA   *Two Ages,* trans. Howard V. Hong and Edna H. Hong. Princeton: Princeton University Press, 1978.

UDVS   *Upbuilding Discourses in Various Spirits,* trans. Howard V. Hong and Edna H. Hong. Princeton: Princeton University Press, 1993.

WA   *Without Authority,* trans. Howard V. Hong and Edna H. Hong. Princeton: Princeton University Press, 1997.

WL   *Works of Love,* trans. Howard V. Hong and Edna H. Hong. Princeton: Princeton University Press, 1995.

Introduction

Though his writings are often brilliantly poetic and often deeply philosophic, Kierkegaard was neither a poet nor a philosopher, but a preacher, an expounder and defender of Christian doctrine and Christian conduct.

W. H. Auden[1]

Away from the aesthetical! . . . Away from speculation!

Walter Lowrie[2]

The five volumes discussed in the work that follows were written by Kierkegaard and are surely among his most widely read and discussed texts. But he published them under three different pseudonyms, and most emphatically requested that we not attribute to him anything written by them (*CUP* 1:626-27). I have honored that request. Yet I have entitled the book *Kierkegaard's Concept of Faith*. How so?

There is an obvious sense in which the accounts of faith offered to us by the pseudonymous authors are also Kierkegaard's. The ideas they contain had to be thought up by some actual person before they could be attributed

---

1. W. H. Auden, ed., *The Living Thoughts of Kierkegaard* (New York: D. McKay Co., 1952), p. vii.

2. Chapter titles, respectively, for works written in 1841-44 and, more specifically, the Climacus writings of 1844-46, in Walter Lowrie, *Kierkegaard* (New York: Harper & Brothers, 1962), 1:232-90 and 2:295-346. Cf. *PV,* 5-6. I prefer Lowrie's 'aesthetic' to the Hongs' 'esthetic' and shall use it throughout, even when citing the Hongs' translations.

to some fictitious person, just as the actions and words of characters in a novel had to be thought up by its author before they could be attributed to the characters. Moreover, it is Kierkegaard who thinks it is worthwhile to present these fictitious writers and their ideas to us for our reading pleasure or perhaps some more serious purpose. Similarly, it is Dostoyevsky who first creates the words and deeds of three very different brothers, Ivan, Dmitri, and Alyosha, and then presents them to us. Perhaps each of these is autobiographical, representing an aspect of Dostoyevsky's character, though we would be foolish simply to identify him with any of them. Unless we are writing an intellectual biography, we do not read Dostoyevsky's novels to learn about him. We read for the pleasure of meeting such characters and, perhaps, for some more serious purpose such as learning about human existence, that is, about ourselves.

So the ideas about religious faith or, more specifically, Christian faith, found in the writings of our three pseudonyms, are Kierkegaard's, not in the sense that he is giving us his personal credo (though we must not preclude a priori a deep sympathy with the authors he creates), but in the sense of thinking them up, inscribing them, and presenting them to us by publishing them. To what end? In what sense does he think it worth our while to consider them?

Kierkegaard seeks to answer this question in two essays published together in *The Point of View (PV)*. The short version was published in 1851 (after all the works considered here had been published) under the title *On My Work as an Author (PV, 5-26)*. The longer, much more personal version was published posthumously in 1859 as *The Point of View for My Work as an Author (PV, 29-97)*, with a Supplement (*PV*, 103-26). In these essays he makes several important claims about his authorship, which he dates from the publication of *Either/Or* in 1843.

First, he repeatedly insists that his authorship be interpreted and evaluated as a whole, a totality. This means not only viewing the earlier works in the light of the later ones and vice versa, but also the aesthetic writings in relation to the religious writings and vice versa. He calls these the writings of his left hand and his right hand, respectively (*PV*, 36). By the former he does not mean just those writings that present the aesthetic stage or existence sphere but rather all the pseudonymous writings in their use of indirect communication in contrast with the religious writings that employ direct communication and are published under his own name (*PV*, 7).[3]

---

3. See the discussion of indirect communication in chapter 10 below.

Kierkegaard is famous for his polemics against the speculative philosophy of Hegel and his followers. But in certain respects he is himself deeply Hegelian, and this is nowhere more emphatically the case than in his holism. Like the homiletics professor whose mantra is "a text without a context is a pretext," Kierkegaard rejects an atomistic view of meaning, truth, and human existence. Everything is what it is by virtue of its relations to what it is not. So, unlike the New Critics, for whom every poem is a self-contained world unto itself, Kierkegaard insists that his writings be read as a whole.

Second, he insists that from start to finish he is a religious author and, more specifically, that his writings have a distinctly Christian meaning. The claim is

> that I am and was a religious author, that my whole authorship pertains to Christianity, to the issue: becoming a Christian, with direct and indirect polemical aim at that enormous illusion, Christendom, or the illusion that in such a country all are Christians of sorts. . . . Thus my entire work as an author revolves around: becoming a Christian in Christendom. (*PV*, 23, 90; cf. 8, 12, 31)

In other words, even when accounts of what faith is are offered to us by fictitious authors who insist that they do not have it (Johannes de Silentio, Johannes Climacus), the point of offering such accounts to the public and the potential benefit of reading them are to make aware or to become aware of what Christian faith truly is and how it has been betrayed by Christendom.

Third, Kierkegaard insists that he has been a religious author from the very beginning and rejects the notion that he began as an aesthetic author and only as he got older became a religious author (*PV*, 29-31, 44). As evidence he reminds us,

> The directly religious was present from the very beginning; *Two Upbuilding Discourses* (1843) is in fact concurrent with *Either/Or.* And in order to safeguard this concurrence of the directly religious, every pseudonymous work was accompanied concurrently by a little collection of 'upbuilding discourses' — until *Concluding Postscript* appeared, which poses the issue, which is *the issue* . . . of the whole authorship: *becoming a Christian.* (*PV*, 7-8)[4]

4. Kierkegaard published groups of two, three, and four "upbuilding discourses" to accompany pseudonymous works in 1843-44, collected in *Eighteen Upbuilding Discourses*

This does not mean that he had the whole authorship planned out in advance. Rather, he places great emphasis on the role of "Governance" in his authorship. He senses that he has been guided by God in ways of which he was not aware at the time (*PV,* 76-77; cf. 74).

Fourth, Kierkegaard insists that he is not a teacher but a learner. "I call my whole work as an author my own upbringing and development, but not in the sense as if I were now complete or completely finished with regard to needing upbringing and development" (*PV,* 12). So he describes himself as a "fellow-pupil" (*PV,* 79). As it turns out, this has involved him in several distinct roles. It is perhaps especially in relation to the aesthetic, that is, pseudonymous works that he describes himself as a spy, since a certain deception, a working incognito was deemed necessary to undermine the illusion that Christendom had become (*PV,* 53-54, 87n., 92). And it is no doubt especially in relation to the religious, signed works that he describes himself as a penitent (*PV,* 24, 62, 79).

Fifth, Kierkegaard suggests that although the aesthetic and the religious, the pseudonymous and the signed, the indirect and the direct are both present from the very beginning of his authorship, his personal upbringing nevertheless involves a journey from the one to the other. "A person does not reflect himself into being a Christian but out of something else in order to become a Christian" (*PV,* 93). Kierkegaard describes that journey as follows:

> The movement the authorship describes is: *from* 'the poet,' from the aesthetic — *from* 'the philosopher,' from the speculative — *to* the indication of the most inward qualification of the essentially Christian; **from** the *pseudonymous Either/Or,* **through** *Concluding Postscript,* with *my name as editor,* **to** *Discourses at the Communion on Fridays,* of which two were delivered in Frue Church. (*PV,* 5-6)[5]

(*EUD*), and *Three Discourses on Various Occasions (TDIO)* to accompany *Stages on Life's Way (SLW)* in 1845. For the correlation between the pseudonymous and signed works, see *PV,* xxiii-xxvii. For a discussion of Anti-Climacus as a pseudonym after *Postscript,* see *PV,* 6n.

5. Kierkegaard often describes this journey. It is "*back* from the aesthetic to becoming a Christian . . . [and in *Postscript*] *back* from the system, the speculative, etc. to becoming a Christian" (*PV,* 55). The authorship "is not the work of the poet passion or of the thinker passion, but of devotion to God, and for me a divine worship" (*PV,* 73). "The task that is to be assigned to most people in Christendom is — away from 'the poet' or from relating oneself to or having one's life in what the poet recites, away from speculative thought, from having one's life imaginatively . . . in speculating (instead of existing) to becoming a Christian" (*PV,* 78).

In the same year that he wrote this, 1851, he also prefaced the last group of his communion discourses by saying, "A gradually advancing author-activity that began with *Either/Or* seeks here its decisive point of rest at the foot of the alter."[6] Every reader of Kierkegaard should know that he considered his communion discourses to be the telos of his authorship.[7] (Perhaps in today's culture the movement toward the faith that comes to the altar is **from** popular culture and scientific naturalism insofar as these are the current moral equivalents of the aesthetic and the speculative.)

Kierkegaard repeatedly describes this movement as an "emptying" (*PV*, 35, 77, 85, 88). In the older Lowrie translation we read instead of a "catharsis."[8] Kierkegaard says that the aesthetic writings needed to be "taken into custody by the religious; the religious put up with this emptying out of the poetic but continually pressed on, as if it would say, 'Aren't you soon finished with that?'" (*PV*, 85-86). He even wonders if the aesthetic not only needs to be emptied out but is also "something that must be repented" (*PV*, 88). It seems that he takes this journey quite personally, as if there is something of both the poet and the philosopher in him that needs to be teleologically suspended, subordinated to something higher. This will come as no surprise to his readers.

Kierkegaard also tells us that in making this journey he lost the ability to be an "interesting" author.

> I lose the interesting, to be a riddle, whether this defense of Christianity carried to the extreme was not the most subtly devised form of an attack. This interesting I lose; in its place is substituted what is anything but interesting, *direct communication,* that the issue was and is: becoming a Christian. . . . And now, now I am not at all interesting any longer. That what it means to become a Christian should *actually* be the fundamental idea in the whole authorship — how boring! (*PV*, 91-92)[9]

6. *Discourses at the Communion on Fridays,* trans. Sylvia Walsh (Bloomington: Indiana University Press, 2011), p. 125.

7. Fortunately, all thirteen of these, originally scattered in Danish editions and in the Hongs' translations, have been gathered into a single volume and superbly translated with a helpful introduction by Sylvia Walsh. See previous note.

8. *The Point of View for My Work as an Author,* trans. Walter Lowrie (New York: Harper & Row, 1962), p. 18.

9. Cf. *PV*, 61-62 for an account of how Kierkegaard sought to support his aesthetic writings by living a lifestyle, in public, that was "interesting and pungent."

The "interesting" is an essential category of the aesthetic stage.[10] Perhaps this is the reason why Kierkegaard calls the pseudonymous texts with their indirect communication his aesthetic authorship even when, as in the texts before us, the subject matter is the religious stage.

Finally, Kierkegaard refuses to appeal to authorial authority in support of his claims about the meaning of his writings. "From the very beginning I have enjoined and repeated unchanged that I was 'without authority.'" This pertains not only to the truth of the claims made in and by the works but also to the interpretation of their meaning. "I regard myself rather as a *reader* of the books, not as the *author*" (*PV*, 12). He tells us that he is "accustomed to take a completely objective attitude to my own [literary productions]" and that their claims must be validated from the standpoint of "a third party, as a reader" (*PV*, 33).[11] In other words, we shouldn't just take him at his word; we should read his authorship as a serious presentation of what Christian faith truly is, in contrast with what Christendom has made of it, only if we as readers can make sense of it in those terms. In *Point of View* he writes as a reviewer, and we are invited to read the works for ourselves and judge whether his interpretation is faithful or misleading.

There has been no shortage lately of interpreters who challenge Kierkegaard's reading of his own texts in *Point of View*. These interpretations have been called literary readings, for they place great emphasis on such literary features as pseudonymity, indirect communication, and irony. They have also been called postmodern or deconstructive, for they place great emphasis on internal tensions within texts and the resultant ambiguity or even undecidability of meaning that results. For example, Roger Poole writes, "Kierkegaard writes text after text whose aim is not to state a truth, not to clarify an issue, not to propose a definite doctrine, not to offer some meaning that could be directly appropriated. . . . The aim of the aesthetic texts is not to instruct, or to inform, or to clarify, but on the contrary to divert, to subvert, and to destroy clear biographical intelligibility."[12]

10. See especially "Rotation of Crops," *EO* 1:285-300. The young aesthete writes, "Boredom is the root of all evil" (*EO* 1:289), reinforcing his amoral interpretation of good and evil.

11. On Kierkegaard's relation to the "death of the author" discussions by Derrida, Foucault, and Barthes, see my "Kierkegaard and the Anxiety of Authorship," *International Philosophical Quarterly* 34, no. 1 (March 1994): 5-22. Reprinted in *The Death and Resurrection of the Author?* ed. William Irwin (Westport, CT, and London: Greenwood, 2002), pp. 23-43.

12. Roger Poole, *Kierkegaard: The Indirect Communication* (Charlottesville: University of Virginia Press, 1993), pp. 6 and 9. The first part of this quotation is cited as typical of deconstructive readings by C. Stephen Evans, *Kierkegaard: An Introduction* (New York: Cambridge

Fenger, Garff, and Mackey take aim directly at *Point of View,* suggesting that its signed author, Søren Kierkegaard, is just another pseudonym, engaging in playacting and producing literary fiction.[13] I take such views to be misguided, but I do not here attempt any direct refutation of them. I rather attempt to show that they are quite unnecessary. My claim is that the pseudonymous texts under consideration here make perfectly good sense when read as Kierkegaard suggests we read them, that they have a common problematic about what Christianity is and what it means to become a Christian in Christendom, that they make a rich variety of claims about these matters, and that these claims are coherent with one another.

This coherence claim does not mean that they are synonymous and interchangeable or that they represent a system in the sense of completeness and closure.[14] The image I have had in mind throughout the writing of this monograph is that each thesis, expressed in the form of "faith as . . . ," is but one facet of a complex gem. But I do not purport to present the entire gem; there are other texts not discussed and much more that can be said about the ones I do discuss.

I am also fond of the parable of the "six blind men from Hindustan,"[15] each of whom had hold of part of an elephant. Each took the part with which he was familiar to be the whole, so

> Though each was partly in the right,
>   they all were in the wrong.

University Press, 2009), p. 13, and by Mark Tietjen, *Kierkegaard, Communication, and Virtue: Authorship as Edification* (Bloomington: Indiana University Press, 2013), ch. 2. This latter volume, which cites the second part as well, develops an explicit and sustained critique of deconstructive readings and thereby a cogent defense of Kierkegaard's claim that his writings, taken as a whole, are best read as having a serious religious purpose.

13. See Henning Fenger, *Kierkegaard: The Myths and Their Origins,* trans. George C. Schoolfield (New Haven: Yale University Press, 1980); Joakim Garff, "The Eyes of Argus: *The Point of View* and Points of View on Kierkegaard's Work as an Author," trans. Jane Chamberlain and Belinda Ioni, in *Kierkegaard: A Critical Reader,* ed. Jonathan Rée and Jane Chamberlain (Malden, MA: Blackwell, 1998); and Louis Mackey, *Points of View: Readings of Kierkegaard* (Tallahassee: University Presses of Florida, 1986).

14. For a thoughtful account, in dialogue with Poole, Fenger, and Garff, of what kinds of unity we should and should not seek in Kierkegaard's authorship, see George Pattison, *Kierkegaard's Upbuilding Discourses: Philosophy, Literature and Theology* (New York: Routledge, 2002), pp. 4-9.

15. Easy to find on the Internet. I have used it in *Whose Community? Which Interpretation? Philosophical Hermeneutics for the Church* (Grand Rapids: Baker Academic, 2009), pp. 25-26.

The error to be avoided here is perhaps not so much this one of taking any one part to be the whole[16] as it is assuming that my twelve facets or any other such list gives us the whole elephant or, if you prefer, the whole gem. I make no claim to have offered "the complete Kierkegaard"; nor do I suggest that "the complete Kierkegaard," if such a thing were *per impossible* to be found, would give us the whole answer to the question what Christianity is and what it means to become a Christian. Each facet (each "faith as . . .") is a perspective. Each pseudonym is a complex perspective, made up of more than one facet. Kierkegaard's authorship as a whole is a multiply complex perspective, and, given our hermeneutical situation, each interpretation of that authorship is one perspective among other possible ones. As he himself insists, this is true of Kierkegaard's own reading of his authorship. My claim is simply that his reading is a faithful and illuminating one. His authorship on his reading of it makes claims that are important for philosophy of religion, for theology, and, most of all, for religious life as it might be lived by individuals wishing to be faithful.

This does not mean ignoring the literary features of the authorship. Climacus writes, "But the presence of irony does not necessarily mean that the earnestness is excluded. Only assistant professors assume that" (*CUP* 1:277n.)[17] I not only agree; I take this to signify the more general truth that the literary features on which deconstructive readings focus are not incompatible with the seriousness of purpose Kierkegaard attributes to his texts. N.B. "to his texts." The issue is not a psychological thesis about the author's conscious purpose at the time of writing; it is rather a semantic issue about the intention of the texts, what they are trying to say.

There is, however, one specific passage about which I must say something. Johannes Climacus concludes his *Concluding Unscientific Postscript* with a kind of postscript, entitled "An Understanding with the Reader." In it he insists that he is not a Christian but a humorist (*CUP* 1:617). Then he tells us, "I have no opinion except that it must be the most difficult of all to become a Christian. As an opinion it is no opinion" (*CUP* 1:619). We must notice two things here. First, Climacus does have an opinion, and it conforms to what Kierkegaard tells us in *Point of View* his authorship is about. Second, the sense in which it is no opinion is not that it makes no substantive claim but that it "does not have any of the qualities that ordi-

---

16. Though Pattison rightly warns against this. See note 14 above.

17. The passage is self-referentially consistent. The satire on assistant professors is used to make a serious point about the compatibility of the comical and the serious.

narily characterize an 'opinion' " (*CUP* 1:619). This is because (1) it does not flatter him, (2) it does not insult the Christian, and (3) it does not insult the attacker of Christianity. In other words, it is not a piece of ideological self-congratulation. This little satire illustrates once again Climacus's persuasion that the comical is not incompatible with a serious purpose, and it anticipates the view that Kierkegaard himself will shortly develop about the public and public opinion in the *Corsair Affair* (see *COR*).

Then Climacus comes to the punch line towards which he has been working: "what I write contains the notice that everything is to be understood in such a way that it is revoked" (*CUP* 1:619). Should we conclude that, to say nothing about Kierkegaard himself, not even Climacus has any substantive claims about the nature of faith to communicate (whether directly or indirectly), that he writes only to illustrate the fragility of meaning, its ambiguity, or even its undecidability?

Such a conclusion seems to me entirely unnecessary. There are less tendentious readings of the revocation. For example, Ed Mooney suggests a different reading, based on Climacus's own view that "the secret of communication specifically hinges on setting the other free" (*CUP* 1:74). The pseudonyms occupy unique perspectives. "None can — or does — claim final moral or religious authority to possess the truth."[18] In other words, like Kierkegaard, Climacus knows that he writes "without authority," and this helps to explain the revocation.

Moreover, right after Climacus's concluding postscript, Kierkegaard adds in his own name "A First and Last Explanation" in which he first acknowledges that he is the author of the pseudonymous works to date and then distances himself from them by asking us to attribute these texts to the pseudonymous authors and not to him (*CUP* 1:626-27). So Mooney writes, "In its final pages we have two gestures that distance the writer's own authority from the printed word in order, as I see it, to promote a reader's freedom to interpret."[19] In other words, the revocation is a double authorial disavowal of the authority to decide the meaning of a text in a fixed and final way. But such hermeneutical humility does not entail that the author has nothing positive to say, only that he speaks from a finite and at best penultimate perspective.

18. Edward F. Mooney, "Exemplars, Inwardness, and Belief: Kierkegaard on Indirect Communication," in *International Kierkegaard Commentary*, vol. 12: *Concluding Unscientific Postscript to "Philosophical Fragments,"* ed. Robert L. Perkins (Macon, GA: Mercer University Press, 1997), p. 136.

19. Mooney, "Exemplars, Inwardness, and Belief," p. 136.

In a footnote, Mooney develops this suggestion in an important way. "The distancing gestures of both Climacus and Kierkegaard are, of course, incomplete. The *Postscript* is not withdrawn from publication. It remains for sale in bookstores." There may be something ironical about the revocation and the distancing. "If so, they are not to be taken entirely straightforwardly, but as freedom-enhancing existence-communications open to interpretation on roughly the same level as the rest of the *Postscript*."[20] Does not Climacus himself say that "to write a book and to revoke it is not the same as refraining from writing it" (*CUP* 1:621)?

I have always found this complex act of publishing a book with a revocation at the end to be illuminated by the courtroom scene familiar from movies and television. The attorney asks the witness a question that immediately evokes an objection, no doubt anticipated. Before the judge has a chance to rule, the attorney says, "I withdraw the question." But the withdrawal is quite impossible; everyone understands that the judge's injunction, "The jury will disregard the previous question," cannot be obeyed. The implication of the question has been planted in their minds, and it does its work even without the authority of the official record, from which it has been stricken. Objectively it has been banished; subjectively it remains very much alive.

Similarly, whether the reader reads the *Postscript* before or after the revocation, the reading cannot simply be erased. The double withdrawal means that the text is offered to us by Climacus and Kierkegaard without their *imprimatur,* that is, "without authority." As readers we are left alone with the text and its claims, which is what I take the purpose of pseudonymity to be in the first place. The hope is that we will not be influenced by the fact that Climacus is an interesting writer, both as a poet and as a philosopher, or that Kierkegaard is a famous writer.

In much the same spirit, Andy Burgess offers a somewhat different reading of the revocation. His point of departure is Climacus's insistence that "one does not prepare oneself to become aware of Christianity by reading books or by world-historical surveys, but by immersing oneself in existing" (*CUP* 1:560). The danger to be avoided is this: "If [Climacus] succeeds in portraying the error in speculative theology in philosophical terms, his portrayal of Christianity may itself be taken to be a ladder to paradise that can substitute for simple faith. *Postscript* would then replace Hegel's *Phenomenology*."[21]

20. Mooney, "Exemplars, Inwardness, and Belief," p. 136n.
21. Andrew J. Burgess, "The Bilateral Symmetry of Kierkegaard's *Postscript,*" in Per-

Climacus would appreciate the prayer of Henri Nouwen, and Kierkegaard even more so, since his reflections come in the form of a prayer.[22]

> O Lord Jesus Christ, Son of the living God, have mercy on me, a sinner. I
> am impressed by my own spiritual insights. I probably know more about
> prayer, meditation, and contemplation than most Christians do. I have
> read many books about the Christian life, and have even written a few
> myself. Still, as impressed as I am, I am more impressed by the enormous
> abyss between my insights and my life.[23]

Seen in this light, the revocation downplays the importance of the
theoretical analyses offered by Climacus, not to obliterate them but to put
them in their proper place. To read, to understand, and to accept them is
not to have faith. At most they can provide "some kind of guide book for the
philosophically sophisticated believer."[24] C. S. Lewis provides a helpful metaphor for this notion. In response to the complaint that theology is abstract
and even arid in comparison with direct religious experience, he immediately grants the point. Compared to the real experience of places worth
seeing, a map is "something less real . . . a bit of coloured paper." So you will
not "get anywhere by looking at maps without going to sea." But it is equally
true that you will not "be very safe if you go to sea without a map."[25]

Climacus and Kierkegaard distance themselves from their philosophical and theological analyses to emphasize the limitation of maps; but they
publish them to offer the benefits of maps. The maps that accompany fantasy fiction are as fictitious as the stories they support; they can be helpful
for reading. The maps put out by Mapquest or Rand McNally are unreal in
a very different sense; just to the degree that they are good maps they can
be helpful for life.

---

kins, ed., *International Kierkegaard Commentary,* vol. 12: *Concluding Unscientific Postscript to
"Philosophical Fragments,"* p. 341.

22. Fortunately, over a hundred of the prayers scattered throughout Kierkegaard's writings have been collected in a single volume, *The Prayers of Kierkegaard,* ed. Perry D. LeFevre
(Chicago: University of Chicago Press, 1956). It is hard, if not impossible, to read these prayers
and assume that Kierkegaard is only playacting, even when writing in his own name.

23. Henri Nouwen, *A Cry for Mercy: Prayers from the Genesee* (New York: Random
House, 2002), p. 36. In the next paragraph, Nouwen adds, "Sometimes I even have the painful
feeling that the clearer the vision, the more aware I am of the depth of the canyon."

24. Burgess, "Bilateral Symmetry," p. 342.

25. C. S. Lewis, *Mere Christianity* (New York: Macmillan, 1952), pp. 119-20.

Alastair Hannay seems to be at least in the same ballpark as Burgess in his reading of the revocation. He sees it as an attempt to point beyond the objective thinking contained in *Postscript* to the subjective thinking it seeks to evoke. "*Postscript* is of course very far from being a piece of subjective thinking itself . . . the attitude it calls for in the reader initially is of a conventionally objective kind." Is this what Christianity is? Are these the difficulties of becoming a Christian? "Accordingly neither writing a book like *Postscript* nor acknowledging the truth of what it says is the kind of thing *Postscript* is really about . . . we might say that what *Postscript* is about transcends the realm of ideas, which means that the ideas it develops must be left behind." Or, to be more precise, "it is to be forever revoked in order for the idea to assume its properly living form in the womb of the single reader's self-understandings," which would be subjective thinking.[26] Rejecting more radical readings of the revocation, Hannay suggests, "Perhaps, then, we should be content with the uncomplicated thought already aired that the objective form of *Postscript's* discussion is in some sense inappropriate to the kind of truth-finding that Climacus is out to elucidate."[27]

In keeping with these suggestions, I take the revocation in the postscript to the *Postscript* to be an attempt to avoid hermeneutical dogmatism and to remind the reader of the crucial difference between subjective and objective thinking (see especially chapters 9 and 10 below). This leaves us free to read Climacus (and the other pseudonyms) as making rather specific theoretical and existential claims on us who dare to read them. In doing so we become responsible for responding to them hermeneutically (what they mean), epistemically (what truth, if any, they contain), and existentially (taking a stance toward them in our lives).

Note to the reader: My hope is that those interested in reading Kierkegaard will find this volume helpful whether they bring only a little philosophical background to that task or a lot. As much as possible, I've used the notes for material that presupposes more rather than less. For philosophically trained readers they are an important part of my interpretation. For those with less background they can be safely ignored.

---

26. Alastair Hannay, "Johannes Climacus Revocation," in *Kierkegaard's "Concluding Unscientific Postscript": A Critical Guide*, ed. Rick Anthony Furtak (New York: Cambridge University Press, 2010), pp. 50-51. Cf. my essay, "Climacus on Subjectivity and the System," in the same volume, pp. 132-48.

27. Hannay, "Johannes Climacus Revocation," p. 57.

PART ONE

Johannes de Silentio

CHAPTER 1

Faith as the Task of a Lifetime

Although *Fear and Trembling* retells the story of Abraham's near sacrifice of Isaac as told in Genesis 22 and Hebrews 11, it is not about sacrifice. And although it contains the (in)famous account of the teleological suspension of the ethical, it is not about ethics. It is about faith and Abraham as the knight of faith. Abraham is, of course, no Christian, but no fewer than four books in the New Testament (Romans, Galatians, Hebrews, and James) portray Abraham as a hero of faith. So while his story has no specifically Christian content, it has the form of biblical faith sufficiently for Kierkegaard to assume that it is relevant for his overwhelmingly "Christian" readership. Not that any of his readers was overwhelmingly Christian, a matter of great importance for understanding the treatise, but rather, numerically speaking, his audience overwhelmingly identified itself as Christian. A subsequent pseudonym, Climacus, will satirize this assumption overtly. Johannes de Silentio, the pseudonymous author of *Fear and Trembling,* will probe and question this self-assurance. He repeatedly tells us that he lacks the humility and courage to make the movements of Abraham's faith. "I wonder if anyone in my generation is able to make the movements of faith? . . . I honestly confess that in my experience I have not found a single authentic example" (*FT,* 34, 38).

Silentio's disclaimer makes him an outsider looking at the life of faith. This means that *Fear and Trembling* is not a work of Christian theology, in which a teaching scholar in the church offers an interpretation of the Christian faith to inspire and to instruct and especially to inform preaching. So what kind of writing is it? Kierkegaard calls it a dialectical lyric, which isn't exactly a familiar philosophical genre. But we can fit it without too much difficulty into several genres with which we are familiar.

Fear and Trembling can be read as a treatise in *phenomenology à la Husserl.* It is the quest for an eidetic intuition, the apprehension and articulation of the form of a particular mode of intentional experience. And, since Silentio does not affirm the validity or veridicality of this experience, however much he is in awe of it, we can think of his account as under the phenomenological reduction, the *epoche.*[1]

We can also read our text as an example of *hermeneutical phenomenology à la Ricoeur.* The difference is that instead of seeking to follow Husserl's program, "back to the things themselves," by approaching them directly, one does so indirectly through earlier cultural deposits, interpreting them in the light of prior interpretations. The path leads along "the detour through the contingency of cultures, through an incurably equivocal language, and through the conflict of interpretations."[2] It requires "the long detour of the signs of humanity deposited in cultural works" and of "the detour of understanding the cultural signs in which the self documents and forms itself . . . [so that] reflection is nothing without the mediation of signs and works."[3] The authors of Genesis (including redactors), of Hebrews, and of James offer the interpretations by which Silentio's interpretation is mediated.[4]

A third genre that helps illumine our text is *ideology critique à la Marx.* Silentio's account will portray reason as anything but pure, universal, disinterested, and objective. He will take more seriously than Hegel the latter's claim, "Whatever happens, every individual is a child of his time; so philosophy too is its own time apprehended in thoughts."[5] And he will have his own version of the Marx/Engels thesis that "the ruling ideas of each age have ever been the ideas of its ruling class."[6] It is no accident that *Fear and Trembling* begins, in its very first sentence, with a critical reference to "our age" or that his question (above) is whether "anyone in my generation"

1. See Jeffrey Hanson, ed., *Kierkegaard as Phenomenologist: An Experiment* (Evanston: Northwestern University Press, 2010).

2. Paul Ricoeur, *Freud and Philosophy: An Essay on Interpretation,* trans. Denis Savage (New Haven: Yale University Press, 1970), p. 42.

3. Paul Ricoeur, *Hermeneutics and the Human Sciences,* trans. and ed. John B. Thompson (New York: Cambridge University Press, 1981), pp. 143, 158-59.

4. I omit the Pauline accounts in Romans and Galatians because Silentio is not interested in justification by faith alone. He is more nearly in agreement with James 2:18, "Show me your faith apart from your works, and I by my works will show you my faith."

5. *Philosophy of Right,* Preface.

6. Found first in *The German Ideology* and then in *The Communist Manifesto.* See *Karl Marx: Selected Writings,* 2nd ed., ed. David McLellan (New York: Oxford University Press, 2000), pp. 192 and 260.

really has faith. That what passes as "reason" turns out to be the doubly contingent self-interested, self-congratulatory self-interpretation of (1) the present age as seen by (2) its dominant elite means quite simply that "reason" is ideology in a rather Marxist sense.

Silentio's "Marxism" will have a more Nietzschean flavor. Instead of protesting against alienation and exploitation, he will suggest that, compared to Abraham, the present age is nothing more than "wretched contentment."[7] In any case, the "attack upon Christendom" associated with Kierkegaard's final polemical pamphlets begins not later than *Fear and Trembling,* and the theory and practice of any Abrahamic monotheism will be countercultural just to the degree that they remain faithful to their Abrahamic roots. The fact that Abrahamic monotheism is the basis for this form of social critique indicates that neither Marxian nor Nietzschean atheism has a monopoly on it. Its origins, in fact, go back to such Hebrew prophets as Isaiah, Amos, Hosea, and Jeremiah.[8]

Still another genre that almost fits is that of *existential psychoanalysis.*[9] Since Silentio does not commit himself to the ontology presupposed by Abraham's faith, he does not practice existential psychoanalysis in the sense in which Anti-Climacus does in *Sickness unto Death;* he cannot be said to have psychic or spiritual health as his direct goal. But by calling faith a passion and, indeed, the highest passion, he poses the question of transphysical health most sharply. Abrahamic faith is either a pathology of the passions or the true foundation of the soul's health. Silentio is the Socrates whose narrative poses this question insistently.

---

7. This lament reverberates through Nietzsche's *Thus Spoke Zarathustra.* See Prologue, Section 3; On the Pale Criminal; and On the Higher Man, Section 3. Edward Mooney writes that in *Fear and Trembling,* Kierkegaard seeks "to raise doubts about his countrymen's understanding of ethics and faith, to awaken them from spiritual complacency, to probe the possibilities for individual life in an age that threatens to level all to a sleepy collective mediocrity." *Knights of Faith and Resignation: Reading Kierkegard's "Fear and Trembling"* (Albany: SUNY Press, 1991), p. 2.

8. See "Prolegomena to Any Future Philosophy of Religion That Will Be Able to Come Forth as Prophecy" and "Kierkegaard as a Prophetic Philosopher" in my *Kierkegaard's Critique of Reason and Society* (Macon: Mercer University Press, 1987), pp. 1-27.

9. Sartre uses this phrase to indicate the practical significance of his phenomenological ontology in *Being and Nothingness.* The phrase is also used in connection with psychiatric theorizing that draws on Heidegger and a variety of other existential philosophers, including Kierkegaard. Ludwig Binswanger and Medard Boss are important here. See Rollo May, ed., *Existential Psychology,* 2nd ed. (New York: Random House, 1969) and Rollo May, Ernest Angel, and Henri F. Ellenberger, eds., *Existence* (New York: Basic Books, 1958).

*   *   *

The bulk of *Fear and Trembling* is sandwiched between a brief Preface and a brief Epilogue. The Preface begins with a complaint that in "our age" everything in the world of ideas can be had at such a bargain price that perhaps no one will find it worthwhile to buy (*FT,* 5). The Epilogue begins with a reference to Dutch merchants who sank a few cargoes in order to raise the price and then asks, "Do we need something similar in the world of the spirit?" (*FT,* 121). Silentio is posing the question whether in "our age" faith hasn't been so cheapened as to be all but worthless. It seems as if he wishes to supplement Bonhoeffer's account of cheap grace with his own account of cheap faith.[10]

This cheapening takes place through the Hegelian notion that faith is easily achieved by the many and that the higher task of the intellectual elite is to "go further" than faith to the speculative system that attains the status of science. It is here that we find the first of what I shall present as Silentio's five theses about faith: **Faith is the task of a lifetime.**

Silentio resists the notion that faith is to be surpassed with two analogies. In the Preface he satirizes the notion of going beyond doubt, as the Danish Hegelian Martensen had purported to do. But the ancient Greeks understood that doubt was "a task for a whole lifetime" and was "not acquired in days and weeks" since it involved denying "the certainty of the senses and the certainty of thoughts." For Pyrrho, the goal of doubt was to free oneself from commitment to any belief at all. No easy task!

The closest analogy to this kind of doubt is not Descartes' artificial, temporary doubt as a method rather than an actual experience; it is rather the Buddhist no-self doctrine that calls on disciples to rid themselves of the belief that anything has a lasting identity. One does not first achieve this extremely difficult goal and then go on to study Buddhist metaphysics. Rather, Buddhist metaphysics and the accompanying narratives are the "expedient" or "skillful" means for achieving this radical, fundamental change of conscious experience. Silentio's implicit suggestion is that metaphysics is not a higher stage than the spirituality of faith, which needs to "go further," to surpass itself in that direction; rather, it is properly understood and evaluated as the "expedient" or "skillful" means in the service of the spirituality of faith. Insofar as theology is metaphysics in the service of spirituality, it is, so far as faith is concerned, the highest form of knowledge but not, qua

10. Dietrich Bonhoeffer, *The Cost of Discipleship* (New York: Macmillan, 1963).

knowledge, the highest human achievement. The contrast with Hegel could not be sharper when Hegel writes that "philosophy must beware of the wish to be edifying."[11]

In the Epilogue the analogy is with love that is portrayed as the task of a lifetime. We never learn to love so completely that we can "go further" to higher tasks. Just as the tyro who says "I learned how to play golf (or chess or poker) yesterday" is ridiculous, so anyone who says "I learned how to love my parents (or my siblings, or my spouse, or my children) yesterday" is ridiculous.

Similarly, the Hegelians who want to "go further" than faith are ridiculous and the legitimate target of satire.[12] So, in the Preface Silentio satirizes those who purport to have gone further than faith. "In our age [N.B.], everyone is unwilling to stop with faith but goes further. It perhaps would be rash to ask where they are going, whereas it is a sign of urbanity and culture for me to assume that everyone has faith, since otherwise it certainly would be odd to speak of going further. It was different in those ancient days. Faith was then a task for a whole lifetime" (*FT,* 7). In the Epilogue he poses quite bluntly the crucial question implicit in his satires: "Are we so sure that we have achieved the highest?" (*FT,* 121).

Gilbert Ryle's distinction between task words and achievement words is helpful here.[13] Task words signify an activity that is still ongoing, while achievement words signify activities that have been brought to successful completion. Thus in the pairs *hunting-finding, treating-healing, traveling-arriving,* and *running-winning,* the former terms are task words, while the latter are achievement words. It is clear that, for Silentio, 'faith' is a task word. The word 'task' is especially prominent in the Epilogue. But in both the Preface and the Epilogue, faith is not just a task but, like doubt and love, properly understood, the task of a lifetime. It is never fully mastered; there

---

11. G. W. F. Hegel, *Phenomenology of Spirit,* trans. A. V. Miller (Oxford: Clarendon, 1977), p. 6. A large number of Kierkegaard's writings, pseudonymous and otherwise, have 'edification' or 'upbuilding' (alternative translation) in their title or subtitle. This is a fundamental difference between the system and Kierkegaard's authorship(s).

12. The use of satire throughout Kierkegaard's writings reflects the view that sometimes the best philosophical argument is laughter. See *CUP* 1:512-13, 2:263n.754, in which Lord Shaftesbury suggests that the question, *"Is it not ridiculous?"* can never be ruled out a priori.

13. Ryle employs this distinction throughout *The Concept of Mind* (New York: Barnes and Noble, 1949). He has a therapeutic purpose. "Primarily I am trying to get some disorders out of my own system. Only secondarily do I hope to help other theorists to recognize our malady and to benefit from my medicine" (p. 9).

is always more to learn. It is never fully perfected; there is always the challenge to become more faithful.

The theme of "going further" than faith has been identified above as Hegelian. In what sense? In a book that provides a masterful account of Kierkegaard's relation to the Danish Hegelians, Jon Stewart argues the general thesis that "the bulk of his criticism is *aimed* at his Danish contemporaries and not at Hegel himself." More specifically, with reference to the period from *Either/Or* to *Concluding Unscientific Postscript* (which includes *Fear and Trembling*), he claims that what is normally taken as a critique of Hegel is "*directed* primarily at other sources and not at Hegel himself." With reference to the "odd use of Hegel" in the main body of *Fear and Trembling*, he claims that it "in fact has very little to do with Hegel himself but is rather a part of Kierkegaard's continuing polemic against Martensen and the beginning of his polemic against Heiberg." Finally, with reference to the Preface's polemic against those who would go further than doubt and faith, Stewart writes, "This Preface signals to the reading public immediately that the author of the work is a critic of Heiberg, Martensen, Nielsen, and the other Danish Hegelians."[14] Reference to Hegel is conspicuously absent in this fourth formula, though in context the reader is bound to read "and not Hegel himself." The other three do mention him, but they do so in two different ways. The first two concern where the critique is "aimed" or "directed" and draw the negative conclusion, "not at Hegel himself." This seems to be a psychological thesis about whom Kierkegaard had in mind when critiquing Hegelian thought. Stewart makes a good case for thinking that Kierkegaard had Martensen especially in mind in his satires about "going further." But, of course, it doesn't follow that he didn't have Hegel himself in mind as well; and, in any case, the more interesting question philosophically is not the momentary state of Kierkegaard's consciousness but whether the critique makes genuine contact with Hegel's thought. The

14. Jon Stewart, *Kierkegaard's Relations to Hegel Reconsidered* (New York: Cambridge University Press, 2003), pp. 38, 33-34, 306, 310; emphasis added. For critical examinations of the claim that the Hegel critique in Kierkegaard's writings concerns the Danish Hegelians and not Hegel himself, see my review in *Søren Kierkegaard Newsletter* 48 (September 2004): 10-15, and Robert L. Perkins's review in *International Journal for Philosophy of Religion* 56 (2004): 55-57. For a more sympathetic reading of Stewart, which essentially repeats his central thesis, see Jamie Turnbull, "Jon Stewart's Relations to Kierkegaard Reconsidered," *Søren Kierkegaard Newsletter* 58 (November 2011): 2-4. Another indispensable source on the Danish Hegelians is Bruce H. Kirmmse, *Kierkegaard in Golden Age Denmark* (Bloomington: Indiana University Press, 1990).

third statement suggests that it does not. It "has very little to do with Hegel himself." This deep ambivalence runs throughout Stewart's general "not Hegel but the Danish Hegelians" thesis.

Even among Kierkegaard scholars, the question whether Kierkegaard was especially thinking of this Danish Hegelian or that one when writing a particular passage is interesting but not terribly important. Far more important for any reader of Kierkegaard is the substantive question whether his critique of "Hegelian" thought effectively engages the thought of Hegel himself, and, if so, with what force. This is true for two reasons. First, unlike the Danish Hegelians, both Kierkegaard and Hegel are part of the philosophical canon of the west, and their quarrel, like that between Plato and Aristotle regarding the forms or between Kant and Anselm or Leibniz regarding the so-called ontological argument is at once part of our cultural heritage and a matter of ongoing philosophical significance (if not necessarily in just the way originally posed). Second, in this connection, Hegel is more than just Hegel. He is a prime example of a major part of the Enlightenment Project. The phrase "religion within the boundaries of mere reason" is not just the title of a book by Kant; it describes the central theme or task of Enlightenment philosophy of religion. The most powerful seventeenth-century version is Spinoza's;[15] the most powerful eighteenth-century version is Kant's; and the most powerful nineteenth-century version is Hegel's.

It is worth noting that each of these three is deeply incompatible with the other two. This is ironic. It was the exclusive particularism of positive, institutional religion and the linkage between this and religiously motivated and legitimated violence that the Age of Reason sought to overcome by virtue of the supposed fact that reason was universal, while faith was particular. The names Judaism, Christianity, and Islam, along with Protestant and Catholic, were all too familiarly linked to religious persecution and wars of religion. But insofar as the three versions of religion just mentioned (along with a variety of others such as the English Deists) were mutually exclusive, "reason" turned out to be more particular than universal. We would have to speak of reason^s, reason^k, and reason^h. "Reason" begins to look like a variety of faiths, so that corresponding to Judaism, Christianity, and Islam, there

15. One might add John Locke's name alongside Spinoza's. See Nicholas Wolterstorff, *John Locke and the Ethics of Belief* (New York: Cambridge University Press, 1996), giving equal time to empiricism and rationalism in the seventeenth century. The argument here would remain unaffected. One would simply have to add the reason of Locke, that is, reason^l, to the list below, for Locke's view of reason and the religion of reason is at odds with each of the other three.

would be Spinoza's reason, Kant's, and Hegel's.[16] By linking Hegelianism to "our age," Kierkegaard calls attention to the particularity and contingency of this version of reason and develops a mode of ideology critique both like and unlike Marx's.

Given this sense in which Hegel is more than just Hegel but also a major version of the religion of reason, Kierkegaard's critique of Hegelian philosophy of religion can and should be read as a response to this broader Enlightenment project and not only an intramural Danish debate just to the degree that it engages Hegel's own thought.

In the Preface Silentio effectively engages Hegel himself in two ways. First, in describing his target he uses three terms that are utterly essential to Hegel's own account of his philosophy: 'speculation,' 'science,' and especially 'system,' a term whose frequency turns the entire final paragraph into a satire. This is not just the lingo of the Danish Hegelians. Hegel's system in three parts, Logic, Philosophy of Nature, and Philosophy of Spirit, appears under the title *Encyclopedia of the Philosophical Sciences*. The Preface and Introduction to the *Phenomenology of Spirit* contain Hegel's most extended meta-discourse on what he takes to be the proper nature of philosophical thought. They can be fairly summarized as saying that philosophy achieves[17] its true nature as a *speculative system* that attains the status of *science*. Just what he means by this and just how forceful Kierkegaard's critique may be can only be worked out in detailed analysis. But a critique of the notion that philosophy has a speculative, scientific system as its task and, now finally, in "our age" its achievement, cannot be shunted off as having "very little to do with Hegel himself." Kierkegaard would have had to be deeply ignorant of Hegel's own thought (and we know he was not) to be thinking only of the Danish disciples.

A second direct hit on Hegel himself (whose force, of course, remains to be evaluated) occurs in the middle of the Preface's last paragraph, in which Silentio humbly and satirically distances himself from any ability to

---

16. A further irony lies in the fact that this project has been carried out in postmodern contexts as well. See, for example, Martin Heidegger, "Phenomenology and Theology," in *Pathmarks,* ed. William McNeill (New York: Cambridge University Press, 1998), pp. 39-62, and Jacques Derrida's "religion without religion" project as developed in such texts as *The Gift of Death,* trans. David Wills (Chicago: University of Chicago Press, 1995), and "Faith and Knowledge: The Two Sources of 'Religion' at the Limits of Reason Alone," in *Acts of Religion,* ed. Gil Anidjar (New York: Routledge, 2002), pp. 40-101.

17. 'Philosophy' is an achievement word for Hegel. Hence the later satire by Climacus over whether the system is finished.

understand the system, much less produce one himself. "Even if someone were able to transpose the whole content of faith into conceptual form, it does not follow that he has comprehended faith, comprehended how he entered into it or how it entered into him" (*FT, 7*).

Hegel's earliest writings on religion are a virtually Nietzschean diatribe against biblical religion. His hostility to Judaism would sound anti-Semitic were it not for the fact that, like Nietzsche, he immediately points to ways in which Christianity has inherited rather than overcome the slave mentality of its ancestors. But shortly before writing the *Phenomenology of Spirit* (1807), he found a way to speak favorably of Christianity while keeping a great gulf fixed between himself and mainstream orthodoxy and piety.[18] It was the claim that religion and philosophy have the same content but different forms. Religion has the form of representations *(Vorstellungen),* while philosophy has the form of concepts *(Begriffe).* Christianity is the highest form of religion, but it is not the highest form of knowledge. *Vorstellungen* are not the "proper" form of truth, so it is necessary to translate the language of religion (representations), including systematic theology, into the language of speculative philosophy (concepts) in order to achieve absolute knowing, the true content in its true form. In other words, religious discourse, in both its lay and academic modes, is an inferior apprehension of the truth and needs to be upgraded, reinterpreted, corrected by philosophy. This is Hegel's version of the Enlightenment project of "religion within the limits of reason alone."[19]

Hegel is not as clear about the difference between representations and concepts as we would like. He often mentions the use of images from sense perception in the former,[20] but it is not sense experience as such that is the problem. It is rather the form of sense experience in which the object is distinct from and over against the subject. Thus there arises a threefold distinction between representations and concepts. (1) Unlike concepts, rep-

---

18. Most immediately in their Lutheran forms.

19. Hegel places this thesis at the very beginning of his system. See *Encyclopedia Logic,* trans. T. F. Geraets, W. A. Suchting, and H. S. Harris (Indianapolis: Hackett, 1991), §§1-6. Cf. *Phenomenology of Spirit,* trans. A. V. Miller (Oxford: Clarendon, 1977), ch. 7, and *Hegel's Lectures on the Philosophy of Religion,* ed. Peter C. Hodgson (New York: Oxford University Press, 2007), 1:396-406. In the one-volume edition (Oxford, 2006), the pages are 144-54. Pagination is the same in the earlier issue by University of California Press, 1984 (three volumes) and 1988 (one volume) respectively.

20. For this reason *Vorstellung* has often been translated as 'pictorial thinking.' But this is not to get to the heart of the matter.

resentations assume a divine transcendence that can be expressed in the language of the here and the beyond (Jenseits) and thus between presence and absence. Hegel carries out a sustained polemic against anything and everything jenseitig. (2) Representations have the form of consciousness (object over against and distinct from subject), while concepts have the form of self-consciousness in which the human spirit becomes increasingly aware of itself. (3) Accordingly, what religion perceives as a unique, contingent historical event, philosophy understands as a universal ontological necessity.

Thus, in the *Phenomenology of Spirit*, Hegel takes the doctrine of the incarnation, that Jesus of Nazareth is the God-man, fully human and fully divine, to be the central truth of Christianity. "The divine nature is the same as the human, and it is this unity that is beheld [in Jesus]."[21] In its religious form, which is not adequate to its content, this signifies a truth about a unique individual, Jesus of Nazareth. In its philosophical form, in which the true content achieves its true form, it represents a general truth about human nature, not in its individual mode but in that corporate, collective, intersubjective selfhood that Hegel calls spirit. Thus the claim is that the human spirit is the divine spirit and that it becomes itself fully through the historical unfolding of its social objectifications (Objective Spirit) and of its three moves of self-consciousness (art, religion, and philosophy — Absolute Spirit).

It is clear that the form of religious thought and discourse is very different from the thought and discourse of the speculative system of philosophical science. But it now looks as if the content has changed as well, and not minimally. What Hegel presents as the highest form of the Christian religion seems much closer to Feuerbachian atheism than to any of the Abrahamic monotheisms, including historical Christianity.[22] Christianity has been improved so much that it is no longer recognizable.

21. *Phenomenology of Spirit*, p. 460. Cf. my commentary in *History and Truth in Hegel's Phenomenology*, 3rd ed. (Bloomington: Indiana University Press, 1998), pp. 201-7.

22. For Feuerbach what believers take to be a superior being "up there" or "out there" is nothing more than the projection of our ideals of ourselves pushed to their limit or, perhaps, imagined without limitation. Thus, "theology is anthropology." See *The Essence of Christianity*, trans. George Eliot (New York: Harper and Brothers, 1957). In *History and Truth*, I have developed a similar parallel between Hegel and Durkheim, according to whom religion is society's objectification of its own self-image. The "Freudian" character of both Feuerbach and Durkheim is that for religious consciousness this takes place unconsciously and thus has the form, as Hegel puts it, of consciousness rather than self-consciousness.

Silentio will make this kind of critique later, when we come to the third place at which he lands a direct hit on Hegel himself. But here he makes a different point, this one about appropriation. Anticipating his colleague, Johannes Climacus *(Philosophical Fragments* and *Concluding Unscientific Postscript)*, he complains that in their eagerness to convert Christianity into the system, the Hegelians have smothered the existential question of the individual's relation to the truth. Even if the thinker could succeed in translating religious *Vorstellungen* into philosophical *Begriffe*, "it does not follow that he has comprehended faith, comprehended how he entered into it or how it entered into him" (*FT*, 7).

CHAPTER 2

Faith as Trust in Divine Promises

To know that faith is the task of a lifetime is not to know anything specifically about faith. The same can be said about learning to doubt, to love, and to play chess, or poker, or golf. What is the specific task that constitutes faith?

Silentio answers this question — with constant reference to Abraham, of course — by making two contrasts: the knight of faith is first contrasted with the knight of infinite resignation and then with the tragic hero. In these contrasts we get the second and third theses about faith: **Faith is trust in divine promises** and **Faith is obedience to divine commands**.[1] These are the tasks specific to faith. This chapter deals with the first of them, the next chapter with the second.

Two important corollaries should be noted at the outset. First, faith is trans-cognitive. It presupposes certain factual beliefs, including the belief that there is a God, that God has made certain promises, and that God has issued certain commands. Second, faith presupposes a fully personal God, one who is capable of entering into covenantal relations by performing such speech acts as promising and commanding. Not every referent of the term 'God' can do this. One thinks of the gods of Aristotle, Spinoza, and Hegel.[2]

---

1. In *The Babylonian Captivity of the Church*, Martin Luther writes, "Why, the whole Scripture is concerned with provoking us to faith; now driving us with commands and threats, now drawing us with promises and consolations. In fact, everything in Scripture is either a command or a promise. The commands humble the proud with their demands, the promises exalt the humble with their forgiveness." *Luther's Works*, vol. 36: *Word and Sacrament II*, ed. Abdel Ross Wentz (Philadelphia: Fortress, 1959), p. 124.

2. George Steiner writes, "It is the Hebraic intuition that God is capable of all speech-acts except that of monologue." *Real Presences* (Chicago: University of Chicago Press, 1989), p. 225.

These two corollaries give rise to the claim that faith involves both "be-lief that" and "belief in," but in such a way as to make the latter primary. Faith may well have its creedal expression, but it is not reducible to belief or even primarily belief as cognitive assent to certain propositions. It is rather a personal relation to a personal God. That is why James can say, "Even the demons believe — and shudder" (James 2:19). They are, as James sees them, entirely orthodox, but they don't have faith. They have the correct beliefs that God is thus and so, but they lack faith because they don't have the appropriate beliefs in God, expressed in trust and obedience. It is not an accident that in Kierkegaard's Christian context, the Apostles' and Nicene Creeds begin, respectively, "I *believe in* God," and "We *believe in* one God." The creeds tell us that it is not all about creeds.

The second thesis about faith, that it is trust in divine promises, is de-veloped in what can be seen as the third and fourth introduction to Silen-tio's little book, the Eulogy on Abraham (Panegyric, Speech in Praise of Abraham) and the Preliminary Expectoration[3] (Preamble from the Heart).[4] In the first of these, Silentio reminds us of Abraham's life after his decisive, covenantal encounter with God and before the trial of Genesis 22 in which God asks him to sacrifice Isaac, the son of promise.

> By faith Abraham emigrated from the land of his fathers and became an alien in the *promised* land. . . . By faith he was an alien in the *prom-ised* land. . . . By faith Abraham received the *promise* that in his seed all the generations of the earth would be blessed. . . . Abraham became old, Sarah the object of mockery in the land, and yet he was God's chosen one and heir to the *promise* that in his seed all the generations of the earth would be blessed. . . . He accepted the fulfillment of the *promise,* he ac-cepted it in faith, and it happened according to the *promise,* according to his faith. (*FT,* 17-18; emphasis added)

The agenda for Abraham's life was completely changed by the threefold promise of God, the promise of a land, of a son, and of a blessing through the son. Abraham's faith was his trust in the promising God, his confidence

3. 'Expectoration' here means outpouring from the heart, not spitting; it derives from the Latin, meaning to drive from the chest.
4. After the Preface, the second introduction, Exordium (Attunement, Prelude), sug-gests possible versions of the Abraham story in which he is not the knight of faith. On reading the text as having four introductions, see John Lippitt, *Routledge Philosophy Guidebook to Kierkegaard and "Fear and Trembling"* (New York: Routledge, 2003), p. 15.

that God was up to something good and would fulfill these promises. Accordingly, we hear no "dirge" (*FT*, 17) of lamentation from one who lives as an alien and an exile, no

> By the waters of Babylon —
> > there we sat down and there we wept
> > when we remembered Zion.
> On the willows there
> > we hung up our harps. . . .
> How could we sing the LORD's song
> > in a foreign land? (Ps. 137:1-2, 4)

By faith he experienced exile not as God's judgment or abandonment but as the path to the good things God had promised. Moreover, in spite of the long delay in which the promised son became more and more impossible (Silentio's argument requires this grammar), he did not waver and give up on the promise (*FT*, 18).

The corollaries to the promises were the commands: first, to leave his native land and emigrate to somewhere not yet specified, and second, to wait in confident hope for the increasingly impossible birth of a son. The son eventually is born. The impossible becomes actual. The story has a happy ending. Until. Without any further promise there comes a further command, to take Isaac to the land of Moriah and offer him as a sacrifice. We know that Abraham travels with Isaac for three days with the intent to do this, until at the last moment he is stopped by God. So we already see the third thesis emerging: **Faith is obedience to divine commands**. This is how trust in the divine promises manifests itself. Paraphrasing Peirce's definition of belief as "that upon which a man is prepared to act,"[5] we can say that trust is that upon which one continues to act.

But Silentio is in no hurry to give us his reflection on this third thesis. He will do so in the three problems that make up the main body of his text after the four introductions. Before turning to that task, he offers us further reflection on faith as trust in divine promises by comparing faith with infinite resignation. Anticipating that theme in the next section, the Prelimi-

---

5. *Collected Papers of Charles Sanders Peirce*, ed. Charles Hartshorne and Paul Weiss (Cambridge, MA: Harvard University Press, 1960), 5:7. The definition is actually that of Alexander Bain, here quoted by Peirce, who adds, "From this definition, pragmatism is scarcely more than a corollary."

nary Expectoration (Preamble from the Heart), he writes in the Eulogy on Abraham that "it is great to give up one's desire, but it is greater to hold fast to it after having given it up; it is great to lay hold of the eternal, but it is greater to hold fast to the temporal after having given it up" (*FT,* 18).

Then, to make sure we're paying attention, he concludes his eulogy with the reminder that Abraham "got no further than faith" (*FT,* 23). He got no further because 'faith' is a task word and not an achievement word. It signifies an incomplete rather than a successfully completed activity. Silentio has just alluded to the way in which Abraham's faith holds strong through that ultimate test in which he is asked to return the son of promise to the God who promised. He gets Isaac back. Surely, we might think, his faith has become an achievement. Memory and rest can replace expectation and patient waiting.

But no. There is still the promise that God will provide a blessing for all people through his seed, the son Isaac. This does not happen during Abraham's lifetime; indeed, he doesn't even know just what form this blessing will take. Jews, Christians, and Muslims will subsequently give different answers to this question. But he knows none of them. He can remain faithful only by continuing to trust that God will fulfill that promise in God's own time and way, whenever and whatever that may be. If with Heidegger life is always lived *unterwegs* (on the way) because it is being-toward-death, for Abraham, in faith, it is always lived *unterwegs* because God's promises, even when partially fulfilled, are never in this life completely fulfilled. So faith is the task of a lifetime.

It is in the Preliminary Expectoration or Preamble from the Heart that Silentio develops the contrast between the knight of infinite resignation and the knight of faith. They are both knights because their virtue or excellence is, in the language of Aristotle, moral virtue and not intellectual virtue. They are doers and not merely knowers, participants and not merely observers, agents and not merely thinkers. (Of course, as we shall see, this does not mean that faith belongs to what Kierkegaard will present, in a variety of works, as the ethical stage on life's way or existence sphere.)

In the earlier Eulogy, Silentio had contrasted the poet or orator with the hero. "The poet or orator can do nothing that the hero does; he can only admire, love, and delight in him" (*FT,* 15). Nietzsche puts the same point in reverse. "The fact is that *if* he were [a hero], he would not represent, conceive, and express it: a Homer would not have created an Achilles nor a Goethe a Faust if Homer had been an Achilles or Goethe a Faust."[6] In

---

6. Friedrich Nietzsche, *On the Genealogy of Morals,* trans. Walter Kaufmann (New York: Vintage Books, 1967), Third Essay, Section 4.

both cases the contrast is between those who merely admire greatness and those who do great things. To speak of the "knight" of faith is to assimilate Abraham with Achilles and Faust, not with Homer or Goethe. Implicit is a critique of those who with Hegel satisfy themselves with understanding the system and those who with Lutheran orthodoxy satisfy themselves that their beliefs are orthodox. Inspired by Abraham, Silentio asks, "What have you done about it? How has it changed your life?"

At the outset of his Preliminary Expectoration Silentio revives this theme with a brief meditation on the "old adage: 'Only one who works gets bread'" (*FT,* 27). He comments that in the external world this does not hold. People often get various rewards they haven't earned. Perhaps Kierkegaard is thinking of himself, living off the wealth created by his father's hard work. But in the world of spirit, he insists, "it holds true that only the one who works gets bread. . . . There is a knowledge that presumptuously wants to introduce into the world of spirit the same law of indifference under which the external world sighs. It believes that it is enough to know what is great — no other work is needed" (*FT,* 27).

Faith is action, reducible to neither admiration nor knowledge. Neither the poet nor the philosopher, as such, has faith. The point of reflection on the Abraham story is neither to praise him nor to understand him but to imitate him. To do so rightly is to have faith, but to "go beyond" him to poetry or philosophy, along with Kierkegaard's romantic and idealistic contemporaries, is not to go on to something higher but to abandon a difficult task for an easier one. Theology is not immune to this retreat in the face of difficulty. "Philosophy goes further [than faith]. Theology sits all rouged and powdered in the window and courts its favor, offers its charms to philosophy" (*FT,* 32). There is a theology that accepts the Hegelian offer of tutelage, or, more generally, that seeks to become scientific and intellectually respectable by giving hermeneutical hegemony to some contemporary philosophy. Putting delicacy aside, Silentio does not merely accuse it of being too timid to think for itself out of its own resources. He calls it a whore.

We need to locate Kierkegaard in a particular historical narrative in order to appreciate his giving this theme so strongly to Silentio. It is the history of Protestant pietism. In seventeenth- and eighteenth-century Germany it developed as a reaction to Lutheran orthodoxy,[7] which was perceived as being all but exclusively concerned, in its conflict with Calvinism

---

7. Sometimes referred to, along with its Calvinist counterpart, as Protestant scholasticism.

and Catholicism, with orthodox beliefs and creedal purity. Pietism placed the greater emphasis on holy living (good works) and especially on the inner, affective dimensions of faith. When Kierkegaard or his pseudonyms emphasize passion, subjectivity, and inwardness, they betray an affinity, not accidental, with this tradition.

It began in Germany at Halle under Philipp Jacob Spener (1635-1705) and August Hermann Franke (1663-1727). More important for the Danish context is the pietism of Count N. L. Zinzendorf (1700-1760), whose followers came to be known as Herrnhuters. It is Herrnhuter pietism that developed in Denmark in the early eighteenth century and almost a century later became the spiritual home of Kierkegaard's father, Michael Pedersen Kierkegaard. Knowing the enormous spiritual influence he had on his son Søren, we can be sure that Søren's religious upbringing had a strongly pietist orientation, and we can see its influence early on and throughout his writings.

The oft-quoted Gilleleie journal entry from August 1835 expresses the spirit of pietism profoundly.

What I really lack is to be clear in my mind *what I am to do,* not what I am to know, except in so far as a certain understanding must precede every action. The thing is to understand myself, to see what God really wishes *me* to do; the thing is to find a truth which is true *for me,* to find *the idea for which I can live and die.* What would be the use of discovering so-called objective truth, of working through all the systems of philosophy . . . and so construct a world in which I did not live, but only held up to the view of others; — what good would it do me to be able to explain the meaning of Christianity if it had *no* deeper significance *for me and for my life;* what good would it do me if truth stood before me, cold and naked, not caring whether I recognized her or not, and producing in me a shudder of fear rather than a trusting devotion? I certainly do not deny that I shall recognize an *imperative of understanding* and that through it one can work upon men, *but it must be taken up into my life,* and *that is* what I recognize as the most important thing.[8]

8. *The Journals of Kierkegaard,* ed. Alexander Dru (New York: Harper & Row, 1958, 1959), p. 44; emphasis in original. This is what Johannes Climacus will call truth as subjectivity in *Concluding Unscientific Postscript,* but N.B. — at the beginning and end of this passage, Kierkegaard emphasizes the importance of objective truth in its role of penultimate importance. There is a curious affinity with Jonathan Edwards here. John E. Smith says that Edwards was "by no stretch of the imagination an existentialist" but "was wrestling with the same problem. He saw that an

An important pietist movement in Kierkegaard's own Denmark arose around N. F. S. Grundvig. Kierkegaard distanced himself from this movement and its leader. But "however much [Grundvig and Kierkegaard] differed in their radicality and their final vision, [they] shared a strong distaste for the official Golden Age ecclesiastical establishment."[9] By the nineteenth century the rationalistic theologies of the Enlightenment had become the target of pietism more than Lutheran orthodoxy, and with Kierkegaard more specifically the Danish Hegelians and Hegel himself who had carried out the Enlightenment project in his own distinctive and creative way. But whether the immediate target was Lutheran orthodoxy, Enlightenment rationalism, or Hegelian Idealism, the pietist critique was aimed at the ways in which these theologies made the life of faith too easy by making some orthodoxy, some right cognition, primary. Religion was all but entirely a matter of the intellect, whereas for pietism the role of the will and of the affections was the end to which true belief was the means.

We return to the Preliminary Expectoration and the contrast between the knight of infinite resignation and the knight of faith. Both have been required to give up their dearest for the sake of the highest. Part of the exposition of resignation comes in the form of a parable of a lad who falls in love with a princess whom he must give up, having never had her, because "the relation is such that it cannot possibly be realized, cannot possibly be translated from ideality into reality" (FT, 41).

As a knight of infinite resignation, he is resigned. That is to say, he gives up the beloved without anger, bitterness, or resentment. He does not "sulk" but finds "joy and peace and rest in [his] pain" (FT, 49; cf. 45).[10] He is reconciled with existence (FT, 45).[11] But this resignation is not just any old giving

---

understanding which excludes first-person experience is doomed to be lost in abstraction and forfeit its relevance for religion . . . [he] makes it clear that understanding can be preserved within religion if it is not taken as a purely theoretical power which ignores the experience of the unique individual." Editor's introduction to Jonathan Edwards, *A Treatise Concerning Religious Affections* (New Haven: Yale University Press, 1959), pp. 46, 44.

9. Bruce H. Kirmmse, *Kierkegaard in Golden Age Denmark* (Bloomington: Indiana University Press, 1990), p. 485. For this context see Kirmmse's index under pietism, awakenings, Herrnhuterism, rationalism, and Grundvig.

10. With reference to Abraham's earlier willingness to leave his homeland and become an exile and alien in response to the promise and command of God, Silentio writes that there "is no dirge by Abraham" (FT, 17).

11. Sharon Krishek puts it nicely. The acceptance of loss in resignation "means that one does not try to deny the loss or render it insignificant . . . at the same time it also means to be at peace with this painful existence — not to rebel against it or become bitter and angry

up. It is infinite resignation. This presupposes that "the knight will then have the power to concentrate the whole substance of his life in the meaning of actuality into one single desire." If one lacks this concentration one "acts as shrewdly in life as the financiers who put their resources into widely diversified investments in order to gain on one if they lose on another — in short, he is not a knight" (*FT,* 43).[12] The lad who gives up the princess is a model of infinite resignation because "this love is the entire substance of his life" (*FT,* 41).

Infinite resignation is a necessary condition for faith. It is "the last stage before faith,[13] so that anyone who has not made this movement does not have faith." We might say that both knights say with Job, "the LORD gave, and the LORD has taken away; blessed be the name of the LORD" (Job 1:21). The knight of faith "does exactly the same as the other knight did: he infinitely renounces the love that is the substance of his life, he is reconciled in pain. But then the marvel happens; he makes one more movement" (*FT,* 46).

This "one more movement" actually signifies a fourfold difference between infinite resignation and faith. First, Silentio imagines himself as the knight of infinite resignation, for, as he insists, he lacks the courage and humility of faith and wonders whether "anyone in my generation is able to make the movements of faith" (*FT,* 33-34; cf. 49).[14] "The moment I mounted the horse, I would have said to myself: Now all is lost, God demands Isaac, I will sacrifice him and along with him all my joy" (*FT,* 35). Resignation is the end of hope, the loss of a future.

By contrast, Abraham believes, "by virtue of the absurd," that he will get Isaac back.[15] The promise of God keeps hope alive. Abraham still has a future.

But resignation's loss of hope and a future is not despair. It is the withdrawal of the self out of time and into eternity. The lad's love for the princess

---

with regard to it." *Kierkegaard on Faith and Love* (New York: Cambridge University Press, 2009), p. 54.

12. Cf. the long occasional discourse best known from a subheading, "Purity of Heart Is to Will One Thing" in *UDVS,* 5-154.

13. We should no doubt take this "before" in a structural and not a temporal sense.

14. In a puzzling move, Silentio begins by describing himself as a tragic hero, though he will shortly use the tragic hero to illustrate a very different dimension of Abrahamic faith. But by the end of the paragraph, it is clear that he is talking about infinite resignation. Perhaps infinite resignation is a necessary condition for being a tragic hero as well as for faith.

15. We shall have to return to this notion of the absurd when we discuss the relation of faith to reason.

becomes "the expression of an eternal love" and is "transfigured into a love of the eternal being" (*FT*, 43). For "what I gain in resignation is my eternal consciousness" and "my eternal consciousness is my love for God" (*FT*, 48). Infinite resignation is a kind of religion, perhaps an analog of Religiousness A in *Concluding Unscientific Postscript*. Both are contrasted with biblical faith. Imagining himself performing the movement of infinite resignation, according to which "all is lost," Silentio adds, "yet God is love and continues to be that for me, for in the world of time God and I cannot talk with each other, we have no language in common" (*FT*, 35). It is a loving God who requires the resignation, whose providence, for example, keeps the lad and his princess apart. Hence the absence of anger, bitterness, and resentment. But the knight of infinite resignation relates to this God only in eternity, only when by a kind of reverse kenosis[16] he has emptied himself of everything temporal and reduced himself to his "eternal validity." This sounds a lot like the God of the English deists and perhaps of Kant, a God who does not act in the world of human history and personal, temporal existence.[17] We aren't told just what the lad's love for the princess looks like when it has become "the expression of an eternal love" (*FT*, 43). We only know that in time it remains an unfulfilled dream, a fantasy. "He is no longer concerned about what the princess does, and precisely this proves that he has made the movement infinitely" (*FT*, 44).

By contrast, and this is the second difference, Abraham's faith was not just that he would get Isaac back but that somehow he would get Isaac back in time, *in this life*. "He did not have faith that he would be blessed in a future life, but that he would be blessed here in the world. God could give him a new Isaac, could restore to life the one sacrificed" (*FT*, 36). We find nothing about this hope of resurrection in the Genesis account.[18] But Silentio draws on the epistle to the Hebrews, where we read,

16. 'Kenosis' is the Greek term for the emptying of Philippians 2:7, according to which Christ Jesus emptied himself of divine power and privilege in order to become fully human.

17. Kant writes, "For if God should really speak to a human being, the latter could still never *know* that it was God speaking." Kant, *The Conflict of the Faculties*, in *Religion and Rational Theology*, ed. Allen W. Wood and George di Giovanni (New York: Cambridge University Press, 1996), p. 283. See Allen W. Wood, "Kant's Deism," in *Kant's Philosophy of Religion Reconsidered*, ed. Philip J. Rossi and Michael Wreen (Bloomington: Indiana University Press, 1991), pp. 1-21.

18. Belief in bodily resurrection comes long after Abraham in the history of Judaism. By the time of Jesus it was a disputed matter, the Pharisees affirming it and the Sadducees denying it. For a historical analysis of beliefs about life after death in ancient paganism, the

By faith Abraham, when put to the test, offered up Isaac. He who had received the promises was ready to offer up his only son, of whom he had been told, "It is through Isaac that descendants shall be named for you." He considered the fact that God is able even to raise someone from the dead. (Heb. 11:17-19)

Silentio puts great emphasis on the worldliness of Abraham. He does not withdraw from time to eternity, from the body to the soul. "Yet Abraham had faith, and had faith for this life. In fact, if his faith had been only for a life to come, he certainly would have more readily discarded everything in order to rush out of a world to which he did not belong. But Abraham's faith was not of this sort" (*FT*, 20).

Accordingly, Silentio stresses, almost to the point of parody, the immersion of the knight of faith in worldly life here and now. To Silentio's surprise,

he looks just like a tax collector! His stance . . . belongs entirely to finitude; no spruced-up burgher walking out to Fresberg on a Sunday afternoon treads the earth more solidly. He belongs entirely to the world; no bourgeois philistine could belong to it more. . . . He finds pleasure in everything. . . . Sunday is for him a holiday. He goes to church. No heavenly gaze or any sign of the incommensurable betrays him; if one did not know him, it would be impossible to distinguish him from the rest of the crowd. . . . In the afternoon he takes a walk to the woods. He enjoys everything he sees . . . one would take him for a mercantile soul enjoying himself . . . his gait is as steady as a postman's. On the way, he thinks that his wife surely will have a special hot meal for him . . . roast lamb's head with vegetables. . . . The stranger leaves him thinking that he surely is a capitalist . . . one would swear it was the butcher . . . and yet, this man has made and at every moment is making the movement of infinity. He drains the deep sadness of life in infinite resignation, he knows the blessedness of infinity, he has felt the pain of renouncing everything, the most precious thing in the world, and *yet the finite tastes just as good to him as to one who never knew anything higher . . . he has this security that makes him delight in it as if finitude were the surest thing of all.* (*FT*, 39-40; emphasis added)

<hr />

Old Testament, and post-biblical Judaism, see N. T. Wright, *The Resurrection of the Son of God* (Minneapolis: Fortress, 2003), chs. 2-4.

This is why Silentio can call the knight of faith the "only happy man, the heir to the finite" (*FT,* 50).

We have seen that, like the life of faith, the life of infinite resignation alone is a religious life. But here is the third and most fundamental difference. The two knights serve two very different gods. The knight of faith makes that "one more movement," the faith that he will get the beloved (Isaac or the princess) back *in this life,* and this movement is made (a) "by virtue of the absurd" and (b) "by virtue of the fact that for God all things are possible" (*FT,* 46). When we come to explore the relation of faith and reason in *Fear and Trembling,* we will have to notice the close linkage between the God of faith and the absurd. For now we will have to notice that the God of faith is an agent and a speaker in this world, in time. This God made Isaac's birth possible in the first place and might resurrect him if that should prove necessary; and this God made the promises to Abraham that are the basis of his faith. We hear nothing of such agency from the essentially deist God of infinite resignation, so "all is lost"; and in infinite resignation one must say that "in the world of time God and I cannot talk with each other, we have no language in common" (*FT,* 35). This God is too remote to keep promises and too impersonal to make them in the first place.

This difference is illustrated in the story of the resurrection of Lazarus in John 11. The disciples try to dissuade Jesus from going to Bethany, near Jerusalem, where there had been recent attempts to stone him. But Thomas says, "Let us also go, that we may die with him" (v. 16). He is a knight of infinite resignation. Although he thinks that "all is lost" now, his loyalty to Jesus forbids clinging to life at the cost of betrayal. Jesus, by contrast, says, "Our friend Lazarus has fallen asleep, but I am going there to awaken him" (v. 11). He believes that divine power can raise the dead not just at the end of the age but even now, and he believes that power is at work in him. That power in him might well signify his own divinity, but the belief in that power by one who is human enough to weep in response to Mary's weeping (vv. 31-36) signifies a Jesus who is a knight of faith.

The fourth and final difference between resignation and faith is almost a corollary to the third. Silentio keeps telling us that although he is in awe of Abraham he cannot himself make the movements of faith because he lacks the courage of faith (*FT,* 33-34). We might take this to mean that he is less virtuous, less spiritually developed than Abraham, or any of his (Silentio's) contemporaries who imitate Abraham by having faith, if there are any.

But I think we must take his insistence in a stronger sense, especially in the light of his account of infinite resignation as a form of human autonomy. In infinite resignation, which is a "substitute for faith," I "find myself and again rest in myself" (*FT,* 35); "he who loves God without faith reflects upon himself; he who loves God in faith reflects upon God" (*FT,* 37); and "one who has resigned infinitely is sufficient to oneself" (*FT,* 44). Resignation does not require faith, "for what I gain in resignation is my eternal consciousness. This is a purely philosophical movement that I venture to make when it is demanded and can discipline myself to make. Because every time some finitude will take power over me, I starve myself into submission until I make the movement. . . . This movement I make all by myself. . . . It takes purely human courage to renounce the whole temporal realm in order to gain eternity" (*FT,* 48-49).

When we read these passages in connection with the one where Silentio calls faith a "miracle" (*FT,* 37),[19] it looks as if infinite resignation is a natural human capacity while faith is not. It looks as if the deist God of the former is, strategically speaking, an attempt to remain religious while retaining the autonomy with which modernity had become so enamored. By contrast, for Silentio, faith is to be understood as a result more of divine agency than of human agency. Given the Pauline polemic against salvation as a reward for good works, it is easy to read Ephesians 2:8 — "For by grace you have been saved through faith, and this is not your own doing; it is the gift of God" — as suggesting that salvation and the grace that bestows it are gifts of God. Silentio seems to be suggesting that the very faith by which this gift is received is itself a gift, something we cannot produce out of our own resources.

Before turning from thesis 2, **Faith as trust in divine promises**, to thesis 3, **Faith as obedience to divine commands**, it will be worth our while to look at John Davenport's claim that the "main point" of *Fear and Trembling* "is to present the essence of 'faith' as *eschatological* trust."[20] In the next chapter I will challenge the claim that the contrast between the knight of faith and the knight of infinite resignation is the "main point" of our text. To say so is to overlook the explicit claim that this contrast is "preliminary," that this section is a "preamble." It is also to suppress the reason why what

19. On the relation between Silentio's conception of faith as a miracle and Hume's discussion of miracles, see Michelle Kosch, *Freedom and Reason in Kant, Schelling, and Kierkegaard* (Oxford: Clarendon, 2006), pp. 184-86. This is in connection with the need for what Johannes Climacus calls "the condition" in *Philosophical Fragments.* See chapter 7 below.

20. John J. Davenport, "Faith as Eschatological Trust in *Fear and Trembling*," in *Ethics, Love, and Faith in Kierkegaard,* ed. Edward F. Mooney (Bloomington: Indiana University Press, 2008), p. 198.

follows, the contrast between the knight of faith and the tragic hero, is for Silentio, if not for all readers, the main point.

But here I want to raise a different issue. Davenport's emphasis on faith as trust is right on target. What I want to challenge is the appropriateness of calling this trust eschatological. Davenport knows that it is important not to Christianize Abraham. So he emphasizes that his account "abstracts from the differences among religious creeds concerning salvation, 'last things,' or the hereafter." He knows that "eschatology" typically "is associated with last battles and final judgment, whereas God's promise to Abraham (before Isaac is born) is not that he will be judged and will enter heaven or that the world will be renewed in a cosmic apocalypse." He cites the crucial passage from *Fear and Trembling*: "He did not have faith that he would be blessed in a future life, but that he would be blessed here in the world" (*FT*, 36).[21]

But once the term 'eschatology' has been emptied of all these connotations of a final culmination of history; of a final judgment; of a transition from earth to heaven, from the present age to the (messianic) age to come, or from time to eternity, its use is more misleading than illuminating. Davenport cites a phrase from the text that does the job quite adequately: Abraham's faith is "trusting expectancy" (*FT*, 19). Why call this expectancy eschatological? Davenport appeals to "the general structure" underlying normal eschatological discourse, "namely, trust in the ultimate accomplishment of the Good by divine power." He argues that Abraham's faith "performs the same eschatological function that faith in salvation beyond death does for Christians," namely trust that "the future state, ultimate outcome, or final end is a *victory of the good*."[22] But this double use of 'ultimate' lets the cat out of the bag. Language sometimes overcomes its users. Here is the implication of a final culmination of history of which we find no trace in the Abraham story, either in its biblical form or in Silentio's retelling. All we find there is the hope for a universal blessing, but that is not the same as an "ultimate outcome, or final end [as] a *victory of the good*."

Davenport appeals to Silentio's claim that if the ethical universal "is the highest that can be said of man and his existence, then the ethical is of the same nature as a person's eternal salvation" (*FT*, 54), noting that "eternal salvation" is "an eschatological concept."[23] But he has already told us that he is abstracting from such notions, which, in any case, do not appear in

21. Davenport, "Faith as Eschatological Trust," pp. 198-201.
22. Davenport, "Faith as Eschatological Trust," pp. 200-201; emphasis in original.
23. Davenport, "Faith as Eschatological Trust," p. 199.

Abraham's case. Just in case we are tempted to Christianize Abraham, Silentio has already emphasized the this-worldly character of his faith. The reference to eternal salvation occurs, not in Silentio's analysis of Abraham, but in his construal of Hegel, who claims to be a Christian thinker. Silentio is suggesting that he is not. If the ethical universal is the highest, in Hegel's sense of *Sittlichkeit*,[24] "then no categories are needed other than what Greek philosophy had or what can be deduced from them by consistent thought. Hegel should not have concealed this, for, after all, he had studied Greek philosophy" (*FT*, 55).

Messianic Judaism and Christianity will doubtless read the promise of universal blessing eschatologically, but we need to follow Davenport's advice not to "Christianize" Abraham better than he has done. A further indication of the way in which Davenport is betrayed by his own use of the language of eschatology comes when he appeals to Alastair Hannay for support. The latter's account is "an anticipated apocalyptic turning *within history,* not merely in the next life or the cosmic end of time: for, as Hannay says, 'in the end' does not include 'in the hereafter' for Abraham."[25] Davenport has failed to abstract, as promised, from the language of an end or culmination of history that can be called apocalyptic, of which I find no trace in *Fear and Trembling*. He can hardly expect his readers to do so.

So what do we have if we do follow Davenport's good advice rather than his practice? We have an account of faith as trust in divine promises, a "trusting expectancy" that is hard to distinguish from hope. Faith has a future and is not the despair that says, "All is lost." If faith is informed by messianic Judaism or Christianity, it will have good reason to include eschatological promises within the object or content of faith. But we will also have a warning from Abraham/Silentio not to overlook any possible promises that might be called pre-eschatological, promises that are not only this worldly but penultimate.

24. For an account of ethical life *(Sittlichkeit)* as the laws and customs of one's people, see chapter 3 below.
25. Davenport, "Faith as Eschatological Trust," p. 206.

Faith as Obedience to Divine Commands

It is well known that Kierkegaard develops, in a variety of texts, a theory of the three stages on life's way or existence spheres: the aesthetic, the ethical, and the religious. These stages or modes of being-in-the-world are best understood as different criteria for what counts as the good life. The aesthetic may include an interest in the arts, but that is not essential. What all forms of the good life have in common are criteria in which good and evil, right and wrong play no fundamental role. The good life is amoral, and its goal is, for example, the interesting as distinct from the boring life. The young aesthete in *Either/Or* expresses his philosophy as follows: "Boredom is the root of all evil" (*EO* 1:285). Good and evil, right and wrong are central to the ethical and religious stages. For the ethical these are defined by the society or community to which one belongs, while for the religious they are defined by God. So we might say that the three spheres (for they are not stages in the developmental sense) posit three different absolute points of reference respectively: I myself, my society, and God.

At the beginning and the end of the Preliminary Expectoration, Silentio tells us why it is preliminary, and he does so with reference to the theory of the stages or existence spheres. His treatise is a commentary on the difference between the ethical, as interpreted by Hegel, and the religious, as embodied in Abraham's faith. "If faith cannot make it a holy act to be willing to murder his son, then let the same judgment be passed on Abraham as on everyone else. . . . The ethical expression for what Abraham did is that he means to murder Isaac; the religious expression is that he means to sacrifice Isaac" (*FT,* 30). Just before turning to the three problems that make up the main body of his text, after the four introductions, Silentio speaks of "the prodigious paradox of faith, a paradox that makes a murder into a holy and God-pleasing act, a paradox that gives Isaac back to Abraham again, which no thought can grasp" (*FT,* 53).

We shall explore the categories of the paradox and the absurd when turning to the relation between faith and reason. For now it is important to notice that the two paradoxes mentioned are not one and the same. The paradox that gives Isaac back to Abraham is the one highlighted in the contrast between the knights of infinite resignation and of faith. We have just examined it and found no reference to murder. Abraham is a knight of faith because, in addition to the resignation that is willing to give up Isaac without anger, bitterness, or resentment, he believes that he will get Isaac back in this life because God has promised and with God all things are possible. The account abstracts entirely from the fact that Abraham is to give Isaac up by killing him. Otherwise the parable about the lad and the princess wouldn't fit at all. It is only about giving up and (not) getting back.[1]

Now the plot thickens. It is no longer just about giving up and getting back but about the difference between murder and sacrifice (see *FT,* 55, 57). For Problem I, the crucial contrast will be between the knight of faith and the tragic hero. Each of the three tragic heroes who will appear, Agamemnon, Jephthah, and Brutus, killed one of his children. The difference between them and Abraham is not that they actually did it while Abraham eventually did not.[2] The passage just cited above indicates that for Silentio Abraham is to be evaluated on the basis of what he meant to do, and he clearly meant to kill Isaac if it came to that. The difference is that the three tragic heroes are justified, at least in their own context, in a way that Abraham is not and cannot be.

So why are the first paradox and the first contrast preliminary to the second paradox and second contrast? One way to put it is that the first, having abstracted from the issue of killing and focusing only on giving up, presents only an abstract, incomplete account of faith. The faith that goes

---

1. "Many a father has lost his child, but then it was God, the unchangeable, inscrutable will of the Almighty, it was his hand that took it. Not so with Abraham! A harder test [*Prøve*] was reserved for him, and Isaac's fate was placed, along with the knife, in Abraham's hand" (*FT,* 22).

2. In some versions of the Greek story, Agamemnon goes through with the sacrifice of his daughter, Iphigenia. In others, including Euripides', who apparently has been reading Genesis, she is replaced at the last minute by a deer. For Silentio the difference would not matter, since the last-minute replacement of Isaac by the ram caught in a thicket (Gen. 22:13) does not in the least get Abraham off the hook.

beyond infinite resignation is only an aspect, a necessary but not sufficient condition of authentic Abrahamic faith. Only when it is integrated into the dimension to which Silentio now turns our attention do we have the whole picture of faith. Only when trust in divine promises enacts itself in obedience to divine commands, with all that entails (which is what the three problems are about) do we have faith fully present.

Another way to see the preliminary character of faith as the movement beyond infinite resignation is rather Kantian. In the Abraham story, faith as trust in divine promises is about happiness, and Silentio says that "the knight of faith is the only happy man, the heir to the finite, while the knight of resignation is a stranger and an alien" (*FT,* 50). The joy of infinite resignation is "not the joy of faith, and with comparison with that, it is unhappy . . . for if [the knight of infinite resignation] had gotten Isaac again, [he] would have been in an awkward position. What was the easiest for Abraham would have been difficult for [infinite resignation] — once again to be happy in Isaac!" (*FT,* 34-35).

By contrast, faith as obedience to divine commands is about worthiness to be happy. There is no happiness in the obedience that journeys three days to Mount Moriah. Silentio regularly describes it as filled with anxiety and distress (for example, *FT,* 63, 65, 74-75, 113).[3] For Abraham "weeping may spend the night, but joy comes [only] in the morning" when he does get Isaac back.[4] To speak of Abraham's worthiness to be happy is not to imply that Abraham somehow earned the promised blessings, that God somehow owed them to him. It is only to suggest that the obedience that begins with his emigration and concludes, so far as our narrative takes us, with the trip to Mount Moriah is a fittingly grateful response to the gifts graciously promised.[5]

In either case, what the text does not allow is those interpretations that make the contrast between faith and resignation the main point of *Fear and Trembling* (of which more hereafter).

---

3. And paradox, indicating a pain for the intellect as well as for the loving heart of a father. It is in these terms that Silentio describes the faith of the Virgin Mary (*FT,* 65).

4. Psalm 30:6 (30:5, NRSV), from the Psalter in the *Book of Common Prayer.*

5. Perhaps this is why Paul is not so different from James, after all. James famously writes, "So faith by itself, if it has no works, is dead. But someone will say, 'You have faith and I have works.' Show me your faith apart from your works, and I by my works will show you my faith" (James 2:17-18). Paul begins his epistle to the Romans, in which he argues so strongly that salvation is a gift of grace and not something earned by good works, with a reference to "the obedience of faith" (ὑπακοὴν πίστεως, Rom. 1:5). He sees obedience as an integral aspect of faith.

The main point comes in the contrast between the ethical and the religious, or, more concretely, between Abraham and Hegel as developed in each of the three problems that make up the main body of the text. Silentio tells us this in several ways. First, each of the three problem discussions begins with essentially the same argument. The ethical is the universal. If this is the highest, then Hegel is right, but Abraham is lost and cannot be justified, much less praised (*FT,* 54-55, 68, 82). Second, for the ethical or social morality, Silentio uses *det sædelige* or *Sædelighed,* the Danish equivalent of Hegel's *das Sittliche* or *Sittlichkeit,* normally translated as 'ethical life' and meaning the laws and customs of one's people.[6] Third, Silentio gives the following as examples of the ethical as the universal: the nation, the state, society, the church, and the sect (*FT,* 57-59, 74, 79). In other words, the ethical as the universal is not something like a Platonic form or a Kantian principle; it is rather a concrete universal, some historically particular community to which individuals belong and whose laws and customs are the norms for their lives.[7]

The urge to assume that by "the ethical" Silentio means any ethics that expresses itself in purportedly universal principles, independent of anything historically particular or conditioned, seems irrepressible, however clearly the text precludes that reading of "the ethical" as "the universal." In particular, readers of *Fear and Trembling* want to find in it a contrast between Kantian ethics and biblical faith.[8] But the text does not allow such a generalized contrast between ethics and Abrahamic faith. Silentio identifies

6. As developed in the *Phenomenology of Spirit,* the *Philosophy of Right,* and the *Philosophy of Spirit.* In the latter two its three moments are not principles but social institutions: family, civil society, and the state.

7. Silentio says that the ethical is the universal and thus applies to everyone at all times (*FT,* 54). If he left it at that his concept of the universal would fit Platonic, Kantian, or any other form of rational ethics. But when he goes on to define the universal so explicitly in terms of various communities and with explicit reference to Hegel, he effectively qualifies the "everyone" and "at all times" to mean everyone and at all times within this or that particular community or society.

8. See, for example, Ronald M. Green, *Kierkegaard and Kant: The Hidden Debt* (Albany: SUNY Press, 1992). John Lippitt suggests that the contrast is between faith and Kantian or Hegelian ethics more or less equally. *Routledge Philosophy Guidebook to Kierkegaard and "Fear and Trembling"* (New York: Routledge, 2003), pp. 82-89. Ed Mooney takes the issue to concern the subjectivity that does not remain "*within* the confines of rational ethics," and with reference to the contrast between the subjective and the universal writes, "Mainstream Platonic and Kantian traditions in ethics deny any rational or justificatory status to the 'subjective' or 'particular.'" Mooney, *Knights of Faith and Resignation: Reading Kierkegaard's "Fear and Trembling"* (Albany: SUNY Press, 1991), pp. 73-74.

a very specific concept of ethical life in order to make a very specific point, the main point of *Fear and Trembling.*

We can see that point clearly if, taking seriously the Hegelian character of the ethical in our text, we substitute 'society' (or 'community') for 'the universal,' and 'God' for 'the absolute,' in order to get the following passage:

> The paradox of faith, then, is this: that the single individual is higher than [society], that the single individual — to recall a distinction in dogmatics rather rare these days — determines his relation to [society] by his relation to [God], not his relation to [God] by his relation to [society]. The paradox may also be expressed in this way: that there is an absolute duty to God, for in this relationship of duty the individual relates himself as the single individual absolutely to the absolute. (*FT,* 70)

Neither Platonic ethics, as usually read, nor Kantian ethics, nor utilitarianism, nor intuitionism, nor classical natural law theory see themselves as making the laws and customs of a particular society the highest norms for human life.[9] They purport to embody a pure reason that inhabits "the view from nowhere," uncontaminated by the particularity and contingency of any actual society. They claim to present an ahistorically universal truth to which every society and every individual is responsible.

Hegel rejects this view of ethics in favor of a thoroughly historical conception of human reason. "Whatever happens, every individual is a child of his time; so philosophy too is its own time apprehended in thoughts."[10] He applies this principle even to his logic. He bemoans, in the opening sentence of his *Science of Logic,* that the

> complete transformation which philosophical thought in Germany has undergone in the last twenty-five years and the higher standpoint reached by spirit in its awareness of itself, have had but little influence as yet on the structure of logic. . . . If it is remarkable when a nation has become indifferent to its constitutional theory, to its national sentiments, its ethical customs and virtues, it is certainly no less remarkable when a nation loses its metaphysics, when the spirit which contemplates its own

---

9. Legal positivism would be closer to Hegel except that it lacks the notion of a teleological fulfillment of the historical process.

10. G. W. F. Hegel, *Philosophy of Right,* trans. T. M. Knox (Oxford: Oxford University Press, 1942), p. 11 (preface).

pure essence is no longer a present reality in the life of a nation . . . logic shows no traces so far of the new spirit which has arisen in the sciences no less than in the world of actuality. However, once the substantial form of the spirit has inwardly reconstituted itself, all attempts to preserve the forms of an earlier culture are utterly in vain; like withered leaves they are pushed off by the new buds already growing at their roots.[11]

In other words, philosophy, including its most formal, fundamental principles, is and ought to be relative to the standpoint of spirit in the historical development of its self-consciousness, and N.B. spirit here is the spirit of a nation or culture.

Hegel had expressed this idea earlier in his *Phenomenology of Spirit*.

To show that now is the time for philosophy to be raised to the status of a Science would therefore be the only true justification of any effort that has this aim. . . . If we apprehend a demand of this kind in its broader context, and view it as it appears at the stage which self-conscious Spirit has presently reached, it is clear that Spirit has now got beyond the substantial life it formerly led in the element of thought. . . . Besides, it is not difficult to see that ours is a birth-time and a period of transition to a new era. Spirit has broken with the world it has hitherto inhabited and imagined. . . . The gradual crumbling that left unaltered the face of the whole is cut short by a sunburst which, in one flash, illuminates the features of a new world.[12]

In applying this idea that "philosophy too is its own time apprehended in thoughts" to Plato, Hegel applies it to every ethics whose claim to universality is the claim to flow from some ahistorical, "pure" reason. "[S]ince philosophy is the exploration of the rational, it is for that very reason the apprehension of the present and the actual, not the erection of a beyond, supposed to exist, God knows where, or rather which exists . . . in the error of a one-sided, empty, ratiocination. In the course of this book I have remarked

11. *Hegel's Science of Logic,* trans. A. V. Miller (New York: Humanities, 1969), pp. 25-26; cf. pp. 42, 51. Hegel identifies logic with metaphysics, speaking of "the science of logic which constitutes metaphysics proper or purely speculative philosophy" (p. 27).

12. *Hegel's Phenomenology of Spirit,* trans. A. V. Miller (Oxford: Oxford University Press, 1977), pp. 3-7. Hegel later says that the idea that philosophy must be a system and that substance is essentially spirit is "the most sublime concept and the one which belongs to the modern age and its religion" (p. 14; translation altered).

that even Plato's *Republic,* which passes proverbially as an empty ideal, is in essence nothing but an interpretation of the nature of Greek ethical life."[13]

Hegel regularly argues that, just to the degree that Kant keeps practical reason ahistorically pure, it is unable to justify any determinate content.[14] If any specific duties are to be found, they will have to be imported, without notice and without warrant, from the moral understanding of various historical communities and their traditions, especially as expressed in particular religious communities and philosophical traditions. Hegel uses the term 'reflection' here in a double sense. It refers to reflective, discursive thought, as distinct from immediate moral sense or judgment; and it refers to the fact that even as discursive thought (theology or philosophy as distinct from what Kant calls "healthy human understanding") the content will be a reflection of and thus conditioned by the historical context out of which it grows and on which it is dependent.

Kierkegaard, throughout his writings, pseudonymous and otherwise, agrees with Hegel on this point.[15] This is why he can be read as ideology

13. Hegel, *Philosophy of Right,* p. 10. "In his *Republic,* Plato displays the substance of [Greek] ethical life in its ideal beauty and truth; but he could only cope with the principle of self-subsistent particularity, which in his day had forced its way into Greek ethical life, by setting up in opposition to it his purely substantial state. . . . The principle of self-subsistent, inherently infinite personality of the individual, the principle of subjective freedom, is denied its right in the purely substantial form which Plato gave to spirit in its actuality" (p. 124, Remark to §185). In other words, the "pure" reason that purports to soar above the historically concrete, contingent, and particular world of the cave into the sunlight of uncontaminated universality is a fiction. It is the actual masquerading as the ideal, the particular masquerading as the universal. The new principle comes from Christian and Roman sources, and the Greek view must be *aufgehoben* or teleologically suspended in these subsequent historical developments in order for the particular to move toward the genuine universality of teleological fulfillment.

14. Hegel, *Phenomenology of Spirit,* pp. 252-62, "Reason as lawgiver" and especially "Reason as testing laws"; G. W. F. Hegel, *The Encyclopaedia Logic,* trans. T. F. Geraets, W. A. Suchting, and H. S. Harris (Indianapolis: Hackett, 1991), §52 (with addition); and *Hegel's Lectures on the History of Philosophy: The Lectures of 1825-1826,* ed. Robert F. Brown (Berkeley: University of California Press, 1990), pp. 244-46.

15. Thulstrup is simply wrong when he presents as his major thesis that "Hegel and Kierkegaard have in the main nothing in common as thinkers, neither as regards object, purpose, or method, nor as regards what each considered to be indisputable principles." Niels Thulstrup, *Kierkegaard's Relation to Hegel,* trans. George L. Stengren (Princeton: Princeton University Press, 1980), p. 12. Jon Stewart is right to reject this view. *Kierkegaard's Relation to Hegel Reconsidered* (New York: Cambridge University Press, 2003), pp. 14-27. But it does not follow that Thulstrup's view was the "standard view" in 2003 or that Kierkegaard's critique of "Hegel" was only aimed at and only effectively engaged the Danish Hegelians. See the discussion in chapter 1 above.

critique.[16] Marx and Engels will later put it this way: "The ideas of the ruling class are in every epoch the ruling ideas, i.e. the class which is the ruling material force of society is at the same time its ruling intellectual force."[17] The only (crucial) difference between Marx and Engels on the one hand and Hegel and Kierkegaard on the other is that the latter pair, while thinking that 'reason' is always a reflection of a historically particular world, and therefore neither 'pure' nor utterly universal, do not put this in terms of economic classes but leave open the possibility of a wide variety of conditioning factors.

At this point we need to remember, as we saw in chapter 1 above, that *Fear and Trembling* is framed between satires in "our age" (*FT*, 5) and "the present generation" (*FT*, 121). Silentio wants to concentrate our attention, not on some generic notion of the ethical, but on that specific variety that makes the laws and customs of a particular society the highest norms for its members and seeks to transubstantiate this particularity into a universality by calling itself "Reason" or perhaps "Pure Practical Reason."

We might say that *Fear and Trembling* continues the "attack upon Christendom" whose beginning could be placed at the end of *Either/Or*.[18] In the second volume of *Either/Or*, Judge William embodies the ethical stage in two very long letters to the young man, known only as A, who has embodied the aesthetic stage in the first volume. Two significant features of the good judge's letters are the moral complacency they exhibit ("Wretched contentment!" Kierkegaard must have thought)[19] and the Hegelian character of his ethical self-understanding.

The clearest indication of the latter is that, in urging the young aesthete to choose the ethical, he does not urge him to adopt some moral principle or highest maxim such as Kant's Categorical Imperative, the Golden Rule, or the command of neighbor love. So far as his moral self-understanding has any specific content, it is entirely in terms of a social institution, mar-

16. See the relevant discussion in chapter 1 above.

17. *Karl Marx: Selected Writings*, ed. David McLellan, 2nd ed. (New York: Oxford University Press, 2000), p. 192 (from *The German Ideology*, a draft not published until 1932) and p. 260 (in *The Communist Manifesto*, 1848). In the latter Marx and Engels write, "Law, morality, religion are to [the proletariat] so many bourgeois prejudices, behind which lurk in ambush just as many bourgeois interests" (p. 254).

18. *Either/Or* and *Fear and Trembling* were published in February and October of 1843 respectively. The first contrasts the aesthetic and the ethical stages, while the latter contrasts the ethical with the religious.

19. For this link between Kierkegaard and Nietzsche, see chapter 1 above.

riage. Thus, in urging the young aesthete to choose the ethical, he urges him to choose marriage. What is Hegelian about this is clear. When Hegel gives a systematic account of ethical life *(Sittlichkeit)*,[20] he does so in terms of three social institutions: family, civil society (the private sector of a capitalist economy), and the state. In the *Philosophy of Right* he introduces us to ethical life with one of the few sustained analyses of marriage in the western philosophical tradition.[21]

So how does the "attack upon Christendom" begin at the end of *Either/ Or?* After the two very long letters, the judge sends to his young friend a sermon by a pastor who was "stuck out in a little parish in the heath in Jylland." It is entitled "The Upbuilding That Lies in the Thought That in Relation to God We Are Always in the Wrong." It is a meditation on Jesus first weeping over Jerusalem and then "cleansing" the temple by driving out the money changers (*EO* 2:337-41). The text portrays Jesus' virtual despair over the established center of religious life in his day and his anger at those who ran the temple, the very center of this center.[22]

What Judge William does not see, but the reader is supposed to see, is that the homily is an ultimatum,[23] a final word, a last judgment, not on the amoralism of the young aesthete but on the good judge himself. God is not a factor in the former's world, so he cannot think of a relation to God of any sort. The judge, by contrast, is very devout and talks a lot about God. But he leaves the impression that while God is very much a part of

20. In the *Philosophy of Right* and the *Philosophy of Spirit* (part three of his system, the *Encyclopedia of the Philosophical Sciences).*

21. See "Hegel's Radical Idealism: Family and State as Ethical Communities," in my *Hegel, Freedom, and Modernity* (Albany: SUNY Press, 1992), pp. 37-54.

22. "The Temple was the focal point of every aspect of Jewish national life. Local synagogues and schools of Torah in other parts of Palestine, and in the Diaspora, in no way replaced it, but gained their significance from their implicit relation to it. . . . But the Temple was not simply the 'religious' centre of Israel — even supposing that a distinction between religion and other departments of life could make any sense at the period in question. It was not, shall we say, the equivalent of Westminster Abbey, with 'Buckingham Palace' and the 'Houses of Parliament' being found elsewhere. The Temple combined in itself the functions of all three — religion, national figurehead, and government. . . . The high priest, who was in charge of the Temple, was as important a political figure as he was a religious one." N. T. Wright, *The New Testament and the People of God* (Minneapolis: Fortress, 1992), pp. 224-25. Cf. the central importance of the temple in Wright's *Jesus and the Victory of God* (Minneapolis: Fortress, 1996), chs. 9 and 11. This non-separation of "church" and state resembles Hegel's *Sittlichkeit.* See *Philosophy of Right,* the long Remark to §270.

23. The section is so titled, presumably by Victor Eremita, the pseudonymous discoverer and editor of the papers that make up the two volumes.

his world, he is so complacent (wretched contentment!) in his piety and civic virtue, which are but two sides of the same coin, that he cannot really imagine himself in the wrong against God.[24] The established order, into which he has been thoroughly and successfully socialized, is pretty much identical with the Kingdom of God. If the ethical universal is the highest, "then the ethical is of the same nature as a person's eternal salvation" (*FT*, 54). In other words, socialization is salvation because "the ethical is the divine" (*FT*, 60).[25]

Judge William is the embodiment of Christendom. A critique of a Platonic or Kantian ethic leaves it untouched, for those philosophies do not represent its self-understanding. But a critique of Hegelian ethics is a direct assault on the Christendom that equates socialization with salvation and assumes that being on good terms with one's society — church and nation in this case[26] — is all that can be asked of one. As we shall see, Anti-Climacus will make this kind of critique even more fully explicit in *Practice in Christianity.* But its presence already in *Fear and Trembling* is lost when "the ethical" is assimilated to some Platonic or Kantian ethics.

Incidentally, this is the third place where Silentio's argument makes direct and effective contact with Hegel himself and not just the Danish Hegelians.[27]

In Problem I,[28] Silentio poses the question whether there can be a teleological suspension of the ethical (in the religious). If not, Hegel is right and the universal (his universal) is the highest; but in that case Abraham is lost and what he intends is not sacrifice but murder. What, then, is a teleological suspension? Quite simply, it is what Hegel calls an *Aufhebung.* It is a movement in which what takes itself or is taken to be something that stands alone and is sufficient unto itself is contextualized, is relocated as part of some larger whole of which it is not the organizing principle. Thus, in the *Philosophy of Right,* the family is *aufgehoben* in civil society; civil society

---

24. Perhaps Kierkegaard is thinking of Judge William when he has Vigilius Haufniensis write, "But for ethics the possibility of sin never occurs" (*CA*, 23).

25. Silentio speaks of socialization as the "mediation" of the individual into the universal and then denies that faith can be understood in these terms (*FT*, 60, 62, 66, 70-71). This is because there is something in the individual, so far as faith is concerned, that is "incommensurable" with the universal, with society (*FT*, 55, 69)

26. See note 22 above.

27. For the first two points of contact directly with Hegel and the critique of Jon Stewart on this point, see chapter 1 above.

28. Why the Hongs use 'problema' in an English translation escapes me entirely.

is *aufgehoben* in the state; and, finally, the state is *aufgehoben* in universal history.[29]

This structure had already appeared in the second volume of *Either/Or*, but not by either its Hegelian or its Kierkegaardian name. Judge William regularly insists that the aesthetic is *aufgehoben* or teleologically suspended in the ethical. What that means, first of all, is that in the ethical the aesthetic is "dethroned" (*EO* 2:226). But that does not mean that it is "annihilated" (*EO* 2:31; cf. 271), or "repudiated" (*EO* 2:61), or "excluded" (*EO* 2:177), or "destroyed" (*EO* 2:253). Rather, it means that in the ethical it is "ennobled" (*EO* 2:21, 30, 57, 61) or "transfigured" (*EO* 2:31, 56, 94, 253, 271). It becomes part of a larger whole whose organizing principle it is not. Judge William uses the image of concentric circles to express this notion of a subordinate part (*EO* 2:29-30, 47-48, 55, 57, 60).

> In the ethical, the personality is brought into a focus in itself; consequently, the aesthetic is absolutely excluded or *it is excluded as the absolute,* but relatively it is continually present. In choosing itself, the personality chooses itself ethically and absolutely excludes the aesthetic; but since he nevertheless chooses himself and does not become another being by choosing himself but becomes himself, *all the aesthetic returns in its relativity.* (*EO* 2:177; emphasis added)[30]

Perhaps Silentio has been reading *Either/Or*, for he applies this structure to the relation between the ethical and the religious, the norms that express the essence of some particular human society or community and the norms that come from a special divine revelation not reducible to any society's values. To repeat, if there is no *Aufhebung* or teleological suspension of the ethical in the religious, if the latter cannot trump the former, then Hegel is right. The concrete social universal is the highest, and "the ethical is the divine" (*FT*, 60); but Hegel "is wrong in not protesting loudly and clearly against Abraham's enjoying honor and glory as a father of faith when he

---

29. Though it doesn't yield a happy translation, the standard comment is that what is *aufgehoben* is at once cancelled and preserved. Fair enough, but both 'cancelled' and 'preserved' need to be nuanced. As we shall see, what is *aufgehoben* is cancelled as absolute in stand-alone self-sufficiency and preserved as a relative, subordinate part of a more complex totality whose first principle it is not. Thus, structurally speaking, Hegel denies absolute autonomy to both family and civil society and historically denies it to the state.

30. I prefer 'aesthetic' to the Hongs' 'esthetic,' and here, as elsewhere, I alter their translation to reflect that.

ought to be sent back to a lower court and shown up as a murderer" (*FT,* 54-55).[31] Silentio is stipulating, in effect, and for purposes of his argument, that Abraham lives in a culture where child sacrifice is not accepted.[32]

The biblical story of Abraham assumes, as Silentio puts it, that there is a teleological suspension of the ethical in which "that which is suspended is not relinquished but is preserved in the higher, which is its τελος" (*FT,* 54).[33] To apply Judge William's language to this *Aufhebung,* we can say that the ethical is "ennobled" and "transformed" when it plays the role of servant rather than master to the religious.

This means three things. First, the paradox of faith is that the individual is higher than the universal, but only "*after* having been in the universal" (*FT,* 55). In other words, the knight of faith is not like the aesthete who has never been "subordinate as the single individual to the universal" (*FT,* 56). He has been socialized and takes the laws and customs of his society seriously. They have normative significance for him. That is why Abraham's trip to Mount Moriah is filled with anxiety, distress, and paradox (*FT,* 63, 65, 74-75, 113). The world in which what he intends is condemned as murder is a world in which he still lives. He is no blithe spirit.

---

31. In his 1824 lectures on the philosophy of religion, Hegel praises Abraham, along with Job, for the fear of the Lord that is the beginning of wisdom and "one essential aspect of freedom." It is expressed in an "absolute trust, or infinite faith." *Hegel's Lectures on the Philosophy of Religion,* vol. 2: *Determinate Religion,* ed. Peter C. Hodgson (Berkeley: University of California Press, 1987), pp. 441-47. In his early theological writings Hegel had portrayed Abraham as utterly alienated and servile, as if he had been reading Nietzsche on slave morality and its religion. G. W. F. Hegel, *Early Theological Writings,* trans. T. M. Knox (Chicago: University of Chicago Press, 1948; reissued by University of Pennsylvania Press in 1971), pp. 182-89. Kant famously rejects any teleological suspension of his quite different universal, and accordingly condemns Abraham, both in *Religion within the Bounds of Mere Reason* and in *The Conflict of the Faculties,* found in *Religion and Rational Theology,* The Cambridge Edition of the Works of Immanuel Kant, trans. and ed. Allen W. Wood and George di Giovanni (New York: Cambridge University Press, 1996), pp. 124, 203-4, 282-85.

32. Apart from Genesis 22, there are sixteen passages in the Hebrew Bible in which "child sacrifice is condemned as an abomination before God." Louis Jacobs, "The Problem of the *Akedah* in Jewish Thought," in *Kierkegaard's "Fear and Trembling": Critical Appraisals,* ed. Robert L. Perkins (University: University of Alabama Press, 1981), p. 1. But these reflect Mosaic legislation. What the ethical culture that Abraham brought with him from Ur of the Chaldees had to say about child sacrifice is not so clear.

33. On the idea that the religious is the proper goal of the ethical, see C. Stephen Evans, "Faith as the *Telos* of Morality: A Reading of *Fear and Trembling,*" in *International Kierkegaard Commentary,* vol. 6: *"Fear and Trembling" and "Repetition,"* ed. Robert L. Perkins (Macon, GA: Mercer University Press, 1993), pp. 9-27.

But that world is only penultimate for the individual, and it is only when he is raised above the universal *after* having been subordinated to it that he "stands in an absolute relation to the absolute" (*FT,* 56). N.B. The individual who is raised above the universal is not the isolated, atomic individual sometimes attributed to Kierkegaard. His theory is as much a theory of the self as essentially relation as Hegel's. But where Hegel collapses the difference between God and society, Kierkegaard keeps them separate, and in faith as the teleological suspension of the ethical allows the relation to God to trump the relation to society. Only the former relation is absolute and ultimate.

Second, to see the individual as capable of being higher than the universal in relation to God as absolute is to find in the individual a "residual incommensurability" vis-à-vis the ethical universal (*FT,* 55; cf. 69, 82). This world both is and is not his home. He does not fit into it without remainder.

Third, Silentio sometimes uses Hegel's language for this incommensurability. The individual cannot be "mediated" into the universal (*FT,* 60, 62, 66, 82). The aesthete and the knight of faith share an incommensurability and remain unmediated into the universal. But while the aesthete stands wholly outside the ethical and allows it no normative significance, the knight of faith is partially or penultimately within the universal while resisting any full absorption by, or by virtue of, a relation to something higher. In faith it is not the individual as such that is higher than the universal, but the individual in relation to Someone higher.

While there is an implicit comparison between the knight of faith and the aesthete in this part of Silentio's argument, the explicit comparison is with the tragic hero. Agamemnon, Jephthah, and Brutus are tragic heroes. Each actually kills a son or daughter, and each for a different reason. But each of their reasons might be called a *raison d'état*. Their love for their children (an aesthetic good) and their duty toward them (an ethical good)[34] are trumped by their duty toward the state, their political community. But this teleological suspension of the family in the state does not take the tragic hero out of the ethical but only moves the tragic hero from one, lower level to a higher level.[35] Families who send their fathers and sons (and now their

---

34. "There is no higher expression for the ethical in Abraham's life than that the father shall love the son" (*FT,* 59).

35. The term *raison d'état* implies a certain overriding or trumping, usually some national interest thought to override what would otherwise be a legal or moral requirement. For the tragic hero it is one ethical requirement overridden by another ethical requirement, but the higher requirement grows out of the needs of the state, the larger community.

mothers and daughters) off to war are like the tragic hero. A need of the state takes precedence over the needs, desires, and responsibilities of the family, and men and women "abandon" their families, possibly never to return.

What distinguishes the tragic hero from the knight of faith is that the former is justified within the ethical sphere. The norms arising out of citizenship not only trump those of the family but provide a justification whose legitimacy all fellow citizens can be expected to understand and approve. The three tragic heroes killed their children, but they did not commit murder, and all their friends and neighbors can see this for themselves. So it is possible to weep with the tragic hero, but not with Abraham. With him we encounter the *horror religiosis* (*FT,* 61). For he does not have the benefit of such a justification. No *raison d'état* calls for the sacrifice of Isaac, and so, from the ethical point of view — to which Abraham, in fear and trembling, is not immune — the killing he intended remains murder.

Silentio told us that he could make the movement of infinite resignation by himself but not the act of faith exhibited by Abraham. That act, he said, is a miracle (*FT,* 37). Now he tells us, "A person can become a tragic hero through his own strength — but not the knight of faith. . . . Faith is a marvel" (*FT,* 67).

In Problem II, Silentio poses the question, *"Is there an Absolute Duty to God?"* (*FT,* 68). We can see immediately that this is another form of the question whether there is a teleological suspension of the ethical. For in Problem I it is the paradox of faith that the individual stands in an absolute relation to the absolute, who, for Abraham, is God (*FT,* 56, 62).[36]

Returning to the theme of incommensurability, Silentio puts it in terms of Hegel's claim that the outer (*das Äussere,* sometimes the *für sich,* the for itself, the explicit, the fully developed) is and ought to be higher than the inner (*Das Innere,* sometimes the *an sich,* the in itself, the implicit, the undeveloped). Thus the adult is higher than the child. Silentio assimilates the inner-outer dyad to the individual-universal dyad. Thus the ethical task is for the "single individual to strip himself of the qualification of interiority and to express this in something external. . . . The paradox of faith is that there is an interiority that is incommensurable with exteriority, an interi-

---

36. This formula reappears in Problem III (*FT,* 93, 98, 113). At the end of his third problem Silentio states his conclusion: "Thus either there is a paradox, that the single individual as the single individual stands in an absolute relation to the absolute, or Abraham is lost" (*FT,* 120).

ority that is not identical, please note, with the first but is a new interiority"
(*FT*, 69).[37]

Here the inner is that dimension of the individual that is incommensurable with the ethically universal, the external, the public. Once again, the
religious is set off from the aesthetic, without naming the latter. In *Fear and
Trembling* no figure like the knight of infinite resignation or the tragic hero
stands for the aesthete. But Abraham is once again set off from the aesthete.
The first inwardness is the total incommensurability or eccentricity of the
aesthete to the ethical, the refusal to grant the latter any normative force.
Faith is a *new* inwardness that comes *after* the individual has granted just
such force to the ethical; but this new interiority signifies the religious incommensurability of the individual to the social totality, which is not identified with the divine.

This brings Silentio to the passage cited above as the main point of *Fear
and Trembling*, according to which faith means that we determine our relation to society (the universal) by our relation to God (the absolute) rather
than the other way around (*FT*, 70).[38] This means that the duty to God is the
absolute duty, and "if this duty is absolute, then the ethical is reduced to the
relative. From this it does not follow that the ethical should be invalidated;
rather, the ethical receives a completely different expression, a paradoxical
expression, such as, for example, that love to God may bring the knight of
faith to give his love to the neighbor — an expression opposite to that which,
ethically speaking, is duty" (*FT*, 70; translation altered).[39] In other words,
having at first interpreted the teleological suspension of the ethical in terms
of an absolute duty to God, Silentio here reverses field and derives the *Aufhebung* of the ethical in the religious from the notion of an absolute duty to God.

37. At the beginning of Problem III, Silentio will make essentially the same distinction in
terms of a first immediacy and a later immediacy (*FT*, 82). The Hongs' note 6 at *FT*, 69 refers
to passages elsewhere in Kierkegaard's writings where he makes the distinction between a
first and second immediacy.

38. It is true that Kant, not least when he speaks of Abraham (see note 31 above), makes
our relation to God dependent on and derivative from his ethical universal. So to praise Abraham's faith is to challenge Kant's theology. But in *Fear and Trembling* this is at best indirect,
for unlike Silentio, Kant does not interpret reason as ideology or the ethical as the laws and
customs of a historically particular society. Silentio takes aim at a nineteenth-century view
of reason, not an eighteenth-century view. With Hegel and Marx he has made the historical
turn.

39. "The ethical expression for [Abraham's] relation to Isaac is that the father must love
the son. This ethical relation is reduced to the relative in contradistinction to the absolute
relation to God" (*FT*, 70-71).

To illustrate this notion of a love "opposite" to the ethical understanding of love, Silentio cites Luke 14:26: "'If any one comes to me and does not hate his own father and mother and wife and children and brothers and sisters, yes, and even his own life, he cannot be my disciple.' This is a hard saying. Who can bear to listen to it?" (*FT*, 72).[40] He glosses this as follows: the absolute duty to God "can never lead the knight of faith to stop loving . . . the ethical expression for what he is doing is: he hates Isaac. But if he actually hates Isaac, he can rest assured that God does not demand this of him, for Cain and Abraham are not identical. He must love Isaac with his whole soul. Since God claims Isaac, he must, if possible, love him even more, and only then can he *sacrifice* him" (*FT*, 74).[41] This is one of the many passages where Silentio speaks of the distress, anxiety, and paradox experienced by Abraham in his trial.

Silentio concludes Problem II with the reminder that unless there is an absolute duty to God that renders the ethical relative, Abraham is lost.

Problem III poses the question: *"Was It Ethically Defensible for Abraham to Conceal His Undertaking from Sarah, from Eliezer, and from Isaac?"* (*FT*, 82).[42] The answer is No. The ethical requires disclosure and does not tolerate hiddenness. "If there is no hiddenness rooted in the fact that the single individual as the single individual is higher than the universal, then Abraham's conduct cannot be defended" (*FT*, 82). Silentio has distinguished the ethical from the religious in terms of universal-individual, relative-absolute, commensurable-incommensurable, mediated-immediate. To these he now adds the dyad disclosure-hiddenness. While neither the left hand nor the right hand categories are exactly synonymous, they do cluster closely together as signs of the ethical and the religious respectively.

Silentio has been telling us all along about Abraham's silence. He does

---

40. Translated from the Danish, I presume.

41. Silentio writes, "Next I would describe how Abraham loved Isaac. . . . I hope to describe [this fatherly love] in such a way that there would not be many a father in the realms and lands of the king who would dare to maintain that he loved in this way. But if he did not love as Abraham loved, then any thought of sacrificing Isaac would surely be a spiritual trial" (*FT*, 31).

42. The biblical narrative indicates that Abraham hid his intention from Isaac. Silentio throws in Sarah and Eliezer, the servant, to make more explicit that it is the family that gets trumped in Abraham's hiddenness, if it can be justified by a teleological suspension of the ethical that presupposes an absolute relation to God as absolute. Using Hegel's language, in Abraham's culture a servant is more nearly a member of the family than a burgher in civil society.

not speak because he cannot speak, and he cannot speak because no one will be able to understand him (*FT*, 10, 21, 60, 71, 76, 79-80). Silentio now makes that point his central theme. He clearly does not mean that Abraham's family lacked the linguistic competence, in whatever language they spoke, to understand an announcement by Abraham to the effect that he was taking Isaac to Mount Moriah to offer him as a burnt offering to God. The question throughout the three problems is whether Abraham can be justified and rightly honored as the father of the faithful[43] in spite of the fact that in terms of the ethical he is a murderer. So the inability of Abraham's family to understand him means that they could not understand how he could be justified. The demand of the ethical for disclosure is the requirement that one's actions be justified, or at least justifiable, in the public forum governed by the laws and customs of one's people. This the tragic hero can do.

Silentio, who does not share the classical view of reason as the "view from nowhere," as unsituated insight into unchanging, universal truth, has an appropriately conversational view of reason. The tragic hero has the benefit of what we could call a Habermasian justification.[44] "In the first place, he has the consolation that every counterargument has had its due, that he has given everyone an opportunity to stand up against him. . . . He can be sure that everything permitted to be said against him has been said ruthlessly, mercilessly" (*FT*, 113-14), and yet he can say, "This is what I am doing, and this is why it is right. I'm sure you all can see that." Abraham does not have this consolation.

We might even say that Silentio also has a Gadamerian theory of conversational reason at work. When Iphigenia is about to be sacrificed by Agamemnon, "she submits to her father's resolve; she herself makes the infinite movement of resignation, and they now have a mutual understanding. She can understand Agamemnon, because the step he is taking expresses the universal" (*FT*, 115). That is to say, she can understand how he is justified in terms of the norms shared by the whole community to which her family belongs. We can imagine that this "mutual understanding" (what Gadamer

43. We might well add — in the three monotheisms that bear his name: Judaism, Christianity, and Islam.

44. For Jürgen Habermas's conversational theory of reason, see Habermas, *The Theory of Communicative Action*, 2 vols., trans. Thomas McCarthy (Boston: Beacon, 1984 and 1987); Habermas, *Moral Consciousness and Communicative Action*, trans. Christian Lenhardt and Shierry Weber Nicholsen (Cambridge, MA: MIT Press, 1990); and Seyla Benhabib and Fred Dallmayr, eds., *The Communicative Ethics Controversy* (Cambridge, MA: MIT Press, 1990).

would call *Verständigung*)[45] was not immediate, and we can imagine the conversation between father and daughter that brought it about. Abraham has no such conversation available to him. For him no interest or value of the larger society or culture trumps his duty to protect his son's life so far as he is able.

We might anticipate that Silentio, having abandoned the view of reason as unsituated insight into unchanging, universal truth, and finding that he cannot replace it with some (now widespread) conversational interpretation of reason in the case of Abraham, will find it difficult to reconcile the latter's faith with reason. Like Hegel, he treats the former as a chimera, and it turns out that the teleological suspension of the ethical is also the teleological suspension of conversational reason. Abraham is very lonely indeed, humanly speaking, precisely because of his utterly essential and absolute relation to God as absolute.

Silentio now turns our attention more explicitly than before to the contrast between the religious and the aesthetic.[46] While disclosure is characteristic of the ethical, both the aesthetic and the religious involve hiddenness. Just as we have seen Silentio distinguish a first interiority from a new interiority and a first immediacy from a second immediacy, so we can expect him here to say of the aesthetic and the religious that in their similarity they are vastly dissimilar. Where hiddenness prevails over disclosure there is an incommensurability between the individual and the ethical universal, but the two incommensurabilities are dramatically different.

45. "There would be no speaker and no art of speaking if understanding *(Verständigung)* and consent *(Einverständnis)* were not in question . . . there would be no hermeneutical task if there were no mutual understanding *(Einverständnis)* that has been disturbed and no agreement *(Verständigung)* that those involved in a conversation must search for and find again together." Hans-Georg Gadamer, "On the Scope and Function of Hermeneutical Reflection," in *Philosophical Hermeneutics,* ed. David Linge (Berkeley: University of California Press, 1976), p. 25; cf. p. 7; translation altered. See the section entitled "Understanding and Agreement" in Jean Grondin, "Gadamer's Basic Understanding of Understanding," in *The Cambridge Companion to Gadamer,* ed. Robert J. Dostal (New York: Cambridge University Press, 2002), pp. 39-42. In his famous non-debate with Derrida, Gadamer writes, "The interpreter has no other function than to disappear completely into the achievement of full harmony in understanding [*Verständigung*]. The discourse of the interpreter is therefore not itself a text; rather it *serves* a text." "Text and Interpretation," in *Dialogue and Deconstruction: The Gadamer-Derrida Encounter,* ed. Diane P. Michelfelder and Richard E. Palmer (Albany: SUNY Press, 1989), p. 41.

46. See Robert L. Perkins, "Abraham's Silence Aesthetically Considered," in Perkins, ed., *International Kierkegaard Commentary,* vol. 6: *"Fear and Trembling" and "Repetition,"* pp. 155-76.

Silentio turns to the literary form of the aesthetic, in particular the comic and tragic narratives we find in novels, plays, operas, and so forth. Here we find the first mark of aesthetic hiddenness. It falls under the more general aesthetic category of the interesting (*FT*, 82-83). Silentio draws on Aristotle's account of reversal of fortune (περιπέτεια) and discovery or recognition (άγνώρισις).[47] The hiddenness that is eventually discovered and that often leads to a reversal of fortune, producing comedy or tragedy, has its place in literary narratives because of the way it makes them interesting. The story of Oedipus is Aristotle's obvious, prime example of a discovery that leads to a reversal from good to bad fortune. When Oedipus discovers whom he has killed and whom he has married, his life is ruined. Given Kierkegaard's love of Mozart, the opposite movement can nicely be illustrated from *The Marriage of Figaro*. The discovery that Marcellina is Figaro's mother rescues Figaro from a terrible fix and showers good fortune on him. Then, in the final scene, the discovery that 'Susanna' is really the Countess in disguise and that the 'Countess' is really Susanna in disguise brings good fortune to everyone in Mozart's überhappy ending.

Silentio gets carried away and gives six examples of aesthetic hiddenness, one from an example he makes up and the others from Euripides, Aristotle, the Danish legend of Agnes and the merman, the book of Tobit, and the Faust legend. The result is that Problem III is one-and-a-half times as long as Problems I and II together, quite unnecessarily.

Perhaps the most interesting case is that of Agnes and the merman, for it shows a second possible mark of aesthetic hiddenness: the demonic.[48] The aesthetic in general, and the interesting in particular, are not evil. The aesthete has abstracted from good and evil as fundamental categories for evaluating one's being-in-the-world. But just for this reason the aesthetic has no defense against evil and thus the demonic, when evil becomes the basis of one's life. Such is the seducer, the merman, at least when seen from an ethical or religious perspective. As Silentio tells the story, slightly altered, Agnes is quite willing to be taken. But as the merman is about to take her down into the sea as his booty, he sees her as "trusting with all her soul . . . in absolute faith and in absolute humility . . . she entrusts her whole destiny to him in absolute confidence." The merman "cannot withstand the power of innocence . . . and he cannot seduce Agnes." Instead he takes her home

---

47. Aristotle, *Poetics*, ch. 11.

48. For more detailed analysis, see Sharon Krishek, *Kierkegaard on Faith and Love* (New York: Cambridge University Press, 2009). See 'Agnes' and 'Merman' in her index.

as if he had had no sexual intentions (*FT*, 94). In fact, "he can never seduce again" (*FT*, 96). He has been overtaken by repentance, true repentance at least insofar as it resulted in a dramatic change of behavior.

The merman's problem is that Agnes's innocence has evoked a conscience in him, as if by some kind of Platonic recollection. He is no longer comfortably ensconced in the aesthetic world of the seducer from *Either/ Or* 2. He hasn't exactly chosen to live in the light of good and evil, as Judge William admonished A to do. We can almost say that he has been seduced into the ethical, for repentance is not an aesthetic category. It is this birth of conscience that represents the possibility of the demonic, as seen not only from outside but perhaps even by the merman himself. "But immediately two forces struggle over him: repentance, Agnes and repentance. If repentance alone gets him, then he is hidden; if Agnes and repentance get him, then he is disclosed" (*FT*, 96).

How so? This hiddenness, after repentance and the birth of conscience, but without acknowledgment and confession, is the demonic in this case. The demons, we can assume, know themselves to be evil; they are not aesthetes for whom the category is inoperative. But they do nothing to change their condition. By active repentance the merman has done what they never do. But by keeping it hidden, pretending "that he only wanted to show her how beautiful the sea is when it is calm" (*FT*, 94), he fails to break through to the ethical, which calls for disclosure, the public, linguistic, conversational application of ethical norms to one's behavior. One might well be skeptical of a repentance that is only verbal and without any corresponding action. But Silentio suggests that a repentance that is active but nonverbal is equally incomplete and inauthentic.

Repentance and Agnes. Conscience and confession. Inwardness that passes over into the outwardness of the linguistic, cultural universal. This would seem to be the merman's salvation, a teleological suspension of the aesthetic in the ethical. But Silentio says that's not quite right. Rather,

> when the single individual by his guilt has come outside the universal, he can return only by virtue of having come as the single individual into an absolute relation to the absolute. . . . Sin is not the first immediacy [aesthetic innocence as, for example, in an infant]; sin is a later immediacy [a declaration of independence from ethical and religious norms]. In sin, the single individual is already higher (in the direction of the demonic paradox) than the universal. . . . An ethics that ignores sin is a completely futile discipline, but if it affirms sin, then it has *eo ipso* exceeded itself.

Philosophy teaches that the immediate should be annulled. This is true enough, but what is not true is that sin is directly the immediate, anymore than faith is directly the immediate. (*FT*, 98-99)[49]

Why should we read the merman's repentance in terms of sin and thus of a violated God relation instead of merely the resurfacing of a repressed socialization that remains within the ethical? Why must his confession go beyond Agnes to Someone Absolute? It is not easy to say. The suggestion above that conscience is born in him by something like a Platonic recollection suggests contact with norms that transcend the social order. But is such a reading necessary? Or has Silentio simply been misled by a familiar association of 'repentance' and 'sin'? Vigilius Haufniensis, the pseudonymous author of *The Concept of Anxiety*, writes, "Repentance is the highest ethical contradiction, partly because ethics requires ideality but must be content to receive repentance, and partly because repentance is dialectically ambiguous with regard to what it is to remove, an ambiguity that dogmatics for the first time removes in the Atonement" (*CA*, 117). In other words, "Who can forgive sins but God alone?" (Luke 5:21).

No doubt Silentio and Haufniensis are expressing something Kierkegaard deeply believes; but whether Silentio has shown, without appeal to theology, that repentance entails sin and thus a movement to the religious and the God relation is not clear. In any case, if the merman were to remain silent in his repentance, confessing to neither Agnes nor God, he would surely represent an aesthetic hiddenness that goes beyond the literarily interesting toward the demonic. It is miles removed from Abraham's silence. It is, on Silentio's analysis, precisely Abraham's obedience to the command of God that renders him silent. So far as the binding of Isaac is concerned, he has no need for repentance, confession, and forgiveness.

Steve Evans says that "it is a mistake to take *Fear and Trembling* as giving us a positive account of faith." This is a tautology as Evans presents it, for he writes, "To really understand the positive character of the religious life, including of course faith, one must understand sin." He appeals to the fact that only in the writing of later pseudonyms, Johannes Climacus in *Concluding Unscientific Postscript* and Vigilius Haufniensis in *The Concept of Anxiety*, is sin treated adequately in the authorship and that in *Fear and*

49. In a note, Silentio writes, "As soon as sin emerges, ethics founders precisely on repentance; for repentance is the highest ethical expression, but precisely as such it is the deepest ethical self-contradiction" (*FT*, 98n.). Cf. *CA*, 17, 117 and *CUP* 1:288, 532-34.

Trembling "sin was used occasionally to throw light on Abraham's ethical suspension, but no more than that."[50] We can concede that Silentio does not even attempt to give a sustained analysis of the concept of sin, though we should not overlook that he does (a) indicate that sin is an essential component in the religious sphere and (b) that it involves an absolute relation to the absolute.[51]

Perhaps Evans would have made his point more precisely if he had said that *Fear and Trembling* does not give us a *complete* account of the religious sphere. For it surely gives us a positive account insofar as the last two theses we have explored so far go a long way toward giving a positive, affirmative account of the religious. That faith is the task of a lifetime is important, but it tells us nothing specific to faith. There are other such tasks. But that faith is trust in divine promises and obedience to divine commands tells us a great deal about biblical religion, and perhaps all of the Abrahamic monotheisms. This account will become still more specific with the two theses that remain: **Faith is incommensurable with reason** and **Faith is the highest passion**.

But before we turn to the first of these remaining theses, three issues arising out of the account given so far need our attention. So we turn to three questions *in medias res.*

50. Evans, "Faith as the *Telos* of Morality," p. 22. See *CUP* 1:268. Evans quotes from the older Swenson/Lowrie translation rather than the Hongs'.

51. See also the discussion by Silentio (cited just above) of sin as a second immediacy and as the reality that shatters the complacency of the ethical. It may be that he gives us no comprehensive analysis of sin, but it may well be unfair to him to reduce him to a poet who provides no "detailed information about the character of Christian existence." The points he makes about sin are important "details." But Evans is surely right that we "should not look to [Silentio's] story to develop a Christian ethic." Evans, "Faith as the *Telos* of Morality," p. 23.

CHAPTER 4

Interlude — Three Questions *In Medias Res*

It might seem as if the account of the religious given to this point, so far from being insufficiently positive, is too positive, or perhaps too particular. Biblical faith, the faith of Abraham, may well be trust in divine promises and obedience to divine commands, but Silentio makes no suggestion that what his "present age" lacks is trust in *these* promises and obedience to *these* commands. Later believers will believe themselves to be inheritors of some of the promises to Abraham. Thus, for example, in his *Benedictus*, Zechariah interprets the birth of John the Baptist as a fulfillment of the covenantal promise to Abraham (Luke 1:72-73), and Mary, in her *Magnificat*, interprets the upcoming birth of Jesus in the same way (Luke 1:54-55). But the promise of a son in one's old age and the command to offer this son as a burnt offering are not general features of biblical religion. They belong to Abraham alone. The promise of a son who would be the Messiah belongs to Jewish and Christian faith; and that he would turn out to be "the Lamb of God who takes away the sin of the world!" (John 1:29) belongs to Christian faith. But these are not the promises to Abraham as he would have understood them. Nor were subsequent believers commanded to practice child sacrifice.[1]

So suppose I do not want to condemn Abraham as a murderer (*FT*, 53, 55, 57) nor merely admire him as a poet or orator would (*FT*, 15, 27-28); rather, I want to imitate him in the life of faith. What would it mean for Silentio's contemporaries or ourselves, for that matter, to seek to grow in faith by imitating Abraham, the father of the faithful?

It might be helpful at this point to suggest that, without knowing it,

1. See chapter 3, note 32, above.

Silentio is practicing what has since come to be called epistemological particularism. This is a philosophical approach to knowledge that is more trusting than skeptical toward common sense. It is associated with Thomas Reid, G. E. Moore, Roderick Chisolm, and Ernest Sosa, among others.[2] It takes the question, What do we know? to be prior to the question, How do we know?

The opposite perspective is often called methodism, not as a religious tradition but as the reversal of the priority of the two questions. Before we can know what we know, what to count as genuine knowledge, we have to (a) identify the method or process by which genuine knowledge comes into being and (b) test the candidates for knowledge by this criterion. Epistemic particularism says, by contrast, that we know that some of our beliefs are genuine knowledge with greater certainty than any beliefs we may have about the proper method or procedure. Thus, G. E. Moore refuted skepticism about the independent reality of a world not reducible to our mental representations or ideas[3] by showing one of his hands and then the other and concluding from the fact that there are two external objects that there is an external world of such objects.[4] For particularism we don't first establish criteria and then decide with their help what counts as knowledge; we rather identify some very clear cases of knowledge and then seek to infer the criteria (plural — no assumption that all knowledge is of the same kind) that would justify these instances if there were such a need and that can then be applied to cases that are not so clearly authentic knowledge.

Silentio, who is more a social critic than an epistemologist, wants to challenge his contemporaries with an account of genuine religion. This is not an abstract, theoretical account of religion in all its possible and actual forms; it is rather an inquiry into the religion that might be a live option for his contemporaries. This would be biblical religion or, even more specifi-

2. Reformed epistemology has at least one foot in this camp. See Alvin Plantinga, *Warranted Christian Belief* (New York: Oxford University Press, 2000), in the light of *Warrant and Proper Function* (New York: Oxford University Press, 1993). It is no accident that Nicholas Wolterstorff, Plantinga's colleague in developing Reformed epistemology, is the author of *Thomas Reid and the Story of Epistemology* (New York: Cambridge University Press, 2001).

3. Bishop Berkeley's *esse est percipi*, to be is to be perceived.

4. G. E. Moore, "A Defense of Common Sense" and "Proof of an External World," in *Philosophical Papers* (London: Collier Books, 1962), pp. 32-59 and 126-48 respectively. The showing of the two hands belongs to the second paper, but epistemic particularism is present in both. Cf. Roderick M. Chisolm, *The Problem of the Criterion* (Milwaukee: Marquette University Press, 1973).

cally, Christianity. For he is addressing Christendom. So, as an epistemic particularist, he zeroes in on Abraham, the father of the faithful in Genesis and the paradigm of faith in no fewer than four books of the New Testament (Romans, Galatians, Hebrews, and James).[5]

The three theses we have examined (so far) can be seen as the three criteria he has extracted from the Abraham story (so far).[6] Nothing can count as genuine biblical faith that is not (a) the always unfinished task of a lifetime, (b) trust in divine promises, and (c) obedience to divine commands. We see immediately that the criteria are more general than the particular instances whose interpretation they have become.[7] This calls for something similar to what Nicholas Wolterstorff has called a double hermeneutic.

The general hermeneutical context for Wolterstorff is what he calls authorial discourse hermeneutics. He wants to distinguish this sharply from the psychologism of "romantic" hermeneutics, according to which a text externalized the inner, psychic life of its author and interpretation reverses the movement and with the help of the text enters into that inner life. He writes,

> The myth dies hard that to read a text for authorial discourse is to enter the dark world of the author's psyche. It's nothing of the sort. It is to read to discover what assertings, what promisings, what requestings, what commandings, are rightly to be ascribed to the author on the ground of her having set down the words that she did in the situation in which she set them down. Whatever the dark demons and bright angels of the author's inner self that led her to take up this stance in public, it is that stance itself that we hope to recover, not the dark demons and bright angels.[8]

To interpret a text is to try to identify the speech acts expressed in its inscription.

The theological context for Wolterstorff's analysis is biblical interpretation in which the interpreter takes the Bible to be the Word of God, that is,

---

5. Not to mention the references from Luke just cited from the *Benedictus* and the *Magnificat*.

6. 'Extract' is a fudge word, non-committal with regard to these alternatives.

7. I have spoken of the criteria as arising from the particular instances by inference and by interpretation. I don't think these are equivalent, but for now leave open the question which is a better account.

8. Nicholas Wolterstorff, *Divine Discourse: Philosophical Reflections on the Claim That God Speaks* (New York: Cambridge University Press, 1995), p. 93.

the bearer of divine speech acts, most particularly promises and commands. The double hermeneutic, both parts of which are necessary to genuine understanding, can be expressed in terms of two questions: What *did* the human author say back then? and What *is* God saying to us now through this ancient discourse? Note well the shift from past to present tense.[9]

But this double hermeneutic is not necessarily tied to a theological context. Gadamer expresses it in a non-theological context when he says that interpretation is both reproductive and productive.[10] The reproductive activity we can call exegesis. It asks how the author and the original audience would have understood the text. Following Gadamer, we can call the productive activity application. It asks how we can and should understand the text today, assuming that different contexts can and should generate different readings. It wants to know how we are addressed today by this text, be it the *Iliad* or *Long Day's Journey into Night*.

We find the same non-theological double hermeneutics in Derrida. He writes,

> To produce this signifying structure [the meaning of a text] obviously cannot consist of reproducing, by the effaced and respectful doubling commentary [i.e., exegesis], the conscious, voluntary, intentional relation that the writer institutes in his exchanges with the history to which he belongs thanks to the element of language. This moment of doubling commentary should no doubt have its place in a critical reading. To recognize and respect all its classical exigencies is not easy and requires all the instruments of traditional criticism. Without this recognition and this respect, critical production would risk developing in any direction

---

9. The situation is somewhat complicated by the fact that for Wolterstorff what God *said*, say, to the Corinthians, through Paul's epistles, is not necessarily the same as what God *says* to us now. "I cannot in general just assume that what God said to me in my situation, or to my group in our situation, by way of this text is exactly the same as what God said to other earlier readers and interpreters in their situations." *Divine Discourse*, p. 185. So there is what the author said back then, what God said back then (and at other various times in the past), and what God says to us today. But this nuance will not concern us, since we're interpreting *Fear and Trembling* and not the Bible.

10. Hans-Georg Gadamer, *Truth and Method*, 2nd ed., trans. Joel Weinsheimer and Donald G. Marshall (New York: Crossroad, 2004), pp. 296: "Not just occasionally but always, the meaning of a text goes beyond its author. That is why understanding is not merely a reproductive but always a productive activity as well."

at all and authorize itself to say almost anything. But this indispensable guardrail has always only *protected,* it has never *opened,* a reading.[11]

Here again we find exegesis (reproduction) and its question — How was the text originally understood by its author and intended readers? — affirmed as utterly necessary; at the same time it is limited as insufficient. For Wolterstorff, Gadamer, and Derrida, to read is not merely to engage in an antiquarian task but to open oneself to what a text can and should say to us long after its author is dead.[12]

If we put together our epistemological particularism and double hermeneutics, we can answer the question how Silentio's contemporaries or we ourselves might imitate Abraham even though this does not entail that we expect a child in our old age or that we are willing to sacrifice whatever child we may have. By virtue of the fact that the criteria of genuine faith are more general than the specifics of Abraham's faith, it is possible for us to practice a double hermeneutic with reference to Abraham. What promises and commands did God address to Abraham in terms of which his faith becomes specific? And what promises and commands does God address to us in very different circumstances that give determinate content, at least in part, to our (possible) faith? We obviously cannot answer this question through the exegesis of *Fear and Trembling,* but that task can provide something like a Derridean guardrail to protect us from going off track. For example, if Silentio is on the mark, faith cannot be reduced to doctrinal assent; for assent is obviously not trust or obedience. Nor can faith be identified with any action or actions, moral or ritual, that are understood as achievements rather than tasks, leaving our faith to be but a fact about our past history.[13]

11. Jacques Derrida, *Of Grammatology,* trans. Gayatri Chakravorty Spivak (Baltimore: Johns Hopkins University Press, 1974), p. 158.

12. Wolterstorff rejects the notion of textual meaning on the grounds that it fails to take seriously enough the author's role as the origin of the speech acts inscribed in the text. *Divine Discourse,* ch. 8. But the text is the primary, sometimes the only, access we have to those speech acts. Talk of textual meaning acknowledges that it is through the text that we access the author's speech acts.

13. A subsequent pseudonym, Johannes Climacus, will satirize the idea that adulthood consists in having all one's existential tasks finished and behind one. "For most people, life changes when they have come to a certain point in their searching. They marry, they enter occupations, in consequence of which they must out of decency finish something, must have results. . . . So they believe that they themselves actually have arrived. . . . One who is existing is continually in the process of becoming. . . . Only he really has style who is never finished" (*CUP* 1:85-86).

N.B. To say that faith is not reducible to X or identified with Y is not to say that X and Y are not important or not somehow included within faith as ingredient, or perhaps as necessary but insufficient conditions.

In summary answer to our first question, we can say that Silentio's account offers us both positive and negative guidance for imitating Abraham's faith in a context very different from his. How compelling we find Silentio's guidance and how seriously we seek to be guided by it are, of course, up to each of us individually. For each of us is "that single individual" to whom Kierkegaard addresses his writings (see *PV,* 103-26).

Our second question arises out of the fact that Silentio defines faith in part as obedience to divine commands. Does this mean that he is proposing a divine command ethics, according to which it is the divine command that makes what is right right and what is wrong wrong?[14] Any tight linkage between moral obligation and divine commands raises what can be called the Euthyphro dilemma: Are the right and the good right and good because they are commanded by God or are they commanded by God because they are right and good?[15] The dilemma is as follows: if the former is the case, these values appear to be arbitrary, while if the latter is the case it appears that God is subject to something outside and independent of God.

The question arises most naturally in connection with *Works of Love,* where Kierkegaard, in his own name, presents a general ethical theory centered on the divine command, "You shall love your neighbor as yourself."[16] But Silentio does not present us with an ethical theory of any kind. His ac-

---

14. The term 'divine command ethics' is regularly applied to any such theory, but 'metaethic' would be a more accurate term, for what is at issue is not immediately the content of right and wrong but what it is that constitutes right and wrong as such.

15. Plato's *Euthyphro,* 10a: "Is the pious [or holy, τὸ ὅσιον] loved by the gods because it is pious, or is it pious because it is loved by the gods?"

16. For helpful discussion in the context of *Works of Love,* see M. Jamie Ferreira, *Love's Grateful Striving: A Commentary on Kierkegaard's "Works of Love"* (New York: Oxford University Press, 2001), and C. Stephen Evans, *Kierkegaard's Ethic of Love: Divine Commands and Moral Obligations* (New York: Oxford University Press, 2004). Evans calls attention to the literature that discusses Kierkegaard's relation to divine command theory. In addition to attributing a version of this theory to Kierkegaard, Evans defends it, following Robert Adams's double claim that (1) for a theist, God and the Good are identical, so that God is not subject to anything external, and (2) the commands of a *loving* God are not arbitrary in any problematic way. By contrast, Ferreira is reluctant to attribute a divine command ethic to Kierkegaard. She concludes her discussion of Kierkegaard's "You *shall* love" by saying, "Thus far we do not have reason to consider *Works of Love* as propounding a divine command ethic or a simple ethics of obedience" (p. 42).

count of the ethical sphere presupposes that of Judge William in *Either/Or,* who distinguishes it from the aesthetic by the fact that good and evil, right and wrong, are essential categories for human existence. But even less than Judge William does Silentio tell us what is good and what is right in any general, determinate way. So it might well be a mistake to look for a meta-ethical account of the relation of divine commands to moral obligations.

Jamie Ferreira writes, "The story of Abraham and Isaac in *Fear and Trembling seems* to portray just such a divine command ethic: what makes it right to sacrifice Isaac is that, and only that, God commands it."[17] What is right about this is that it is, at first glance, tempting to attribute a divine command meta-ethic to Silentio, even in the absence of any general normative ethical theory. But we should resist this temptation, for it is without warrant. To be sure, the text supports the claim "what makes it right to sacrifice Isaac is that, and only that, God commands it." No other ground seems remotely plausible. But it goes beyond the evidence available to us to assume that this is a general, meta-ethical principle for Silentio. This is especially true in light of the relative validity of the ethical sphere. We have duties derived from the laws and customs of our people (society, nation, state, church, sect, *Volk*) so long as these are not trumped by a special command from God. But nothing Silentio says about *Sittlichkeit* suggests that it presupposes a divine command meta-ethic. In any case, he insists that he is not a philosopher.

There is, to be sure, a general principle nearby in *Fear and Trembling,* derived, as suggested above, in accord with Silentio's epistemological particularism. Faith is in part and in essence obedience to divine commands, so for faith it is always the case that if God commands something it is obligatory. A divine command is a sufficient condition for obligation. No exemptions are implied, much less suggested. But it does not follow that a divine command is a necessary condition of obligation, that what makes any commanded action obligatory "is that, and only that, God commands it." One might say, using Thomist categories, that some actions are obligatory by virtue of the natural law, some by virtue of human law (like driving on the right- or left-hand side of the road), and some only by divine law, expressed in specific revealed commands (like circumcision or baptism). I am

---

17. Ferreira, *Love's Grateful Striving,* p. 40; emphasis added. She wisely warns us against reading this single instance into a general principle in *Works of Love.* By the same token, even if the latter text does presuppose to some significant degree a divine command meta-ethic, that would provide no warrant for reading it back into *Fear and Trembling.*

not suggesting that Silentio is a Thomist, only that the question of a divine command meta-ethic in Kierkegaard properly belongs in the discussion of *Works of Love,* where at least we have an ethical theory of some determinacy whose meta-ethical foundations can be explored.

Our third question is what to do with interpretations of *Fear and Trembling* that make the contrast between infinite resignation and faith the main point of Silentio's text. The simple answer is to refute and reject them. To identify the main point in this way is to overlook the explicit claim that this contrast is "preliminary," that it occurs in a "preamble," one of the four introductions to the main text as developed in the three problems. It is also to suppress the reason why what follows, the contrast between the knight of faith and the tragic hero, is for Silentio, if not for all readers, the main point. In doing so it misses the primary "attack upon Christendom" to be found in *Fear and Trembling.*

Consider Edward Mooney's book *Knights of Faith and Resignation: Reading Kierkegaard's "Fear and Trembling,"* presented (in 1991!) as the first "book-length commentary in English on *Fear and Trembling.*"[18] We suspect that something has gone wrong from the very title of the book.

Our anxieties are not lessened when we read that "Kierkegaard takes this occasion to range widely beyond the biblical text [Genesis 22] — to raise doubts about his countrymen's understanding of ethics and faith, to awaken them from spiritual complacency . . . that threatens to level all to a sleepy collective mediocrity." This would be very much on target as an attack upon Christendom if Mooney didn't continue, "His 'knight of faith' and 'knight of infinite resignation' are gallant heroes ready to battle for a worthy self, a self properly related to itself, to its social and personal context, and to God."[19] The fact is that the contrast between these two knights is not about the relation between ethics and religion. The knight of infinite resignation is not the representative of the ethical;[20] that task falls to the tragic hero in texts that are not designated as "preliminary." The knight of infinite resignation has a view of the proper relation to himself and to God, but society is not part of the equation, and just for that reason the contrast with the knight of faith is not a warning against "collective mediocrity." There is no suggestion in the text that the individual who resigns the dearest for the sake of the

18. Edward F. Mooney, *Knights of Faith and Resignation: Reading Kierkegaard's "Fear and Trembling"* (Albany: SUNY Press, 1991), p. ix.

19. Mooney, *Knights,* p. 2.

20. He might be seen as the representative of a certain form of the religious analogous to Religiousness A in *Postscript.*

highest, without resentment and without hope, is somehow an expression of the spiritlessness of the present age. The knight of infinite resignation is a hero in the eyes of Silentio.

Mooney tells us that the imagery of a mother weaning her child in the Exordium (second preface) "reinforces *Fear and Trembling*'s fundamental themes." After a quotation from *Concluding Unscientific Postscript* about resignation, he continues, "More specifically, *resignation* of something of utmost value (in this case, the child to be weaned), coupled with the assurance that it will be *returned,* is Johannes de Silentio's basic characterization of faith. Faith is the process of weaning the child and welcoming its return. It is a *'double movement'* of *giving up and getting back.*"[21]

The imagery of weaning does indeed prefigure the analysis of the Preliminary Outpouring about giving up and getting back (by virtue of the absurd). But it is strange, to say the least, to find the main point of a book in one of its introductions that is explicitly labeled as "preliminary." With reference to the dialectic of giving up and getting back, Mooney later acknowledges that it gives us only "a preliminary, if prominent sketch of faith."[22] That is an accurate statement. But it is too late; he has already committed himself to an untenable strategy for reading the main body of the text. "Here is the fundamental contrast that underlies the argument of *Fear and Trembling,* the contrast between resignation and faith. . . . In 'Problemata' the ordeal of faith is traced out in terms of its challenge to reason, ethics, and speech. Love, reason, and affiliation at first appear *lost* — and then, uncannily, *returned.*"[23] Quite apart from the sense that love, reason, and affiliation are not returned in the form in which they are lost, the fundamental categories around which the three problems revolve are not loss and return, giving up and getting back, but the terrifying alternative, murder or sacrifice, and the question expressed thereby: Are the norms that arise within our communal life the highest requirements and justifications for our actions, or can they be trumped by divine commands not reducible to social (even ecclesial) norms? It is in these terms, not giving up and getting back, that ethics and reason are put in question in the three problems. To subsume the problems under the categories of loss and return is to miss the point of the problems and thereby the main point of *Fear and Trembling.*

21. Mooney, *Knights,* p. 31; emphases his. I would emphasize "fundamental themes" and "basic characterization."

22. Mooney, *Knights,* pp. 58-61; quotation p. 61.

23. Mooney, *Knights,* p. 39; emphases his.

John Davenport similarly makes the contrast between faith and infinite resignation (a) the central theme of *Fear and Trembling* and (b) the key to understanding the teleological suspension of the ethical. For him "the transition from the ethical to the religious . . . is the movement from the 'Knight of Infinite Resignation,' who exemplifies a kind of limiting point within the ethical, to the 'Knight of Faith' instantiated by Abraham . . . the main point of *Fear and Trembling* . . . is to present the essence of 'faith' as *eschatological* trust."[24] My objection to this move is much stronger than my earlier quibble about his use of the term 'eschatological.' One can easily drop the term 'eschatological' and replace it with the notion that faith is (among other things, N.B.) "trusting expectancy" (Davenport) or hope and have "a preliminary, if prominent sketch of faith" (Mooney). But to make faith as the teleological suspension of infinite resignation the key to faith as the teleological suspension of the ethical is to miss the main point of the book.

It seems that Davenport has been spooked by "irrationalist" readings of *Fear and Trembling* by interpreters such as Alasdair MacIntyre and Brand Blanchard. On their view the linkage between divine commands and moral or religious obligation in *Fear and Trembling* means that Kierkegaard identifies faith with "total submission to 'the arbitrary fiats of a cosmic despot'" and the "blind fanaticism" of obedience to "a God who demands our allegiance to his own inscrutable authority."[25]

As we look at his analysis we do well to remind ourselves of three things. First, there is no strong divine command (Davenport's SDC) metaethic in *Fear and Trembling*, namely the general claim that a divine command is the necessary and sufficient condition for (categorical, moral, or/ and religious) obligation. Second, a weaker principle is implied, if not stated theoretically, by Silentio (who insists he is not a philosopher), namely that a divine command is a sufficient condition for obligation. Within the horizon of biblical faith, and most particularly within the story of Abraham,[26] if God commands it, it becomes my duty. No other ground seems remotely

---

24. John J. Davenport, "Faith as Eschatological Trust in *Fear and Trembling*," in *Ethics, Love, and Faith in Kierkegaard*, ed. Edward F. Mooney (Bloomington: Indiana University Press, 2008), pp. 196 and 198. Cf. Davenport, "Kierkegaard's *Postscript* in the Light of *Fear and Trembling*: Eschatological Faith," in *Revista Portuguesa de Filosofia* 64, no. 2-4 (2008): 879-908.

25. Davenport, "Faith as Eschatological Trust," pp. 196-97.

26. Silentio might acknowledge other examples, such as the command to Jonah to go and preach to Nineveh or the call of Paul to become the apostle to the Gentiles. "If I proclaim the gospel, this gives me no ground for boasting, for an obligation is laid on me, and woe to

available to acquit Abraham of the charge of murder. We may not like this fact about the Bible or about Silentio's telling of the Abraham story, but that is no reason to deny its presence in both.

An advantage of such a weak divine command theory, by contrast with the stronger version (SDC), is that it is not vulnerable to the following critique:

> Modern ethical theories such as deontologies, consequentialisms, social contract theories, divine command theories, and more recent virtue ethics theories . . . are artificial regimentations of the ethical concepts in which some one privileged concept is assigned a foundational or quasi-foundational role, and the attempt is then made to derive all the other important concepts from the privileged one. I think this procedure is fundamentally flawed, in part because the concepts just don't work in the way supposed.[27]

Third, "arbitrary" commands do not automatically signify irrationalism, despotism, or blind fanaticism, at least if by arbitrary is meant imperatives that are neither entailed nor justified by some general principle of reason. No such principle, psychological or moral, is available to parents in deciding how large an allowance to give to a child of a particular age, whether or not to make the allowance contingent on faithful performance of specified chores, or, if the option is for such a linkage, which chores should be specified. But we don't think of parents as despots when they make these decisions, especially if they are loving parents.[28] They have purposes in mind that pertain to the child's good, even if they have no neat algorithm to make their decisions for them and no guarantee that they have made the wisest choices. The sense in which the decisions are arbitrary is quite harmless. Of course, given the imperfect wisdom and love of human

me if I do not proclaim the gospel!" (1 Cor. 9:16). This obligation clearly does not come from some universal, rational ethics.

27. Robert C. Roberts, "Philosophy, Understanding, and Being a Person," in the newsletter of the University of Notre Dame Center for Philosophy of Religion, Spring 2012, pp. 2-3.

28. This is why the divine command meta-ethic defended by Adams and Evans (see note 16 above) restricts itself to the commands of a loving God. Davenport calls this "agapic command ethics" (ACE) but wants no more to do with it than with SDC. Davenport, "Faith as Eschatological Trust," p. 207. N.B. There are weak and strong versions of ACE. According to the former a divine command is sufficient to generate an obligation, while according to the latter such a command is both necessary and sufficient.

parents, their decisions may be, as Aristotle or Goldilocks might put it, too "soft" or too "hard" instead of "just right." But they are not *ipso facto* "despotic" claims to an obedience of "blind fanaticism." Unless, of course, one wants to eliminate the concept of obedience entirely from human life.

Davenport has another reason to stay away from any form of divine command theory. "As Lippitt points out, all divine command readings ignore this key element in the story: they leave unclear 'the significance of God's substituting the ram' for Isaac."[29] But that is to ask Silentio and his commentators to do everything at once. Reflection on the significance of the ram properly belongs to the preliminary contrast between faith and infinite resignation and to the account of faith as trust in divine promises. Reflection on the role of divine commands in the life of faith properly belongs to the primary contrast between the knight of faith and the tragic hero, according to which only a divine command not reducible to social morality can acquit Abraham of the charge of murder. There is no reason why this discussion in the problems or our reflection on various forms of divine command theory should throw light on the significance of the ram. Abraham's actions and their underlying intention are not justified by the appearance of the ram. The burning question is whether Abraham was justified in setting out for Mount Moriah with the intention of sacrificing Isaac (with the hope but without any certainty that the command would be revoked). There is no need to set up an either/or between faith as trust in divine promises and faith as obedience to divine commands. In Silentio's view, biblical faith is both. Obedience without trust is not faith; trust without obedience is not faith.

In keeping with his account of what the main point of *Fear and Trembling* is, Davenport offers an account of the teleological suspension of the ethical and the absolute relation to the absolute (Problems I and II) that "depends on a clear understanding of 'infinite resignations.'" Accordingly, he claims that "the telos toward which the ethical is suspended in Kierke-gaardian faith is the *promised eschatological outcome* in which the highest ethical norms will be fulfilled by an Absolute power that transcends human capacities."[30] What makes the (intended) killing of Isaac sacrifice instead of murder is the hope that it will not "permanently end Isaac's life in this

---

29. Davenport, "Faith as Eschatological Trust," p. 212. The quotation is from John Lippitt, *Routledge Philosophy Guidebook to Kierkegaard and "Fear and Trembling"* (New York: Routledge, 2003), p. 147.

30. Davenport, "Faith as Eschatological Trust," p. 199.

world."[31] In Problems I and II faith remains absurd because of its relation to the eschatological promise. Abraham's salvation and justification, and thus the key to the story, is in the freeing of Isaac, not his binding.[32] Abraham's faith "does not consist in the willingness to sacrifice Isaac, but in the belief that he will *somehow* get Isaac back."[33] It does not consist "in transgressing lower or less enlightened normative systems, trumping communal mores, or challenging established human orders."[34] The command to sacrifice is "the obstacle [to faith] rather than the telos toward which the ethical (in all its senses [?]) is suspended: Abraham's fulfillment of the universal obligation to love one's child is apparently *blocked* by the singular command to Abraham."[35]

The problem with all these claims is that they insist on fitting Problems I and II (the teleological suspension of the ethical, clearly identified as social morality, the laws and customs of one's people, and the absolute duty to God) in terms of the contrast between faith and infinite resignation. But in these problems those categories, which are central in preliminary texts, have been replaced by a new contrast, that between the knight of faith and the tragic hero. Here the question is whether there are norms of obligation and justification in which the killing of one's child or the intended killing of a son or daughter is obligatory and justified. Silentio's argument is that, for the tragic heroes he presents, social morality provides such norms insofar as the requirements of the larger community trump the desires and duties of family life; there is no suggestion that they fall short of faith by a lack of eschatological hope. But for Abraham, the universal in that sense provides neither obligation or justification. The only thing that could is an absolute duty to God that is higher than and not reducible to the duties of one's *Sittlichkeit (FT, 68)*. Nor can this duty be identified with eschatological hope. That theme belongs to earlier portions of the text. Abraham's faith is distinguished from infinite resignation by his trust (by virtue of the absurd) that the God for whom all things are possible will keep the promises pertaining to Isaac. Abraham's faith is distinguished from that of the tragic hero by his obedience (once again by virtue of the absurd, but a different absurdity) to a divine command incommensurable with the norms of his culture.

31. Davenport, "Faith as Eschatological Trust," p. 201.

32. Davenport, "Faith as Eschatological Trust," pp. 203, 205.

33. Davenport, "Faith as Eschatological Trust," p. 206. What is the textual support for this either/or?

34. Davenport, "Faith as Eschatological Trust," p. 208.

35. Davenport, "Faith as Eschatological Trust," p. 212.

Silentio tells us that there is "no higher expression for the ethical in Abraham's life than that the father shall love the son" (*FT,* 59). For Abraham, as distinct from the tragic hero, there is no *raison d'état* that trumps his obligation as a father. But his duty to love Isaac is not *"blocked"* by the "singular command" to sacrifice him.

> The absolute duty can lead one to do what ethics would forbid, but it can never lead the knight of faith to stop loving. Abraham demonstrates this. In the moment he is about to sacrifice Isaac, the ethical expression for what he is doing is: he hates Isaac. But if he actually hates Isaac, he can rest assured that God does not demand this of him, for Cain and Abraham are not identical. He must love Isaac with his whole soul. Since God claims Isaac, he must, if possible, love him even more, and only then can he *sacrifice* him, for it is indeed this love for Isaac that makes his act a sacrifice by its paradoxical contrast to his love for God. . . . Only in the moment when his act is in absolute contradiction to his feelings, only then does he sacrifice Isaac. (*FT,* 74)

The paradox here stems from the fact that in the teleological suspension "the ethical is reduced to the relative. From this it does not follow that the ethical should be invalidated; rather, the ethical receives a completely different expression, a paradoxical expression, such as, for example, that love to God may bring the knight of faith to give his love to the neighbor — an expression opposite to that which, ethically speaking, is duty" (*FT,* 70). The question here is not about eschatological hope; rather, it is about who defines what love of neighbor shall mean. Is it the norms of my society and culture or the command of God that may differ from the former and in its absoluteness trump them? Far from the command of God to sacrifice Isaac blocking Abraham's fulfillment of his duty to love Isaac, it is the ethical that is the temptation, a veritable obstacle if I allow it to become absolute (*FT,* 60).

It now becomes clearer what is lost when the square peg of Problems I and II is forced into the round hole of the contrast between resignation and faith. It is true that Kierkegaard[36] has more than Hegel and his followers as his immediate target. But the other target is not Kant.[37] It is a Christen-

36. Here I mean to speak of the author behind the pseudonym in order to suggest that the attack upon Christendom that Kierkegaard later develops both pseudonymously and in his own name is already at work in *Fear and Trembling.*

37. It is true that Abraham's faith is incommensurable with Kant's ethics, as Kant himself famously noticed. See chapter 3, note 31, above. But given Kant's "Hegelian" understanding of

dom that is all too Hegelian in its treating social morality *(Sittlichkeit)* as absolute in its authority rather than relative, while at the same time speaking a lot about God. For Kierkegaard the problem with his present age was not the absence of eschatological trust, but the bourgeois complacency that equated civic virtue with genuine faith. Protected by immersion in a social order that had been effectively deified, the individual was immune to the fear and trembling of ever being alone before God.

Sharon Krishek is another interpreter who takes the contrast between resignation and faith to be the central point of *Fear and Trembling.* Drawing on the contrast between the knight of infinite resignation and the knight of faith, she writes of the double structure of faith in terms of resignation and faith, resignation and repetition, and giving away and getting back. She quotes Silentio, "Through resignation I renounce everything. . . . By faith I do not renounce anything; by faith I receive everything" *(FT,* 48-49).[38] She is on solid ground when she says that this double movement is "an essential part of Kierkegaard's analysis of faith," that "the concept of resignation is crucial for a correct understanding of faith," and *"Resignation is a permanent component within faith."* But we can only be skeptical when she says that this contrast is "the core of *Fear and Trembling,*" and all the more so when she makes it "the basis on which Kierkegaard construes his famous discussion regarding the 'teleological suspension of the ethical.'"[39]

One strength of Krishek's analysis of the movement from resignation to faith is that she supplements the categories of giving up and getting back with the concept of trust in the promises of God as the context and ground of the former. Thus she highlights faith as trust in divine promises.[40] But there are two problems with the development of this promising move.

First, Krishek is keenly aware of the problem raised by the specificity of the promises made to Abraham. How can he be a paradigm of faith for Kierkegaard's contemporaries (or ourselves) who have not been promised a land and a son in old age? (Ominously, she sees the problem only in relation

---

reason as historically conditioned and particular, any Kierkegaardian critique of Kant would be indirect, and, in any case, Kierkegaard seems focused on his immediate context.

38. Sharon Krishek, *Kierkegaard on Faith and Love* (New York: Cambridge University Press, 2009), pp. 5-6, 14, 46, 76, 130. She sees this double structure as an analog of romantic love, the central concern of her book.

39. Krishek, *Kierkegaard on Faith and Love,* pp. 46-47, 76. She rightly refers here to Problem I and to Problems II and III as its implications.

40. Krishek, *Kierkegaard on Faith and Love,* pp. 95-99, 104, 106.

to the divine promises and not also to the divine commands given to Abraham, to leave home and to sacrifice Isaac.) But when, following the method of epistemic particularism, she moves from the promises specific to Abraham to promises addressed to subsequent children of Abraham, she gets too abstract for the sake of universality. Following Hannay, Kellenberger, and Davenport, she suggests that to those of us who come after Abraham, the promise is "that it would be 'all right' no matter what," "that all will be well — all will be well with 'everything,' " that there will be "a perfect realization of the ideals of ethics . . . an ultimate realization of the good."[41]

But this sounds more like a general, vague, deistic belief in divine providence rather than biblical faith. Are not the promises that come to those who would follow in the faith of Abraham after him far more specific than this? Are there not the messianic promise that comes through David, the promise of a new covenant that comes through Jeremiah, and the promise of an outpouring of the divine spirit that comes through Joel? Do not Christians, who recite the Apostles' Creed, trust in the promises of "the forgiveness of sins, the resurrection of the body, and the life everlasting. Amen"?[42] If these latter promises sound too much like Davenport's "ultimate" happy ending, are there not the promises of Christ: "I am with you always, to the end of the age" (Matt. 28:20) and "I will ask the Father, and he will give you another Advocate, to be with you forever. This is the Spirit of truth . . . [who] will teach you everything, and remind you of all that I have said to you" (John 14:16-17, 26)? These promises are for the here and now, prior to any "ultimate" or "eschatological" triumph of the good. In short, the promises of biblical faith for those who follow Abraham are concrete and specific, not by being addressed to a single individual, to be sure, but by having a quite determinate content, given through divine revelation from a God who speaks.

The second problem with Krishek's reading of faith as trust in divine promises is more pressing in the present context. It concerns her commitment to read the teleological suspension of the ethical in terms of the dialectic of resignation and faith. We can see in advance that this will be deeply problematic. The categories she has to work with are (a) resignation and repetition or giving up and getting back and (b) faith as trust in divine promises. But that is not what the teleological suspension of the ethical is

---

41. Krishek, *Kierkegaard on Faith and Love,* pp. 97-99.

42. These three promises are already prominent in some forms of Second Temple Judaism.

about. In the Eulogy on Abraham and the Preliminary Expectoration or Outpouring, where Silentio develops the contrast between infinite resignation and faith, he warns us three times that something quite different lies ahead.

> Many a father has lost his child, but then it was God, the unchangeable, inscrutable will of the Almighty, it was his hand that took it. Not so with Abraham! A harder test [*Prøve*] was reserved for him, and Isaac's fate was placed, along with the knife, in Abraham's hand. (*FT,* 21-22)

> If faith cannot make it a holy act to be willing to murder his son, then let the same judgment be passed on Abraham as on everyone else. . . . The ethical expression for what Abraham did is that he meant to murder Isaac; the religious expression is that he meant to sacrifice Isaac — but precisely in this contradiction is the anxiety that can make a person sleepless, and yet without this anxiety Abraham is not who he is. (*FT,* 30)

> In order to perceive the prodigious paradox of faith, a paradox that makes a murder into a holy and God-pleasing act, a paradox that gives Isaac back to Abraham again . . . in order to perceive this, it is my intention to draw out in the form of problemata the dialectical aspects implicit in the story of Abraham. (*FT,* 53)

This last quotation brings the Preliminary Outpouring to a close and introduces Problem I. It, along with the other two passages just cited, makes it clear that Silentio is going on to something new, something that calls for new categories: the ethical and the religious, murder and sacrifice. In the earlier discussion, Silentio argued that "the knight of faith is the only happy man, the heir to the finite, while the knight of resignation is a stranger and an alien" (*FT,* 50). But now it is not a question of happiness; it is rather a question of how it is possible that Abraham's intended act could be "a holy and God-pleasing act." It is a question of how Abraham's act could be justified, a question of norms. That is why the alternatives of murder and sacrifice are identified with the difference between the ethical and the religious, two different sources of norms for human action: social practices and divine revelation. In contrast to the knight of infinite resignation, the knight of faith is surely a representative of the religious sphere. But nowhere is the former identified with the ethical sphere, especially in the Hegelian form in which it is presented by Silentio.

The representative of the ethical sphere is the tragic hero. What distinguished him from Abraham is that his act of killing his child is authorized by the laws and customs of his society. His family and friends weep with him, but they understand that he is doing the right thing. Abraham, by contrast, does not have this comfort, so if there is not a teleological suspension of the ethical, if the norms of one's social order cannot be trumped by divine revelation, Abraham is lost, a murderer and not a hero of any kind. The question is about a hierarchy of norms, those that are relative and those that are absolute.

The first of the three quotations given together above highlights this difference in an important way. On the one hand there is the challenge of responding in faith to losses suffered at the hand of another, namely God. The self is passive in the loss.[43] Resignation is acceptance, without resentment and anger, of the loss of what one loves. If, in the context of belief in God's goodness, resignation is matched with hope, we get faith.[44] But the self remains passive in the loss and we do not yet have Abraham.

On the other hand, and this is what the three warnings point to, when we get to the problems and to the teleological suspension of the ethical, the loss is carried out by the self's own agency. The analysis of resignation abstracts from this crucial aspect of the Abraham story. That is why the parable of the lad who loved a princess is appropriate. But this part of the Abraham story comes back with a vengeance when his agency is restored to the narrative and the pressing question becomes, not How do you deal with the losses you suffer? But How can this act of killing be anything but murder? Is there a norm higher than the social norms that provide Abraham with

43. Krishek nicely generalizes from Abraham's loss by emphasizing the inevitability of loss in relation to finite goods.

44. Job seems to be a good example of the resignation that is not yet faith, especially when he says, "the LORD gave, and the LORD has taken away; blessed be the name of the LORD" (Job 1:21). Two months after publishing *Fear and Trembling*, along with *Repetition*, Kierkegaard published an edifying or upbuilding discourse on just this text, "The Lord Gave, and the Lord Took Away; Blessed Be the Name of the Lord" (*EUD*, 109-24). It focuses on Job's suffering in the double sense of experiencing pain and of being passive in doing so. Job is an actor, to be sure, and his "significance by no means consists in what he said but in what he did . . . not in his having said it but in his having acted upon it" (*EUD*, 109). But, unlike Abraham, when we get to the full story, Job is not asked to be the agent of his own suffering. For an illuminating commentary comparing this reading of the Job story with those in *Repetition*, see Andrew Burgess, "Repetition — A Story of Suffering," in *International Kierkegaard Commentary*, vol. 6: *"Fear and Trembling" and "Repetition*," ed. Robert L. Perkins (Macon, GA: Mercer University Press, 1993), pp. 247-62.

no justification? According to Krishek, Abraham's faith does not violate any ethical ideal.[45] According to Silentio, Abraham violates the *Sittlichkeit* in which he finds himself and can only be judged, by his family, his friends, and himself, as a murderer. That is why he acts in fear and trembling, filled with anxiety. Only if these norms are relative and in his case trumped by a higher obligation can he be a hero of faith.

Krishek notices that Silentio presents the ethical sphere in Hegelian terms. But, following Stephen Mulhall, she suggests that "maybe the problem begins precisely with Johannes' uncritical presupposition according to which Hegel's theory of the ethical is indeed the ultimate one." So she asks, "is the ethics that *Fear and Trembling* refers to only the Hegelian *Sittlichkeit*? After all, the 'suspended' duties not to kill and to love one's son seem to be valid from *any* ethical point of view."[46]

Apart from forgetting Silentio's insistence that Abraham never ceased to love Isaac, Krishek is surely right. For example, Abraham is deeply problematic within the Kantian understanding of the ethical, as Kant himself was not hesitant to point out.[47] But it does not follow that Silentio is "uncritical" in focusing our attention so pointedly on the Hegelian understanding of the ethical sphere. He (and Kierkegaard) may well have at least two good reasons for doing so.

First, he (they) may accept the Hegelian view that "Whatever happens, every individual is a child of his time; so philosophy too is its own time apprehended in thoughts," along with its corollary, "In the course of this book I have remarked that even Plato's *Republic*, which passes proverbially as an empty ideal, is in essence nothing but an interpretation of the nature of Greek ethical life."[48] In other words, Plato (and by implication Kant and a whole host of other ethical theorists) mistakenly take their reflections to be the result of "pure" reason that reflected itself out of anything historically particular and contingent; they fail to see that what they call 'reason' is in fact the historically specific ideas that reflect and legitimize the cultural community (or communities) to which they belong — what Marx calls ideology. Thus, for example, Kant fails to see that "pure practical reason" is in fact a somewhat secularized version of basic Christian ethics with a Lutheran pietist flavor.

---

45. Krishek, *Kierkegaard on Faith and Love*, p. 106.

46. Krishek, *Kierkegaard on Faith and Love*, pp. 103-4.

47. See chapter 3, note 31, above.

48. See chapter 3, notes 10 and 13, above.

Second, insofar as Silentio (and Kierkegaard) do have more than a Hegelian meta-ethics in mind — the laws and customs of one's society as one's highest norms — they may well not be thinking of other ethical theories but of their contemporary society, which they see as entirely too Hegelian to be Christian. One need not be a philosopher to think and act as if the norms into which one has been socialized in what Hegel calls the universal — state, society, nation, church, sect — are the highest norms. "As long as I am a law-abiding, productive citizen and a reasonably faithful church member, God could not ask anything more of me, and surely it would be impolite of God to suggest that we in our complacent self-assurance have subtly equated ourselves with God as the Absolute. That would be to suggest that our piety is idolatry! The prophetic strand of biblical religion that makes such a charge is always about 'them,' never about 'us.'"

Given the critique of "the present age" found in *Fear and Trembling*[49] and elsewhere in Kierkegaard's writings, pseudonymous and direct, it seems to me highly likely that Silentio's insistent identification of the ethical sphere with its Hegelian interpretation expresses his (and Kierkegaard's) understanding of "reason" as ideology and a consequent critique of Hegelian theory and Danish practice along these lines. The question posed by *Fear and Trembling* is thus not just whether anyone of Silentio's contemporaries has a faith that truly imitates Abraham's, but more specifically whether contemporary piety isn't to some significant degree idolatrous. To shift attention away from the role of the Hegelian ethical in *Fear and Trembling* by saying, however rightly, that Abraham is in trouble with other ethical theories is to ignore the two good reasons Silentio (and Kierkegaard) have for focusing so sharply on the Hegelian interpretation of the ethical sphere.

Mooney, Davenport, and Krishek are brilliant scholars. All of us who read Kierkegaard are in their debt. But on the point where I have taken issue with them here, it seems to me that they lead us away from the very heart of *Fear and Trembling*.

---

49. See the discussion in chapter 1, above, of Silentio as practicing Marxian-Nietzschean ideology critique.

CHAPTER 5

Faith as the Teleological Suspension of Reason

So far we have three theses about faith as presented by Silentio:

Faith is the task of a lifetime.
Faith is trust in divine promises.
Faith is obedience to divine commands.

Now we can add a fourth:

Faith is the teleological suspension of reason.

In the next chapter we will get our fifth and final thesis:

Faith is the highest passion.

That there is a tension between faith and reason in *Fear and Trembling* is clear enough. Our task is to clarify its nature. I shall argue that this tension doesn't in any meaningful sense make Kierkegaard or his pseudonyms who express this tension into irrationalists, unless by 'irrationalist' one means "anyone who doesn't conform to my particular interpretation of human reason and its powers." But in that case we've abandoned philosophy as careful thinking in favor of politics as manipulative name-calling. But first, a terminological clarification.

In chapter 1 I suggested that reason is not one thing but many. For example, Spinoza, Kant, and Hegel all give us a version of what Kant calls "religion within the boundaries of mere reason." But each of these is deeply incompatible with the other two, since each invokes a different conception of reason. Of course, these are not the only three versions of reason. I suggested that philosophers acknowledge this by using subscripts or superscripts to indicate which version of reason they are invoking, especially when they purport to be the voice of Reason. This would seem to be required by the virtues of honesty and humility.

But there is a useful, generic way of speaking about many varieties of reason at once. In the medieval and especially in the modern period it became increasingly automatic to distinguish reason from faith, or reason from revelation, or philosophy from theology as follows. Reason (and philosophy as its expression) is the exercise of the human intellect unaided, which is to say, not dependent on any divine revelation not already available to the human intellect.[1] By contrast, faith (and theology as its expression) is dependent on divine revelation, the thoughtful reception of (purported) truth not available to unaided human intellect. God shows us truth that we cannot discover for ourselves. While this way of speaking has the unfortunate tendency to encourage the thoughtless assumption that human reason is one thing and not many, it is not incompatible per se with the recognition that it comes in at least as many varieties as Heinz has pickles or Baskin-Robbins has flavors. In any case, this way of distinguishing faith from reason has become such a standard usage that it is regularly used even by those who think that the human intellect is perfected rather than perverted when it is humbly dependent on divine revelation.[2] Accordingly, the tension between faith and reason will be understood here along these lines. 'Reason' will signify any and all versions of human intellectual activity that purport to operate independently of divine revelation.

It is tempting to think that faith takes God into account and that reason does not, and that accordingly the distinction between faith and reason would map directly onto the distinction between religious and secular

---

1. Thus 'reason' is a way of speaking of knowledge as recollection. Some theologies distinguish general from special revelation so that the human intellect in its universal essence is already a source of divine revelation distinct from that which comes in specific acts in history and prophetic and apostolic interpretations of those acts, along with the scriptural witness to those acts and those interpretations. In what follows, 'revelation' will be understood as special revelation.

2. In other words, faith is reason at its very best, since it does not exclude the highest source of knowledge. For a sustained argument that faith is or at least can be knowledge and not something less than and opposed to knowledge, see Alvin Plantinga, *Warranted Christian Belief* (New York: Oxford University Press, 2000).

standpoints or epochs. But it is not that simple. As the concept of general revelation implies,[3] it is possible to give reason absolute hegemony over all claims of faith to being addressed by divine revelation and still have a God on the scene who is not wholly immanent within human history and experience. Deism in general and Kant in particular are examples of this possibility.[4] While these may be seen as part of a movement toward a secular society and culture, it would be strange to call them secular in and of themselves.[5] So the distinction is epistemic and not primarily ontological.

We have already noticed the satirical polemic against the system (Hegel and his Danish followers) in Silentio's Preface. But that is only a particular interpretation of reason. The first hint that there is a tension between Abraham's faith and reason in some more nearly generic sense comes in the Exordium. Silentio imagines a man who reads the story of the binding of Isaac and wishes he could have been there as an eyewitness. What concerned this man "was not the beautiful tapestry of imagination [apparently the aesthetic force of the story] but the shudder of the idea" (*FT*, 9).

Kierkegaard often, pseudonymously and otherwise, uses abstract, Platonic/Hegelian language when speaking of the religious: the idea, the infinite, the eternal, the absolute. The God of Abraham is surely more concrete, more personal than these terms suggest. But they can be applied to the biblical God, and I suspect that Kierkegaard speaks this way not mindlessly but deliberately. He wants to suggest that even if our God-talk is abstractly metaphysical, or onto-theological, as Heidegger has taught us to say,[6] it can and should have more bite than Hegelian philosophy or an all too Hegelian Christendom manage to notice. In this connection Kierkegaard regularly evokes Socrates.

This "shudder of the idea" reverberates throughout *Fear and Trembling*. Thus Silentio finds himself "shattered" and "paralyzed" (*FT*, 33) when thinking about Abraham, whom he approaches with "a *horror religiosis*" (*FT*, 61). It is a story of "terror," the "terrible," and "the terrifying" (*FT*, 72, 75, 77), of the "dreadful" and "dreadfulness" (*FT*, 78, 114).

3. See note 1 above.

4. See chapter 2, note 17, above.

5. Michael Allen Gillespie writes, "Secularization theorists [of modernity] understood that some vestiges of religion might persist, but they imagined these would all essentially be forms of deism or Unitarianism." *The Theological Origins of Modernity* (Chicago: University of Chicago Press, 2008), p. 271.

6. See the title essay in my *Overcoming Onto-Theology: Toward a Postmodern Christian Faith* (New York: Fordham University Press, 2001), pp. 1-28.

Two subsequent writers come immediately to mind. Rudolf Otto describes the holy as the *mysterium tremendum et fascinans.* The mysterious element of the holy he parses in terms of the "wholly other." The *tremendum* signifies the "awefulness," the "overpoweringness," the "absolute unapproachability," the "majesty," the "urgency" of the holy, the "dread" and "shuddering" it evokes. Paradoxically, the holy that frightens or repels in these ways is also "fascinating" and "uniquely attractive."[7] Otto speaks of this as the "non-rational" (not irrational) element in religion.[8]

In somewhat the same spirit, Jean-Luc Marion speaks of saturated phenomena; these include but are not limited to religious phenomena. What they have in common with Otto's holy as wholly other is that they burst the bounds of the classical definition of truth as *adequatio intellectus et res.* None of our language or conceptualities is adequate to the realities they intend and describe, not by virtue of some defect of the intellect, but by virtue of an excess, an overflowing of the "object" of the intellect. It is too rich, too full, even too wild to be captured without remainder by our terms and our theories.[9]

When Silentio uses language that evokes the thought of Otto and Marion, the emphasis is on the emotional aspect rather than the epistemic, the *tremendum* more than the *mysterium.* But we should notice two things. First, it is not the God of Abraham who calls forth these experiences of fear and trembling in Silentio, but Abraham himself as the knight of faith. Second, Silentio repeatedly tells us that he cannot understand Abraham. He might have said something like this. "When I encounter a character like Judge William in that fascinating recent book, *Either/Or,* I can understand his piety. But when I come to Abraham I cannot understand his faith. It is a marvel, a miracle, and, indeed, a *mysterium tremendum.* As you can tell, I find Abraham utterly fascinating. I can't stop thinking about him. But I have

7. Rudolf Otto, *The Idea of the Holy,* trans. John W. Harvey (New York: Oxford University Press, 1958), pp. 13, 19, 23, 25, 31.

8. Otto, *The Idea of the Holy,* pp. 1-4. Simon D. Podmore stresses the importance of Otto's notion for understanding Kierkegaard. See Podmore, *Kierkegaard and the Self before God* (Bloomington: Indiana University Press, 2011), pp. 43-49, 68-89, and 111-19.

9. See Jean-Luc Marion, "The Saturated Phenomenon," in *Phenomenology and the "Theological Turn": The French Debate,* trans. Bernard G. Prusak and Thomas A. Carlson (New York: Fordham University Press, 2000), pp. 176-216; *Being Given: Toward a Phenomenology of Givenness,* trans. Jeffrey L. Kosky (Stanford: Stanford University Press, 2002), pp. 199-221; and *In Excess: Studies of Saturated Phenomena,* trans. Robyn Horner and Vincent Berraud (New York: Fordham University Press, 2002).

to confess, he scares me to death, not least because I can't fit him into any of my conceptual cubby-holes."[10]

It is important to notice the sense in which this theme in *Fear and Trembling* expresses the tension between faith and reason. It is not that faith is a matter of surface emotions, while reason is a matter of deep insight. It is precisely what Abraham knows that makes things so difficult for him and so difficult for Silentio to understand. "He knew that it was God the Almighty who was testing [*prøvede*] him; he knew it was the hardest sacrifice that could be demanded of him; but he knew also that no sacrifice is too severe when God demands it — and he drew the knife" (*FT*, 22).

So what is the tension? It is the discrepancy between Abraham's faith and the view of reason as the human power to understand everything and leave no mysteries unresolved.[11] Such a view of reason is anything but self-evident, and it is not clear how one could establish it by means of argument and evidence. To adopt it is to adopt an a priori presupposition in the Kantian sense, except for the fact that this a priori is hard to construe as a condition of the possibility of experience. It is to adopt a prejudice (pre-judgment) in the Gadamerian sense, along with the realization that this places one in a hermeneutical circle that is but one option among others.[12] It places one within what Ricoeur calls "the conflict of interpretations,"[13] where there is

---

10. I remember some years ago teaching *The Idea of the Holy*. At one point I said, without having planned to do so, "If it isn't scary, it isn't God."

11. Kant and Hegel have just such a view. For Hegel what is mysterious to sense and understanding is not mysterious to speculative reason. See *Hegel's Lectures on the Philosophy of Religion, One-Volume Edition: The Lectures of 1827*, ed. Peter C. Hodgson (New York: Oxford University Press, 2006), pp. 422-25. Kant's view is not quite so absolute. He admits the possibility of mysterious realities, but insists that making them integral to religious life is harmful, servile anthropomorphism and delusion. See *Religion within the Boundaries of Mere Reason* and *Lectures on the Philosophical Doctrine of Religion*, both in *Religion and Rational Theology*, The Cambridge Edition of the Works of Immanuel Kant, ed. Allen W. Wood and George di Giovanni (New York: Cambridge University Press, 1996), pp. 65, 96, 164-71, 190-91, 204, 209, and 482.

12. Or perhaps a "proposal" in the sense of C. G. Hempel. The empiricist or logical positivist criterion of cognitive meaning stated that only analytic statements or those at least in principle capable of empirical testing (verification or falsification) had cognitive meaning and could be either true or false. Noting that this principle was itself neither analytic nor empirically testable, Hempel suggested that it should be considered a "proposal." This internal critique of the positivist interpretation of reason took a lot of wind out of its sails. See Hempel, "Problems and Changes in the Empiricist Criterion of Meaning," *Revue Internationale de Philosophie* 41 (1950): 41-63.

13. Paul Ricoeur, *The Conflict of Interpretations*, ed. Don Ihde (Evanston: Northwestern University Press, 1974).

no a priori guarantee of a right to hegemony over other interpretations. It appears that it is by an act of "faith" that Spinoza, Kant, and Hegel affirm the triumph of reason over mystery in matters religious. Obviously in this context 'faith' does not signify dependence on divine revelation but something like belief that can be seen to be risky and without guarantees. Much human knowledge rests on trust in the testimony of others (for example, the daily newspaper), and such knowledge is a form of 'faith' in this sense.

We might call this textual stream in *Fear and Trembling* a "preliminary" indication of the tension between faith and reason. For in it Silentio does not use the three crucial terms in which he otherwise articulates that tension: 'madness,' 'the absurd,' and 'paradox.' He just tells us that Abraham is a phenomenon that exceeds his understanding. He satirically says of the man who was utterly fascinated with the Abraham story despite "the shudder of the idea," presumably himself, "He did not know Hebrew; if he had known Hebrew, he perhaps would easily have understood the story and Abraham" (*FT*, 9). In other words, the failure of understanding is not due to some defect or deficiency on the part of the one who seeks to understand but is due to the nature of what is to be understood, but can't be.

It is in the Eulogy on Abraham that Abraham's faith is described as "madness." In two paragraphs, Silentio describes how that faith was "unreasonable" even before the command to sacrifice Isaac (*FT*, 17-18). The decision to emigrate from his homeland and become an alien and exile made no sense according to "worldly understanding." Emigration is entirely reasonable under certain circumstances, such as, say, the Irish potato famine or the Nazi persecution of the Jews. But Abraham has no such rationale. All he has is his faith, his trust in God's promises, and his obedience to the divine command to go. Silentio here places emphasis on the promises: the promised land and the promised son. Abraham's trust in these promises is "unreasonable" by the standards of "worldly understanding," by which we can understand human reason or intellect unaided by divine revelation (the promises and the command).

Just before these paragraphs, Silentio eulogizes Abraham as "great by that power whose strength is powerlessness, great by that wisdom whose secret is foolishness, great by that hope whose form is madness" (*FT*, 16-17). Let us look first at the wisdom/foolishness paradox. It immediately evokes Paul's sustained contrast in the first two chapters of 1 Corinthians of the wisdom of the world with the wisdom of God, which appears to be foolish from the perspective of worldly wisdom. But "God's foolishness is wiser than human wisdom" (1 Cor. 1:25).

Just four months after the publication of *Fear and Trembling*, Kierke-gaard preached a sermon in Trinity Church, Copenhagen, on this Pauline theme. It deserves more attention than it has gotten. His text is 1 Corin-thians 2:6-9 about the "hidden wisdom of God" that is not "the wisdom of the world."[14] It begins with the prayer, "Father in Heaven! We know indeed that Thou dwellest in light, and that Thy Nature is clarity; but for that very reason Thou art mysterious to us, even in Thy revelation."[15] Later he writes,

> The glory of which we are speaking was certainly not very acceptable to the earthly eye, since it was a stumbling-block to the Jews and foolishness to the Greeks. The eye which saw it, therefore, was not the earthly eye, but the eye of faith, which confidently peered through the terror in order to see what no earthly eye can discover if he who gazes is ignorant of what there is to see.[16]

Here Kierkegaard (in his own name) articulates the principle that is al-ready at work in *Fear and Trembling* and that will be characteristic of all his discussion of faith and reason, pseudonymous and otherwise. The divine revelation to which the Bible bears witness and, in so doing, becomes the Word of God is mysterious, offensive (stumbling-block), foolishness, even madness, not intrinsically but in relation to and from the perspective of a merely human standpoint, in this case the "earthly eye." Where "reason" claims autonomy and self-sufficiency for itself, it will find divine revelation to be "unreasonable." Indeed, it ought to, for if it did not, divine revelation would turn out to be nothing but another name for human reason. But then Abraham is lost. For the promises and commands that give him his agenda and even his identity are not inherent in the human intellect. There was no potato famine or persecution of the Jews to motivate his emigration, nor any new biological discoveries to ground his trusting expectation of a child in his old age and, even more importantly, Sarah's.

So we should not be surprised when, after having described Abraham's faith as madness (*FT*, 17), Silentio should assimilate it to "the divine mad-ness that was admired by the pagans" (*FT*, 23). Socrates sums up that ad-miration in the *Phaedrus* (244d), when he speaks of "the superiority of the

---

14. Following the translation given with the sermon in Søren Kierkegaard, *Johannes Cli-macus, or De Omnibus Dubitandum Est and A Sermon*, trans. T. H. Croxall (Stanford: Stan-ford University Press, 1958), pp. 159-73.

15. Kierkegaard, *A Sermon*, p. 159.

16. Kierkegaard, *A Sermon*, p. 165.

heaven-sent madness over man-made sanity." Like Paul, he seems to think that there is a divine wisdom that can only appear to "man-made sanity" as madness.[17]

Silentio speaks of madness on two other occasions. In Problem II he speaks of the madness of Abraham and the knight of faith insofar as, in taking himself to have an absolute duty to God, he raises himself as the individual above the universal; and in Problem III Silentio uses this language in his treatment of Sarah, from the book of Tobit. But in the Preliminary Outpouring and in Problems I and II, the language of the absurd and of paradox takes over. I take these three terms to be interchangeable in signifying the incommensurability of faith to human reason in its independence of divine revelation. Whenever reason purports to be autonomous vis-à-vis a God who makes promises and gives commands, faith as trust in such promises and obedience to such commands is bound to appear unreasonable.

At the outset of the Preliminary Outpouring, Silentio introduces his two key terms. He tells us that he is "shattered" and "paralyzed" by the paradox that is Abraham, before whom "I sink down." Anticipating subsequent formulas, he writes, "I by no means conclude that faith is something inferior but rather that it is the highest, also that it is dishonest of philosophy to give something else in its place and to disparage faith" (*FT,* 33). Dishonest? A harsh judgment, perhaps warranted by the realization that the system, which "goes beyond" faith, is more reasonable than faith only in a tautologous sense that follows from the way reason and faith have been defined. That it is an open question to be discussed whether it is better to be reasonable in this sense, philosophy does its best not to notice or to acknowledge.[18]

Then Silentio, in telling us once again that he does not have faith in the Abrahamic sense, writes, "I cannot shut my eyes and plunge confidently into the absurd." This is because he lacks the courage and humility to do so, not because he is intellectually undeveloped (*FT,* 34; cf. 49, 73).[19] We regularly hear that Abraham gets Isaac back "by virtue of the absurd" (*FT,* 37,

---

17. Perhaps Socrates is thinking of Cassandra, Trojan daughter of King Priam and Queen Hecuba. She was given the gift of prophecy by Apollo and rightly foretold the fall of Troy. But when she displeased Apollo, he put a curse on her. She was taken to be insane and no one would believe her prophecies, though they were a divine revelation.

18. Perhaps Sartre's notion of bad faith is appropriate here.

19. Silentio regularly links faith to courage and humility, suggesting (a) that it should be conceived as a virtue, (b) that it is more nearly akin to the moral virtues than to the intellectual virtues, and (c) that he apparently holds to some form of a unity of the virtues thesis.

40, 48-50). This means that there is something absurd about the faith that confidently trusts that he will get Isaac back.

Three passages on this theme highlight the relativity of this absurdity, the fact that we are not dealing with an inherent absurdity but with something that is bound to appear absurd from some standpoint outside of faith.[20] Right after the first mention of resignation by name,[21] Silentio directs our attention to Abraham's faith that goes beyond resignation in expecting to get Isaac back. "He had faith by virtue of the absurd, for human calculation was out of the question, and it certainly was absurd that God, who required it of him, should in the next moment rescind the requirement" (FT, 35-36). What is clear is that by the absurd Silentio understands that which goes beyond merely "human calculation." What is not so clear is that Abraham's hope that God would not in the final analysis make him go through with the sacrifice was absurd or unreasonable. He might have sensed that this was a test and hoped that, when God saw his willingness to do what God asked him to do, the command would be rescinded. But, Silentio might respond, Abraham confidently expected that he would get Isaac back either this way or some other way, and there is no basis in human calculation for that certainty; it has its ground only in Abraham's trust in God's promise. In that case what is absurd is not that God should withdraw the requirement at the last minute, but the faith that was assured that somehow Abraham would get Isaac back.

The next passage takes us immediately to that "some other way." Abraham "did not have faith that he would be blessed in a future life but that he would be blessed here in the world. God could give him a new Isaac, could restore to life the one sacrificed. He had faith by virtue of the absurd, for all human calculation ceased long ago" (FT, 36).[22] Human calculation might hope that the test would be cancelled at the last minute, though confident certainty that he would get Isaac back somehow required a faith that goes beyond such reasoning. But to hope for a bodily resurrection already goes beyond reason and, a fortiori, so does the confident certainty that this is a

20. We might speak here of a different language game (Wittgenstein), a different hermeneutical circle (Gadamer), or a different paradigm (Kuhn).

21. Resignation is described in substance but not by name in the Eulogy on Abraham (FT, 17-18).

22. There is no hint of this resurrection theme in the Genesis story, but Silentio draws on Hebrews 11:17 and 19: "By faith Abraham, when put to the test, offered up Isaac. He who had received the promises was ready to offer up his only son. . . . He considered the fact that God is able even to raise someone from the dead."

possible way for God to be faithful to the promises made to Abraham. At least this faith is incommensurable with reason as Silentio understands it, for he writes, "But to be able to lose one's understanding and along with it everything finite, for which it is the stockbroker, and then to win the very same finitude again by virtue of the absurd — this appalls me" (*FT*, 36). That reason is the stockbroker of the finite suggests that Silentio has something like a Humean or Kantian understanding of reason. Miracles in general and bodily resurrections in particular fall outside the realm of possible knowledge within those horizons.

But what about the Hegelian conception of reason, which purports to be the broker of the infinite? Silentio's argument suggests that, so far as Abraham's faith is concerned, the distinction is without a difference. For the system does not take us from the naturalism of Hume's *Treatise* or Kant's *Critique of Pure Reason* to the supernaturalism for which bodily resurrection is a real possibility. For its claim to infinity turns out to be simply the positing of conceptual access to the totality of finite nature and finite human history.[23] It does not take us from the worlds of nature and history to the God who is an agent irreducible to natural causes and historical agencies. So from the standpoint of all three of these giants of modern philosophy, Abraham's faith will of necessity appear absurd.

The third passage once again presents Abraham making that "one more movement" beyond infinite resignation, and doing so

> by virtue of the absurd, by virtue of the fact that for God all things are possible. The absurd does not belong to the differences that lie within the proper domain of the understanding. It is not identical with the improbable, the unexpected, the unforeseen. The moment the knight executed

23. The same can be said of Spinoza's infinity. Hegel says that "thought must begin by placing itself at the standpoint of Spinozism; to be a follower of Spinoza is the essential commencement of all Philosophy. . . . You are either a Spinozist or not a philosopher at all." Spinoza has the "true infinity," since "'infinite' is not to be taken here in the sense of the indeterminate many, but positively, as a circle is perfect infinity in itself." *Hegel's Lectures on the History of Philosophy*, trans. Elizabeth S. Haldane and Frances H. Simson, vol. 3 (London: Routledge and Kegan Paul, 1896), pp. 257, 283, and 263. Since Hegel takes history into account and not just nature, he insists that the category of substance be teleologically suspended in the category of spirit. So Spinoza is the beginning or commencement of philosophy, not its culmination. In the system, the logic presents the category of the infinite. G. W. F. Hegel, *The Encyclopedia Logic*, trans. T. F. Geraets, W. A. Suchting, and H. S. Harris (Indianapolis: Hackett, 1991), pp. 149-52, 165-66, and 173 (§§94-95, 104, and 111). Then comes the Philosophy of Nature, and finally the Philosophy of Spirit.

the act of resignation, he was convinced of the impossibility, humanly speaking . . . for the understanding continues to be right in maintaining that in the finite world where it dominates this having was and continues to be an impossibility. The knight of faith realizes this just as clearly; consequently, he can be saved only by the absurd, and this he grasps by faith. (*FT*, 46-47)

Silentio could not be clearer. What is possible for God, and therefore not intrinsically absurd, is impossible from the standpoint of reason or the understanding; for the latter speaks "humanly," which means that it restricts itself to "the finite world" from which the agency of a God who could raise the dead has been excluded. Whether this exclusion is *de jure* (overtly asserted) or *de facto* (implied by silence), the result is the same. Abraham's faith is absurd.

As we have just seen, this would be true from the standpoint of Hume, of Kant, or of Hegel. And of Abraham! He would insist as strongly as any modern philosopher that, apart from the reality and activity of a God who does not show up in their thought, what he is doing makes no sense at all.

We can see this logic of absurdity at work in Shakespeare's *Hamlet*. In Act I Claudius is scolding Hamlet for being a melancholy Dane. He sees his nephew's sustained mourning as "impious stubbornness" and "unmanly grief." It is, he says,

> To reason most absurd, whose common theme
> Is death of fathers, and who [reason] still hath cried,
> From the first corse [corpse] till he that died today,
> "This must be so." (I.ii.94-106)

But well before Marcellus announces, "Something is rotten in the state of Denmark" (I.iv.90), Hamlet has a premonition that it is so. First, in his "O that this too too solid flesh would melt" soliloquy, he bemoans the unseemly haste with which his mother, Gertrude, has married his uncle.

> She married. O most wicked speed, to post
> With such dexterity to incestuous sheets.
> It is not, nor it cannot come to, good. (I.ii.156-57)

Then, when Horatio tells him of the appearances of his father's ghost, Hamlet has an intimation of immorality. Once again he soliloquizes.

My father's spirit in arms! All is not well:
I doubt some foul play. Would the night were come!
Till then sit still my soul: foul deeds will rise,
Though all the earth o'erwhelm them, to men's eyes. (I.ii.254-57)

Of course, Hamlet doesn't know the half of it. But by the time the whole truth comes out, we can see that Hamlet's "absurd" melancholy is very much attuned to the way things really are, while Claudius's "reason" is the masquerade for family life and political life that are both immoral and criminal but hardly reasonable.[24]

The language of the absurd dominates the contrast between faith and infinite resignation. But there are two references to paradox in the Preliminary Outpouring. Right after the passage just discussed, Silentio tells us that faith is not some natural optimism, "not the spontaneous inclination of the heart but the paradox of existence" (*FT,* 47). He does not gloss his concept of "the paradox of existence," but it seems to refer to the tension of living in a world in which explanations are normally restricted to natural causes or historical agencies but from which a miraculous, divine agency has not been excluded.[25]

At the very end of the Preliminary Outpouring, Silentio speaks of the "prodigious paradox of faith, a paradox that makes a murder into a holy and God-pleasing act, a paradox that gives Isaac back to Abraham again" (*FT,* 53). In speaking of Abraham getting Isaac back, Silentio is looking back to the contrast just concluded between faith and infinite resignation. In speaking of the dialectic of murder and a holy act, he is looking ahead to the very different contrast between Abraham as the knight of faith and the tragic hero. We move from faith as trust in divine promises to faith as obedience to divine commands and how, in this particular case, such obedience could be justified. This is a new question that did not arise in the previous, prelim-

24. N.B. In relation to the discussion of faith as a passion in the next chapter, it should be noted that it is Hamlet's emotional life that is "attuned" to the truth and disclosive of it. Heidegger is relevant here. He writes, "What we indicate *ontologically* by the term 'state-of-mind' [*Befindlichkeit*] is *ontically* the most familiar and everyday sort of thing; our mood [*Stimmung*], our Being-attuned." As if he has been reading Hamlet, Heidegger adds that it is in "a bad mood" that "Being has become manifest as a burden." He speaks of the "primordial disclosure belonging to moods." *Being and Time,* trans. John Macquarrie and Edward Robinson (New York: Harper & Row, 1962), ¶29.

25. It would seem to be a redundancy to call divine agency miraculous, since, as Silentio and his Abraham understand it, it is not reducible to natural causation or historical agency.

inary contrast. Or, we might say, the earlier contrast raises the question of a metaphysical justification of a particular belief, while the latter concerns the question of a moral justification of a certain action. As I have been arguing, it is important that we keep the two issues separate if we are to be faithful to the text.

As we turn to Problems I and II, which develop the teleological suspension of the ethical and its immediate corollary, that we have an absolute duty toward God, 'paradox' becomes the primary term for designating the unreasonableness of faith, although 'absurd' and 'madness' put in cameo appearances (*FT*, 56, 59, 76-77). I see no substantive significance in this change, since, for example, what is a paradox in one paragraph is absurd in the same or the next (*FT*, 56, 69).

It is in Problem I that we encounter the teleological suspension or *Aufhebung* of the ethical as the domain in which the laws and customs of one's people are the highest norms for action. The ethical is the concrete universal, the community whose values sustain, guide, judge, and reward the individual. We recall that Silentio has identified five such communities: the nation, the state, society, the church, and the sect (*FT*, 57-59, 74, 79). If Abraham is not to be lost, these cannot be the highest sources of normativity for his life. Thus the paradox here is that the individual is higher than the universal (*FT*, 55-56, 62).

Two things to notice about this elevation: First, it is about a "justification" of action that supersedes any justification that the universal (Hegel's *Sittlichkeit*) can offer (*FT*, 55-56). Unlike Abraham, the tragic hero has the latter and therefore does not need any superseding norm, any teleological suspension of the ethical. Second, again we must notice the significance of the "after" (*FT*, 55-56, 99). The aesthete places himself above the ethical by refusing to take good and evil, right and wrong as criteria of the good life. There is no paradox here, only the opposition between a moral and an amoral outlook. By contrast, the knight of faith not only takes good and evil, right and wrong to be essential criteria of the good life, but also accepts the authority of his communities in defining them. The paradox of faith is that "after" this, he relativizes these norms in favor of an "absolute relation to the absolute" (*FT*, 56). He experiences anxiety, distress, and paradox because he is committed to norms that can, and in Abraham's case do, conflict (*FT*, 63, 65, 74-75, 113).

But why speak of paradox and absurdity here? What is unreasonable about saying, "The revealed will of God has a higher claim on me than the laws and customs of my people"? If there is a God anything like Abraham's, wouldn't it be highly unreasonable to elevate merely human norms above the commands of God? In any case, doesn't the tragic hero experience a similar tension? Does he not say, "My love and duty to the state supersedes my love and duty to my family; the family is a source of normativity, but only relatively and not absolutely"?[26]

The answer is fairly clear. Abraham's faith as a teleological suspension or relativizing of the ethical is unreasonable only in relation to a definition of reason according to which the ethical universal is the highest, not-to-be-trumped standard for human action. When reason is ideology as the mirror and legitimizer of some social reality, faith will always be unreasonable in principle, for it will always say, "We must obey God rather than any human authority" (Acts 5:29). As the teleological suspension of the ethical, faith becomes the teleological suspension of reason. N.B. This means that reason's authority is not abolished but rather relativized.

Silentio sees the concept of reason as ideology at work theoretically in Hegelian philosophy and practically in the "wretched contentment" of Christendom,[27] the "our age" (*FT*, 5) and the "present generation" (*FT*, 121) with which he begins and ends his little book. He uses the language of unreason — madness, absurdity, and paradox — not because he shares such a view of reason, but because he wants his readers to notice the deep incompatibility between its explicit or implicit hegemony (Hegel and Christendom, respectively) and biblical faith.[28] So the epistemic corollary of his "If the universal is the highest, then Abraham is lost" is "If that is reason, then biblical faith is and ought to be unreasonable."

One of the ways ideologies set themselves up as the legitimizers of some established order is by calling themselves reason (at least in the modern

26. In Hegelian terms, this tension is resolved by mediation, the proper subordination of the individual to the universal. Just as intelligibility requires the subsumption of the particular under the abstract universal, the concept, so practical rationality requires the subordination of the individual to the concrete universal, the community. But Silentio insists that Abraham's paradox cannot be mediated (*FT*, 56, 66; cf. 70-71).

27. On "wretched contentment," see chapter 1, note 7, above.

28. I have argued elsewhere that Silentio and his successor, Johannes Climacus, do not so much argue for the view of biblical faith that they describe and analyze in such detail as insist on its fundamental difference from various counterfeit versions. See "Johannes and Johannes: Kierkegaard and Difference," in *International Kierkegaard Commentary*, vol. 7: *"Philosophical Fragments" and "Johannes Climacus,"* ed. Robert L. Perkins (Macon, GA: Mercer University Press, 1994), pp. 13-32. In effect they throw down an either/or. On the notion of a counterfeit religion, see William Desmond, *Hegel's God: A Counterfeit Double?* (Burlington, VT: Ashgate, 2003).

world). Silentio sees no reason to accept this self-congratulatory designation without Socratic self-examination. His strategy, as I see it, is to shift the burden of proof. Instead of assuming that Christianity must somehow show itself to be reasonable, it is the ideological concept of reason that needs to show us why we should adopt it.[29] Does not every established order become evil just to the degree that it absolutizes itself, confuses itself with God or the kingdom of God?

Silentio did not live to witness the crimes against humanity perpetrated in the twentieth and twenty-first centuries by self-absolutizing nationalism, tribalism, and racism; self-absolutizing communism; self-absolutizing democratic capitalism; and self-absolutizing sectarianism. But he gives us the tools for understanding them. Whenever what is not God confuses itself with God, humanity becomes inhuman. Silentio shows why religion should protest against this idolatry. Reading him in a later context, we can see that, even if we are not Abrahamic monotheists, there is good reason to be on guard against letting anything finite and relative take itself to be infinite and absolute. At best there is intellectual confusion in such a move, at worst intellectual dishonesty.

Problem II doesn't add anything substantively new to this analysis. As a corollary to or even synonym for the teleological suspension of the ethical, Silentio here speaks of an absolute duty to God. But already in Problem I he had articulated the Abrahamic paradox in terms of "an absolute relation to the absolute" in a context where this absolute was clearly not some abstract metaphysical principle but a personal God who makes promises and gives commands (FT, 56). Silentio does make explicit that this does not invalidate the ethical universal but only relativizes it, and that for faith it is the relation to God that governs our relation to society, whereas for reason, at least in its distinctive modern forms, it is the other way around (FT, 70). Once again: either/or.

Similarly, Silentio revisits the earlier (and later) theme that the knight of faith cannot make himself understood by those around him since it is not by virtue of some communal life and language they share that he can be justified. First, Silentio notes that one consequence of this is a lack of security (FT, 76, 78). The knight of faith is not surrounded by a social support system that reassures him that he is doing the right thing. In the language

---

29. The same thing happened when the logical positivist verification criterion of meaning was said to be a "proposal." Instead of ethical and religious discourse having to prove somehow that it is cognitively meaningful and thus capable of truth or falsity, the burden shifted to the positivists to show why we should adopt their "proposal." See note 12 above.

of the sociology of religion, he lacks the "plausibility structure" that is the "base" which gives reality and stability to the life-world and which is constantly renewed in "conversation."[30] That is why the silence of Abraham in Problem III is so serious.

Second, Silentio calls our attention to an all but inevitable reaction to a sense that one is beginning to become isolated: sectarianism.

> The true knight of faith is always absolute isolation; the spurious knight is sectarian. This is an attempt to jump off the narrow path of the paradox and become a tragic hero at a bargain price. The tragic hero expresses the universal and sacrifices himself for it. In place of that, the sectarian Punchinello has a private theater, a few good friends and comrades. (*FT*, 79)

It may seem that Silentio exaggerates when he speaks of the "absolute isolation" of the knight of faith. After all, isn't he a member of several communities that provide a "plausibility structure" for his life of faith? Yes, of course, but. . . . None of these communities, whether religious or secular, has any more than relative authority; each is always open to the possibility of being the temptation to be overcome if faith is to remain vital. The "absolute isolation" of faith is not the whole of what Silentio says. That theme needs to be taken in dialectical tension with the real, if relative, significance of communities, sacred and secular, in the life of faith.

Silentio has fun satirizing the sectarian, and the satire is serious sociology. What is perhaps more important is the way he undermines the distinction between church and sect that, since Troeltsch, has been standard fare in the sociology of religion.[31] Without denying the differences between large, big-tent, mainstream (often state) churches and small, more narrowly defined, peripheral religious communities, he shows their logic and psychology to be the same. They offer to the devout individual a group home that provides the security of a collective, conversational plausibility structure. Vis-à-vis Abraham, either kind of religious community — no less than the political and social communities, typically secular in modernity — is a temptation to faith. They represent the all too real possibility of seeking one's justification from a merely human source.

---

30. Peter L. Berger, *The Sacred Canopy: Elements of a Sociological Theory of Religion* (Garden City, NY: Doubleday, 1967), pp. 45-48 and 17. On conversational rationality, see chapter 3, notes 44 and 45, above.

31. Ernst Troeltsch, *The Social Teaching of the Christian Churches*, trans. Olive Wyon, vol. 2 (New York: Harper & Row, 1960), p. 993.

Finally, so far as Problem II is concerned, Silentio tells us that the "true knight of faith is a witness, never the teacher" (*FT*, 80). In *Philosophical Fragments*, Climacus distinguishes the divine teacher from the human teacher. The former gives the learner the truth both by giving a truth the learner does not already possess *and* by giving the condition or the ability to recognize it as the truth. Therefore "the learner owes the teacher everything" (*PF*, 30). The human teacher, by contrast, operates within the framework of Platonic recollection. Like Socrates with the slave boy in the *Meno*, the teacher can give the learner a new truth, but cannot give the ability to recognize it as such. If the learner does not already have the condition, learning cannot occur. But if the truth is already within the learner, that is, if the learner already possesses the ability to recognize the truth as the truth and thus to "recollect" it, the teacher is "something accidental, a vanishing point, an occasion," and the learner is "sufficient unto himself" (*PF*, 11). It doesn't matter whether it was Mr. Williams, my high school geometry teacher, or Miss Schillerup, the substitute, who first presented me with the proof of the Pythagorean theorem and was thus the occasion for my learning. What matters is that I had the ability to recognize the proof as compelling. Otherwise I would have been nothing more than a parrot who had been taught to say, "The square of the hypotenuse. . . ."

Silentio doesn't tell us just what he understands by teaching when he denies that capacity to the knight of faith, and we have no warrant for assigning to him the meaning that Climacus gives us. Using the latter as a foil, however, I want to suggest a sense in which, within the ethical, the human teacher can indeed be a teacher and not merely an occasion. This will give content to the claim that the knight of faith can be only a witness and not a teacher. The prima facie plausibility of such a reading is that it makes the distinction between the teacher and the witness derivative from the distinction between the ethical and the religious stages as it has been developed in Problems I and II, at whose conclusion the former distinction occurs.

Within the ethical, the teacher gives to the learner the truth and the ability to recognize it as the truth, though not in the sense of Platonic recollection. In situations where it makes sense to speak of indoctrination, catechesis, socialization, or acculturation, the teacher is the one who passes on to the learner the laws and customs of the people or what we might call the lore of the tribe, its practices of cognition and comportment.[32] The basis of

---

32. I am using 'practices' here in the technical sense developed by Alasdair MacIntyre in *After Virtue* (Notre Dame: University of Notre Dame Press, 1981), pp. 175-89.

learning is not recollection such that the learner is "sufficient unto himself," but rather authority such that "the learner owes the teacher everything," since it is the teacher's authority and not the learner's insight that governs the situation.

We need not see the situation as "authoritarian" in some pejorative sense. The authority of the teacher can be grounded in the learner's desire to belong and, perhaps, an instinctive tendency to imitate. In some contexts, of course, these natural incentives to recognize the authority of the teacher are supplemented by a system of rewards and punishments. But whatever the mix and whatever the degree of success in the process by which the individual is "mediated" into the universal, just to the degree that it does succeed, it does so because the teacher gives the truth to a learner who does not already possess it. This is possible by virtue of the teacher's authority, which is derived from being the authoritative voice of a community that the learner has some incentive to belong to. The learner does not accept the truth because of the inherent ability to recognize it as such; rather, the learner recognizes the truth as such by means of accepting it on the teacher's authority. The learner is not a parrot but one whose belief structure is enlarged by the teacher's instruction.

If the knight of faith speaks out of his faith, he is not trying to pass on the lore of the tribe, nor does he have the authority to do so as its authoritative voice. By virtue of his "incommensurability" with the ethical sphere, he is eccentric to the circle that defines the relevant universal. But, of course, he lives in a circle that, while not concentric, overlaps the ethical sphere and its rationality. So he might be a school teacher teaching the pledge of allegiance to the flag to school children, and he might do so just as another teacher who wants nothing to do with faith. But if he decides to speak from his faith as well, he might say something like this:

> It's a good thing to pledge allegiance to the flag and to the republic for which it stands. They are gifts for which we should be thankful, and we are indebted for them and to them. But that republic is human, all too human, and its authority over us is only relative and never absolute. Our only absolute allegiance is to God, which is why we say "under God" in the pledge. To remind ourselves of this important mental reservation, it is a good idea always to pledge allegiance with our fingers crossed.

That this instructor is not a teacher in the sense I'm suggesting we should attribute to Silentio will be clear when parents or a principal hear about this and he loses his job. It would be interesting to know what happens to him if he does this in a parochial school or as a Sunday school teacher.

To say that our instructor speaks as a witness and not as a teacher is to say that he speaks without authority, without the support of some sociological plausibility structure.[33] Positively, it is to say that he speaks on his own authority, that he tells us what he has experienced and what he believes without any appeal to what "we" think about the matter. In a courtroom, for example, we expect a witness to tell us what he or she has seen or heard without any appeal, overt or implicit, to the interests of any group, be it the police department or some racial/ethnic majority or minority community.[34] The witness is not there in the capacity of their representative but solely to speak as an individual. It is this civil function to which Silentio appeals to distinguish the knight of faith from those who teach on behalf of some ethical community, religious or secular.

I have been arguing throughout that Abraham's faith is unreasonable — madness, absurd, paradox — not intrinsically but relatively, that is, only in relation to some interpretation of reason or understanding from which some essential of biblical faith has been excluded a priori. Steve Evans calls attention to a passage from Kierkegaard's later papers (1850) that makes this point. "The absurd is a category, the negative criterion of the divine or of the relation to the divine. When the believer has faith, the absurd is not the absurd — faith transforms it. . . . Therefore, rightly understood, there is nothing at all frightening in the category of the absurd" (*JP* 1:10). Evans's comment deserves to be quoted at length.

> This is consistent when we recognize the social, historically conditioned character of "reason" and "the ethical" in Kierkegaard's treatment. Insofar as God transcends the social order, and insofar as the social order attempts to deify itself and usurp divine authority, there is a necessary opposition between faith and "reason," just as there is a tension between faith and what in *Fear and Trembling* is called "the ethical."

33. Since Kierkegaard so often insisted that he spoke "without authority," that is to say, in his context, not as a clerical representative of the state church nor as a professorial representative of the state university, it is appropriate that one collection of his essays and discourses is published under the title *Without Authority*. See *WA*.

34. In later writings Kierkegaard will draw on the link (in Greek) between a witness and a martyr. I think the weaker sense of a witness in a courtroom is more helpful for getting at what Silentio is after here.

In other words, faith is the teleological suspension of reason. Evans continues:

> So the believer understands and must not forget that in faith he is committed to something that cannot be defended by appeal to values and modes of thinking enshrined in the social order. He is indeed called to a lonely journey to Mt. Moriah. However, the believer does not see the journey as absurd, for he has faith. From the perspective of faith, the relativity and historical character of "reason" and "the ethical" become clear, and new ways of thinking and acting open up, which may be judged by society as "irrational" and "unethical" but may be seen by the "single individual" as fulfilling in a more authentic way the ideals that society claims to support.[35]

Silentio gives us the premises from which to draw this kind of conclusion, and it is terribly important to make these points over against readings that dismiss Kierkegaard as an irrationalist. But Silentio does not draw these conclusions. Instead of Kierkegaard's "nothing at all frightening in the category of the absurd," Silentio emphasizes the anxiety, distress, fear, trembling, terribleness, and dreadfulness of Abraham's experience of faith. Similarly with Evans's comment, "However, the believer does not see the journey as absurd, for he has faith." Silentio insists that, while the knight of faith has gone beyond "reason" and "the ethical," he does so only "after" having been immersed in them and without abandoning them. They remain part of his identity. The only conclusion we can draw is that there is something within the knight of faith that does "see the journey as absurd" and that feels it in a way reflected in Silentio's psychological trauma language. Our answer to Evans's question, "Is faith still absurd?"[36] has to be thoroughly dialectical: No and Yes. After all, the book is about faith and its title is *Fear and Trembling*.

35. C. Stephen Evans, "Faith as the *Telos* of Morality: A Reading of *Fear and Trembling*," in *International Kierkegaard Commentary*, vol. 6: *"Fear and Trembling" and "Repetition,"* ed. Robert L. Perkins (Macon, GA: Mercer University Press, 1993), p. 24.

36. Evans, "Faith as the *Telos* of Morality," p. 23.

CHAPTER 6

Faith as the Highest Passion

In *The Book of Common Prayer,* the collect for the fifth Sunday in Lent could bring Silentio to mind.

> Almighty God, you alone can bring into order the unruly wills and affections of sinners: Grant your people grace to love what you command and desire what you promise; that, among the swift and varied changes of the world, our hearts may surely there be fixed where true joys are to be found; through Jesus Christ our Lord, who lives and reigns with you and the Holy Spirit, one God, now and for ever. *Amen.*[1]

First, the God to whom the prayer is addressed is the God of promise and command. "Unruly wills and affections" would seem to belong to us insofar as we do not trust the divine promises or obey the divine commands. In Silentio's terms, no matter how "ethical" we are, we lack faith. In the language of the prayer, we are sinners.

Second, to bring our wills and affections into a right relation to the God of promise and command is not within our power. It requires gracious divine agency, and it is for this grace that the prayer prays. We recall Silentio's insistence that he cannot make the movement of faith and that this movement is a "miracle" and a "marvel."

Third, the heart of the matter is, well, the heart and its "fixations," not the intellect in some purely cognitive sense. The heart is a fundamental category of biblical religion, and it signifies the deepest inner source of our

---

1. *The Book of Common Prayer* (New York: Seabury, 1979), p. 219.

life, especially the will and the affections, our desires and our loves, what we want and what gives us joy.[2] Silentio's way of saying that faith is a matter of the heart is his fifth thesis about faith: **Faith is a passion**. As I shall argue, this means, among other things, that faith is a matter of our emotional life.

The most obvious difference between the prayer and Silentio's account of faith is that the emotion highlighted in the prayer is joy,[3] while for Silentio, as we have noted, the emotions associated with faith are fear, trembling, anxiety, and distress. We read that "the knight of faith has the passion to concentrate in one single point the whole of the ethical that he violates, in order that he may give himself the assurance that he actually loves Isaac with his whole soul." Whereas the tragic hero is "secure," the knight of faith exposes himself to "sleeplessness" and "dreadfulness" (*FT*, 78).

Kierkegaard, as it turns out, writes a lot about joy in his own name;[4] so it is perhaps misleading to identify him as "the melancholy Dane."[5] But Silentio is surely a candidate for that title. We need to keep in mind that his critique of Hegelian philosophy and of Christendom involves a sustained stress on the *mysterium tremendum* rather than the *fascinans*, the repelling rather than the attracting force of the sacred. He thinks his audience sees Christianity as all about comforting the afflicted (or even comforting the comfortable) and not about afflicting the comfortable.

Silentio — and Kierkegaard, for that matter — are in tune with Jon-

---

2. There is an obvious link here with Aristotle, whose concept of moral virtue involves bringing our actions and emotions into conformity with reason. *Nichomachean Ethics*, II.6 and II.9. Some translations of Aristotle read "passions and actions," but since I am going to distinguish passions from emotions, I won't make the two terms interchangeable.

3. Love is also an emotion, but it is more than that and here is closer to desire than to emotion.

4. He writes six "upbuilding discourses" on joy in *Upbuilding Discourses in Various Spirits* and seven "Christian discourses" on joy in *Christian Discourses*. All of these are on the theme of joy in the midst of suffering, so it is clear that Christian joy is in tension with worldly joy, mirroring the relation of faith and reason in Kierkegaard's writings, including *Fear and Trembling*.

5. Simon D. Podmore writes that "this oft-repeated legend for Kierkegaard — 'the melancholy Dane' — represents a perception that only sees half the face, as it were, of one of modern theology and philosophy's most insightful exponents of the *triumph of faith over despair*." He notes the origin of this moniker in P. T. Forsyth's reference to "the great and melancholy Dane in whom Hamlet was mastered by Christ," and bemoans the fact that "the darker aspect has prevailed and the second part of Forsyth's 'dialectic,' which redeems Kierkegaard from the melancholy of the first, fades, unheeded, into obscurity." Podmore, *Kierkegaard and the Self before God: Anatomy of the Abyss* (Bloomington: Indiana University Press, 2011), p. xi; emphasis in original.

athan Edwards, who writes, "True religion, in great part, consists in holy affections."[6] Similarly, Robert Roberts writes,

> Whatever else Christianity may be, it is a set of emotions. It is love of God and neighbor, grief about one's own waywardness, joy in the merciful salvation of our God, gratitude, hope, and peace. So if I don't love God and my neighbor, abhor my sins, and rejoice in my redemption, if I am not grateful, hopeful, and at peace with God and myself, then it follows that I am alienated from Christianity, though I was born and bred in the bosom of the Presbyterian Church, am baptized and confirmed and willing in good conscience to affirm the articles of the Creed.[7]

I am not going to equate passion with emotion. But I do want to suggest that, when Silentio tells us that faith is a passion, he points us in the direction of Edwards's affections and Roberts's emotions. So let us first look at what Silentio tells us about faith as a passion.

His topic sentence, as it were, is that faith is a "prodigious passion," even the "supreme" or "highest passion" (*FT,* 23, 121). Moreover, passion is not peripheral. It is what "unites all human life" as what is "essentially human" (*FT,* 67, 121).[8]

Silentio links this theme with his critique of those who would "go further" than faith to reason as something higher, especially in the form of speculative philosophy (*FT,* 7, 23, 121). Silentio "easily envisions his fate in an age that has crossed out passion in order to serve science" (*FT,* 7).[9] In a closely related move, he anticipates Kierkegaard's own critique of the "present age" in *Two Ages.* Silentio writes, "What our generation lacks is not reflection but passion." The "leap" requires passion, whereas "mediation" does not (*FT,* 42n.). He asks whether "the present generation" has not "perfected

---

6. Jonathan Edwards, *A Treatise Concerning Religious Affections,* ed. John E. Smith (New Haven: Yale University Press, 1959), p. 95.

7. Robert C. Roberts, *Spirituality and Human Emotion* (Grand Rapids: Eerdmans, 1982), pp. 1-2.

8. It is not clear whether we should read this as saying that passion is what we all have in common or that it is what gives to each of us whatever degree of coherence or integrity we have as persons.

9. This occurs in a paragraph that refers to "the system" nine times and identifies the heart of Hegel's philosophy of religion — "to transpose the whole content of faith into conceptual form," that is, from the *Vorstellungen* of the religious life to the *Begriffe* of speculative philosophy. See the discussion in chapter 1 above.

the art of self-deception." "Are we so sure that we have achieved the highest?" Has the present generation understood that the "essentially human is passion" and that "the highest passion in a person is faith" (*FT*, 121)? In an early draft of the Epilogue, Silentio speaks of those who want to "go further, as if it were an easy matter to bring about a more unbelieving, more correctly, a less believing, age than our own, whose insipid rationality has pumped all passion out of life" (*FT*, 257).[10] The contrast between passion and reflection that underlies all these comments suggests that it involves the self who is actively, we might say existentially, engaged in becoming itself as distinct from the self who has become a spectator, disengaged not only from the world but especially from itself.[11]

Silentio thus tells us how important he takes passion to be. He also tells us what it is not. It is not an "aesthetic emotion," a "spontaneous inclination of the heart" (*FT*, 47). Nor is faith a matter of "the qualifications of feeling, mood, etc. that belong to interiority," for it is "an interiority that is not identical, please note, with the first but is a new interiority" related to the paradox and the absurd (*FT*, 69). But Silentio does not tell us what passion is. So if we want to know how his passion relates to Edwards's affections and Roberts's emotions, we will have to develop a vocabulary not found in the former's text.

I shall distinguish passion from emotion and emotion from feeling. I do not claim that these distinctions correspond to ordinary usage, which is anything but precise and consistent,[12] or that they correspond to the way

10. In interesting passages not pertinent to our immediate concern, Silentio tells us that every movement of infinity requires passion. These include infinite resignation, Socratic ignorance, irony, humor, and repentance (*FT*, 42n., 51, and 99). In telling us how he is "shattered," "repelled," and "paralyzed" by the paradox that is Abraham, Silentio describes his own thought as passionate (*FT*, 33).

11. Jonathan Edwards distinguishes the faculty of disinterested cognition from the other faculty, sometimes called the heart. By it "the soul does not merely perceive and view things, but is in some way inclined with respect to the things it views or considers; either is inclined to 'em, or is disinclined, and averse from 'em; or is the faculty by which the soul does not behold things, as an indifferent unaffected spectator." *Religious Affections*, p. 96. While this indicates that the heart's perspective is not that of disinterested cognition, it fails to capture the way the self is itself at issue in Kierkegaardian passion. As Heidegger puts it, "Dasein . . . is ontically distinguished by the fact that, in its very Being, that Being is an *issue* for it." *Being and Time*, trans. John Macquarrie and Edward Robinson (New York: Harper & Row, 1962), ¶4, p. 32. For an analysis of the pathology of a schizoid self that splits itself into an active self in the world and a disengaged, observer self outside the world, see R. D. Laing, *The Divided Self* (New York: Penguin Books, 1965).

12. Martha Nussbaum notes "our casual and frequently loose use of words such as 'feel-

any single philosopher of the emotions uses these terms. These distinctions represent a heuristic. If they are warranted, it will be because they are conceptually coherent and because they throw light on the relation of faith, as Silentio presents it, to our emotions or affections.

The following simple story may prove useful for illustrating various aspects of the analysis to follow. Suppose I have a passion for fly-fishing. Perhaps it isn't my highest passion, but it prevails over a good many of my desires. It is strong enough to say that it is an important part of my personal identity. It's one of the first things people think about when they think of me. If I see some of my equipment in my neighbor's garage and think he stole it, I will be angry. If I am reminded that I lent it to him and haven't needed it since, that anger will dissipate (unless the idea of stolen gear is a cover for a deeper, unconscious ground for my anger). If another friend invites the first friend to a weekend at his cottage, near a fabulous trout stream, but leaves me out, I will feel envy and resentment. If I get home and find an e-mail inviting me to join them, the envy and resentment will be replaced by gratitude. My passion for fly-fishing has a variety of emotional consequences depending on the circumstances.

By passions I shall understand what matters to us, what is important to us, what we care about deeply enough to be part of our identity. Roberts suggests that our passions "constitute our character, our inmost self. Passions differ from other concerns in determining a person's actions and emotions over relatively long stretches of his life, and roughly by being 'higher' in the order of his cares." In other words, a passion is to some significant degree "overriding" in relation to other things that matter to us.[13] In the background here is Heidegger's analysis of Dasein (the critter that each of us is) as care[14] and especially Frankfurt's analysis in "The Importance of What We Care About."[15]

Frankfurt suggests that, in their preoccupation with matters epistemological and ethical, philosophers have paid insufficient attention to "a third branch of inquiry, concerned with a cluster of questions which pertain to another thematic and fundamental preoccupation of human exis-

ings,' 'emotions,' and 'passion.'" *Upheavals of Thought: The Intelligence of Emotions* (New York: Cambridge University Press, 2001), p. 8.

13. Roberts, *Spirituality and Human Emotion*, p. 19.

14. *Being and Time*, Division One, Section VI, but see numerous other references in the index.

15. This is the title essay of Harry G. Frankfurt's *The Importance of What We Care About* (New York: Cambridge University Press, 1998), pp. 80-94.

tence — namely, *what to care about.*" This third branch "resembles ethics" but "differs significantly from ethics. . . . Ethics focuses on the problem of ordering our relations with *other people*" in terms of right and wrong and moral obligation. "We are led into the third branch of inquiry, on the other hand, because we are interested in deciding what to do with *ourselves* and because we therefore need to understand what is *important,* or, rather, what is *important to us.*"[16]

Two caveats. First, this may sound as if this "third branch of inquiry" is an exercise in amoral, or, as Kierkegaard would say, aesthetic narcissism. And, of course, it could be. In my list of what I care about, right and wrong, good and evil, and the rights and needs of my neighbor might be conspicuously missing. But they need not be. I may care deeply about moral issues, abstractly, and about my neighbors, concretely. We should take Frankfurt's emphasis on *"ourselves"* and *"important to us"* not to exclude a love of God and neighbor from what we care about but rather to emphasize that what we care about concerns who we are, our identity. We are not disengaged spectators in our caring; rather, we are ourselves at issue.

Heidegger points out that Kant's three questions from the first critique,[17]

What can I know?
What should I do?
What may I hope?

evoke a fourth question in his lectures on logic:[18]

What is the human being? *(Was ist der Mensch?)*[19]

We could say that Frankfurt's three questions also evoke a fourth as follows:

What can I know?
What should I do?
What do I care about?
Who am I?

16. Frankfurt, "Importance of What We Care About," pp. 80-81.
17. At *Critique of Pure Reason,* A 804-805 = B 832-833.
18. *Kant's Werke (Akademie Textausgabe)* (Berlin: Walter de Gruyter, 1968), 9:25.
19. Martin Heidegger, *Kant and the Problem of Metaphysics,* trans. Richard Taft (Bloomington: Indiana University Press, 1997), p. 145.

In any case, the existential overtones of Frankfurt's fourth question suggest that, perhaps ironically, he is closer to Kierkegaard than to Heidegger/ Kant.[20]

Second, Frankfurt speaks of an "inquiry" oriented toward "deciding what to do with *ourselves*." Fair enough; caring is a legitimate topic for philosophical reflection. But we should not overlook the fact that if and when we ever undertake such an "inquiry" it will be as those who always already care about a variety of matters, and care deeply enough about some of them that they signify our identity. One needn't be a philosopher to be defined in good measure by one's cares or concerns.

This way of thinking about our passions breaks the ancient tie, due largely to the Stoics, between 'passion' and 'passivity.' To make this point Jamie Ferreira cites a definition of 'passion' from the *Oxford English Dictionary* as "an eager outreaching of the mind towards something; an overmastering zeal or enthusiasm for a special object."[21] Our passions are a mix of activity and passivity. As Ferreira puts it, "a passion is not something over which we have no control — we are not mere victims — but it is equally not something which we decide to have or not have in the same way we decide to have steak rather than cheese soufflé for dinner."[22]

By emotions I mean such mental states as "appetite, anger, fear, confidence, envy, joy, affection, hatred, longing, emulation, [and] pity." The list is Aristotle's.[23] They are sometimes referred to as passions or feelings, though for purposes of analysis I will distinguish them from both.

With the help of our story we can see the relation between passions and emotions. In my usage, passions are not so much emotions but dispositions to have emotions. A dispositional property is always present, even when it is not actualized in some episode. Thus, glass is always brittle, but this shows itself only when it is struck with sufficient force by some hard object. My passion for fly-fishing is like this. It is always a part of who I am, but it is not always manifest in my consciousness (or my actions). But given the right trigger, in our story a belief, then another belief, and then an invitation, it produces an appropriate emotion. The emotion need not

20. On the other hand, the Heidegger of *Being and Time* can be fairly summarized as saying, not Dasein cares, but Dasein is care, in which case the close link between our cares and our personal identities is reestablished.

21. M. Jamie Ferreira, *Transforming Vision: Imagination and Will in Kierkegaardian Faith* (Oxford: Clarendon, 1991), p. 23.

22. Ferreira, *Transforming Vision*, p. 25.

23. *Nichomachean Ethics*, bk. 2, ch. 5.

be absolutely appropriate; my passion may be deeply problematic and the belief may be false. But given the passion and the belief, it is not surprising that the anger, envy, and gratitude arise. There's a visible fit among them. Thus in Roberts's definition of emotions as "concern-based construals" or seeings-as, the concern (or care) is the disposition and the construal is the episode.[24] In my anger, for example, I see my neighbor as a scoundrel. Similarly, in Rick Furtak's definition of emotions as "perceptions of significance," the significance comes from the passion as a disposition of care or concern and the perception is the occurrent or episodic manifestation of that disposition.[25] Here, too, seeing-as language is appropriate. Frankfurt highlights the complexity of the situation. "The fact that someone cares about a certain thing is constituted by a complex set of cognitive, affective, and volitional dispositions and states."[26]

Contemporary philosophical reflection on the emotions often begins in dialogue with the ancient Stoics. Two points are important for our purposes. First, the Stoic ideal of *apatheia,* or freedom from the passions, is a wholesale rather than a retail assault on our emotional life. The life of reason must be dispassionate, not because this emotion is too strong or that one is related to the merely trivial, but because all of what counts as passions on a Stoic analysis grows out of cares or concerns (what I'm calling passions) for what is beyond our control. This leaves us vulnerable to pain and compromises the ideal of autonomy and the goal of happiness. The war against the passions must be fought at the dispositional (wholesale) level rather than the episodic (retail) level.[27] We must learn not to care about

---

24. Robert C. Roberts, *Emotions: An Essay in Aid of Moral Psychology* (New York: Cambridge University Press, 2003), p. 64. He adds that "concerns, cares, desires, loves, interests, attachments, and enthusiasms are dispositions to emotions; when we construe circumstances in terms that touch or impinge on our concerns, the construals are emotions" (pp. 79-80).

25. Rick Anthony Furtak, *Wisdom in Love: Kierkegaard and the Ancient Quest for Emotional Integrity* (Notre Dame: University of Notre Dame Press, 2005), p. 6.

26. Frankfurt, "Importance of What We Care About," p. 85. Roberts distinguishes emotion from passion as follows with reference to our next pseudonym, Johannes Climacus: "Climacus thinks of proper personal formation as in large part a matter of proper *passional* formation — the proper formation of interests, enthusiasms and concerns, and of the various emotions that arise from these." Roberts, "Dialectical Emotions and the Virtue of Faith," in *International Kierkegaard Commentary,* vol. 12: *Concluding Unscientific Postscript to "Philosophical Fragments,"* ed. Robert L. Perkins (Macon, GA: Mercer University Press, 1997), p. 73.

27. "Sometimes the Stoics go no further than to censure emotional responses that are disproportionate because we are excessively concerned about paltry objects. This argument might be called a *structural* critique . . . (as opposed to the *fundamental* thesis which dismisses

anything we cannot control, not to let such matters matter or be important to us. Then we will not be vulnerable to the "upheavals of thought" that disturb our peace of mind.[28]

There is an important insight here, namely, an awareness of "the importance of what we care about," of the dispositional dimension of our emotional life. But contemporary philosophers are apt to side with Aristotle against the Stoics and to believe that emotional integrity is not to be found in the wholesale extirpation of the emotions but in their proper formation. Thus, Aristotle famously says that "it is a hard task to be good . . . anyone can get angry — that is easy . . . but to do all this to the right person, to the right extent, at the right time, for the right reason, and in the right way is no longer something easy that anyone can do. It is for this reason that good conduct is rare, praiseworthy, and noble."[29] Frankfurt is an Aristotelian in this sense insofar as he takes the questions, What is worth caring about? and Am I justified in making something or other important simply by caring about it? to be hard questions, not susceptible to easy, categorical, negative replies.

Furtak is more aggressive in his attack on the Stoic ideal. Claiming that to be rational is to be passionate, not apathetic,[30] he insists "that we cannot sustain the emotions that hold us together without accepting the risk of suffering emotions that tear us apart." He compares the Stoics to Byron's "men without a heart" and to Camus' Mersault in *The Stranger*, who is without grief at his mother's death. Furtak speaks of "nihilistic indifference" and of a remedy that is "just as bad as the initial affliction."[31]

Nussbaum is also an Aristotelian in this sense, and she illustrates Furtak's point powerfully with reference to love and grief in her treatment of her own grief over her mother's death.[32] As we shall see, Kierkegaard also sides with Aristotle against the Stoics on this point, and it is not an accident

---

all externals [what is beyond our control] as categorically unimportant." Furtak, *Wisdom in Love*, pp. 19-20. I call these two the weak and the strong Stoic theses and agree that the strong thesis is fundamental to Stoicism.

28. The ancient skeptics' goal of *ataraxia*, tranquility, is closely related to the Stoic ideal of *apatheia*. The quoted phrase "upheavals of thought" is the title of an important study of emotions. See note 12 above.

29. *Nichomachean Ethics*, bk. 2, ch. 9.

30. Notice the title of C. Stephen Evans's commentary, *Passionate Reason: Making Sense of Kierkegaard's "Philosophical Fragments"* (Bloomington: Indiana University Press, 1992).

31. Furtak, *Wisdom in Love*, p. xii. The passage cited at note 7 above shows Roberts also to be an Aristotelian on this point.

32. Nussbaum, *Upheavals of Thought*, especially in part 1, section 1, pp. 19-89.

that two "Aristotelian" philosophers of emotion, Roberts and Furtak, are Kierkegaard scholars.

Although Furtak speaks the language of disposition and episode,[33] it seems to me that he weakens the distinction by treating the former as itself an emotion. He speaks of love as "the emotion which is prior to all other emotions. If love did not lead us to care for the people, places, and things of this world, we could not be disposed to respond to one set of circumstances with jealousy, to another with joy, and so on." Thus, "all other emotions (the secondary emotions that follow from love, which is their primary condition) are consequences of the way that we encounter the world in light of our cares."[34] It makes sense to distinguish love as a disposition from love as an episode. It is true all the time that I love my wife, my children, and my grandchildren. But I am not at every moment feeling warm tenderness, or anxious concern, or deep gratitude toward them. There are times when they are not even on the radar screen of my consciousness. In the dispositional sense it seems to me mistaken to speak of love as an emotion, even a primary emotion. Just as in Kant the condition of the possibility of experience is not itself an experience, so here the condition of the possibility of various emotions is not an emotion.

There is a second reason why the Stoics play such a large role in contemporary philosophy of the emotions: they recognize that emotions are not merely a matter of feeling or affect but are also cognitively significant. A preliminary indication of this significance is the fact that emotions tend to presuppose beliefs and thus typically to be vulnerable to change as those beliefs change. When I no longer thought that my neighbor had stolen my fishing gear, I ceased to be angry at him. Nor need this change be left to happenstance. "If passions are formed (at least in part) out of beliefs or judgments, and if socially taught beliefs are frequently unreliable, then passions need to be scrutinized in just the way in which other socially taught beliefs are scrutinized."[35] The perception that grounds an emotion "might

---

33. "Once a person has developed a primary affective disposition, he or she is thereby susceptible to all the varieties of passionate experience." Furtak, *Wisdom in Love,* p. 5.

34. Furtak, *Wisdom in Love,* pp. 10-11.

35. Martha Nussbaum, *Therapy of Desire: Theory and Practice in Hellenistic Ethics* (Princeton: Princeton University Press, 1994), pp. 28, 46, 9. She follows Stoic usage here, speaking of passions where I would say emotions and speaking as if emotions simply are beliefs, a view most clearly held by Chrysippus. Robert Solomon holds this latter belief, while Nussbaum herself holds that "emotions include in their content judgments that can be true or false" and that beliefs are "constituent parts of what the emotion *is.*" See Robert C. Solomon,

contain a right view of the object, or it might not." Thus, "emotions, like other beliefs, can be true or false, and (an independent point) justified or unjustified, reasonable or unreasonable." They are not "immune to rational critique."[36]

We should notice that the beliefs thus closely involved with emotions are of two sorts. There are the factual beliefs that trigger a particular disposition, such as my belief that my neighbor has stolen my fishing gear; and there are normative beliefs on which our passions are dependent, that certain things are worth caring about. While the criteria for these two kinds of belief are surely different,[37] both are subject to rational critique in the sense just described (unless one has a purely non-cognitivist theory of normative claims). Regarding the second kind of belief, Frankfurt notes that "there are two distinct (albeit compatible) ways in which something may be important to a person. First, its importance to him may be due to considerations which are altogether independent of whether or not he cares about the thing in question. Second, the thing may become important to him just because he does care about it. Correspondingly, there are two distinct sorts of ground on which a person who thinks it worthwhile to care about a certain thing [the normative belief] might attempt to justify his view."[38] So the situation is complex, but the point is the same: emotions are not "immune to rational critique."

I have called this vulnerability of emotions to rational critique a "preliminary indication" of their cognitive significance. We can deepen our understanding of this significance if we note that emotions are themselves cognitions. Even if we take the normative and factual beliefs presupposed by emotions to be only necessary conditions and not either identical with or essential ingredients in the emotions,[39] it will remain the case that emotions are themselves intentional. They are "of" or "about" their object. Thus I am angry "at" my friend, envious "of" my other friend, and eventually grateful "to" the first friend. These emotions are interpretations of their object; they see it as something or other; they construe it in a particular way. They have what we could call a propositional content.

The Passions (Garden City, NY: Doubleday, 1977), pp. 185-87 (cited by Roberts, *Emotions*, p. 83, n. 13) and Nussbaum, *Upheavals of Thought*, pp. 1, 34-36, and *Therapy of Desire*, p. 88 in the context of ch. 3 as a whole.

36. Nussbaum, *Upheavals of Thought*, p. 2.
37. See Furtak, *Wisdom in Love*, p. 9.
38. Frankfurt, "Importance of What We Care About," p. 92.
39. See note 35 above.

Because she sees emotions as such "complex" and "rich" intentionalities,[40] Nussbaum describes her theory of emotions as "cognitive-evaluative" and "cognitive-intentional."[41] We might see in the former a reference to the relation of the emotions to the passions from which they arise, while the latter directs our focus toward the emotions themselves. In either case we are encouraged to see "emotions as *thoughts*" and as "value-laden ways of *understanding* the world."[42]

Within the agreement that emotions are cognitive in themselves and thus both vulnerable to changing beliefs and susceptible to rational critique, there is a disagreement to be noted. It is not about whether emotions are intentional but whether that intentionality is best understood in terms of belief and judgment or by analogy with perception.

Perhaps because of her intensive study of the Stoics, Nussbaum consistently uses the language of belief and judgment.[43] Belief or judgment involves assent to, or assertion of, or agreeing to, or acceptance of some propositional content; and typically we do believe the propositional content of an emotion (whether we see the belief as the emotion's ground or as an essential ingredient in it). Thus, when I am angry at my neighbor for stealing my fishing gear, I believe that he has stolen it. So far so good. But Roberts argues that this is insufficient grounds for interpreting the cognitive dimension of emotions in terms of beliefs or judgments. Beliefs and propositions are not fundamental to our emotional life, which is not best conceived in terms of propositional attitudes.[44] If we speak of the intentionality of emotions we should do so in terms of seeing-as or construal by analogy with perception.

Roberts gives two reasons for this policy. First, from a phenomenological point of view, emotions involve appearings. In my anger, my neighbor appears to me as a thief, just as in my gratitude my friend appears to me as a benefactor. The ancient language for such appearings is *phantasia,* and a modern model is the Gestalt switch. The difference between seeing the figure as a duck or a rabbit is not a matter of belief or judgment but simply a difference of appearance (in this case not even triggered by a change of belief).[45] There is a measure of "direct presence" or "immediacy" in my

40. Nussbaum, *Therapy of Desire,* pp. 79, 82, 86, and 88; *Upheavals of Thought,* p. 2.
41. Nussbaum, *Upheavals of Thought,* pp. 3, 11, 23, 77.
42. Nussbaum, *Upheavals of Thought,* pp. 16 and 88; emphasis added.
43. In both *Therapy of Desire* and *Upheavals of Thought.*
44. Roberts, *Emotions,* p. 38.
45. Roberts, *Emotions,* pp. 70-72, 75, 83, 92.

relation to the object of my emotions that is necessarily the case with my beliefs or judgments.[46]

The second reason Roberts gives is that, even if emotions typically involve assent to their propositional content, this is not necessary. In the case of phobia, for example, I can be afraid even though I do not believe that I am in danger.[47] That is why, when I ride one of those elevators with a glass side opening to the atrium that rises who knows how many stories, I stand close to the doors and away from the glass sides opposite. I don't believe I am in any greater danger than when I'm in a completely enclosed elevator, but I feel fear in the one case but not in the other. We could add guilt to Roberts's phobia example. Depending on one's history, it is possible to feel guilty even when one does not believe that one is doing anything wrong.

Furtak agrees with Roberts and adds a third consideration. He argues that seeing-as is prior to propositions and language.[48] We can take this quite literally and note that some infants experience fear in the presence of bearded men or clowns. They "see" them as dangerous, but not because they affirm the propositional content of their emotion. That would presuppose linguistic competence. The most we could say is that there is a propositional content implicit in the emotion that under different circumstances could be asserted or agreed to. But the perception is there even when the belief is not. So, even with respect to linguistically competent adults, Furtak can say that our cares are not necessarily articulated;[49] and we can add that this is equally true of the emotions that arise out of our cares.

Roberts notes that Nussbaum speaks the language of seeing-as, and indeed she speaks of emotions as ways of seeing.[50] But this does not mean any implicit concession to Roberts's perception theory. All it means is that, in ordinary philosophical usage, such notions as seeing-as or construal are not strictly defined. If one uses these terms to speak of beliefs or judgments, one is breaking no linguistic rule. It is just that the metaphor of seeing is more stretched when used with reference to assent than when used with reference to appearings. It also means that when Roberts seeks to restrict the meaning of seeing-as and construal to the perception metaphor, this re-

---

46. Roberts, *Emotions*, pp. 84 and 88. Since perception is a metaphor here, seeing-as does not signify vision in a literal sense or even spatial proximity. Having seen my gear in my neighbor's garage, I "see" him as a thief even while he is still at work.

47. Roberts, *Emotions*, pp. 84, 90-91.

48. Furtak, *Wisdom in Love*, p. 14.

49. Furtak, *Wisdom in Love*, p. 15.

50. Roberts, *Emotions*, p. 87; Nussbaum, *Upheavals of Thought*, pp. 28, 30.

striction is merely stipulative. In the context of his theory, such a stipulation is perfectly in order, but it has no argumentative force. The case will have to be made on the type of considerations already mentioned, and I take that case to be a very strong one.

In spite of imprecise ordinary usage that treats 'passions,' 'emotions,' and 'feelings' as more or less interchangeable terms, I have set out to distinguish them for heuristic purposes. So I have distinguished passion, as the disposition to have various emotions relative to what we care about, from emotions, as the occurrent, episodic, affective manifestation of some passion. I have emphasized the cognitive character of emotions in three ways: (1) they tend to be changeable in response to changed beliefs and for this reason susceptible to rational critique; (2) they are intentional, "of" or "about" some object of which they are an interpretation, a construal, a seeing-as; and (3) while they are intimately related to one's beliefs, they are best thought of themselves as more like perceptions than beliefs or judgments. It is now time to distinguish emotions from feelings.

There is an obvious sense in which emotions are feelings, the heart of our affective life. I feel angry at my friend; I feel envious of my other friend; and then I feel grateful toward that first friend. But there are two reasons not simply to identify emotions with feelings.

The first is that there are feelings that are not intentional-cognitive and do not grow out of our passions. Philosophers sometimes refer to "raw feels" as the class that includes tickles, itches, aches, nausea, the soreness of a sore throat, and the pains of cut flesh or a smashed finger. Although each of these is its own distinctive feeling, phenomenologically or qualitatively different from the others, we are not tempted to call them emotions, and for the reasons just given.

Nussbaum frequently identifies phenomena more or less of this sort that she sharply distinguishes from emotions: "blind surges," "animal energies," "bodily tugs, stabs, and flashes," "moods," and "unthinking energies."[51]

Two special cases perhaps deserve comment. First there is desire or appetite. It will be recalled that Aristotle included appetite in his list, while Nussbaum includes it along with the other items just mentioned as not an emotion, especially when desire or appetite has a clear bodily origin.[52] It seems that the feelings of hunger and thirst, in their qualitative difference from each other, are not seeings-as or construals, and they surely do not de-

51. Nussbaum, *Therapy of Desire*, p. 369, and *Upheavals of Thought*, pp. 1, 16, 24.
52. Nussbaum, *Therapy of Desire*, p. 319n., and *Upheavals of Thought*, p. 24.

rive from our passions. On the other hand, when I feel hungry, that feeling will inform my seeing some things as edible and others as not. Moreover, some of our non-bodily desires, such as the desire to be included on that fishing weekend, do arise out of our passions. So it's a bit muddy here. Perhaps the best we can do is say that desire is sometimes like the raw feels that are not emotions and sometimes it is like the perceptions that are.

The other tricky case is sensation. Here, too, Nussbaum wants to exclude it from the ranks of emotion.[53] But Furtak identifies the problem clearly. "One of the most difficult, and crucial, distinctions to make in this area is that between meaningless sensations and meaningful perceptions." His answer is helpful and easy to anticipate. "Granted, my anger is (in one sense) a chemical episode, and there is something it is like for me to be angry, but neither of these details considered by itself is enough to justify the conclusion that what I am undergoing is anger. The physical aspect and the raw feel of an emotion may be variable and hard to decipher; rather, what will be common to all cases of anger is a certain kind of intentional attitude."[54] But is sensation, in this sense, something that occurs by itself as a discrete event; or is it always already part of a "meaningful perception" of some sort?

Consider the curious case in the movie *The Gods Must Be Crazy* of the Coke bottle that falls among tribespeople who don't even have the concept of a bottle, much less of a cola bottle. It is not their emotional reaction to the bottle that concerns us here, but the relation between sensation and perception. Two different seeings-as can be distinguished: our seeing it as a Coke bottle and their seeing it as some mysterious, religiously significant object. So we have two different perceptions, construals, seeings-as. But we might want to say that, apart from the brain activity, which may or may not be the same in the two cases, there is something that is the same, the something it is like to be appeared to by an object that is in fact a Coke bottle but is not necessarily seen as such. We are talking about a state of consciousness that is not (yet) an intentional, interpretive construal, a seeing-as. If this is what we mean by sensation, then it appears that it does not occur by itself but always as part of a larger complex that includes brain activity and intentionality. In other words, if I abstract the feeling of anger from its cognitive dimension and make it a "meaningless sensation" rather than a "meaningful perception," I no longer have the perception of anger.

53. Nussbaum, *Therapy of Desire*, p. 369.
54. Furtak, *Wisdom in Love*, p. 12.

Wilfrid Sellars suggests something like this in his famous attack on "the myth of the given." His target is sense data empiricism and thus sensation as the act of sensing (*seeing* red), together with its "object" (seeing *red*), which Sellars prefers to call the sense content or sense datum. But his analysis is pertinent to raw feels as well, for he speaks of "the simple ability to *feel a pain* or *see a color*."[55] In his introduction to Sellars's text, Richard Rorty writes, "The fundamental thought which runs through this essay is Kant's: 'intuitions without concepts are blind.'"[56]

Kant is probably best read as saying that intuitions occur only as aspects of a more complex situation that involves concepts as well. Thus he writes, "The understanding can intuit nothing, the senses can think nothing. Only through their union can knowledge arise."[57] Since Kant tends to equate knowledge with experience as judgment, this would seem to be a phenomenological as well as an epistemological point. Intuitions (immediate awareness of something particular) are not experiences or cognitions but abstractions from the experiences or cognitions in which they are ingredient.

Sellars seems to be thinking along these same lines. He writes, "Thus, the non-inferential knowledge of particular matter of fact might logically imply the existence of sense data (for example, *seeing that a certain physical object is red* might logically imply *sensing a red sense content*) even though the sensing of a red sense content were not itself a cognitive fact and did not imply the possession of non-inferential knowledge."[58] The notion that sensations are implied can be taken to mean that we do not encounter them directly but posit them by an analysis in which we abstract them from a more complex totality. Even for classical sense-datum theories, sensing was "taken to belong to a higher level of complexity" such that, for Sellars at least, its cognitive dimension could not "be analyzed without remainder — even in principle — into non-epistemic facts."[59] Perhaps this is the meaning of the cryptic qualifier, "if there is such a thing" with reference to sensing and "if there are such facts" with reference to "the fact that a sense content is a *datum*."[60]

---

55. Wilfrid Sellars, *Empiricism and the Philosophy of Mind* (Cambridge, MA: Harvard University Press, 1997), p. 20.

56. Sellars, *Empiricism and the Philosophy of Mind*, p. 3.

57. Kant, *Critique of Pure Reason*, A 51 = B 75.

58. Sellars, *Empiricism and the Philosophy of Mind*, p. 16.

59. Sellars, *Empiricism and the Philosophy of Mind*, p. 19.

60. Sellars, *Empiricism and the Philosophy of Mind*, pp. 15 and 18.

Here we have the second reason not simply to equate emotions and feelings. Insofar as feelings are like sensations, not independent experiences but abstractions from more complex wholes which are perceptions or like perceptions, seeings-as, we can distinguish emotions from feelings.

So let us return to Silentio's claim that faith is a passion, a "prodigious," "supreme," or "highest" passion. According to the conceptual scheme just developed, that means that Abraham's faith is an expression of what he cares about most deeply, what matters and is important to him at the very core of his being. And what might that be? His relation to God. More particularly, it is the relation in which he "relates himself as the single individual absolutely to the absolute" (*FT,* 70), and it is the concern to make sure that this relationship is always his absolute relation.

The overriding character of passion as care is in sharp focus. Silentio's account anticipates that of a subsequent pseudonym, Johannes Climacus, for whom the task of faith is "*Simultaneously to Relate Oneself Absolutely to One's Absolute τέλος and Relatively to Relative Ends*" (*CUP* 1:387; cf. 407, 414, 422, 431). For Abraham does have relative relations, values, and commitments. There is, to begin with, his family, and Silentio emphasizes that in his whole ordeal Abraham never ceases to love Isaac. There is also his society and its cultural values. Silentio stipulates that child sacrifice is not an accepted practice and that tragic heroes are justified in killing or intending to kill their children only with reference to a higher claim *within* the cultural hierarchy of values and norms (the good and the right). It is precisely because these values and commitments are very real for Abraham that he experiences the overriding character of his passion for God in fear, trembling, anxiety, and distress.

These are the emotions to which Abraham's passion gives rise, and it is a disturbing list. If we compare it with the lists given above by Aristotle and Roberts, we cannot help but be struck by their negative character. Even if Roberts, in giving a list of emotions proper to Christian life, were to replace grief with guilt and remorse so as to emphasize that it is grief over sin that he has in mind, his list would be more balanced than Silentio's and would indeed tilt toward positive emotions: love, joy, gratitude, hope, and peace.

Why such a dour picture of faith as a passion for God? Is Silentio a prophet of gloom and doom? Is he, as suggested above, the real melancholy Dane? Or perhaps Abraham's God is a kind of cosmic Scrooge! I want to suggest that the first of these suggestions is the best. To do so I turn to Part One of *Christian Discourses,* which Kierkegaard published in his own name. It is entitled "The Cares of the Pagans" and is Kierkegaard's most extensive reflection on the importance of what we care about. In the earlier translation by Walter Lowrie,[61] we find "anxieties" instead of "cares," so we are dealing with a special subset of what Frankfurt has in mind, namely those things that matter to us because they disturb our peace of mind. They are what the Stoics thought all passions/emotions were: threats to tranquil happiness.[62] But the things we worry about are surely things that we care about and that are important to us, even if the reverse is not necessarily true.

If we ask what inter-textual help we can get from this portion of *Christian Discourses* for understanding Silentio's claim about faith as a passion, we must ask what Kierkegaard is up to here. At first the answer is obvious. In each chapter he describes a particular anxious care that he attributes to the pagan. By contrast, he affirms each time, *"the Christian does not have this care."* We seem to have an argument for the spiritual superiority of Christians to those of other religious or perhaps secular commitments. But the more closely one reads, and the more closely one looks around oneself in an allegedly Christian country, and the more closely one looks at oneself if one identifies as a Christian, the clearer the irony becomes. The true Christian would not have these cares, but among actual Christians they appear all too typically. That is why the essay I contributed to the *International Kierkegaard Commentary* on this volume is entitled "Paganism in Christendom."[63] Like Anti-Climacus, the pseudonymous author of *Sickness unto Death,* to whom we shall come in due course, Kierkegaard thinks that what passes for Christianity shows itself on close examination to be more nearly some form of paganism. In other words, we here encounter his "attack upon Christendom."

The specifics of his analysis in *Christian Discourses* are not particularly helpful in reading *Fear and Trembling.* What is important, however, are two

---

61. *Christian Discourses,* trans. Walter Lowrie (New York: Oxford University Press, 1940).

62. These "anxieties" are not the anxiety that is sometimes distinguished from fear on the grounds that fear is intentional and has an object — we're afraid *of* the dark, or of recession, or of cancer — while anxiety is a vague dis-ease, possibly intense, without any identifiable source. In each chapter of Part One Kierkegaard identifies the intentional object of the pagans' cares or anxieties: poverty, abundance, lowliness, loftiness, presumptuousness, self-torment, and, finally, indecisiveness, vacillation, and disconsolateness (a curious trio).

63. *International Kierkegaard Commentary,* vol. 17: *"Christian Discourses" and "The Crisis and a Crisis in the Life of an Actress,"* ed. Robert L. Perkins (Macon, GA: Mercer University Press, 2007), pp. 13-33.

assumptions Kierkegaard shares with Frankfurt, namely (1) that what we care about, our passions, are important insofar as they constitute our identity as much as our beliefs and actions, and (2) that it is possible and, in a certain normative sense, necessary that we should care about what we care about, that we should engage in critical reflection about our passions and not treat them passively as some kind of *fait accompli*. As Roberts put it above, if my beliefs are fully orthodox and my behavior, moral and ritual, is fully in line with social and ecclesial expectations, but my passions and the resultant emotions are not authentically Christian, then I am not authentically Christian. Christian formation has not only an epistemic and ethical dimension but also an affective dimension, so that, as Edwards puts it, "True religion, in great part, consists in holy affections."[64]

This is how we can best understand the one-sidedness of Silentio's account of the emotional side of faith in terms of fear, trembling, anxiety, and distress. He is a prophet of doom and gloom insofar as he takes his primary audience, individuals who in Christendom have not become individuals before God as Abraham was, to have selectively eliminated the features of God that keep God from being tamed. God has not been allowed to be the *mysterium tremendum,* the scary God who does not fit within the bounds of "reason," the language game of the best and the brightest of the present age, a proud and very pious culture.[65]

Silentio insists that he doesn't have faith; so he doesn't claim to be a Christian in Lutheran Denmark where faith is the hallmark of being a Christian. But he uses Abraham, who himself is not a Christian, to call Christendom to a faith it hasn't taken seriously enough. No, that's not quite right. Christendom cannot have faith. Silentio calls each individual in Christendom to a faith each professes but hasn't taken seriously enough.

64. See note 6 above.

65. See the discussion in chapter 5 above. On Kierkegaard as a prophetic philosopher, see my *Kierkegaard's Critique of Reason and Society* (Macon, GA: Mercer University Press, 1987), chs. 1 and 2, pp. 1-27.

PART TWO

Johannes Climacus

CHAPTER 7

Faith as the Reception of Revelation

We come to our second pseudonym, Johannes Climacus, named after the monk who in the sixth century became abbot of the famous monastery at Mount Sinai and wrote *The Ladder of Divine Ascent,* a classic of Orthodox spirituality.[1] In Eastern monasteries it was read aloud each year at Lent. Perhaps this is Kierkegaard's suggestion that we read the two works from Climacus as instruction in the spiritual life and especially as calls to repentance, although, given their form, they are not candidates for inclusion in the Classics of Western Spirituality series in which *The Ladder* is to be found.

That form, the genre, we might say, is first epistemological reflection (objectivity, *Philosophical Fragments*) and then existential reflection (subjectivity, *Concluding Unscientific Postscript*). The division of labor is not quite that neat. In the Preface to *Fragments,* Climacus echoes Silentio in satirically distinguishing his fragments (scraps, tidbits, crumbs) sharply from the system, even going to the point of insisting that, with regard to the system and its world-historical significance for the new era or new epoch, he does not even have an opinion that would be of interest to any others, much less any knowledge, to say nothing of a system of the sciences. Instead, "I can stake my own life, I can in all earnestness trifle with my own life. . . . All I have is my life, which I promptly stake every time a difficulty appears. Then it is easy to dance, for the thought of death is a good dancing partner, my dancing partner" (*PF,* 5-8). Here we encounter

---

1. John Climacus, *The Ladder of Divine Ascent,* trans. Colm Luibheid and Norman Russell (Mahwah, NJ: Paulist, 1982).

123

existential subjectivity, but we will have to wait for his second volume to get sustained reflection on it. Apart from a teasing reference to the leap (*PF,* 43), a concept in which the epistemic and existential come together in *Postscript,* Climacus pretty much remains the epistemologist in *Fragments.* *Postscript,* by contrast, deserves to be considered the founding text of existentialism by making 'existence' a technical term designating human life as a very individual task that goes beyond the biological, sociological, and especially the epistemic dimensions of our being-in-the-world. But Climacus thinks of existence with constant reference to the epistemic issues he raised in the earlier text.

In *Fragments,* the question of faith and reason becomes the question of revelation and recollection. It is as if Climacus has been reading *Fear and Trembling.* How does Abraham know what promises to trust or what commands to obey? Silentio's answer is simply and straightforwardly biblical: God told him. Or, to use theological language, the promises and commands came to him through divine revelation. But as a philosopher, Climacus wants some conceptual analysis of this concept; he wants to know what the logic or grammar of 'revelation' might be. Since he is a great admirer of Socrates,[2] the Platonic theory of knowledge as recollection is near at hand for purposes of contrast. It is a theory in which human reason is able to be what the term has come to signify in modernity, autonomous and self-sufficient. It is able to learn the truth without any dependence on the gift of divine revelation. So Climacus decides to see if he can elucidate the concept of revelation by thinking what a theory of knowing would be that does not turn out to be a version of the recollection theory.

Climacus sketches the recollection theory with reference to the famous scene in Plato's *Meno* in which Socrates "teaches" the slave boy the Pythagorean theorem. Socrates draws a figure two feet by two feet, and the boy can recognize that its area is four square feet. Socrates asks for the figure that would contain twice the area, eight square feet. The boy carelessly suggests that the sides be doubled, but can easily see, with help from the diagram drawn by Socrates, that the area is sixteen rather than the desired eight feet. So he splits the difference and suggests sides of three feet; but once again, with the help of Socrates' diagram, he can see that the new area is nine rather than eight square feet. The boy is stuck, a vivid illustration of Socratic ignorance; for at first he thought he knew when in fact he didn't. His

2. I like to think he was turned on to Socrates by reading Kierkegaard's dissertation, *The Concept of Irony with Continual Reference to Socrates.*

progress consists in having learned that he doesn't know what he previously thought he knew. Socrates claims that in "numbing him like the sting ray" (84b) he has not harmed him but helped him.

Then Socrates draws a new diagram, consisting of four of the original squares put together to form a new square, four feet by four feet. He then draws a diagonal through each of the four smaller squares; each of these diagonals immediately becomes the hypotenuse of two facing right triangles. With the help of this diagram, the boy can see that the square of each of these hypotenuses is equal to the sum of the squares on the other two sides. He can then calculate the length of the hypotenuse. The four hypotenuses form the sides of another square within the large square, but turned to look like a diamond, and this inner square has the desired area of eight square feet.

Socrates insists that he did not teach the boy anything but simply reminded him of what he already knew, implicitly, in order to help him "remember" or "recollect." Climacus puts it this way: "The ignorant person merely needs to be reminded in order, by himself, to call to mind what he knows. The truth is not introduced into him but was in him" (*PF,* 9). He was able to see for himself which answers were wrong and which was right.

Expanding on this, Climacus summarizes the Socratic view in four theses:

(a) The truth is already within us.
(b) The "teacher" does not give the learner the truth, but is "something accidental, a vanishing point, an occasion" (*PF,* 11).

This is what Climacus calls a "maieutic" relation and why Socrates insists that he does not give birth but is only a midwife. The boy might have learned the theorem from someone else or even discovered it himself, as, presumably, Pythagoras did.

(c) Since the learner is "sufficient unto himself" and the teacher is merely a trigger for recollecting, this does not take us to the concept of revelation (*PF,* 11).
(d) As a result, the learner's "self-knowledge is God-knowledge" (*PF,* 11).

This last thesis obviously calls for comment, for learning the Pythagorean theorem hardly seems like either self-knowledge or God-knowledge. It is clear that when Climacus speaks of learning the truth he is not speaking of just any old true proposition but rather of something like what he will call "essential knowing" in *Postscript*.[3] It is that understanding of self (Who am I? — see chapter 6 above) in relation to whatever is ultimate, absolute, infinite, eternal that is the common quest of theology and the great traditions of philosophy. If that knowledge, by analogy with geometry, has the form of recollection such that the learner is "sufficient unto himself," then self-understanding would be the knowledge of God; for when I have brought to the surface of full consciousness all that is already within me I will know all there is to know of whatever is divine.[4] Clearly reason as recollection is something quite distinct from faith as response to revelation as the gift of truth one does not already possess.

To tell us what faith is as distinct from reason in this sense, Climacus sets up a thought experiment. "If" we are to have a genuine alternative, what would have to be the case?[5] He pretends to "deduce" this alternative from the concept of a model that does not turn out to be some version of the recollection scheme. As we shall see, he cheats, drawing shamelessly on biblical, Augustinian, Lutheran, and other traditions; but, not trusting the reader to see that he does so deliberately, he exposes himself to outraged objection not once but three times, including at the end of both of his first two chapters in which he develops his alternative to Socrates.[6]

---

3. C. Stephen Evans notes that in the earlier translation by David Swenson (Princeton: Princeton University Press, 1962), the issue is about teaching and learning the "Truth." "The Truth here is closer to what religions have usually termed salvation, and it is also closely related to what Climacus calls the attainment of an 'eternal consciousness' on the title page, and an 'eternal happiness' at other places in the book." Evans, *Passionate Reason: Making Sense of Kierkegaard's "Philosophical Fragments"* (Bloomington: Indiana University Press, 1992), pp. 13 and 27. My treatment of *Fragments* will be highly selective. Evans's volume is a very helpful full commentary.

4. Thus, in the last paragraph of his *Phenomenology*, Hegel describes "absolute knowing" (knowing that is both absolute in itself and knowledge of the Absolute) as "recollection," though this has a historical character foreign to Platonic thought. *Hegel's Phenomenology of Spirit*, trans. A. V. Miller (Oxford: Clarendon, 1977), pp. 492-93. But human knowledge remains autonomous and self-sufficient.

5. This "if," repeated several times, suggests that Climacus is working as a phenomenologist rather than as a theologian. Jean-Luc Marion distinguishes these two aspects of his work by saying that the phenomenologist describes the structure of a *possible* experience, while the theologian, on the basis of faith, affirms the reality of what the experience refers to or purports to present. See Marion, *Being Given: Toward a Phenomenology of Givenness*, trans. Jeffrey L. Kosky (Stanford: Stanford University Press, 2002), pp. 5, 234-36, 242. See also Jeffrey Hanson, ed., *Kierkegaard as Phenomenologist: An Experiment* (Evanston: Northwestern University Press, 2010).

6. See *PF*, 21-22, 35-36, and 53-54. On four other occasions (*PF*, 46-48, 66-71, 89-90, and

The "deduction" proceeds in terms of theses about the moment of learning, the learner, and the teacher, as follows:

1. The moment of learning must be of decisive significance and not merely be an occasion. "A moment such as this is unique. To be sure, it is short and temporal, as the moment is; it is passing, as the moment is, past, as the moment is in the next moment, and yet it is decisive, and yet it is filled with the eternal. . . . Let us call it: *the fullness of time*" (*PF*, 13, 18-19).

This is perhaps a bit misleading. It sounds as if it is of great importance whether I learn the truth of, say, John 3:16 when I am four or fourteen or forty-four. But that is not the point. The point is the quality of the moment in which the learner is taught by the teacher, not its temporal address. It is "filled with the eternal," the point at which the eternal, which by hypothesis is not already within me, enters into my life from beyond me, when I encounter a teacher, as we shall see, who is not a mere occasion or midwife.

2. Since the learner does not already have the truth within, "he has to be defined as being outside the truth (not coming toward it like a proselyte, but going away from it) or as untruth." This means being "polemical against the truth. . . . But this state — to be untruth and to be that through one's own fault — what can we call it? Let us call it *sin*." In that case, however, the learner is "unfree and bound . . . the slave of sin" (*PF*, 13, 15, 17). Here's a vivid example of what I have called Climacus's cheating, drawing on an existing archive and not merely deducing the implications of his hypothesis.

3. There is only one sense in which recollection can be in play here. "That for which the teacher can become the occasion of his recollecting is that he is untruth . . . because I can discover my own untruth only by myself" (*PF*, 14). Like the previous "conclusion," this is dubious as a deduction and a clear instance of Climacus's "cheating" by helping himself to a specific tradition and its vocabulary. Perhaps he is thinking of the Socratic ignorance (as opposed to the Platonic confidence that we can get outside the cave and find the truth by and for ourselves). Socrates seems to think that knowledge has to be recollection but also (1) that our recollective powers are too weak to get us to the truth and (2) that honest reflection can discover this. But he does not make this point by speaking of sin, much less of enslavement to sin, even when some of his interlocutors seem to be "polemical against the truth."

105-10) Climacus invents an interlocutor who objects to the current state of his argument. In all but the next-to-last of these, he introduces the objector with a phrase like "But perhaps someone will say . . ." or "Now if someone were to say. . . ."

4. We come to the crucial point. "Now, if the learner is to obtain the truth, the teacher must bring it to him, but not only that. Along with it, he must provide him with the condition for understanding it. For if the learner were himself the condition for understanding the truth, then he merely needs to recollect" (*PF*, 14). By "understanding the truth" Climacus clearly means not merely comprehending its content as a claim but recognizing it as the truth. That is what the slave boy story is all about. Socrates gives the boy the truth by drawing the right diagram. But he does not need to give him the condition for recognizing it as the truth. That the boy is able to do for himself.[7] Once the truth is staring him in the face, he need not rely on the authority of Socrates; he can see for himself that the first two squares are too large and that only the third is the desired eight square feet. While he needs help in discovering the truth, he needs none in recognizing it; he is a model of epistemic autonomy.[8]

I have often illustrated this for my students in the following manner. I ask them the name of that little girl on whom I had a crush in second grade. They cannot recollect this; they are in untruth (though not by being polemical toward the truth). I remember that recently I could not recall her name, but only that it began with L. So I Googled girls' names beginning with L, and as soon as I came across it, I remembered: it was Linda. But I don't tell the students this. I rather write three names on the board: Laura, Linda, and Lucy. I ask them again to answer my question. They still cannot. I say, "But the truth is staring you in the face. I have just given it to you." The crucial

---

7. Just before a section entitled "The Christian Religion as Natural Religion," Kant describes this situation in which the learner gets help finding the truth but needs no help in order to recognize it as such. "Accordingly, a religion can be *natural*, yet also *revealed*, if it is so constituted that human beings *could and ought to have* arrived at it on their own through the mere use of their reason, even though they *would* not have come to it as early or as extensively as is required, hence a revelation of it at a given time and a given place might be wise and very advantageous to the human race, for then, once the thereby introduced religion is at hand and has been publicly known, everyone can henceforth convince himself of its truth by himself and his own reason." Kant, *Religion within the Boundaries of Mere Reason*, in *Religion and Rational Theology*, ed. Allen W. Wood and George di Giovanni (New York: Cambridge University Press, 1996), p. 178.

8. This autonomy is the neutralization of a double alterity, the otherness of the truth itself to the knower's situation and, more fundamentally, the otherness of the ability to recognize the truth as such, which is not inherent in the learner. Thus Brian Treanor writes, "Socrates' reply to Meno [the doctrine of recollection] is in fact illustrative of how otherness is viewed in the Western tradition. Generally speaking the Western tradition has thought of otherness as something to be conquered." Treanor, *Aspects of Alterity: Levinas, Marcel, and the Contemporary Debate* (New York: Fordham University Press, 2006), p. 5.

factor, it becomes clear, is not so much finding the truth as being able to recognize it as such, which Climacus calls having the condition. I have it, and the Google list becomes the occasion for my recollection. My students do not have it, and the truth, though staring them in the face, goes unrecognized. No big loss. But what if it were the Truth? Not having the condition would be an existential disaster.

So, if the teacher is not to be a Socratic midwife, that is, the maieutic occasion for recollecting what we already know but cannot recall, the teacher must give the learner the truth (unless it is already somehow on the scene, unrecognized); but more importantly, the teacher must give the learner the ability to recognize the truth as such. In any context where the learner already has the condition, we have reverted to some version of the Socratic scheme, and the teacher becomes a mere occasion.

This is why the interpretation of reason as recollection is not restricted to some rationalist version of a priori knowledge. As long as the learner has the capacity to recognize the truth as such, when presented by whatever means with it, we have a version of knowledge as recollection. For the recollection scheme, as presented by Climacus, is not about a priori knowledge in its independence from experience, but about human knowledge in its independence from divine revelation. Recollection signifies the autonomy of the knower, who needs not rely on any external authority.

In his thought-project, Climacus assigns the task of giving to the learner the condition for recognizing the truth as such to the god in time,[9] the as yet unnamed Jesus Christ. In Protestant theology, this role is assigned to the inner witness of the Holy Spirit.[10] In the background is John 14–16, where the Spirit is presented as the teacher who will guide us into the truth. Both Luther and Calvin reject the Catholic view, sometimes attributed to Augustine, that the authority of Scripture as the locus of the Truth derives from the authority of the church. Thus, Luther writes, "This sort of doctrine, which reveals the Son of God, is not taught, learned, or judged by any human wisdom or by the Law itself; it is revealed by God, first by the

---

9. In speaking of "the god" Climacus sticks with a Socratic mode of speech, even while seeking an alternative to Socrates. He will postpone identifying his alternative as Christianity, by name, until *Postscript,* though he expects his readers to recognize it as such long before then.

10. William Barclay points us to the Hebrew background. "Now, in Hebrew thought the Spirit of God had two functions — first, the Spirit revealed God's truth to men; and, second, the Spirit enabled men to recognize and understand that truth when it came to them." *The Gospel of John,* vol. 1, rev. ed. (Philadelphia: Westminster, 1975), p. 145.

external Word and then inwardly through the Spirit. Therefore the Gospel is a divine Word that came down from heaven and is revealed by the Holy Spirit."[11]

Similarly, John Calvin writes, "Scripture Must Be Confirmed by the Witness of the Spirit. Thus May Its Authority Be Established as Certain; and It Is a Wicked Falsehood That Its Credibility Depends on the Judgment of the Church."[12] The subsequent section headings read as follows:

(1) Scripture Has Its Authority from God, Not from the Church;
(2) The Church Itself Is Grounded upon Scripture;
(3) Augustine Cannot Be Cited as Counter Evidence; and
(4) The Witness of the Holy Spirit: This Is Stronger Than All Proof.

Expanding on the fourth, Calvin writes that

> we ought to seek our conviction in a higher place than human reasons, judgments, or conjectures, that is, in the secret testimony of the Spirit . . . the testimony of the Spirit is more excellent than all reason. For as God alone is a fit witness of himself in his Word, so also the Word will not find acceptance in men's hearts before it is sealed by the inward testimony of the Spirit. . . . For even if [Scripture] wins reverence for itself by its own majesty, it seriously affects us only when it is sealed upon our hearts through the Spirit.[13]

11. Martin Luther, *Lectures on Galatians, 1535*, in *Luther's Works*, ed. Jaroslav Pelikan, vol. 26 (St. Louis: Concordia, 1963), p. 73. Cf. p. 213: "They could never attain to the knowledge of God, of themselves, and of their vocation; they never felt the testimony of the Spirit in their hearts." Also, pp. 375-76: "'God has sent the Spirit of His Son into your hearts.' This happens . . . when through the spoken Word we receive fire and light, by which we are made new and different, and by which a new judgment, new sensations, and new drives arise in us. This change and new judgment are not the work of human reason or power; they are the gift and accomplishment of the Holy Spirit, who comes with the preached Word, purifies our hearts by faith, and produces spiritual motivation within us. . . . For if someone experiences love toward the Word, and if he enjoys hearing . . . about Christ, he should know that this is not a work of human will or reason but a gift of the Holy Spirit." Luther also presents the Holy Spirit as our teacher in *Luther's Works*, vol. 26, pp. 79, 440, and 444; vol. 12, pp. 310, 314, 324, 358, and 404; vol. 21, pp. 299-300.

12. John Calvin, *Institutes of the Christian Religion*, trans. Ford Lewis Battles (Philadelphia: Westminster, 1960), heading to I.vii.

13. Calvin, *Institutes*, I.vii.4-5. Cf. II.v.5; III.i.1; III.ii.15; III.ii.33-36; III.ii.41; IV.xiv.8. In this tradition the Westminster Confession of Faith writes (I.5) that while we may be moved to "an high and reverent esteem of the Holy Scripture" by the testimony of the church or by

For Climacus's purpose, the difference between making Jesus Christ the non-Socratic teacher and giving this task to the Holy Spirit is not important. In either case the recollection model is replaced by one in which the ability to recognize the truth as such depends on the active assistance of God, giving the ability to recognize the truth as such, and not on the inherent powers of human reason. When Luther compares the self-authentication of biblical truth with mathematical truth, he can equate them insofar as each

> convinces by its own power without needing any other [human] authorities. Otherwise their self-authentication is completely different. . . . Self-authentication is not an "attribute" of the word; rather it exists only from moment to moment through God's presence and speaking in his word. . . . The self-certainty of reason, the evidential character of rational truths, is far removed from the "testimony of the Holy Spirit."[14]

When Hegel comes to discuss these issues, he uses the classical Protestant language of the witness of the Spirit. In doing so he confirms Climacus's argument that there is a deep gulf fixed between the system and the "Christian" hypothesis he "deduces" from the task of differing from Socrates. Hegel says four things about this witness. First, arguing against making authority or miracles the ground of faith, he makes it clear that the spirit in question is the human spirit.

> But the absolutely proper ground of belief, the absolute testimony to the content of a religion, is the witness of the spirit. . . . The genuine content of a religion has for its verification the witness *of one's own spirit,* [the witness] that this content conforms to the nature of *my spirit. My spirit knows itself,* it knows its essence . . . it is the absolute verification of the eternally true, the simple and true definition of this certainty that is called faith.[15]

Scripture's own inherent excellences, "yet notwithstanding, our full persuasion and assurance of the infallible truth, and divine authority thereof, is from the inward work of the Holy Spirit, bearing witness by and with the Word in our hearts."

14. Paul Althaus, *The Theology of Martin Luther,* trans. Robert C. Schultz (Philadelphia: Fortress, 1966), p. 50.

15. *Hegel's Lectures on the Philosophy of Religion,* ed. Peter C. Hodgson, 3 vols. (Berkeley: University of California Press, 1984-87), 1:389; emphasis added. In the 1824 version of the lectures we read, "Authentic faith can be defined as the *witness of my spirit* . . . which implies that there is no place in it for any other external content" (1:337); emphasis added. In the 1831

Second, this witness has the form of recollection. The truth is already within.

> "We know God immediately; this knowledge is a revelation within us." ... [This] implies that neither positive revelation nor education can bring about religion in such a way that religion would be something effected from outside. . . . Plato's ancient saying is apropos here: that we learn nothing, but only recollect something that we originally bear within ourselves. . . . We are implicitly spirit, for the truth lies within us and the spiritual content within us must be brought into consciousness.[16]

Third, this gives hegemony to philosophy in matters theological.

> The witness of the spirit in its highest form is that of philosophy, according to which the concept develops the truth as purely as such from itself without presuppositions. As it develops, it cognizes — in and through its development it has insight into — the necessity of the truth . . . it is not required that for all of humanity the truth be brought forth in a philosophical way.[17]

We are here reminded of the earlier claim, "Religion is for everyone. It is not philosophy, which is not for everyone."[18]

Finally, it might appear that the distinction between the human and divine spirits, so crucial to Christianity in general and the Reformers in particular, has disappeared. But Hegel has his own version of this distinction, and it pertains to two modes of human thought, depending on the categories it uses. "But if thinking is merely contingent, it abandons itself to the categories of finite content, of finitude, of finite thinking, and is incapable of comprehending the divine in the content; it is not the divine but the finite spirit that moves in such categories."[19] Hegel regularly distinguishes the categories of finitude as "Understanding" from those of infinity as "Reason." So the distinction between the human and divine spirit is the difference

---

version it is "the witness of *our own spirit*" (1:468); emphasis in original. These are student lecture notes, so we should not make too much of the difference between "my" and "our," since either one puts Hegel on the side of Socrates, as the next point makes explicit.

16. Hegel, *Philosophy of Religion*, 1:412-13. Cf. 1:468 (1831), where the witness is identified as Platonic recollection.

17. Hegel, *Philosophy of Religion*, 3:256.

18. Hegel, *Philosophy of Religion*, 1:180.

19. Hegel, *Philosophy of Religion*, 3:261.

between human thought in the philosophically inadequate modes of the Understanding and human thought in the philosophically appropriate categories of Reason. The witness of the spirit remains the witness of the human spirit to the truth already within its rational powers. Where Enlightenment autonomy prevails in this manner, Climacus suggests that Christian faith should respond, "Better well hanged than ill wed." If his readers know their Hegel, they will easily see that Climacus has raised a devastating objection, not to the truth of Hegelian philosophy as such, but to the claim that it is a new and improved version of Christianity. The system should not be welcome in Christendom.

Having developed his alternative to the point where the teacher has to give the learner the condition, Climacus seeks to spell it out in greater detail in further theses as follows:

5. "The teacher, then, is the god himself," for to give the learner the condition to recognize the Truth is an act of creation (*PF*, 15).

6. But since for Climacus sin has become a decisive epistemological category,[20] the teacher will have to be "a *savior*," "a *deliverer*," "a *reconciler*," and "a *judge*" (*PF*, 17-18).

7. Accordingly, the learner can now be designated as a "follower" or "disciple" *(Discipel)* of the teacher. Here we find a strong linkage between the epistemic and the existential, as expressed in the collect for the fifth Sunday of Easter in the *Book of Common Prayer:* "Grant us so perfectly to know your Son Jesus Christ to be the way, the truth, and the life, that we may steadfastly follow his steps in the way that leads to eternal life." Of course, Climacus has not yet identified the teacher as Jesus Christ by name,[21] but he figures it will be no mystery to his readers.

8. As a follower or disciple, the learner has become "a *new* person" who has experienced *"conversion"* through the sorrow of *"repentance"* and a change of being that can be called *"rebirth"* (*PF*, 18-19). These transformations are decisively individual,

> for presumably we can be baptized *en masse* but can never be reborn *en masse.* Just as the person who by Socratic midwifery gave birth to himself

---

20. See my "Taking St. Paul Seriously: Sin as an Epistemological Category," in *Christian Philosophy,* ed. Thomas Flint (Notre Dame: Notre Dame University Press, 1990), pp. 200-226, and the expanded version of this essay, *Suspicion and Faith: The Religious Uses of Modern Atheism* (New York: Fordham University Press, 1998).

21. Christianity is mentioned by name only in the final paragraph of Climacus's little "pamphlet," as he calls it.

. . . and in a more profound sense owed no human being anything, so also the one who is born again owes no human being anything, but owes that divine teacher everything. (*PF,* 19)

With every sentence it becomes clearer that Climacus is borrowing and not deducing (though he is careful to make the logic or grammar of his borrowings such that they do not collapse into the recollection hypothesis). So he constructs an objector who berates him for presenting as his project a set of ideas whose inventor he clearly is not. He immediately "repents" of his shameless borrowing with ironic humility. "I hide my face in shame" (*PF,* 21). Then with ironical courtesy he offers to consider the objector to be the inventor of his project. But guessing that this is not the objector's point, he asks, "Is it not curious that something like this exists, about which everyone who knows it also knows that he has not invented it . . . ? So go ahead and be angry with me and with any other human being who pretends to have invented it, but you do not for that reason need to be angry with the idea" (*PF,* 22). For the present he is content to leave it at that.

In his second chapter Climacus suggests that, by contrast with Socrates, who needs his interlocutors in order to understand himself, the teacher in the alternative does not act out of need but out of love (*PF,* 24-25). If the distinction between *eros* and *agape* is to be drawn in terms of the difference between 'need love' and 'gift love,'[22] then Socrates is the erotic teacher[23] while Jesus Christ (still unnamed) is the embodiment of *agape*. But love is not only the motivation of the teacher who is more than an occasion. "Out of love, therefore, the god must be eternally resolved in this way, but just as his love is the basis, so also must love be the goal" (*PF,* 25). As the hymn writer puts it,

Lord God, your love has called us here
as we, by love, for love were made.[24]

Climacus continues,

The love, then, must be for the learner, and the goal must be to win him, for only in love is the different made equal, and only in equality or in

22. Thus C. S. Lewis in *The Four Loves* (New York: Harcourt Brace Jovanovich, 1960).

23. This comes as no surprise in relation to such dialogues as *Phaedrus* and *Symposium*.

24. Brian Wren, "Lord God, Your Love Has Called Us Here," in *Rejoice in the Lord: A Hymn Companion to the Scriptures,* ed. Erik Routley (Grand Rapids: Eerdmans, 1985), #503.

unity is there understanding. . . . Yet this love is basically unhappy, for they are very unequal, and what seems so easy — namely, that the god must be able to make himself understood — is not so easy if he is not to destroy that which is different. (*PF,* 25)

Unlike unhappy love in the aesthetic sphere, say, Romeo and Juliet, where there is some external barrier to the union of the lovers, here in the religious sphere the problem is that they cannot understand one another. In *Pretty Woman,* Vivian Ward (played by Julia Roberts) cannot understand Edward Lewis (played by Richard Gere), not because their families oppose their relation but because her world is so far removed from his that he may as well be a Martian. Clearly, both for the movie and for Climacus, the equality in which mutual understanding becomes possible is not a transformation of the learner into a teacher such that the former no longer needs the latter.[25] We want to see them united in a love in which each understands the other well enough that they are able to love each other for who they are, independent of their station in life.

Shakespeare's *Othello* provides another example of the problem.

The love between Desdemona and Othello is authentic, yet might have proved catastrophic even in the absence of the demonic genius of Iago. Nothing in Othello is marriageable: his military career fulfills him completely. Desdemona, persuasively innocent in the highest of senses, falls in love with the pure warrior in Othello, and he falls in love with her love for him, her mirroring of his legendary career.[26]

There is no mutual understanding. Neither is able to see the true inner self of the other, so neither is able to love the other in his or her true identity.

These aesthetic examples are but pale analogies. The difference that needs to be overcome in the thought-project of Climacus is what he will shortly call the "absolute difference" between the human and the divine (*PF,*

25. Since this is an erotic relation, the happy ending will be one in which they slowly but surely come to realize that they need each other. So Gere's character is more nearly Socrates than Christ. *My Fair Lady* is perhaps another relevant parable here.
26. Harold Bloom, *Shakespeare: The Invention of the Human* (New York: Penguin Putnam, 1998), p. 448. Othello's account of how Desdemona fell in love with him by means of the stories of his military adventures (*Othello,* I.iii.146-69) concludes with these lines:

She loved me for the dangers I had passed
And I loved her that she did pity them.

44-47; cf. CUP 1:412-13, 492). In *Sickness unto Death* this becomes the "qualitative difference" (*SUD,* 99, 117, 121), the "most chasmal qualitative abyss" (*SUD,* 122), and eventually the "infinite qualitative difference" (*SUD,* 126-27) with which Karl Barth would later shake Protestant theology to its roots.[27]

In order to explore this difference and its overcoming, Climacus, doubtless a fan of *Pretty Woman,* makes up his own story of the king who loved a maiden of lowly station. She cannot close the gap between them; it will have to be up to him. He could bring her to the palace and make her the belle of the ball like Cinderella, giving her a dress as beautiful as she is, seating him next to him at the lavish banquet, and then dancing with her and her alone. This is the "solution" in *Pretty Woman.* But Climacus worries that the lowly maiden would be deceived. She might very well fall in love, but it would be the king's splendor rather than the king himself that would capture her affection (*PF,* 29), or perhaps the idea of being a queen. As if to remind us of the parable's reference, Climacus suggests that it might be the miracles of the god rather than the god himself that the learner learns to love (*PF,* 33). We would have what we might call the Herod syndrome:

> Prove to me that you're divine
> Change my water into wine . . .
> Prove to me that you're no fool
> Walk across my swimming pool.[28]

So Climacus "deduces" that the god will have to close the gap with the learner by means of descent rather than ascent. Here, as before, there is nothing subtle about his borrowings. The god will have to appear "in the form of a *servant*" (*PF,* 31; cf. Phil. 2:7, KJV).

> But the form of the servant was not something put on. Therefore the god must suffer all things, endure all things, be tried in all things, hunger in the desert, thirst in his agonies, be forsaken in death, absolutely the equal

27. Karl Barth, *The Epistle to the Romans,* trans. Edwyn C. Hoskyns (New York: Oxford University Press, 1933, 1968, 1977), p. 10. Kierkegaard also speaks of the "eternal, essential, qualitative difference" (*BA,* 181 = *WA,* 100) and of the "infinite, radical, qualitative difference between God and man" (*JP* 2:113, entry 1383). See chapter 12, note 29, below.

28. "Herod's Song" in Andrew Lloyd Webber and Tim Rice, *Jesus Christ Superstar.* Cf. John 6:26: "Jesus answered them, 'Very truly, I tell you, you are looking for me, not because you saw signs, but because you ate your fill of the loaves.'"

of the lowliest of human beings — look, behold the man. The suffering of death is not his suffering, but his whole life is a story of suffering, and it is love that suffers. . . . O bitter cup — more bitter than wormwood is the ignominy of death for a mortal — how must it be, then, for the immortal one! . . . O consolation in distress to suffer as one guilty — what must it be, then, to suffer as one who is innocent. (*PF*, 32-34)[29]

And the learner's response? If we want to see how the maiden will react if the king's strategy is descent rather than ascent, we might turn to *The Barber of Seville,* where Count Almaviva disguises himself as the student Lindoro to woo the lovely Rosina. But Climacus, as his borrowings show, has long since abandoned his own human parable for the biblical story it is meant to evoke; so he suggests that the learner's response may very well be offense (*PF*, 32). Here we are introduced to a theme that will be important to Climacus in his next chapter, and even more so to Anti-Climacus, our third pseudonym.

The present chapter concludes, however, with another objector complaining that "What you are composing is the shabbiest plagiarism ever to appear, since it is nothing more or less than what any child knows." It is the story of creation and the fall, of incarnation and atonement. By now we know that Climacus will immediately plead guilty.

> Presumably it could occur to a human being to poetize himself in the likeness of the god or the god in the likeness of himself, but not to poetize that the god poetized himself in the likeness of a human being, for if the god gave no indication, how could it occur to a man that the blessed god could need him? . . . This thought did not arise in my heart . . . forgive me my curious mistaken notion of having composed it myself. It was a mistaken notion, and the poem was so different from every human poem that it was no poem at all but *the wonder.* (*PF*, 36)

There is a double irony in Climacus's thought-project. First, there is the irony of his pretended creation of the story (for the alternative to Socrates is indeed, as just noted, a narrative) by "deducing" it from the idea of an alternative to Socrates. Then there is the irony of his obsequious recantation and repentance when challenged by the objectors he creates (*PF*, 21 and 35-36).

---

29. Among other biblical passages evoked in this section are Phil. 2:8; Matt. 4:2; Matt. 27:46; and Matt. 26:39. See *PF*, 286 for a fuller list in the notes.

This raises two points brought into focus by Steve Evans. Both are forms of the question regarding what we should make of this irony.

Some of the early commentators on Kierkegaard in English simply ignored the pseudonymous character of some of his major works and identified the pseudonymous authors with Kierkegaard in spite of his explicit request that we not do so (*CUP* 1:626-27). It has since become mandatory in Kierkegaardian scholarship, not only to honor Kierkegaard's request not to be identified with his pseudonyms (just as novelists might not wish to be identified with any of their characters), but also to take into account the literary gestures of each "author." So we must take Climacus's double irony seriously.

At the opposite extreme from those who straightforwardly identify Kierkegaard with his pseudonyms as straightforwardly putting forth a distinctive philosophy of religion, some more recent interpreters have suggested that the literary features of the pseudonymous authorships undermine the possibility of any substantive claims. Evans's example is Roger Poole, who writes, "Kierkegaard writes text after text whose aim is not to state a truth, not to clarify an issue, not to propose a definite doctrine, not to offer some meaning that could be directly appropriated."[30] This might be on target if it had the insertion of "merely" into the first three clauses and emphasized the "directly" in the fourth. Otherwise, it is terribly misleading. The titles of Climacus's books, *Fragments* and *Postscript* (many times longer than fragments, tidbits, or scraps) are wonderfully ironical. But that does not mean that they are not meant to suggest some quite definite negative judgments about the system and its claim to be science, any more than Mark Antony's oft-repeated irony that the "noble" Brutus "is an honorable man" is not meant to suggest that, despite his reputation, Brutus is anything but honorable.[31] So Evans rightly concludes,

> I want to argue that the literary scholars are quite right to call attention to the ironical character of Kierkegaard's pseudonymous literature, including the writings attributed to Johannes Climacus, but wrong to think that this implies that Kierkegaard's pseudonymous writings do not contain theological and philosophical claims and arguments. . . . Rather, the

30. Roger Poole, *Kierkegaard: The Indirect Communication* (Charlottesville: The University Press of Virginia, 1993), p. 7, quoted in C. Stephen Evans, "The Role of Irony in Kierkegaard's *Philosophical Fragments*," in his *Kierkegaard on Faith and the Self: Collected Essays* (Waco, TX: Baylor University Press, 2006), p. 68.

31. A similar irony runs through *Othello*, where Iago is repeatedly described as "honest."

irony *presupposes* the validity of most of the distinctions and arguments it contains.[32]

Antony's irony not only presupposes that Brutus is less than honorable, but puts this forth as a claim for his audience to recognize as such, however indirectly. Similarly, the ironies in Climacus's titles presuppose that the system is at once comical and catastrophic, in the expectation that the audience will understand this claim, however indirectly. He writes, "But the presence of irony does not necessarily mean that the earnestness is excluded. Only assistant professors assume that" (*CUP* 1:277n.). So, to return to the ironical dialogues at the end of the first two chapters of *Fragments,* the (twice presented) double irony of the shameful claim to authorship shamefully renounced "cannot consist in denying or undermining the claim that Christianity is a revealed religion which cannot be reduced to a set of doctrines to be proven or shown to be probable by human reason," when the latter is understood along the lines of the Socratic hypothesis that knowledge is recollection. It rather presupposes "that Christianity presents itself as a revealed faith that is distinct from any human philosophical doctrine. If the distinction between Christianity and any such doctrine [that is, between revelation and reason as recollection] is not valid, the joke loses its point."[33] This is why Sylvia Walsh can describe *Fragments* as a "jest" while insisting that it is "deadly serious."[34] The fool in Shakespeare's *King Lear* and Rigoletto in the eponymous Verdi opera are entertainers, to be sure, whose task is to amuse; but they are court jesters who all too frequently speak the truth that others are afraid to express.

Happily for Evans, Climacus agrees; so Evans quotes him from *Postscript,* but with reference to a review of *Fragments:*

> The contrast of form, the teasing resistance of the experiment to the content, the inventive shamelessness (which even invents Christianity), . . . the untiring activity of irony, the parody of speculative thought in the entire plan, the satire in making strenuous efforts as if something

32. Evans, "The Role of Irony," p. 69.
33. Evans, "The Role of Irony," p. 75.
34. Sylvia Walsh, "Echoes of Absurdity: The Offended Consciousness and the Absolute Paradox in Kierkegaard's *Philosophical Fragments,*" in *International Kierkegaard Commentary,* vol. 7: *"Philosophical Fragments" and "Johannes Climacus,"* ed. Robert L. Perkins (Macon, GA: Mercer University Press, 1994), p. 33. In *Concluding Unscientific Postscript,* Climacus regularly links jest and earnestness. See *CUP* 1:64, 69-71, 87-89, 102-3, 282, 290, 447.

ganz Auszerordentliches und zwar Neues ["altogether extraordinary, that is, new"] were to come of them, whereas what continually emerges is old-fashioned orthodoxy in its rightful strictness: of all of this the reader finds no hint in the summary.[35]

Here the claim is that irony, parody, and satire are not the abolishing of all claims but the very means of making them (indirectly). This functions to support the claim, coming from "old-fashioned orthodoxy," that Christianity rests on divine revelation and is irreducible to human reason on the recollection model. The force of this latter claim is not that Christianity is true; but it nevertheless has bite. For if the claim is true, then anything that presents itself as rational in terms of recollection is not Christianity but an alternative, a rival, even an enemy. Since both Kant and Hegel, among others, present their philosophies as Christianity that is new and improved by being brought into conformity with their (very different, particular) conceptions of reason (each of which purports to be universal), Climacus's point is to expose such philosophies as being, for better or for worse, something dramatically different from Christianity. That is the thrust of his book's quasi-Shakespearean epigraph, "Better well hanged than ill wed." Christianity is better off when rejected as insufficiently rational than when, in order to prove its reasonableness, it allows some version of autonomous reason to determine what its content can be.

So far then, Evans's first answer to the question of what we should make of Climacus's irony: it is not a barrier to his making substantive claims. But Evans wants to go further. He suggests that in some of the dialogues with his imagined objectors, Climacus presents a kind of apologetic argument for the truth, reasonableness, or plausibility of the Christian story he "deduces" from the idea of differing from Socrates. For example, at the end of his first chapter, Climacus writes, "Is it not curious that something like this [story] exists, about which everyone who knows it also knows that he has not invented it" and that no one else has either. "Yet this oddity enthralls me exceedingly, for it tests the correctness of the hypothesis and demonstrates it" (*PF*, 22).

Evans is not unaware of Kierkegaard's hostility toward apologetics, and

35. Evans, "The Role of Irony," p. 72, quoting *CUP* 1:274-75n. In *Passionate Reason* (p. 18), Evans quotes from the same commentary on the review, "it is only assistant professors who assume that where irony is present, seriousness is excluded" (*CUP* 1:277n.), although this wording is from the earlier Swenson/Lowrie translation.

he might well have added to the passages he cites the following: "Therefore it is certain and true that the first one to come up with the idea of defending Christianity in Christendom is *de facto* a Judas No. 2: he, too, betrays with a kiss, except that his treason is the treason of stupidity. To defend something is always to disparage it. . . . As for Christianity! Well, he who defends it has never believed it" (*SUD,* 87). So Evans qualifies the notion of apologetics he wishes to invoke. It is not a foundationalist apologetics; it offers no knock-down proofs.

Weak foundationalism is simply the belief that some of our beliefs rest on others. Thus Abraham believed that he should sacrifice Isaac because he believed that God had told him to do so, and he believed that he would get Isaac back in this life because he believed that, if necessary, the God for whom all things are possible could and would raise Isaac from the dead. Strong foundationalism is the claim that our most basic, foundational beliefs must be and can be certain and thus final, needing neither revision nor replacement. They are beliefs "to which one might cling, frameworks beyond which one must not stray, objects which impose themselves, representations which cannot be gainsaid."[36] Classical foundationalism is an instance of strong foundationalism, and Evans wisely cites Alvin Plantinga's helpful account. When we combine ancient, medieval, and modern versions of the theory we find that foundational or properly basic propositions must be either self-evident, or evident to the senses, or incorrigible (like the claim that I have an ache or an itch).[37] The sad story of classical foundationalism has been the repeated discovery, not so much that one cannot prove God, freedom, and immortality on such premises, but that one cannot even establish the reality of the external world, or other minds, or the past, or the validity of causal inference. On such foundations, the edifice of knowledge simply crumbles.

So Evans suggests that the alleged apologetics of *Fragments* are of a different sort from classical foundationalist arguments. Although he does not use the language of philosophical hermeneutics as developed by Heidegger, Gadamer, and Ricoeur, among others, it is within this tradition that he

36. Richard Rorty, *Philosophy and the Mirror of Nature* (Princeton: Princeton University Press, 1979), p. 316.

37. C. Stephen Evans, "Apologetic Arguments in *Philosophical Fragments,*" in Perkins, ed., *International Kierkegaard Commentary,* vol. 7: *"Philosophical Fragments" and "Johannes Climacus,"* p. 74. Evans is drawing on Alvin Plantinga, "Reason and Belief in God," *in Faith and Rationality: Reason and Belief in God,* ed. Alvin Plantinga and Nicholas Wolterstorff (Notre Dame: University of Notre Dame Press, 1983), pp. 58-59.

places Climacus. The two key ideas of the hermeneutical turn in philosophy are (1) that our thought has the character of interpretations or construals guided by presuppositions, and (2) that these (revisable or replaceable) presuppositions or prejudices (pre-judgments, a priori anticipations) are borne by traditions. Thus we are always located in some particular language game or worldview, and our thought is inherently perspectival.

The double implication of the hermeneutical character of Climacus's apologetics is that (1) faith is the ground of the arguments' force rather than the other way around, and (2) that one can just as easily respond to the claims in question with offense.[38] Given the fact that 'apologetics' usually suggests arguments intended to bring unbelievers to faith and that, so far as one can tell, the main consumers of Christian apologetic literature are already believers or those who would like to be, it seems to me preferable to call what Climacus is up to by another name, such as, perhaps, faith seeking understanding.[39] Evans almost suggests as much when he writes, with reference to another of Climacus's "arguments," "It does not follow that the argument is pointless even if it is true that the first premise will only be accepted by a person who already accepts the conclusion. The argument might still have value in helping such a person better understand his or her belief."[40]

In the case before us, the premise is that no human is the author of the story Climacus has been telling, and the conclusion is that it must have come as a revelation from God. Climacus is surely wrong when he suggests that everyone knows the premise to be true. From David Friedrich Strauss to the Jesus Seminar there have been those who attribute key aspects of the story to the early Christians, however historically implausible such suppositions may be. And from Feuerbach to Freud there have been projection theories seeking to explain how the "divine" story could have human origins.[41] Shortly after writing *Fragments*, Kierkegaard

38. Evans, "Apologetic Arguments," pp. 71, 73, 77-78.

39. The tradition has deep Augustinian roots; the formula, *fides quaerens intellectum*, comes from Anselm. See Karl Barth's interpretation of the ontological argument for the existence of God in this context: *Anselm: Fides Quaerens Intellectum*, trans. Ian W. Robertson (New York: World Publishing, 1962).

40. Evans, "Apologetic Arguments," p. 79. Cf. *Passionate Reason*, p. 55, where Evans writes with reference to a similar "argument" at the conclusion of Climacus's second chapter, "Climacus is not so much arguing for this bold claim [that his story is *the wonder*] as reminding his presumably Christian readers of it and what it means." But then Evans goes on to add that the strangeness of the story "can be taken as a sign of its truth."

41. Marx, too, but derivatively from Feuerbach. See my *Suspicion and Faith: The Religious Uses of Modern Atheism* (New York: Fordham University Press, 1998), part III.

refers to Strauss and Feuerbach (*BA*, 5); so even if Climacus is innocent of this evidence against his thesis, Kierkegaard is not. Perhaps there is an irony in Kierkegaard's allowing Climacus the exaggeration embodied in his "everyone who knows [the story] also knows that he has not invented it" (*PF*, 22).

In addition to wishing to avoid the false expectations all too likely to be raised by the language of apologetics, in spite of disclaimers, I have a deeper reason for wanting to avoid that language. It pertains to what I take Climacus to be up to. As if to resist the concept of apologetics himself, Climacus tells us in the Moral, with which he concludes his little pamphlet, "This project indisputably goes beyond the Socratic, as is apparent at every point. Whether it is therefore more true than the Socratic is an altogether different question, one that cannot be decided in the same breath, inasmuch as a new organ has been assumed here: faith" (*PF*, 111).[42]

So what are we to make of the fact that Climacus follows up his claim, "everyone who knows [the story] also knows that he has not invented it," by saying that "this oddity enthralls me exceedingly, for it tests the correctness of the hypothesis and demonstrates it" (*PF*, 22)? We could take this to be an ironical claim to something like a foundationalist proof, since it rests on an allegedly universally recognized truth. It would be better, I think, to read this early claim in the light of the later comment in the Moral. In that case, the hypothesis that is confirmed is not that the story is true but rather what Climacus set out to show, namely that it is irreducible to the Socratic assumption that knowledge is recollection. Any story that is not tied to faith in a divine revelation irreducible to the powers and jurisdiction of autonomous human reason is *ipso facto* not the Christian story. It was the purpose of the epigraph, "Better well hung than ill wed," to make it as clear as possible that Climacus's purpose was to rescue Christianity from false friends rather than to make new friends for it or even to help the faithful understand their faith better. The epigraph and the Moral provide the text with alpha and omega points to make sure we don't misunderstand Climacus's agenda.

In this respect I see a deep affinity between the strategies of Johannes de Silentio and Johannes Climacus. In my essay for the International Kierkegaard Commentary volume on *Fragments*, I argued (1) that Silentio argues for the essential difference between the ethical and the religious; (2) that Climacus argues for the essential difference between reason as recollection

---

42. See note 5 above.

and faith in revelation; and (3) that in neither case does Kierkegaard allow them to argue for the superiority, as we might have expected, of the religious and of revelation. They remain content stubbornly to insist on the irreducible difference between the two standpoints. No doubt Kierkegaard has something to do with the fact that each Johannes thinks that, in a situation whose philosophy is Hegel and whose religion is Christendom, it is more important to stress these differences then complacently to assume a harmony verging on identity between Christianity and the socio-cultural reality of the present age and between the faith of the former and the reason of the latter.[43] They see their role more as prophetic protest against those who confusedly and complacently confess a distorted Christian faith than as evangelists seeking to convert or apologists seeking to persuade.[44] Perhaps to speak of apologetics in that context, however legitimate the project of a non-foundationalist apologetics may be, is to distract the reader from the agendas of Johannes and Johannes.

There seems to be good reason to think of Kierkegaard as a philosopher, and the idea that what philosophers do is give arguments for or against various beliefs and practices is deeply ingrained. So the temptation to insist on finding such arguments in Kierkegaard's writings, whether they are thought to be good or bad arguments, is hard to resist. Although she acknowledges that Kierkegaard's writings offer only a "limited defense" of Christianity, Michelle Kosch insists on finding arguments that in order "not to be question-begging" will need to proceed "without presupposing the truth of religious commitments or even the applicability of religious concepts."[45]

Kosch qualifies this in two ways. First, she says that in the pseudonymous writings Kierkegaard's aim was

43. It is worth recalling Simon Podmore's reminder about the pseudonymous writings that they are "from the pen of Kierkegaard and the perspective of [in this case] Johannes Climacus." *Kierkegaard and the Self Before God* (Bloomington: Indiana University Press, 2011), p. 1. It is Kierkegaard who gives us the pseudonyms and their texts because he thinks we should pay careful attention to what they have to say.

44. See my "Johannes and Johannes: Kierkegaard and Difference," in Perkins, ed., *International Kierkegaard Commentary,* vol. 7: *"Philosophical Fragments" and "Johannes Climacus,"* pp. 13-18. I go on to argue that "Johannes Climacus is trying to work out the epistemological ramifications of the critical social theory presented implicitly in the Abraham story as told by Johannes de Silentio" (p. 18).

45. Michelle Kosch, *Freedom and Reason in Kant, Schelling, and Kierkegaard* (Oxford: Clarendon, 2006), p. 139. In the language of apologetics, she finds only a negative apologetics in the pseudonymous authorship.

not to give an argument for the correctness of Christian belief. In fact the project in the pseudonyms is much more modest. Kierkegaard does think that the problem with the views criticized is visible from a general philosophical perspective and that philosophy can have a negative role in paving the way for the sort of belief that becoming a Christian involves.[46]

The second qualification goes like this:

> Some of the position outlined in Kierkegaard's pseudonymous works is motivated purely by religious commitment and has no application apart from the project of leading a certain sort of Christian life. However, for the most part, that position's truth was meant to be judged from the standpoint of the reasonably reflective, but uncommitted, agent.[47]

This seems to me mistaken in two ways and misleading in another. First, the combination of the ideal of avoiding question-begging with that of not presupposing the truth of religious commitments suggests that some neutral, presuppositionless standpoint is possible and that it is to be found in secular thought. But neither Kierkegaard nor his pseudonyms presuppose that such a presuppositionless standpoint is possible, much less that secular thought has an advantage over religious thought in this regard.

Second, it seems to me clear that "for the most part" Kierkegaard's writings, pseudonymous and in his own name, *are* "motivated by religious commitment" and belong to describing and motivating "the project of leading a certain sort of Christian life."[48]

I think philosophy, including the interpretation of philosophical texts, is perspectival, and that objectivity is best served by multiplying perspectives rather than fleeing them with pseudo-claims to neutrality. So I do not reject the project of looking for the kind of arguments we might find in Kierkegaard's diverse authorship if he had written in our situation and accepted the dominant view of what philosophers are supposed to do.[49] But I think it is deeply misleading to suggest that this is what he or his pseudonyms are doing "for the most part." At least so far as Silentio and Clima-

---

46. Kosch, *Freedom and Reason,* pp. 181-82.

47. Kosch, *Freedom and Reason,* p. 141.

48. This is what Kierkegaard himself argues in *Point of View,* although we don't have to take it on his authority. We can see, as I am attempting to do in these chapters, whether the text can support such a claim.

49. Remembering the important qualifications expressed above.

cus are concerned,[50] it seems to me that what they are concerned about "for the most part" is to keep us from blurring the lines between standpoints that are mutually exclusive, to keep the either/or situation in which we so often find ourselves from losing its sharp edge.[51]

Interestingly, Kosch finds it necessary to exempt *Fear and Trembling* from her account of what Kierkegaard is up to "for the most part" in his pseudonymous writings: "It seems to me mistaken to read *Fear and Trembling* as aimed at articulating the shortcomings of the ethical standpoint in a way convincing to an inhabitant of that standpoint. Instead, we should read it as aimed primarily at articulating the constraints imposed by a life of faith, and so presupposing, rather than arguing for, a religious standpoint."[52] The last part of this quotation conforms to her claim that the pseudonyms present no positive apologetics for faith. But the first part runs afoul of her claim that the pseudonymous critiques of alternative standpoints have their force "from a general philosophical perspective." As described here, those in the ethical standpoint will find accounts of its shortcomings to be question-begging.

This latter point seems to me as correct as it is ironical in context. I would only add that we can best make sense of the texts before us if we pay attention to the intended audience of Kierkegaard through Silentio and Climacus. On the one hand, there are the non-academic Christians who make up the bulk of Christendom. They accept, at least nominally, the authority of Scripture, and on that basis they accept that Abraham is a hero of faith and that Jesus is God incarnate. For the most part, at least, they do not need either positive or negative arguments in support of their faith. What they need, in Kierkegaard's view, is to be warned against allowing the established order in (their) contemporary Denmark to be the norm for their "Christian" practice and allowing some fashionable version of the recollection theory (whose name they might not recognize) to be the norm for their "Christian" belief. The dangers to their "faith" come from cultural complacency and certain fashions among the intellectual elite. Their pastors, in particular, are vulnerable to both.

---

50. I believe the same to be true of Anti-Climacus, but that lies ahead of us, not behind.

51. Given the role of teleological suspensions in the theory of the stages, there is no absolute either/or between the aesthetic and the ethical, or between the ethical and the religious, or between Religiousness A and Religiousness B. But there is a sharp either/or between the aesthetic standpoint as absolute and the ethical with the aesthetical included as a subordinate moment. The same can be said for the other two pairs.

52. Kosch, *Freedom and Reason*, pp. 156-60.

On the other hand, there are the intellectual elite themselves, the Hegelians most particularly. They already make the established order the highest practical norm, and speculation in the recollection mode the highest theoretical norm. They need to be reminded that this is not Christianity and that it is misleading, even perhaps dishonest, to present such a standpoint as the new, improved version of Christianity that has finally reached its highest and most fully adequate form.

It is this warning and this reminder that I take to be the goal of Silentio and Climacus as authors. That they stand outside of the faith they describe suggests that Kierkegaard thinks their arguments — not for the truth of Christianity, but for its essential difference from standpoints currently confused with it — should have force "from the standpoint of the reasonably reflective, but uncommitted" reader.

CHAPTER 8

Faith as the Happy Passion That Overcomes Offense

Climacus begins his third chapter with a reference to Socratic ignorance.[1] At *Phaedrus* 229e Socrates admits that he does not know if he is "a more curious monster than Typhon or a friendlier and simpler being, by nature sharing something divine" (*PF,* 37).[2] This gives us a context for and a hint about what Climacus is up to in the claims he is about to make. The two alternatives he will develop, offense and faith, imply two deeply opposing accounts of who we are as human beings.

He begins his account with three theses. First, "paradox is the passion of thought." Second, "the thinker without the paradox is like the lover without passion." Third, the ultimate paradox of thought is "to want to discover something thought itself cannot think" (*PF,* 37).

First, thought is passionate, not dispassionate.[3] We often equate the ideal of scientific objectivity with thought's highest vocation. But this ideal is itself the product of thought's passion for the truth, combined with the sense that desire can distort belief (the hermeneutics of suspicion) and that, at least in some contexts, it can and should be neutralized. For Climacus,

---

1. See the brief discussion in chapter 7 above.

2. In a dialectical spirit that both Socrates and Kierkegaard would welcome, Pascal famously votes for both. "What a chimera then is man! What a novelty! What a monster, what a chaos, what a contradiction, what a prodigy! Judge of all things, imbecile worm of the earth; depositary of truth, a sink of uncertainty and error; the pride and refuse of the universe. . . . Nature confutes the sceptics, and reason confutes the dogmatists. What then will you become, O men! who try to find out by your natural reason what is your true condition? You cannot avoid one of these sects, nor adhere to one of them." *Pensées,* no. 434 (Modern Library edition).

3. Hence the title of Evans's commentary, *Passionate Reason.*

Socrates is the model of a passionate thinker precisely because the question is about himself, his own nature and identity, and this is not a question from which we can or should distance ourselves in dispassionate objectivity. In this regard Kant, of all people, (almost) presents thought as passionate. It is at least interested. He writes,

> All the interests of my reason, speculative as well as practical, combine in the three following questions:
>
> What can I know?
> What ought I to do?
> What may I hope?[4]

Kant tells us that the first question is speculative, the second practical, and the third both speculative and practical. But in his *Logic* he adds a fourth question, "What is man?," adding that the first three refer to and are based on *(beziehen auf)* the fourth. He then adds, interestingly in relation to what Climacus is about to do, that "philosophy must thus be able to determine (1) the sources of human knowledge, (2) the extent of the possible and useful uses of all knowledge, and finally (3) the limits of reason. The last of these is the most necessary but also the most difficult [task] with which the philodox does not trouble himself."[5]

This fourth question undermines or at least overrides the neat distinction between speculative and practical. All three questions as dimensions of the fourth are existential questions. This should not be surprising since the first, presumably speculative question is about God, freedom, and immortality, issues about which we are just fooling ourselves if we think we are dispassionate, objective, neutral spectators.

Second, the thinker's passion is like a lover's passion. Climacus introduces an analogy in support of what will shortly be his third thesis. The paradox of erotic love is that it "wills its own downfall" (*PF*, 39, 48). In *Works of Love*, Kierkegaard presents both erotic love and friendship as forms of self-love. This is because they are "preferential." I seek as a beloved or a friend only those who are in some way attractive to me, who will satisfy

---

4. *Critique of Pure Reason*, A 804-5 = B 832-33. After presenting the four antinomies of pure reason and before presenting his "solution" to them, Kant introduces a section entitled "The Interest of Reason in These Conflicts." A 462 = B 490ff.

5. *Logik*, in *Kant's Werke (Akademie Textausgabe)* (Berlin: Walter de Gruyter, 1968), 9:25. A philodox is a dogmatic person who is in love with his or her own opinions.

some (perceived) need, that is, some desire of mine. I'm in it for what I hope to get out of it in the form of companionship, intimacy, security, status, and so forth.[6] But the paradox of erotic love (Climacus's theme), which is also the paradox of friendship, is that when I succeed in finding a beloved or a friend, when the one I want to be with also wants to be with me, self-love has transcended itself. Now I am concerned about the other's needs and desires. No longer concerned only about my own happiness, I want to make my beloved or my friend happy.

If, as Climacus suggests, the thinker's passion is like the lover's passion it will resemble this paradox, and it is this paradox that is the thinker's passion.

Third, the paradox of thought, like the paradox of self-love in its erotic (and friendship) modes, is the desire to transcend or overcome itself; it is the desire "to discover something thought itself cannot think. . . . But what is this unknown against which the understanding in its paradoxical passion collides and which even disturbs man in his self-knowledge? It is the unknown" (*PF*, 39). As Socrates might put it, thought seeks to know its own ignorance; and as Kant might put it, pure reason seeks by critiquing itself to discover the limits of pure reason.

But to speak merely of the unknown is too abstract for Climacus, as if the issue were some form of skepticism or what, in connection with Derrida, has been called a "generalized apophatics."[7] So, returning to what I have been calling his "cheating," Climacus suggests that we call this unknown *"the god"* (*PF*, 39). The reader realizes immediately that this is the god from Climacus's chapter two who is teacher and savior, to whom the learner owes everything, the not yet named Jesus Christ as God incarnate.[8]

---

6. Levinas speaks of being "absolutely for myself. Egoist without reference to the Other, I am alone without solitude . . . entirely deaf to the Other . . . without ears, like a hungry stomach." *Totality and Infinity: An Essay on Exteriority*, trans. Alphonso Lingis (Pittsburgh: Duquesne University Press, 1969), p. 134.

7. John D. Caputo, *The Prayers and Tears of Jacques Derrida* (Bloomington: Indiana University Press, 1997), §§3-4.

8. At this point Climacus adds a digression against the attempt to prove the existence of God. It employs the hermeneutical principle that thought is never without its presuppositions and thus never neutral and, in that sense, objective. Thus, to prove the existence of God from the works of God (the traditional cosmological or teleological proofs) is already to presuppose that the world has the character of "works" and thus, in a sense, to beg the question. The bearing of this on our exploration of the nature of faith is that if it is argued that faith (as the reception of divine revelation) is not "objective" or "scientific," the reply is that reason (as recollection) is not either. In this context Climacus introduces the notion of the *leap* (*PF*, 43),

The chapter is entitled "The Absolute Paradox," and this paradox is the incarnation, the claim that "[t]his human being is also the god" (*PF*, 45).

What is it that makes this the absolute paradox? It is the (impossible) thought of the "absolutely different" (*PF*, 44-47), the difference presumably being that between the knower and the (un)known. In accord with the ancient principle of knowing that like is known by like, the ultimately unknowable would be the ultimately unlike. But Climacus insists that the absolute difference that generates the absolute paradox with which the understanding collides and experiences its downfall is not ontological but moral.

> But if the god is to be absolutely different from a human being, this can have its basis not in that which man owes to the god (for to that extent they are akin)[9] but in that which he owes to himself or in that which he himself has committed. What, then, is the difference? Indeed, what else but sin. . . . We stated this in the foregoing by saying that the individual is untruth and is this through his own fault. (*PF*, 46-47; cf. 15)

But the paradox embodied in the story Climacus is telling as an alternative to the Socratic model is "even more terrible" than the paradox of the "human being [who] is also the god." To this is added the "duplexity" by which the paradox becomes absolute, "negatively, by bringing into prominence the absolute difference of sin and, positively, by wanting to annul this absolute difference in the absolute equality" (*PF*, 47).[10] In other words, the absolute paradox is the doctrine of the incarnation combined with the doctrine of the atonement, which presupposes the doctrine of the fall and culminates in the doctrine of reconciliation. So Climacus's reference to "old-fashioned orthodoxy in its rightful strictness" should not be surprising.[11] It is succinctly expressed in nine words: "Christ Jesus came into the world to save sinners" (1 Tim. 1:15).[12]

---

suggesting that reason is as much a leap as is faith; it, too, presupposes what it cannot prove, whether it takes the world, for instance, either as works or as brute facts.

9. Climacus seems to be presupposing here something like the Thomistic analogy of being.

10. We recall that equality was the goal of the king who loved the lowly maiden in Climacus's chapter two.

11. See the quotation from *Postscript* in chapter 7 at note 35, above.

12. Conflicting theories, especially of the atonement and the fall, have kept theologians out of the unemployment lines for centuries. Climacus invokes no particular theories but invokes simple, biblical language such as this. The first six words get taken up into theologies

In the analogy, erotic love (and friendship) will their own downfall; that is to say, self-love wills to transcend itself in love for the other. But in this process "self-love has foundered, but nevertheless it is not annihilated but is taken captive . . . but it can come to life again" (*PF*, 48). Two important points here. First, "not annihilated but . . . taken captive" can be read as the claim that when erotic love (and friendship) reach their proper fulfillment, self-love is already *aufgehoben* in love for the other, and need love is already *aufgehoben* in gift love, whether this is explicitly understood or not. But, second, this is not inevitable. Self-love can resist this self-transcendence or lapse back into the immediacy of a self-love that resists its own fulfillment from the start. Then the lover treats the lover (and the friend the friend) as a means to his or her own ends, and self-love, fearing annihilation, resists being taken captive and retains its autonomy in uncompromising self-centeredness.

It is the same with the relation of the understanding to the absolute paradox. For the moment the happy passion, in which the understanding paradoxically fulfills itself in its own downfall as it is taken captive, remains unnamed (*PF*, 48-49, 54), though the suspense is artificial indeed. The reader knows that in Climacus's thought-experiment, that is, seeking an alternative to knowledge as recollection, reason finds its fulfillment in a faith that opens itself to reason's other, namely revelation. Before the happy passion gets named officially, the alternative it will welcome is named in an appendix to chapter three entitled "Offense at the Paradox (An Acoustic Illusion)" (*PF*, 49-54). It is the paradox, indeed, the absolute paradox.

Offense is the "unhappy" relation to the absolute paradox that represents the "misunderstood self-love" of the understanding (*PF*, 49).[13] This, of course, is not the self-understanding of offended consciousness; nor is it, I want to suggest, the verdict of Climacus. It is the verdict that emerges from the alternative to the recollection hypothesis. The alternative knows itself as the (for the moment) unnamed happy passion that welcomes its own downfall by welcoming the absolute paradox (which looks suspiciously like orthodox Christianity). From its perspective, offense, the refusal to welcome the absolute paradox and thereby the downfall of the understanding's autonomy and self-sufficiency, is an unhappy love and the understanding's misunderstand-

---

of the incarnation; the next two into theologies of atonement and reconciliation; the last one into theologies of the fall.

13. The concept of offense was briefly introduced at *PF*, 32. Its fullest development will be found in the writings of Anti-Climacus.

ing of itself.[14] Climacus is still "deducing" the alternative. As I read him, he tries neither to argue for its superiority nor even to indicate his own preference for it. He simply insists on its deep and systematic difference from modernity's reason in its vaunted autonomy and its ideological mirroring of the established order, one dimension of which is Christendom.[15]

We know that the happy passion that welcomes the absolute paradox in its absolute difference and all that that entails will shortly be identified as faith (*PF*, 59, 61). It is significant that the opposite of faith here is not doubt but offense. Especially in light of the role sin plays in the development of the alternative,[16] it should be clear that the issue is not merely epistemic but existential, that the will and not just the intellect is involved, and that the engaged personality of the individual is in play. A later pseudonym, Anti-Climacus, referring to his own work, *Sickness unto Death,* writes that "in modern philosophy there is a confused discussion of doubt where the discussion should have been about despair." Then he adds, "so also the practice has been to use the category 'doubt' where the discussion ought to be about 'offense.' In relation to Christianity the question is "not to doubt or to believe, but to be offended or to believe." Because modern philosophy is abstractly metaphysical, it fails to locate the issue in "the ethical, the religious, the existential" (*PC*, 81n.)

So we have on the one hand the offended consciousness, the unhappy passion that finds the absolute paradox repugnant, even perhaps threatening, for it is a threat to the understanding's aspiration to autonomy. Since we are interested in the historical conflict between faith and reason, let us call this posture Reason, remembering (1) that Climacus speaks instead of understanding (in English translation) and (2) that we are not speaking of reason without qualification but of Enlightenment reason in its desire to be autonomous and self-sufficient.[17] On the other hand we have the happy

14. As a mode of love, offense is a passion. Following the classical notion of the passions as modes of passivity, Climacus insists that offense is a mode of suffering, but not merely so. It is rather the dialectical tension of activity and passivity (*PF*, 50). For discussion of this dimension of the text, see M. Jamie Ferreira, *Transforming Vision: Imagination and Will in Kierkegaardian Faith* (New York: Oxford University Press, 1991), pp. 23-28. By implication, the same will be true of faith. As Paul puts it, it is both a gift (Eph. 2:8 — Calvinists may cheer) and a matter of obedience (Rom. 1:5 — Arminians may cheer).

15. Here I'm reading Climacus intertextually with a backward look at *Fear and Trembling* and a forward look toward *Practice in Christianity,* among other texts.

16. At first in *PF*, 15-19.

17. Since Climacus presents this reason in terms of recollection, we can say that the Enlightenment begins in the Platonic dialogues, especially in the familiar reading of Plato as a speculative optimist, as distinct from a Socrates who combines ignorance with irony.

passion that will shortly be named Faith. Faith is not without reason, but is willing to let its reason suffer the "downfall" in which it is "taken captive" by revelation (*PF,* 48). When it reflects on itself it recognizes that it is the moment in which understanding "surrender[s] itself," "steps aside," or is "discharged" and the paradox "gives itself" (*PF,* 54, 59).

We are now prepared for what Climacus calls the acoustic illusion. In its Enlightenment mode, Reason says that Faith is unreasonable; it is "foolishness" (*PF,* 51-53). It should be supplanted, either (1) replaced by a fully rational religion (or perhaps by atheism), or (2) reinterpreted so as to conform to the requirements of Reason's recollections.[18] But Climacus points out that it is not Reason that discovers that Faith does not conform to it in either of these two ways. It is Faith that long since has insisted that "the message about the cross is foolishness" to those who do not welcome the absolute paradox, and that it is the "wisdom of the world" that is the true foolishness because the message of the cross is "the wisdom of God" (1 Cor. 1:18-21).[19] Offended consciousness is derivative, just as a cartoonist is dependent on the one being caricatured (*PF,* 51). "Yet the understanding has not discovered [the mutual incompatibility of Faith and this version of Reason], since, on the contrary, it is the paradox that discovered it and now takes testimony from the offense. The understanding declares that the paradox is absurd, but this is only a caricaturing. . . . Everything it says about the paradox it has learned from the paradox" (*PF,* 52-53).

Herein lies the acoustical illusion. It looks as if the puppet, Mortimer Snerd, is speaking, but the voice is actually that of the ventriloquist, Edgar Bergen. Analogously, it might seem as if Reason is speaking when the paradox is called unreasonable and absurd; but the voice is actually that of Faith. Faith says to (this version of) Reason, "It is just as you say, and the amazing thing is that you think that it is an objection" (*PF,* 52).[20] Merely to

18. This sentence is my interpretation, not Climacus's, of the Enlightenment project of "religion within the boundaries of mere reason."

19. See Kierkegaard's sermon on a closely related text, 1 Cor. 2:6-9, contrasting the wisdom of the world with the hidden and mysterious wisdom of God. It was preached four months before the publication of *Fragments.* Søren Kierkegaard, *Johannes Climacus, or De Omnibus Dubitandum Est and A Sermon,* trans. T. H. Croxall (Stanford: Stanford University Press, 1958), pp. 159-73.

20. Sylvia Walsh argues that the mistake of Reason goes beyond thinking that by calling the paradox absurd it has raised a substantive objection. Reason fails to notice that the paradox appears to be absurd only to unbelief or to wavering belief. To firm belief it does not appear to be absurd, since it is not inherently absurd. "Echoes of Absurdity: The Offended Consciousness and the Absolute Paradox in Kierkegaard's *Philosophical Fragments,*" in *Inter-*

point out (derivatively) the mutual incompatibility of two points of view is not to argue for either. The "unreasonableness" of Faith consists in its deep divergence from autonomous Reason and its ideas about religion. But what follows from this? Nothing, Climacus suggests. It is a tautology to say that what conflicts with some interpretation of Reason is "unreasonable" by the standards of that version. To revert to the analogy with erotic love (and friendship): only if it has already been independently established that self-love should not surrender its primacy is its "downfall" in caring about the happiness of the beloved (or friend) shown to be an irrational weakness.[21] Similarly, only if it has already been independently established that Reason as autonomous, self-sufficient recollection has a right to hegemony in the realm of our deepest existential questions, does the "foolishness" of faith discredit it.

But why is Enlightenment Reason offended and not merely dubious in relation to something it can neither recollect nor comprehend?[22] Here an intertextual reading might help, drawing on an essay Kierkegaard published several years later than *Fragments* entitled "The Difference Between a Genius and an Apostle." Originally part of a long manuscript published only posthumously and known as *The Book on Adler (BA),* it was published as part of *Two Ethical-Religious Essays* by the pseudonym H.H.[23]

---

national Kierkegaard Commentary, vol. 7: *"Philosophical Fragments" and "Johannes Climacus,"* ed. Robert L. Perkins (Macon, GA: Mercer University Press, 1994), pp. 37-46. To put it this way is, of course, to speak from the standpoint of faith or to describe that standpoint. See the next note.

21. "Independently" here signifies a standpoint neutral with respect to the relative merits of need love and gift love. Analogously, the incompatibility of Faith and Reason would be an "objection," as Climacus puts it, only if Reason's hegemony had already been established from some neutral standpoint. But who, Climacus asks, occupies "the view from nowhere"? For this version of Reason to presuppose that it simply is that point of view is to beg the question at issue.

22. On the allergic reaction of both Kant and Hegel to anything intrinsically mysterious, see chapter 5, note 11, above.

23. It now appears in *WA,* 93-108 and in *The Essential Kierkegaard,* ed. Howard V. Hong and Edna H. Hong (Princeton: Princeton University Press, 2000), pp. 339-49. For helpful discussion of *The Book on Adler* see C. Stephen Evans, "Kierkegaard on Religious Authority: The Problem of the Criterion," in *Kierkegaard on Faith and the Self: Collected Essays* (Waco, TX: Baylor University Press, 2006), pp. 239-60; Stephen N. Dunning, "Who Sets the Task? Kierkegaard on Authority," in *Foundations of Kierkegaard's Vision of Community,* ed. George B. Connell and C. Stephen Evans (Atlantic Highlands, NJ: Humanities, 1992), pp. 18-32; and Stanley Cavell, "Kierkegaard's 'On Authority and Revelation,'" in *Kierkegaard: A Collection of Critical Essays,* ed. Josiah Thompson (Garden City, NY: Doubleday, 1972), pp.

Climacus has been working with the distinction between recollection and revelation. The difference between a genius and an apostle maps onto this distinction quite neatly. The genius belongs to the realm of aesthetics and philosophy and represents two modes of recollection, drawing out into the open what is already inside; by contrast, the apostle belongs to religion, at least to the biblical kind of religion that depends on divine revelation. Whereas for Hegel the three moments of Absolute Spirit are art, religion, and philosophy in an upward trajectory, with art below religion and philosophy above it, for our new friend, H.H., the arts and philosophy are essentially similar, while religion is qualitatively different. The difference is that between immanence and transcendence.

Traditionally, transcendence has signified that which lies beyond, usually with connotations of height,[24] but in recent discussions the emphasis has been more on alterity, that which is different or other. What we have here are two ways of trying to say the same thing wherever height has ceased to be a literally spatial concept; it then becomes a symbol or metaphor for that which is beyond some particular horizon (the natural world, human knowledge and understanding) by being deeply different. The transcendent is neither a part nor the whole of that from which it essentially differs.

This means that the genius is a monad while the apostle is always a dyad, the human messenger essentially linked to the divine source. "A genius lives within himself" (WA, 106), whereas an apostle "is the one who has *divine authority* to *command*" (WA, 107). Apart from the relation to God, the apostle (or prophet) is merely another human voice, and probably not a genius.

Of course this does not mean that the genius is a self-creation *ex nihilo*. The genius may well be deeply immersed in one or more traditions and may even experience "the anxiety of influence."[25] But even if the work of the genius is a "strong misreading" of the work of predecessors, the genius is not

---

373-93. *On Authority and Revelation* is an earlier version of *BA*, trans. Walter Lowrie (New York: Harper & Row, 1966).

24. So it is not surprising that Edwyn Bevan, after an introductory chapter in *Symbolism and Belief* (London: George Allen & Unwin, 1938), follows with two chapters entitled "Height"; or that Mircea Eliade, after an introductory chapter in *Patterns in Comparative Religion* (New York: Sheed and Ward, 1958), follows with these three chapters: "The Sky and Sky Gods," "The Sun and Sun-Worship," and "The Moon and Its Mystique."

25. See Harold Bloom, *The Anxiety of Influence*, 2nd ed. (New York: Oxford University Press, 1997), and *The Anatomy of Influence: Literature as a Way of Life* (New Haven: Yale University Press, 2011).

essentially linked to something qualitatively different. The genius and the predecessors are all human, all too human. It is not the task of the genius to pass on faithfully a message bearing the authority of the traditions or exemplars on which he or she draws. It is the form and content of the work of genius that marks its excellence; for the apostle it is the source (*WA*, 96-97).

Another way to put this is to say that the genius is born, while the apostle is called and appointed (*WA*, 95).

H.H. shows us a consequence of this difference, then gives us both an analogy and an illustration. The consequence concerns the fate of paradox. The genius may introduce something new that is paradoxical vis-à-vis common sense or received knowledge. It may be, for example, the idea that the earth is round. Or, to return to the aesthetic and the philosophical, it may be the new ways of thinking and seeing opened up by a Shakespeare or a Plato. But this paradoxicality is "transitory"; immanence can "assimilate" it, and its paradoxical appearance "vanishes" (*WA*, 94-96). A revelation, by contrast, is something "that passes human understanding" (*WA*, 106) not just temporarily but permanently. If it is "assimilated" it ceases to be itself, or, as Paul might put it, the divine wisdom always distinguishes itself from and stands in judgment on every human wisdom (*WA*, 94-96).[26]

The analogy concerns the command of the king or the father. A "royal command . . . forbids all esthetic and critical impertinence with regard to form and content." By contrast, the poet and thinker are without authority, and their message "is evaluated purely esthetically or philosophically by evaluating the content and the form" (*WA*, 97). Again, "To ask if a king is a genius, and in that case to be willing to obey him, is basically high treason, because the question contains a doubt about submission to authority" (*WA*, 101). Similarly, the son who obeys his father because the latter is a genius, "always profound and brilliant . . . emphasizes something altogether wrong . . . and on that basis he simply cannot *obey* him" (*WA*, 104).

The illustration is the difference between Plato and the apostle Paul. Our essay begins with the sentence, "As a genius, Paul cannot stand comparison with either Plato or Shakespeare" (*WA*, 94). What Plato says about immortality "is actually profound, attained by profound cogitating; but then poor Plato does not have any authority" (*WA*, 103).[27] The implicit con-

---

26. In Kierkegaard's writings as a whole, Christendom can be defined, whether mentioned by name or not, as this assimilation.

27. In a draft for *Johannes Climacus, or De Omnibus Dubitandum Est* (published posthumously), Kierkegaard writes, "In other words, in order for the religious and ethical thesis to have significance, there must be authority. . . . Is talent itself not adequate authority? Phil-

trast is clear. What Paul says about the resurrection of the body is not the product of "profound cogitating"; rather, it comes with the divine authority by virtue of which Paul is an apostle.

H.H. would have been appalled if he could have read Adolf Deissmann's book on Paul.[28] The key to Deissmann's interpretation is the following sentence: "Paul must be classed with the few people regarding whom that much misused phrase 'religious genius' can rightly and fittingly be used."[29] Accordingly Deissmann emphasizes Paul's "genuine humanity," his "unusual gifts," his "hidden greatness," and the "value [and power] of his own personality."[30] In his review, H.H. would have written, "In this manner God is actually smuggled away" (WA, 97).

Deissmann represents the kind of "confusion" Kierkegaard speaks of in his Introduction as editor to *The Book on Adler*.[31] He sees Adler's claim to have received a new revelation as confused, but he is interested in Adler only because he manifests the confusion of the age (BA, 3-4).[32] Kierkegaard hopes that exposing the confusion over the concept of revelation will "elucidate the concept more clearly" (BA, 4). N.B. Kierkegaard sees his new pseudonym, Petrus Minor, as a phenomenologist. He is not arguing that a genuine revelation has taken place in these events or in those writings;[33] he is trying to show what a genuine revelation would have to look like.

The confusion of the age consists in decoupling the concept of revelation from the concept of authority, replacing it, perhaps, with the idea of talent[34] or genius or profundity. But once it becomes clear that revelation

---

osophical talent is adequate authorization for enunciating a philosophical thesis. But something else is required when it involves religious and ethical truths" (PF, 245).

28. Paul Deissmann, *Paul: A Study in Social and Religious History* (New York: Harper & Brothers, 1957).

29. Deissmann, *Paul*, p. 79; cf. pp. 6, 103, 130.

30. Deissmann, *Paul*, pp. 57-59, 77.

31. The unpublished draft manuscript is attributed to Petrus Minor as edited by S. Kierkegaard.

32. The manuscript is entitled "The Religious Confusion of the Present Age Illustrated by Magister Adler as a Phenomenon" (BA, 1).

33. But he does argue that Adler's alleged revelation does not correspond to the unconfused concept of revelation. Of course, his readers did not need to be disabused of Adler's claims but unconfused about the true nature of revelation. So his project is right in step with that of Climacus in PF. Wittgensteinians will appropriately see Petrus Minor as an ordinary language philosopher, seeking to clarify meanings rather than prove moral or metaphysical facts.

34. See note 27 above.

comes with divine authority, of which the apostle is only the messenger,[35] the situation is changed. The issue is no longer doubt but "insubordination" and "disobedience," which is "the calamity of our age," and "the secret in the religious confusion of our age." This is why the "most dangerous" enemies of faith are not "the militia of attackers who want to do away with Christianity" but rather the "missionaries of confusion" (*BA,* 5). When H.H. repeats this theme in terms of "rebelliousness," he identifies these missionaries. "Thus all modern speculative thought is affected by having abolished *obedience* on the one hand and *authority* on the other" (*WA,* 103-4). He doubtless has in mind the Hegelians, but we can remind ourselves that any theory that turns out to be a variation on the recollection theme would be subject to this analysis. "If the authority is not the other (τὸ ἕτερον), if in any way it should indicate merely an intensification within the identity [of the knowing self], then there simply is no authority" (*WA,* 99).[36]

In a later journal entry, Kierkegaard summarizes:

> It is claimed that the arguments against Christianity arise out of doubt. This is a total misunderstanding. [They] arise out of insubordination, reluctance to obey, mutiny against all authority. Therefore, until now the battle against objections has been shadow-boxing, because it has been intellectual combat with doubt instead of ethical combat against mutiny. (*JP* 1:359, entry 778)

This is not to say that there are no genuine epistemic issues. The difference between the recollection and the revelation is between two epistemic models. But from the standpoint of the alternative Climacus has been sketching, and because sin is an important part of that model, the reluctance of the will is a deeper obstacle to faith than the reservations of the intellect.

It is true that Climacus does not thematize the issue of authority and the corresponding themes of insubordination, disobedience, rebelliousness, and mutiny, though, as just noted, his references to sin fit well with this language. But the issue of authority clearly shows its face in the contrast between recollection and revelation. The slave boy needed help discovering the truth, but once it was there, staring him in the face, he was able to recognize it as the truth. He had, as Climacus puts it, the condition. Or, in other words, while the slave boy had to rely on Socrates for help in finding the

---

35. We might say that what the midwife is to recollection, the messenger is to revelation.
36. We are reminded of Climacus's epigraph, "Better well hanged than ill wed."

truth, once it was found he did not have to rely on the authority of Socrates in order to acknowledge it as the truth.[37] By contrast, my students had to rely on my help to give them the truth, the name Linda, and they had to rely on my authority to accept it to be the truth.

This kind of dependence is a routine part of everyday life. We believe things all the time because a relative, or friend, or boss, or subordinate has told us (the time of the meeting, the weather prediction, a juicy piece of gossip). We trust them. Whenever we get the news from a newspaper, the radio, the television, or an online source, we accept facts (and sometimes interpretations) on the authority of others. We do not feel oppressed or offended. In discussing the sources of knowledge, Alvin Plantinga devotes half a chapter to testimony, to beliefs that we accept on the authority of others who attest to them. He quotes Thomas Reid:

> The wise author of nature hath planted in the human mind a propensity to rely upon human testimony before we can give a reason for doing so. . . . And although this natural credulity hath sometimes occasioned my being imposed upon by deceivers, yet it hath been of infinite advantage to me upon the whole; therefore, I consider it as another good gift of Nature.[38]

So reliance on the authority of others for taking the (presumed) truth to be the truth is utterly common and unproblematic. But not always. When children are told that some restriction (a bedtime, a punishment) is for their own good, they may obey, not wishing to pay the price of disobedience. But they may very well do so without belief or acknowledgment. We might say they are offended at parental authority, and doubt would surely not be the right category here. They don't want evidence; they want their parents to loosen up, and any attempt by the parents to argue for their claim is likely only to increase the resentment. Similarly with teenagers in relation to a curfew or body piercings or tattoos or a drinking age. And similarly with

---

37. On the epistemic significance of acknowledgment in relation to doubt, see Stanley Cavell, "Between Acknowledgment and Avoidance," ch. 12 in *The Claim of Reason: Wittgenstein, Skepticism, Morality, and Tragedy* (New York: Oxford University Press, 1979), and "The Avoidance of Love," ch. 10 in *Must We Mean What We Say?*, updated edition (New York: Cambridge University Press, 1976). Also in *Disowning Knowledge in Seven Plays of Shakespeare*, updated edition (New York: Cambridge University Press, 2003), ch. 2.

38. Alvin Plantinga, *Warrant and Proper Function* (New York: Oxford University Press, 1993), p. 77.

adults when another driver calls attention to the rudeness of their driving with a toot of the horn or the government tells them how much they must pay in taxes. At least in some situations we get offended when someone in authority tells us what to do or not to do. We resent it; we take umbrage. We see that authority as an assault on our dignity.

The alternative that Climacus has been developing concerns answers to deeply existential questions: questions of God, freedom, and immortality. Or the three questions Kant identifies as interests of reason:

What can I know?
What ought I to do?
What may I hope?

These three metaphysical themes and these three questions are all dimensions of the fundamental question, Who am I? In spite of his fame as the founder of an existentialism that is seen to have a Cartesian fixation on the individual, Kierkegaard would insist on the equal primacy of the question, Who are we?[39] In relation to the claim of the alternative that in relation to these questions we are both (1) dependent on divine revelation for finding and recognizing the truth and (2) responsible to its authority for acknowledgment of the truth and thus becoming a follower of the god in time who is both teacher and savior, one possibility is offense; the other possibility is faith. Climacus calls the latter a happy passion; relative to the possibility of faith we might call offended consciousness a hostile passion. Offense is not a necessary way station on the path to faith. But it is always a possibility. So faith is the happy passion that overcomes the temptation to offense. Insofar as faith is the task of a lifetime, this temptation is never decisively defeated. Christendom, in Kierkegaardian perspective, can be seen as a lapsing into offense while assuming that one remains faithful. Luther's *simul justus et peccator* (simultaneously justified and a sinner) becomes for Kierkegaard simultaneously faithful and offended.

39. In both the pseudonymous and non-pseudonymous writings.

CHAPTER 9

Faith as the Passionate Appropriation of an Objective Uncertainty

The second book by Johannes Climacus has a title as satirical as the first: *Concluding Unscientific Postscript to "Philosophical Fragments."* To call one's book "fragments" or "crumbs" (an alternate translation) and then to refer to it as a "pamphlet" (*CUP* 1:5, 10, 17) is, in context, to gibe at the Hegelian system. Then to write a sequel and call it a "postscript" to the fragments or crumbs, and an "unscientific postscript" to boot — that is to show irreverence to the holy books of the Hegelian church and the system they purport to present. The satire is the more humorous in that the postscript is almost six times as long as the fragments (though it is also called a "pamphlet" [*CUP* 1:8]). Try to imagine a letter or an email with that ratio.

A quick glance at the table of contents tells the reader that the book has two parts, one devoted to objectivity, the other to subjectivity. A closer look will reveal another asymmetry in that fifteen times as much space is devoted to subjectivity as to objectivity. Climacus tells us right off why. As in *Fragments,* his focus will be on Christianity, but "the issue is not about the truth of Christianity but about the individual's relation to Christianity. . . . The objective issue, then, would be about the truth of Christianity. The subjective issue is about the individual's relation to Christianity" (*CUP* 1:15-17). Anticipating what he will say about subjectivity and echoing Silentio's portrait of the loneliness of Abraham, he writes, "How can I, Johannes Climacus, share in the happiness that Christianity promises? The issue pertains to me alone, partly because, if properly presented, it will pertain to everyone in the same way" (*CUP* 1:17). It is this focus on subjectivity that represents the "new approach to the issue of *Fragments*" (*CUP* 1:17).

In due course Climacus will distinguish these two questions of the truth of Christianity and the individual's relation to it as the what question and the how question. It is his version of the classical distinction between *fides quae creditur* (the faith that is believed, the propositional content affirmed in or by faith, the what of faith) and *fides qua creditur* (the faith by which it is believed, the act of faith, the how). The analysis of subjectivity will be tightly linked, as here, to the how question. We are warned that even if Climacus should speak, as he will, of truth as subjectivity, the point is not about what I should believe or how I should decide what to believe. He is not proposing a subjectivist theology or epistemology. He is rather posing the question whether we are appropriately or authentically living out in our actions and attitudes what we profess to believe, whatever that may be. Augustine's notion of doing the truth *(facere veritatem)*[1] is relevant here, and much of *Postscript* can be read as an analysis of that concept.

We have to take that "much" seriously. The portion of *Postscript* that Climacus devotes to subjectivity is fifteen times as long as the portion he devotes to objectivity. Most of that is devoted to what Jamie Ferreira happily calls *"generic subjectivity"* or "human subjectivity."[2] Just as infinite resignation is the necessary condition for biblical, Abrahamic faith for Silentio, so for Climacus this generic, human subjectivity is the *sine qua non* for Christian faith. It is the genus of which Christianity is a species. A life lived in the mode (or mood in Heidegger's sense)[3] of objectivity, that of the disinter-

1. See Augustine, *Confessions,* X.i.1. Jacques Derrida speaks often of this notion in *Jacques Derrida/Circumfession,* trans. Geoffrey Bennington (Chicago: University of Chicago Press, 1993), pp. 47-48, 56, 137, 233, 300. John D. Caputo makes it a prominent theme in *The Weakness of God: A Theology of the Event* (Bloomington: Indiana University Press, 2006), pp. 118, 268, 272, 276, 296, 299. They both mention the idea in *Augustine and Postmodernism: Confessions and Circumfession,* ed. John D. Caputo and Michael J. Scanlon (Bloomington: Indiana University Press, 2005), pp. 4-5, 9, 23, 33. In spite of deep differences between Derrida and Caputo on the one hand and Augustine and Kierkegaard on the other, I think Kierkegaard would welcome these discussions as signs of a subjectivity that has not been overwhelmed by objectivity as often happens in both modern and postmodern contexts, the absence of an "infinite, personal, passionate interest" in doing the truth (*CUP* 1:55; cf. 29, 33).
2. M. Jamie Ferreira, "The 'Socratic Secret': The Postscript to the *Philosophical Crumbs,*" in *Kierkegaard's "Concluding Unscientific Postscript": A Critical Guide,* ed. Rick Anthony Furtak (New York: Cambridge University Press, 2010), pp. 9-10.
3. See Martin Heidegger's analysis in *Being and Time,* trans. John Macquarrie and Edward Robinson (New York: Harper & Row, 1962), ¶¶29-30. Heidegger's *Befindlichkeit* is translated "state-of-mind" and is the ontological condition for our moods, our "Being-attuned," such as fear.

ested spectator, precludes itself from becoming a Christian even if it affirms orthodox Christian beliefs and engages outwardly in Christian practices (such as attending worship, singing the hymns, reciting the creed, and even staying awake during the sermon). Absent the appropriate inwardness, an "infinite personal, passionate interest" in one's eternal happiness (*CUP* 1:55; cf. 29 and 33), the lay churchgoer stands as much outside the possibility of becoming a Christian as the speculative philosopher, Climacus's primary target. So here again we have an "attack on Christendom" prior to the late polemical pamphlets (that really were pamphlets). Just as an animal cannot be a collie without "first" or "already" being a dog, so Christian faith presupposes that one is "first" or "already" living subjectively. Both Christendom (especially its preachers) and speculative philosophy are like the cat who claims to be a collie and doesn't see how comical this is. Climacus's satires are meant to expose the comedy.[4]

Two points to notice. First, this "generic" subjectivity is also "human subjectivity" because becoming subjective is also the *sine qua non* of being merely human. Climacus hammers away on this point.[5] We might say that he wants to place becoming a Christian on a humanistic foundation, not in the sense of propositions from which to deduce a Christian theology (a foundationalist strategy for answering the what question) but in terms of modes of inwardness that are both (a) possible outside Christianity and (b) that without which Christianity itself is impossible. The importance of this "generic" or "human" subjectivity is indicated by the fact that Climacus devotes a little over five times as much space to it as to specifically Christian subjectivity, in spite of the fact that his primary question is, How do I become a Christian? (*CUP* 1:15-17).

Second, this involves a kind of revision of the theory of stages or existence spheres. Climacus links the subjectivity he describes to the ethical and the religious. That leaves the speculative along with the aesthetic as exterior alternatives to the ethical and religious. Both of these lack that "infinite personal, passionate interest" in doing the truth. So we get, in effect, a double and quadruple theory of the stages.

---

4. Paul Muench suggests that in *Postscript* "Climacus presents his diagnosis of what has gone wrong with Christendom." "Kierkegaard's Socratic Pseudonym: A Profile of Johannes Climacus," in Furtak, ed., *Kierkegaard's "Concluding Unscientific Postscript,"* p. 28.

5. He pleads, "Let us be human beings" (*CUP* 1:114); cf. *CUP* 1:109, 117, 133, 158, 189, 346. He writes, "In the midst of all the jubilation over our age and the nineteenth century there sounds a secret contempt for being a human being — in the midst of the importance of the generation there is a despair over being a human being" (*CUP* 1:355).

Objectivity	Subjectivity
the Aesthetic	the Ethical
the Speculative[6]	the Religious

It is in his discussion of "generic" or "human" subjectivity that Climacus gives us a definition of faith. It is a generic faith, not specifically Christian; but it is as essential to Christian faith as the specifically Christian content. It can perform two functions for our analysis: it can supplement our previous discussions of faith in the writings of Silentio and Climacus, and it can be the focus for gathering and organizing what is most important for our purpose in the massive text that is the *Postscript*.

This definition comes in the (in)famous chapter that affirms "Truth Is Subjectivity." It goes like this:

> *An objective uncertainty, held fast through appropriation with the most passionate inwardness, is the truth,* the highest truth there is for an *existing* person. . . . But the definition of truth stated above is a paraphrasing of faith. Without risk, no faith. Faith is the contradiction between the infinite passion of inwardness and the objective uncertainty. (*CUP* 1:203-4)

Climacus gives a fourfold exposition and defense of the claim that we must think of truth and subjectivity together, even with such a strong connector as "is." The first three lead up to the fourth, which is this definition of truth and of faith as doing the truth *(facere veritatem).*

The first is a satire on the madman who thinks he can prove his sanity by regularly asserting an undisputed, objective truth. So he puts a skittle ball in his coat and every time it bumps him on the behind he says "Boom! The earth is round" (*CUP* 1:195). His doctor is not persuaded that he has been cured, "although the cure certainly could not revolve around getting him to assume that the earth is flat" (*CUP* 1:195).

Climacus moves closer to his target with a satire about the assistant

---

6. See *EO* 2:190, 211-12, where Judge William links German philosophy with the aesthetic mode in that both are forms of despair. Also see Michelle Kosch's comment on this passage in *Freedom and Reason in Kant, Schelling, and Kierkegaard* (Oxford: Clarendon, 2006), p. 147. There is a lot of truth in Kosch's suggestion, "Despite what Kierkegaard himself often says about the tripartite division of stages of existence, there is good reason to think that the most basic division is actually that between views of life that embrace passivity and those that embrace the possibility of action" (p. 155), even if the concepts of existence, subjectivity, and inwardness are not reducible, as she seems to think, to the notion of agency.

professor who, "every time his coattail reminds him to say something, says *de omnibus dubitandum est* [everything must be doubted]," although his systematic writings show "that the man has never doubted anything" and the irony is that "he is not considered lunatic" (*CUP* 1:195).[7]

We might say that the madness of Don Quixote consists in an excess of inwardness, since his "fixed finite idea," the romance of knighthood and chivalry, was hardly worthy of his passion. He is like the teenage girl who lamented, when her parents insisted on going home from the beach earlier than she wished, "You've ruined my entire life." On the other hand, "when inwardness is absent, parroting lunacy sets in, which is just as comic" (*CUP* 1:195). That is the problem with both the madman and the assistant professor. They both think that objectivity is enough, that it is sufficient publicly to affirm what the public will acknowledge to be true. Neither asks what else might be needed to establish, respectively, their sanity or their sagacity. Assuming the truth of what they affirm, neither worries about their proper relation to it.

Early on, Climacus had anticipated the significance of this humor for his concern with faith. Either the individual is "in faith" or not. In the former case "he must in faith be convinced of the truth of Christianity and his own relation to it, in which case all the rest cannot possibly be of infinite interest . . . or he is not in a relationship of faith but is objectively in a relationship of observation and as such is not infinitely interested in deciding the question" (*CUP* 1:21). N.B. Faith requires both objectivity, concern with the truth of Christianity, and subjectivity, concern about one's relation to that (purported) truth. On the other hand, if one is only concerned about the objective element, whether that be the truth of Christianity as defined by Lutheran orthodoxy (Christendom) or by the Hegelian system (speculative philosophy), one doesn't really have faith. Faith is not reducible to propositional assent.[8]

There is a double irony here. "The system presupposes faith as given (a system that has no presuppositions)" (*CUP* 1:14; cf. 50). There is the irony of an allegedly presuppositionless system making such a presupposition;[9] and

---

7. In 1842-43 Kierkegaard drafted but did not publish a treatise entitled *Johannes Climacus, or De Omnibus Dubitandum Est*. It portrays a young man, by no means identical with our pseudonym in spite of his name, completely confused by the notion that modern philosophy begins with doubt. This treatise is included in *PF*.

8. Silentio already made that clear by defining faith as trust in God's promises and obedience to God's commands. See chapters 2 and 3 above.

9. In fairness to Hegel it must be said that the faith he takes to be universally present

there is the irony of presupposing that everyone has faith from a standpoint that precludes faith.

In reflecting on his satire of the madman and the assistant professor, Climacus makes several important points. First, Climacus says that in his analysis

> it is not forgotten, even for a single moment, that the subject is existing, and that existing is a becoming, and that truth as the identity of thought and being is therefore a chimera of abstraction . . . not because truth is not an identity, but because the knower is an existing person, and thus truth cannot be an identity for him as long as he exists. (*CUP* 1:196)

Here we see an important sense in which Kierkegaard can be said to be the father of existentialism. He has his pseudonym use "existence" as a technical term for the distinctive temporality of human life. Thus Climacus speaks of "becoming subjective" and "becoming a Christian," and he presents both as tasks that make life strenuous for those who take them seriously.

We also begin to get a commentary on the "objective uncertainty" clause in the definition toward which we are headed. To speak of the identity of thought and being is not to deny that they can be distinguished. It is rather to affirm that being is the actualizing of what is "first" thought and that thought is thereby able to correspond or be adequate to being. But Climacus asks, Whose thought? and denies that it can be the thought of an existing individual.

---

is not Christian faith but what Jacobi had called an immediate knowledge of God, a certainty whose content is yet to be determined. See Georg Wilhelm Friedrich Hegel, *Lectures on the Philosophy of Religion*, ed. Peter C. Hodgson (Berkeley: University of California Press, 1984-87), 1:384-89, and *The Encyclopedia Logic*, trans. T. F. Geraets, W. A. Suchting, and H. S. Harris (Indianapolis: Hackett, 1991), §63. But Hegel also speaks of having Christian faith as easy and for everyone, while the hard and important task is to go beyond faith to speculative knowledge of its content. Thus, "Religion is for everyone. It is not philosophy, which is not for everyone." *Lectures*, 1:180. And "Religion is the mode, the type of consciousness, in which the truth is present for all men, or for all levels of education; but scientific cognition is a particular type of the consciousness of truth, and not everyone, indeed only a few men, undertake the labour of it." *Encyclopedia Logic*, p. 11 (preface to the second edition). What comes prior to the "scientific cognition" is not just "faith" as the vague, immediate certainty without content, but also the feelings and the representations that give it a specific content. In that sense Hegel does seem to say that in Christendom everyone is already a Christian, and the task for the intellectual elite is to go further.

One of the most famous "existentialist" passages in *Postscript* can be read as a commentary on this denial. Climacus says that *"(a) a logical system can be given; (b) but a system of existence [Tilværelsens System] cannot be given"* (*CUP* 1:109). This means that a system, which presupposes totality or completeness, a place for everything and everything in its place, is possible only by abstracting from the actual to the merely possible, and that when one tries to include actuality, including most especially the actuality of the existing individual, a system becomes impossible.

Once again, Climacus asks, For whom? and goes on to answer his own question. "Existence [actuality] is a system — for God, but it cannot be a system for any existing [*existerende*] spirit. System and conclusiveness correspond to each other, but existence is the very opposite" (*CUP* 1:118). Climacus is a Kantian, who thinks that the difference between divine and human knowledge is fundamental for philosophy.[10] The speculative philosopher who takes the system to be the articulation of the identity of thought and being confuses himself[11] with God. This could be thought of as heresy or even idolatry and blasphemy. Climacus prefers to see it as comical. His is the rhetoric of the ridiculous.

Second, Climacus restricts his epistemic/existential focus to what he calls "essential knowing."

> All essential knowing pertains to existence, or only the knowing whose relation to existence is essential is essential knowing. . . . Therefore only ethical and ethical-religious knowledge is essential knowing. But all ethical and all ethical-religious knowing is essentially a relating to the existing of the knower. (*CUP* 1:197-98)

Two terminological clarifications. Unlike Silentio, Climacus does not seek to set off the ethical sharply from the religious and, in doing so, identify the ethical with Hegelian *Sittlichkeit*, the laws and customs of one's people. Insofar as the latter concerns itself only with outward conformity, it belongs to objectivity rather than to subjectivity, which requires inwardness. By contrast with Silentio, Climacus links the ethical closely to the religious as two species of subjectivity in relation to existence. Further, the distinc-

---

10. For Kant the distinction between appearances and things in themselves on the one hand and the distinction between phenomena and noumena on the other is regularly the distinction between human and divine knowledge. This linkage is overlooked in most commentaries. See my essay, "In Defense of the Thing in Itself," *Kant-Studien* 59, no. 1 (1968): 118-41.

11. The gendered language is fitting here since the philosophers in question are men.

tion made here between the ethical and the ethical-religious is probably best understood as that between an ethics that does not presuppose a religious foundation (like that of Aristotle, Kant, Mill, or Levinas, each of which might be appropriated subjectively) and an ethics that has an explicitly theological ground (like Kierkegaard's in *Works of Love*).[12] It is because both the ethical and the ethical-religious signify tasks for the existing individual that 'existence' as a technical term signifies human life in both its temporality and its tasks. Since these are not only tasks in time but the tasks of human time, becoming subjective and becoming a Christian, they will always be unfinished. Climacus will agree with Silentio that faith is the task of a lifetime; but he will add that becoming human is too.

Third, Climacus takes a swipe at mediation. The term signifies Hegel's holism, a relational ontology and the epistemology and ethics that go with it. Everything is either the infinite whole (Nature for Spinoza, Spirit in its historical unfolding for Hegel) — infinite because there is nothing outside or beyond it — or a finite part of this whole. In *Fear and Trembling*, mediation appeared in its ethical mode. The telos and task for the finite individual is to fit into the ethical totality *(Sittlichkeit)* without resistance or remainder (except for idiosyncrasies that are accidental and not of essential significance). In *Postscript* the focus is epistemic. This means that, as mediation, speculative philosophy seeks to identify the place for everything (Nature or Spirit) and to put everything in its place, drawing a map or a schematic portrait of being's family tree or chain of command.

Climacus grants, at least for the sake of argument, that speculative philosophy can have existence, in the nontechnical sense actuality — nature, society, culture, history, and so forth — in its purview. But speculative philosophy fails to ask how the existing subject, who presumably is not simply identical with speculative thought, relates to it (*CUP* 1:198). Is this the telos and highest task for a human person? Are there not ethical and (perhaps) ethical-religious tasks that are not reducible to the ethical as *Sittlichkeit,* social conformity, as spelled out as one place within the system? Are there not epistemic tasks in which faith goes beyond reason as recollection? That, at any rate, is what Christianity requires, and so, for that matter, does the

---

12. Aquinas's distinction between the cardinal virtues and the theological virtues would appear to have some of both the ethical and the ethical-religious. But his theory of natural law, which has a certain autonomy vis-à-vis revelation, is also set in a theological context as a participation in the eternal law of God. It thus differs from the "modern" natural law of Grotius, Hobbes, and Spinoza. See John Milbank, *Theology and Social Theory: Beyond Secular Reason,* 2nd ed. (Malden, MA: Blackwell, 2006), p. 10. So the situation is quite complex.

generic, human subjectivity currently under discussion. This will become especially clear when we come to speak of Socrates.

Fourth and finally, in a brief paragraph Climacus says that the highest inwardness in an existing individual is passion.[13] An important source of passion is the notion of truth as paradox, and "that truth becomes a paradox is grounded precisely in its relation to an existing subject" (*CUP* 1:199). This thought is adumbrated in the previous paragraph and once again anticipates the discussion of Socrates.

But before we get to Socrates we get Climacus's second commentary on the notion of truth as subjectivity, a parable that reformulates Jesus' parable of the two men who went up to the temple to pray, one in humility, the other in self-righteous arrogance (Luke 18:9-14). Climacus sets up his parable by defining objectivity and subjectivity in terms of the what and the how. To ask the question of truth objectively is to ask about the object of belief, what the believer believes. "*What is reflected upon is not the relation but that what he relates himself to is the truth, the true. If only that to which he relates himself to is the truth, the true, then the subject is in the truth.*" But to ask the question subjectively is to ask about the relationship of the believer to what is believed. "*If only the how of this relation is in truth, the individual is in truth, even if he in this way were to relate himself to untruth.*" Then with reference to the question of God, asked in these two ways, Climacus asks, "Now, on which side is the truth?" (*CUP* 1:199).

This sounds like an either/or situation. But when he turns to his parable, he nuances the situation by asking three times on which side there is "more" truth (*CUP* 1:201). In other words, who is worse off, the person with the right objectivity but the wrong subjectivity, or the person with the right subjectivity and the wrong objectivity? The parable goes like this:

> If someone who lives in the midst of Christianity enters, with the knowledge of the true idea of God, the house of God, the house of the true God, and prays, but prays in untruth, and if someone lives in an idolatrous land but prays with all the passion of infinity, although his eyes are resting upon the image of an idol — where, then, is there more truth? The one prays in truth to God although he is worshiping an idol; the other prays in untruth to the true God and is therefore in truth worshiping an idol. (*CUP* 1:201)[14]

---

13. There is an obvious link to Silentio's claim that faith is a passion, indeed the highest passion. See chapter 6 above.

14. Climacus does not need to commit himself personally to the notion that the Chris-

It can seem as if Climacus is saying that it doesn't matter what you believe as long as you are sincere, or as long as you are passionate about it; the what doesn't matter, only the how. But this is wrong for two reasons. First, his analysis of subjectivity is about getting the how right, not about how to find the right what; and second, we have already seen that at least so far as Christian faith is concerned, one must be concerned about both the objective truth of the what and the subjective truth of the how (*CUP* 1:21).

Still, the rhetorical question, Where is there more truth?, has bite, for the apparently intended answer is that there is more truth in the idolater's prayer than in that of the one-sidedly objective, orthodox Christian. The basis for such a claim is not an indifference to the content of one's faith, the *fides quae creditur,* a "different strokes for different folks" type of relativism. It is rather the claim that the idolater's prayer is a truly human prayer, while in this case the Christian's prayer is defective in a way that renders it subhuman. Climacus uses a political metaphor to make the same point. "Although an outsider, I have at least understood this much, that the only unforgivable high treason against Christianity is the single individual's taking *his relation to it* for granted" (*CUP* 1:16; emphasis added). He accuses both the praying Christian in the parable (Christendom) and speculative philosophy with committing this treason.

For his third gloss on the slogan, "Truth Is Subjectivity," Climacus turns from the fictional pagan in the parable to a real pagan he deeply admires, Socrates, "an ideal model for Climacus's conception of *the* human task," already identified as "becoming subjective."[15] So far we have met the madman, the assistant professor, the praying Christian, and the praying pagan. They are firmly convinced of the objective truth of what they believe. They have found the right what, which corresponds to their subjective certainty but is not dependent on or reducible to it. At least nothing Climacus says about them suggests otherwise. It is only with Socrates that we get a living commentary on the opening phrase in the upcoming definition of truth as subjectivity: "an objective uncertainty."

> But Socrates! He poses the question [of immortality] objectively, problematically: if there is an immortality. So, compared with one of the mod-

---

tian God is the true God, nor does he need to try to prove it. He is writing for an audience that is already persuaded of that.

15. Jacob Howland, "Lessing and Socrates in Kierkegaard's *Postscript,*" in Furtak, ed., *Kierkegaard's "Concluding Unscientific Postscript,*" p. 116.

ern thinkers with the three demonstrations, was he a doubter? Not at all. He stakes his whole life on this "if"; he dares to die, and with the passion of the infinite he has so ordered his whole life that it might be acceptable — *if* there is an immortality. (*CUP* 1:201)[16]

In a long footnote Climacus confesses to "a dubiousness in the design of *Fragments*." There he portrayed only an opposition between Socrates, with his doctrine of knowledge as recollection, and Christianity as dependent on divine revelation.[17] Now he sees a "positive relation" between them,[18] insofar as Socrates is a "model" of the subjectivity that is the *sine qua non* of Christianity and, as we shall see, an "analog" of Christian faith. Instead of a simple either/or relation between Socrates and Christianity, as in *Fragments, Postscript* presents "a specific sort of 'both-and' (which nonetheless differs from 'mediation')."[19] This "positive relation" must not compromise Climacus's claim that the difference between the two is "infinite" (*CUP* 1:206n.). So there is both an either/or and a both/and.

How so? Perhaps Climacus is suggesting that Socrates has the wrong epistemology, knowledge as recollection, but the right appreciation of existence, living with objective uncertainty. Hence the either/or and the both/and. Howland puts this suggestion nicely: "If from the perspective of *Postscript* Socrates is wrong about the nature of the truth (which he identifies with philosophically cognizable being) and wrong about our ability to learn the truth on our own, he is nevertheless fundamentally right about the individual's relation to the truth."[20]

But how are we to square this with Climacus's double claim that (a) to attribute the idea that knowledge is recollection to Socrates is to make a speculative philosopher out of him and (b) that Socrates "continually parts with [this doctrine] because he wants to exist" (*CUP* 1:206n.)?

---

16. Socrates was a great inspiration for Kierkegaard. He writes, "I calmly stick to Socrates. True, he was no Christian, that I know, although I also definitely remain convinced that he has become one. . . . Qualitatively two altogether different magnitudes are involved here, but formally I can very well call Socrates my teacher — whereas I have believed in only one, the Lord Jesus Christ" (*PV*, 54-55).

17. At the end of *Fragments* (*PF*, 109-10), Climacus states explicitly, to no one's surprise, that the thought-project he has been developing in the attempt to go beyond Socrates is Christianity.

18. Ferreira, "The 'Socratic Secret,'" p. 7.

19. Ferreira, "The 'Socratic Secret,'" p. 7.

20. Howland, "Lessing and Socrates," p. 115.

Both of these claims are misleading at best. Climacus is surely right to want to distinguish Socrates from Plato. The thoughtful reader of Plato's dialogues will suspect what numerous scholars have suggested, namely that the Socrates of the *Apology* is more or less the historical Socrates, while the Socrates of the *Phaedo* is really a mouthpiece for Plato (except for the courage with which he dies). It is the former for whom that objective uncertainty, "if there is an immortality," is crucial, whereas the latter, like the modern philosophers of whom Climacus speaks, is armed with arguments for immortality and is rightly seen as a speculative philosopher.

But it is misleading for Climacus to say that the Socrates who chooses existence over speculation "parts with" recollection and the immanence it presupposes, or that his failure to do so would render him a speculative philosopher. Socrates has no other theory of knowledge. His references to the god who warns him occasionally what not to do hardly represent a move to revelation as distinct from recollection, and in any case these negative warnings have nothing to do with immortality. What keeps Socrates from being a speculative thinker like Plato (at least on a familiar, traditional reading of dialogues like the *Phaedo*) are several features of his thought that neither express nor require parting company with the epistemology of recollection and its immanence. That there is a generic subjectivity that can exist in paganism means that it is not incompatible with the notion of knowledge as recollection per se. We can see this in several ways.

First of all there is the famous Socratic ignorance. Climacus himself reminds us of this theme (*CUP* 1:202). At his trial Socrates tells of the claim by the oracle at Delphi that no one was wiser than he, Socrates. When Socrates examined those who were thought to be wise, he regularly found them not to be, and he came to this conclusion: "Well, I am certainly wiser than this man. It is only too likely that neither of us has any knowledge to boast of, but he thinks that he knows something that he does not know, whereas I am quite conscious of my ignorance. At any rate it seems that I am wiser than he is to this small extent, that I do not think that I know what I do not know." This is why he can say that his reputation rests on his wisdom. "What kind of wisdom do I mean? Human wisdom, I suppose. It seems that I really am wise in this limited sense. Presumably the geniuses whom I mentioned just now are wise in a wisdom that is more than human."[21] Climacus reminds us of this theme and tells us that this takes Socrates beyond

---

21. *Apology,* 20d-21d. Those he has just mentioned are the sophists who take money for teaching the young.

being merely a "model" of subjectivity. "Socratic ignorance is an expression of the objective uncertainty; [it is] an analogue to the category of the absurd," and, correspondingly, "Socratic inwardness in existing is an analogue to [Christian] faith" (*CUP* 1:205; cf. 566).

The epistemic humility of Socratic ignorance does not require abandoning the theory of recollection. One need only deny that by its means one can reflect oneself out of time and into eternity so as to attain to an absolute, divine knowing. This is what "Socrates" claims in the *Phaedo*. "We are convinced that if we are ever to have pure knowledge of anything, we must get rid of the body and contemplate things by themselves with the soul by itself." Socrates immediately denies that we can do this in our lifetime, when the soul is contaminated with the body, from which we must continually seek to purify it.[22] But later he seems quite optimistic about the possibility of such purification.

> But when [the soul] investigates by itself, it passes into the realm of the pure and everlasting and immortal and changeless, and being of a kindred nature, when it is once independent and free from interference, consorts with it always and strays no longer, but remains in that realm of the absolute, constant and invariable, through contact with beings of a similar nature. And this condition of the soul we call wisdom.[23]

In the light of the later dialogues it might be claimed that Plato never forgot that philosophy is just that, love of wisdom and not yet wisdom itself. But surely the Socrates of the *Apology* needs to be distinguished from the "Socrates" of the *Phaedo*, with his Project Purification and his arguments for immortality, and this is what Climacus does in *Postscript*. Accordingly Climacus can speak of "a Socratic tryst with the god in the idea on the boundless sea of uncertainty" (*CUP* 1:88). As he puts it, once the existing person enters time "he in no way can take himself back into eternity by Socratically recollecting" (*CUP* 1:207-8). The Socrates on the "boundless

22. *Phaedo*, 66dd-67d.

23. *Phaedo*, 79d. This passage nicely anticipates the way Hegel concludes his system by quoting the passage from Aristotle's *Metaphysics* (xii, 7, 1072b, 18-31) in which the identity of thought and being is expressed as thought thinking itself, a contemplative pleasure that God enjoys always and we sometimes, presumably when we are thinking the Logic. *Hegel's Philosophy of Mind*, trans. William Wallace and A. V. Miller (Oxford: Clarendon, 1971), p. 315. Here is a strong claim that reflection, as recollection, can take us out of time and into eternity, the realm of eternal, unchanging truth.

sea of uncertainty" *(Postscript, Apology)* is not the same as the Socrates who by recollection reflects himself out of time and into eternity *(Fragments, Phaedo).*

In the second place, Climacus might have mentioned the Socratic irony here, since it also places a major qualification on the powers of recollection. It supports Socratic ignorance by exposing the unknowing of those who are so sure they know. That is its role in one of the passages just cited, where Socrates ironically suggests that the sophists, who charge for their teaching, must have a "more than human wisdom." Later Climacus relates Socratic irony to the present discussion. He refers to "an ethicist [who] uses irony as his incognito. In this sense Socrates was an ethicist, but, please note, bordering on the religious, which is why the analogy to faith in his life was pointed out earlier" (*CUP* 1:503).

A third theme crucial for understanding Socrates is paradox. In the context of essential knowledge, paradox "is the objective uncertainty that is the expression for the passion of inwardness that is truth." However,

> the eternal essential truth is not at all paradoxical in itself, but only by being related to an existing person. This is expressed in another Socratic thesis: that all knowing is recollecting. This thesis is an intimation of the beginning of speculative thought, but for that very reason Socrates did not pursue it. . . . Socrates essentially emphasizes existing, whereas Plato, forgetting this, loses himself in speculative thought. (*CUP* 1:205)

Because he avoids this forgetting, Socrates is "way beyond speculative thought." Rather, "he acquires, when rightly depicted, a certain analogous likeness to what the imaginary construction set forth [in *Fragments*] as that which truly goes beyond the Socratic: the truth as paradox is an analog to the paradox *sensu eminentiori;* the passion of inwardness in existing is then an analog to faith *sensu eminentiori*" (*CUP* 1:206n.) One already finds faith and paradox in Socrates, and these are analogous to faith and paradox *sensu eminentiori* (in a more eminent or, we might say, dramatic sense) as found in Christianity. Here Climacus seems "to locate Socratic eros just below Christian faith on a continuum of increasing subjective truth, paradox, and passion."[24] But this does not require the abandonment of knowledge as rec-

---

24. Howland, "Lessing and Socrates," p. 127. Cf. *CUP* 1:209: "When the eternal truth relates itself to an existing person, it becomes the paradox. Through the objective uncertainty and ignorance, the paradox thrusts away in the inwardness of the existing person. But since

ollection; paradox, like the antinomies in Kant, only serves as a barrier to the confusion of human with divine knowing. We ourselves are the measure and criterion for what we can know, even if that falls conspicuously short of the pure, presuppositionless, comprehensive knowledge required and claimed by speculative thought.

Whereas Silentio used 'paradox' and 'absurd' interchangeably (along with 'madness'), Climacus seems to be distinguishing them. Paradox can occur in paganism, as Socrates demonstrates. Climacus appreciates the contradiction between time and eternity. Immersed in temporal existence, the individual is essentially related to eternity both in the form of eternal happiness and in the form of eternal truth, changeless, unconditioned, un-contaminated — in short, divine. But this paradox is only an analog of the paradox *sensu eminentiori* and the absurd, which belong to Christian faith. The latter is absurd or doubly and dramatically paradoxical because it not only places the existing individual in the dialectical tension between time and eternity but also "contains the contradiction that something that can become historical only in direct opposition to all human understanding has become historical" (*CUP* 1:211; cf. 210). This is the Christian claim, central to *Fragments,* that in Jesus of Nazareth God has become a human individual. According to Climacus's "doctrine of analogy," the epistemic difference between Socrates and Christianity maintains the either/or of *Fragments,* while the existential similarity between them supplements this with the both/and of *Postscript.* Socrates is essential to Christian faith, neither because he holds that knowledge is recollection, nor because he abandons this view, but because his kind of subjectivity is a necessary condition of that faith.

Climacus introduced the distinction between the what of objectivity and the how of subjectivity for the sake of his parable. But in his discussion of Socrates as a "model" of subjectivity and an "analog" of Christian faith, he continues to use the distinction for purposes of analysis. In doing so he introduces a fourth and fifth theme for illuminating Socratic "faith," namely decision and striving.

From the objective point of view "there is no infinite decision, and thus it is objectively correct that the distinction between good and evil is canceled" (*CUP* 1:203). On the other hand, it is in subjectivity and only there

---

the paradox is not in itself the paradox, it does not thrust away intensely enough. . . . When the paradox itself is the paradox, it thrusts away by virtue of the absurd and the corresponding passion of inwardness is [Christian] faith."

that decision is found. Accordingly, "[t]he passion of the infinite, not its content, is the deciding factor. . . . In this way the subjective 'how' and subjectivity are the truth" (*CUP* 1:203). For Socrates the decision is whether to live his life as if there is an immortality, a personal existence on the other side of death. There are several things to notice here.

First, just as for Silentio faith is a passion, indeed the "highest passion" (see chapter 6 above), so for Climacus, here as in *Fragments,* faith is a matter of passion, a matter of what we care about deeply enough that it is part of our identity.

Second, it is "the passion of the infinite" because its "object" is of absolute or infinite importance, rendering all other concerns relative and finite.

Third, in the context of "objective uncertainty," this passion is related to a decision about who I am and how I should live my life. This decision is "infinite" for the same reason that the passion is infinite. It is of ultimate importance, rendering all others penultimate.

Finally, this passion and this decision presuppose the infinite, absolute, ultimate importance of the distinction between good and evil in contrast to the objectivity in which that distinction is "canceled." This is a reminder of the theory of the stages or existence spheres. We have seen that what sets off the ethical and the religious from the aesthetic is that for the former, but not for the latter, the difference between good and evil is of prime importance.[25] Now, in keeping with the double/quadruple revision of that theory, the suggestion is that, while the ethical and the ethical-religious take that difference seriously, speculative philosophy does not. It is concerned with matters it takes to be more important. Understanding has become an end in itself and as such has rendered merely relative any individual's concern to be doing the truth by doing good and avoiding evil.

In the case of the Hegelian system that is a double relativity. Concern for personal and social responsibility in terms of good and evil is only relatively important compared with the highest human task, available only to the few, of speculative theorizing. Moreover, good and evil, right and wrong are relative to the society in and by which they are acknowledged. We are reminded that *Sittlichkeit,* ethical life, is a matter of the laws and customs of one's own particular, contingent historical society. These are the senses in which good and evil are "canceled." These last six paragraphs about decision are more extensive than the half paragraph Climacus devotes to the theme at this point. But, as we shall see, he has more to say about it elsewhere.

25. See chapter 3 above.

The same is true about the fifth and final dimension of his use of Socrates as a commentary on his definition of faith: striving. We get only a single sentence. "But at the same moment [as the subject faces the infinite decision], the existing person is in the temporal realm, and the subjective 'how' is transformed into a striving that is motivated and repeatedly refreshed by the decisive passion of the infinite, but it is nevertheless a striving" (*CUP* 1:203).

This notion of striving picks up two important themes in *Postscript*. On the one hand, striving signifies strenuous effort. In an autobiographical interlude that Muench nicely assimilates to Socrates' "apology,"[26] Climacus ironically confesses that he lacks the ability of so many systematic writers to make spiritual life ever easier and decides that his calling is "to make difficulties everywhere" (*CUP* 1:186-87; cf. 130, 241, 587, 619). He will eventually say, "My intention is to make it difficult to become a Christian, yet not more difficult than it is" (*CUP* 1:557; cf. 213, 383-84).[27] It is not surprising that, given his dual focus on "becoming subjective" and "becoming a Christian," he sees his task as making difficulties in both cases.

On the other hand, the notion of striving picks up the temporal theme of always being unfinished. Climacus writes, "Only he really has style who is never finished" (*CUP* 1:86).[28] This pungent aphorism is sandwiched between a brief satire and a bit of philosophical anthropology. Here's the satire:

> For most people, life changes when they have come to a certain point in their searching. They marry, they enter occupations, in consequence of which they must out of decency finish something, must have results. . . . So they believe that they themselves actually have arrived. . . . So off and on they also engage in a little striving, but the last is merely a skimpy marginal note to a text finished long ago. (*CUP* 1:85)

26. Muench, "Kierkegaard's Socratic Pseudonym," p. 33. See *CUP* 1:185-88 and 234-43 for Climacus's autobiography.

27. Climacus immediately adds, "and not difficult for the obtuse and easy for the brainy, but qualitatively and essentially difficult for every human being, because, viewed essentially, it is equally difficult for every human being" (*CUP* 1:557-58; cf. 217, 220-21, 227-28, 566). This spiritual egalitarianism runs through *Postscript* as a critique of Hegel's spiritual elitism, "Religion is for everyone. It is not philosophy, which is not for everyone." See note 9 above.

28. This notion is the theme for my essay on Kierkegaard, "Becoming Real — With Style," in *Styles of Piety*, ed. S. Clark Buckner and Matthew Statler (New York: Fordham University Press, 2006), pp. 76-93. From Margery Williams's *The Velveteen Rabbit* it cites the Rabbit's question whether becoming real happens all at once, to which the Skin Horse replies, "You become. It takes a long time."

The philosophical anthropology begins with an observation and moves on to an imperative and then to a (concluding, unscientific) indicative from which the imperative is derived. It notes that "one continually feels an urge to have something finished, but this urge is of evil and must be renounced. The perpetual process of becoming is the uncertainty of earthly life, in which everything is uncertain" (*CUP* 1:86).

Here it is not the frightening faith of Abraham but the mere generic task of becoming subjective that is the always unfinished task of a lifetime (*CUP* 1:73, 81-82, 158, 161-64, 171n., 179, 182, 428, 443-47).

In summary, there are five themes of thought that protect Socrates from falling into speculative thought as found in Plato and Hegel without having to abandon the notion of knowledge as recollection. Severally and collectively they constitute a barrier to any attempt to back out of time into an eternity of pure, presuppositionless, comprehensive knowledge. But, unlike the appeal to divine revelation, they do not challenge the notion that we are the measure and criterion of whatever "knowledge" may be available to our finite, temporal, contaminated capacities.

So we come at last to Climacus's definition of truth as subjectivity. It was stated at the outset in order to suggest that it is the goal toward which (1) the satire on the madman, (2) the parable about the two kinds of prayer, and (3) the tribute to Socrates are rightly seen to be headed and on which they can be read as commentaries. Or better, even if the definition is the telos toward which the other three explanations of truth as subjectivity are headed, we can read all four as commenting on each other. For three themes from Climacus's direct exposition of his definition have already been borrowed in presenting the first three "commentaries": the analogy of Socratic, generic subjectivity to the absurd and to the Christian paradox; Climacus's task as making things more difficult; and the egalitarian character of existential tasks, for which the intellectual elite have no privileged access or advantage. It is time to repeat the definition and notice several commentaries on it that we have not already anticipated. We recall how it goes:

> *An objective uncertainty, held fast through appropriation with the most passionate inwardness, is the truth,* the highest truth there is for an *existing* person. . . . But the definition of truth stated above is a paraphrasing of faith. (*CUP* 1:203-4)

The first implication of this definition that Climacus gives us is quite simple: "Without risk, no faith. Faith is the contradiction between the infinite passion of inwardness and the objective uncertainty" (*CUP* 1:204). He immediately gives us one of his two favorite metaphors for faith in the midst of objective uncertainty.[29] It is like being "out on 70,000 fathoms of water" (*CUP* 1:204). My cognitive feet can touch no *terra firma*. No foundationalist epistemology, nor any other kind for that matter, can guide whatever subjective certainty I may have to a ground where it becomes objective certainty.

An example of the difference between subjective and objective certainty may be helpful. I am sure that my wife loves me; I do not doubt it in the slightest; I am subjectively certain that this is true. But it is objectively uncertain, and I may be mistaken, just as people were subjectively certain that the earth is flat, though it was objectively uncertain all along and, in fact, false. It is possible that my wife was persuaded to devote her life to science and that our marriage has been a long experiment in which she has pretended to love me in order to test some hypothesis or other. Or perhaps, in the last couple of years, unnoticed by me, she has "lost the joy" and no longer really cares about me. However improbable these logical possibilities may be, and however much evidence can be mustered against them, it remains the case that my belief is objectively uncertain. According to a familiar empiricism, this is true of all matters of fact. According to Climacus, it is true *a fortiori* when the Socratic paradox of eternal truth in relation to a temporally existing individual is involved; and it is true *in sensu eminentiori* when the Christian paradox is involved.

The implication is that speculative philosophy, flying the flags of science and autonomy, is an illegitimate attempt to supplant the objective uncertainty of temporal finitude with a risk-free ascent to eternity by means of eternal truth.[30] But Climacus insists that human existence is temporal and asks about the temporal character of such an ascent. It cannot be a movement forward, since the future is uncertain, a fact we are reminded of with Socrates' "if there is an immortality." So it must be a movement backward as suggested by the language of recollection. "If even Socrates comprehended the dubiousness of taking himself speculatively out of existence back into eternity, when there was no dubiousness for the existing person except that he existed . . . now [in relation to the Christian paradox] it is impossible. He must go forward; to go backward is impossible" (*CUP* 1:208-9). For the existing individual, "the eternal, essential truth is not behind him but has

29. The other is the metaphor of the leap. It will be discussed in the next chapter.
30. Both Plato and Hegel use the language of ascent when talking about philosophy.

come in front of him. . . . The fraud of speculative thought in wanting to recollect itself out of existence has been made impossible" (*CUP* 1:209).

Climacus seems to be implying two things. First, in temporal existence "we walk by faith, not by sight" (2 Cor. 5:7). This faith can be cashed in as sight only in eternity, only in the life to come. Perhaps the notion of eschatological verification is at work here, and speculation is the impatient insistence on having in time what is available only in eternity.

But there is also the implication that speculative philosophy walks by faith and not by sight, however much it seeks to hide this fact from itself. For, given our temporal finitude and our not now being present at the parousia or denouement, both speculative philosophy itself and the claim that it is our highest task are objectively uncertain. Insofar as the speculative philosopher's existential complacency is an appropriation of this "truth," even if it is without passionate inwardness, Plato is a Platonist and Hegel is an Hegelian by means of an act of faith.

Appealing to the Delphic oracle, we might say that Socrates and the authentic Christian are wiser than the speculative philosophers such as Plato and Hegel[31] because, while they all live by faith and not by sight, the former pair acknowledges this and the latter pair does not.

Just for this reason speculative thought wants to come to the aid of Christianity and explain it in such a way as to make it conform to reason. But, Climacus objects, Christianity has presented itself as *the paradox,* as "an absurdity to the understanding," as "a stumbling block to Jews and foolishness to Gentiles" (1 Cor. 1:23).

> Suppose that Christianity was and wants to be a mystery, not a theatrical mystery that is revealed in the fifth act [the point in history when speculative thinking comes to fruition in the system]. . . . Suppose that a revelation *sensu strictissimo* [in the strictest sense] must be a mystery and be recognizable just by its being a mystery, whereas a revelation *sensu laxiori* [in the broader sense], the withdrawing into the eternal through recollection, is a revelation in the direct sense. (*CUP* 1:213)[32]

---

31. Or any other intellectual who thinks that "science" of some sort provides an objective basis for existence that is rationally superior to religious faith.

32. Climacus is referring to his notion that authentic existential communication, which takes into account the subjectivity of the how and not only the objectivity of the what, can only take place indirectly. It cannot be simply the presentation of propositions for the reader's assent. See the discussion in the next chapter. *Laxus* means both wide or spacious and loose or lax. In the present context the latter sense seems more fitting. The idea of a revelation *sensu*

In all of these ways Climacus distinguishes both Socratic, generic subjectivity and Christian, specific subjectivity from the objective posture of speculative thinking that forgets what it is to exist. But he does not take himself to be arguing for the truth of Christian beliefs or the rightness of Christian practices. He remains an outsider. He doesn't try to decide, much less argue, that Christianity is true (*CUP* 1:222, 224, 273, 369, 379, 619). He thinks that Christianity may be true (*CUP* 1:231-32, 234). "But if Christianity is perhaps in the wrong, this much is certain: speculative thought is definitely in the wrong, because the only consistency outside Christianity is that of pantheism, the taking of oneself out of existence back into the eternal through recollection" (*CUP* 1:226; cf. 271n., 361).

We remember the frame of *Fragments*. First there is the motto, "Better well hanged than ill wed." Then there is the Moral with which he concludes: "This project indisputably goes beyond the Socratic, as is apparent at every point. Whether it is therefore more true than the Socratic is an altogether different question, one that cannot be decided in the same breath, inasmuch as a new organ has been assumed here: faith" (*PF*, 111). In that context, where he does not distinguish Socrates from Plato, the Socratic signifies the recollection doctrine in its speculative, Platonic form, without the Socratic qualifications presented in *Postscript*. Socratic/Platonic philosophy in that sense must be sharply distinguished from Christianity. Here he tells us the same thing.[33] He is not trying to make the case for Christianity but for subjectivity. To that end he thinks it crucial to distinguish authentic Christianity, whatever one makes of it, both from speculative philosophy and from the non-academic Christianity of a Christendom that has also forgotten what it means to exist.[34]

---

laxiori takes note of the fact that Hegel speaks of Christianity as the revealed religion. But this doesn't mean a departure from recollection toward revelation in Climacus's sense. It rather means that the mystery is revealed and ceases to be mysterious. See Hegel, *Lectures on the Philosophy of Religion*, 3:422-25, 489, and *Phenomenology of Spirit*, trans. A. V. Miller (Oxford: Clarendon, 1977), pp. 453-78.

33. For this reading of the main point in Climacus and Silentio, see my essay "Johannes and Johannes: Kierkegaard and Difference," in *International Kierkegaard Commentary*, vol. 7: *"Philosophical Fragments" and "Johannes Climacus,"* ed. Robert L. Perkins (Macon, GA: Mercer University Press, 1994), pp. 13-32.

34. This reading of Climacus's purpose refutes the widespread view that a skeptical epistemology is the main point of *Postscript*. Thomas C. Anderson cites several examples. See his "Kierkegaard and Approximation Knowledge," in *International Kierkegaard Commentary*, vol. 12: *Concluding Unscientific Postscript to "Philosophical Fragments,"* ed. Robert L. Perkins (Macon, GA: Mercer University Press, 1997), p. 187.

CHAPTER 10

Faith as a Leap and a Striving

The definition of faith in terms of truth as subjectivity has been asked to serve as the focus for gathering and organizing what is most important for our purpose in the massive text that is the *Postscript*. So let us look for further insight into the meaning of "objective uncertainty." Climacus's discussion of objectivity is, as already noted, very short relative to the space devoted to subjectivity. Climacus discusses two modes of knowing, "the historical point of view" (*CUP* 1:23-49) and "the speculative point of view" (*CUP* 1:50-57).[1]

It is not as a general epistemologist that he chooses these two. As we have seen, he is interested in "essential knowing," the kind that "pertains to existence. . . . Therefore only ethical and ethical-religious knowledge is essential knowing" (*CUP* 1:197-98). He is concerned that, if historical knowing and speculative knowing are confused with Christian faith, the latter will cease to be either faith (as generic subjectivity) or Christian (as specific subjectivity). On the one hand, *"appropriation with the most passionate inwardness"* (*CUP* 1:203) falls by the wayside with the assumption that what really matters is having the right what, the objective truth. On the other hand, one loses sight of the risk involved in grounding one's temporal identity and eternal destiny on something like the Socratic "if" (see chapter 9). So, before his expansive argument for the importance of subjectivity, Climacus speaks briefly about objective uncertainty.

---

1. The fact that Climacus calls these "points of view" is not innocent. It suggests a hermeneutical, well, point of view, according to which all knowing is perspectival and, as such, essentially incomplete.

183

If "appropriation" is the key to subjectivity, "approximation" summarizes what Climacus has to say about historical knowing. This is because it is never finished (*CUP* 1:26, 43). If we think of historical events such as the French Revolution or the American Civil War or the biographies of Cleopatra or Queen Elizabeth I, we see that of the making of historical accounts there is no end; and we see why. New data may emerge; important sources may be shown to be either more or less reliable than previously assumed; new angles of approach may bring either additions to or revisions of previous accounts — or both.

Moreover, we may have to suspend judgment on important questions simply for lack of evidence. Were Anne Boleyn and the five men executed with her guilty of adultery and, in that case, of treason? Modern historians are inclined to think not, but the evidence is not decisive. One of the men confessed — under torture. What are we to make of that? The same can be said for the claim that Richard III killed the princes in the tower who would have posed a threat to his kingship. The jury is still out. Even if a jury of historians tells us that a particular conclusion is beyond reasonable doubt, that verdict may be subsequently overturned for any of several reasons. Apparently no one doubted for centuries that the writings now attributed to Pseudo-Dionysius were written by a contemporary of the apostle Paul. Now that that view has been abandoned, it remains unclear just who the author was, when he (or she?) wrote, and whether he (or she?) was orthodox or heretical. Similarly, it remains an open question who wrote the Epistle to the Hebrews. To speak of approximation is to speak of degrees of certainty, all of which fall short of absolute certainty. For that reason we can speak of objective uncertainty even when we are very sure.

Climacus assumes that the incarnation presents itself as a historical event (hence "the god in time," as he puts it in *Fragments*) that took place during the time of King Herod of Judea, when Augustus was the emperor of Rome and Quirinius the governor of Syria (Matt. 2:1; Luke 2:1-2; cf. Luke 3:1 for further historical reference points). Accordingly, certain historical beliefs about what Jesus did and said and suffered are part of the what of Christian faith. As such they are objectively uncertain. As historical "facts," they obey the logic of historical knowing and remain objectively uncertain. It has even been seriously argued that Jesus of Nazareth did not even exist, in which case, presumably, he would not qualify as God incarnate. Even if this is wildly improbable, it is not logically impossible. Christianity would surely be a greater hoax than, say, the Donation of Constantine or Piltdown man, but such is the nature of historical evidence that it cannot be absolutely precluded. To revert to the jury metaphor, we know that juries can agree that a fact or set of facts has been established "beyond a reasonable doubt." But we also know, especially with the help of DNA, that juries can be wrong and that they cannot reasonably claim that a certain fact or set of facts has been established beyond any possibility of error. Their verdicts remain objectively uncertain even when we remain subjectively certain and are without actual doubts.

But, anticipating Lessing, whom he will shortly discuss, Climacus asks us to consider how it might be if, *per impossible,* we had something like objective certainty about Jesus based on the Bible as our source of historical knowledge. "I assume, then, that with regard to the Bible there has been a successful demonstration of whatever any theological scholar in his happiest moment could ever have wished to demonstrate about the Bible" (*CUP* 1:28). Then he poses the question, "what then? Has the person who did not believe come a single step closer to faith? No, not a single step. Faith does not result from straightforward scholarly deliberation, nor does it come directly; on the contrary, in this objectivity one loses that infinite, personal, impassioned interestedness, which is the condition of faith" (*CUP* 1:29).

But perhaps the person who already believed will have a stronger faith? No, for that individual "much fear and trembling will be needed lest he fall into temptation and confuse knowledge with faith. Whereas up to now faith has been a beneficial taskmaster in uncertainty, it would have its worst enemy in this certainty" (*CUP* 1:29). Climacus reminds us that he has said this before. "What has been intimated here has been emphasized in *Fragments* frequently enough, namely, that there is no direct and immediate transition to Christianity" (*CUP* 1:49). Chapters four and five of *Fragments* are a sustained argument that the historical knowledge of Jesus available to anyone, from eyewitness contemporaries to those who have centuries to observe the impact of Christianity in the world, is one thing; faith is another.

We know that Climacus will tell us that, when it comes to faith, the what by itself, no matter how firmly established or how firmly believed, is not enough; and we know that the how that is needed will be a matter of passionate appropriation. Here, in making that latter point, he introduces an important consequence of the scary juxtaposition of approximation with appropriation. It is not just a matter of risk; it is also a matter of decision. "As soon as subjectivity is taken away, and passion from subjectivity, and infinite interest from passion, there is no decision whatever. . . . All decision, all essential decision, is rooted in subjectivity. At no point does an observer (and that is what the objective subject is) have an infinite need for a decision" (*CUP* 1:33; cf. 21, 27, 34). To the degree that we define ourselves in terms of objectivity, we take ourselves to be intellect. To the degree that we define ourselves in terms of subjectivity as well (for Climacus never proposes subjectivity *instead of* objectivity), we take ourselves to be will as well as intellect.[2]

We might say that Climacus sides with Kant (against Aristotle) in giving priority to practical reason, which issues in action, over theoretical reason, which does not. If we think of will in terms of commitment and resolve,[3] we can recall his suggestion that the pagan who prays with commitment and resolve to a false god is better off than the Christian who prays to the true God without commitment and resolve in complacent, absentminded orthodoxy.

At the outset of his discussion of truth as subjectivity, Climacus returns to the theme of approximation and thus to further reflection on objective uncertainty. This time approximation is not restricted to historical knowledge but applies to empirical knowledge generally.[4] He asks the classical epistemological question: What are the nature and limits of human knowledge? He makes three suggestions about the nature of empirical knowledge.

First, it is temporal. Both the "object" and the subject are in time, "in the process of becoming" (*CUP* 1:189).

Second, it lacks the unconditioned starting point that foundationalist models of knowing require. The careful reader might immediately object that his primary target is Hegel, and Hegel rejects foundationalist models in favor of a holistic model. Every starting point is revised as it is *aufgehoben* (recontextualized, perhaps) in ever more inclusive contexts or horizons of

2. For the sense of will that is relevant here, see John Davenport, *Will as Commitment and Resolve: An Existential Account of Creativity, Love, Virtue, and Happiness* (New York: Fordham University Press, 2007). Although he does not discuss Kierkegaard in great detail here, Davenport is a widely read Kierkegaard scholar and operates within Kierkegaardian horizons. His reference to commitment and resolve can help us not to take Climacus's talk of decision to have overtones of (Sartrean) arbitrariness, as if deciding to become a Christian were like deciding to wear this shirt rather than that one today.

3. See previous note. Of course, Climacus will not speak of subjectivity as practical *reason* because he wants to stress the difference between recollection and revelation. Faith will embody a certain (putative) knowledge, but it will not be reason. Climacus has ceded that term to the recollection theory in all its modes.

4. By empirical knowledge Climacus seems to mean what falls between the formal, static knowledge of logic and mathematics and the metaphysical knowledge of such (putative) realities as God, freedom, and immortality, as Kant would put it. It surely includes historical knowledge.

which it is but a part and not a self-sufficient whole. Only the one, complete whole is, ontologically, true being. This is Hegel's *ens realissimum*, the most real or the truly real being. Since it is the Whole and not the Creator, Hegel can say that "thinking, or the spirit, has to place itself at the standpoint of Spinozism. This idea of Spinoza's must be acknowledged to be true and well-grounded. There is an absolute substance, and it is what is true. But it is not yet the whole truth, for substance must also be thought of as inwardly active and alive, and in that way must determine itself as spirit."[5] Corresponding to this ontological holism is an epistemic holism. Only when we have the whole story do we have the truth. So an attack on foundationalist epistemologies misses Climacus's intended target.

But he has already anticipated this objection. So he writes, "Thus [empirical] truth is an approximation whose beginning cannot be established absolutely, because there is no conclusion that has retroactive power" (*CUP* 1:189). That is the Hegelian claim: the beginning is given a firm foundation, not at the beginning by virtue of its own isolated, atomic character, but at the end by its relation to the whole and all its other parts. But if no beginning is absolute by being self-evident or self-justifying, and no ending can be absolute since both subject and object are in time and the story isn't over, then "every beginning, when it is *made* . . . does not occur by virtue of immanental thinking but is *made* by virtue of a resolution, essentially by virtue of faith" (*CUP* 1:189).

Here again we have that generic notion of faith that not only is not Christian faith but is not even religious faith. Here again we also have the notion that decision (resolution) plays a role in cognition. Taking historical knowledge as our example, we can note that the historian decides to study this event rather than that, to ask these questions rather than those, to consult these sources rather than those, and to consider the work finished (ready for publication) rather than needing further work. The result

---

5. Georg Wilhelm Friedrich Hegel, *Lectures on the History of Philosophy: The Lectures of 1825-1826*, vol. 3: *Medieval and Modern Philosophy*, trans. R. F. Brown, J. M. Steward, and H. S. Harris (Berkeley: University of California Press, 1990), p. 154. In the *Phenomenology*, just after insisting that Substance be understood as self-developing Subject and thus as Spirit, Hegel writes, "The True is the whole. But the whole is nothing other than the essence consummating itself through its development. Of the Absolute it must be said that it is essentially a *result*, that only in the *end* is it what it truly is; and that precisely in this consists its nature, viz., to be actual subject, the spontaneous becoming of itself." *Phenomenology of Spirit*, trans. A. V. Miller (Oxford: Clarendon Press, 1977), pp. 9-11. The examples Hegel gives are organic, not personal: the acorn becoming a tree or an infant becoming an adult; see pp. 6-7.

is relative to these and other decisions and is never the whole story; it is but an approximation. Some narratives may be better than others, but none is ever the whole story. According to Thomas Anderson, Climacus thinks empirical knowledge is arbitrary "because it is the knower who *decides* the 'limits' of his or her investigation of any empirical data."[6] But this is a mistake. What Climacus writes is this: "every beginning, when it is *made* (if it is not arbitrariness by not being conscious of this) . . ." (*CUP* 1:189). What makes a made or chosen beginning arbitrary is not that it is made but that the maker forgets the making and says, in effect, Who? Me? What did I have to do with it?

The third mark of empirical knowledge in the passage before us is its abstractness. Following Hegel, Climacus does not think of abstractness in terms of the difference between instance and kind, for example, between this horse and horseness.[7] To abstract is rather to take the part in isolation from the whole that is its ground and from which it derives its full meaning. If we take the term 'being' abstractly in terms of such isolated facts as "the earth is round" or "Copenhagen is in Denmark," then "nothing stands in the way of abstractly defining truth as something finished" (*CUP* 1:190). But the identity of thinking and being, or the correspondence between them in such cases, is a tautology; "that is, thinking and being signify one and the same, and the agreement [correspondence] spoken of is only an abstract identity with itself" (*CUP* 1:190). In other words, the being in question is the being that is produced by thinking in the process of abstracting parts from the whole and atomizing them (treating them as isolated atoms).[8] It is all too easy for such being to correspond to the thinking that has defined it.

Hegel has no quarrel with giving an empirical realist account of our beliefs about the shape of the earth and the location of Denmark. 'Copenhagen is in Denmark' is true just because Copenhagen is in Denmark. But just as Kant is an empirical realist and a transcendental idealist, denying that at

6. Thomas C. Anderson, "Kierkegaard and Approximate Knowledge," in *International Kierkegaard Commentary*, vol. 12: *Concluding Unscientific Postscript to "Philosophical Fragments,"* ed. Robert L. Perkins (Macon, GA: Mercer University Press, 1997), p. 189.

7. It would be misleading to speak of particular and universal here because Hegel often uses the latter term to signify the whole. This would be a concrete universal as distinct from an abstract universal such as horseness. The examples here are those of Anderson in his attempt to show that Hegel is an empirical realist ("Kierkegaard and Approximate Knowledge," p. 191).

8. Of course, in physics atoms are anything but atomic. They are what they are and they do what they do only as part of the field of forces in which they find themselves.

the former level (where common sense and the sciences operate) we know things as they really are (the thing in itself, noumenal reality), so Hegel is an empirical realist and an absolute idealist, denying that at the former level we know things as they really are.[9]

But unlike Kant, Hegel claims that in speculative philosophy we can know the thing in itself, things as they really are, without "cheating" by abstracting. His holism involves the claim that the system enables us to see things concretely and as a whole. To see concretely here means to practice a thoroughly relational ontology and the corresponding relational epistemology. This means understanding every finite reality (whether a physical object, a social practice, a historical event or epoch, or whatever) in its immediate context and eventually in the one all-inclusive context that Spinoza was trying to express with his metaphysics of the One Substance that he called *Deus sive natura* (God or nature). Hegel might well have called his Whole *Gott oder Geschichte* (God or history).

This does not mean that speculative philosophy pretends to know all of empirical reality in its particular detail. A certain Herr Krug, reading Hegel rather clumsily, challenged him to show how the system could provide a deduction of his (Herr Krug's) pen. In a sarcastic reply worthy of Climacus, Hegel dismisses this as a "naïve," that is, careless or superficial reading.[10] It is not the task of philosophy to discover whether Herr Krug has a pen and, if so, what color it is and whether it leaks. Philosophy teaches us that if we would understand Herr Krug's pen as it really is we must triply contextualize it: in the system of categories spelled out by the Logic; in the order of nature articulated by the Philosophy of Nature; and in the human world of society, culture, and history presented by the Philosophy of Spirit.

The system gives us a picture of the whole that is the context of all contexts, the horizon of all horizons. It is abstract in the sense that its account of, say, the family does not include anything particular about the Westphal family; its account of civil society does not include anything about the South African economy; and its account of the state does not include anything

9. For the very important way in which Hegel distinguishes his "absolute" idealism from Kant's "subjective" idealism, see G. W. F. Hegel, *The Encyclopedia Logic*, trans. T. F. Geraets, W. A. Suchting, and H. S. Harris (Indianapolis: Hackett, 1991), §45, addition.

10. See Hegel's *Philosophy of Nature*, trans. A. V. Miller (Oxford: Clarendon, 1970), note to Remark on §250. Cf. "Wie der gemeine Menschenverstand die Philosophie nehme, — dargestellt an den Werken des Herrn Krug's," in Hegel's *Gesammelte Werke*, vol. 4: *Jenaer Kritische Schriften,* ed. Hartmut Buchner and Otto Pöggeler (Hamburg: Felix Meiner Verlag, 1968), pp. 174-87.

about the Chinese state. But it is not abstract in the sense of suggesting that we can know things as they really are by treating them as isolated atoms.

So how are we to understand Climacus's description of human knowledge as abstract? He writes,

> As soon as the being of truth becomes empirically concrete, truth itself is in the process of becoming and is indeed in turn, by intimation, the agreement between thinking and being, and is indeed actually this way for God, but it is not that way for any existing spirit, because this spirit, itself existing, is in the process of becoming. (*CUP* 1:190)[11]

We could read this as a variation of Herr Krug's position. He might say something like this: "As soon as we turn to finite particulars as such the system can never be finished and the correspondence of thought to being that it proclaims evaporates. Only God could have such infinite, absolute knowledge." But since Hegel never claims to have such infinite omniscience, the critique would completely miss its target, as Herr Krug's did.

A more charitable reading of Climacus and, by implication, Hegel would focus on the theme of becoming. Hegel doesn't think of nature as a whole in terms of becoming, as we are more likely to today in the aftermath of Darwin and the current global warming crisis. But his Philosophy of Spirit in all its dimensions is thoroughly historical, and he even treats Logic as a historical discipline.[12]

So the question whether the system can be finished and thereby express the whole in the mode appropriate to it is the question whether history has completed its unfolding and has become the context of contexts that will not be *aufgehoben* in a larger whole that brings the story to its conclusion. Does history have meaning? Is it a tragedy or a comedy? Or perhaps, in Macbeth's words, a "tale told by an idiot, full of sound and fury, signifying nothing"?[13] Does it end with the heat death of the universe? Or with the heat death of the human race (through global warming or nuclear warfare)? Or with the new Jerusalem as part of a new heaven and a new earth (Rev. 21:1-4)? Only within the horizon of history's completion could we know things as they really are, could thought and being correspond. Climacus's

---

11. Cf. the discussion in chapter 9, above, of *CUP* 1:118, where reality is a system, but only for God.

12. *Hegel's Science of Logic*, trans. A. V. Miller (London: George Allen & Unwin, 1969), pp. 25-26, 42, 51-52.

13. *Macbeth*, V.v.26-28.

claim that only God can have this knowledge is not a claim about God's omniscience of particulars; rather, it is the claim that only God can see anything real *sub specie aeterni*,[14] not from somewhere in the midst of historical time but with a view of history in its totality and finality.

We are considering Climacus as an epistemologist and asking what he has to say about the nature and limits of human knowledge under the rubric of "approximation." We have noted three theses about the nature of empirical knowledge: it is temporal; it lacks the kind of absolute starting point that foundationalist models require (a lack that cannot be made good by Hegel's holist alternative); and it is abstract in the Hegelian sense of isolating "objects" of understanding from the contexts, especially historical contexts, that are essential to their being and their intelligibility.

We can consider the second and third of these as corollaries to the first, for a close look will show that they are expansions on the notion that both the knower and the known are within time, in a process of becoming. Neither is finished. We might express this whole package as the claim that human knowledge is perspectival, viewing a changing reality from somewhere within the flow of historical as well as personal time.[15] So it turns out that

---

14. This Latin term, more usually *sub specie aeternitatis*, means under the aspect of eternity or from the standpoint of eternity. It is fundamental to Spinoza's *Ethics*, where he writes, "It is the nature of reason to perceive things in the light of eternity *(sub quadam specie aeternitatis)*" (Part II, Proposition 44, Corollary 2). This is a corollary to the claim that reason sees things as necessary rather than contingent. Climacus often uses his version of the phrase to signify the spurious claim of the system to have recollected itself, in effect, out of time and into eternity. See *CUP* 1:81, 192, 217, 227, 301, 305-9, 329, 362, 553. Jon Stewart writes, "Climacus uses this phrase several times to describe the aperspectival or absolute perspective of systematic philosophy, which casts its view over all of world history." He suggests that Kierkegaard's more immediate reference is to Martensen. This may well be true, but it doesn't lessen the appropriateness of using the phrase in the interpretation of Hegel himself. See Stewart, *Kierkegaard's Relations to Hegel Reconsidered* (New York: Cambridge University Press, 2003), p. 460; cf. p. 511.

15. This puts Climacus in the company of Nietzsche and Gadamer, among others. As different as their agendas may be, all three spell out the finitude of human knowing in terms of its perspectival limitations. Thomas Nagel puts it this way: "[the problem is] how to combine the perspective of a particular person inside the world with an objective view of that same world, the person and his viewpoint included. It is a problem that faces every creature with the impulse and the capacity to transcend its particular point of view and to conceive of the world as a whole." *The View from Nowhere* (New York: Oxford University Press, 1986), p. 3. Climacus would agree that we have the impulse to do this and the capacity to transcend our viewpoint by supplementing it with the views of others. But he denies that we can succeed in conceiving of the world as a whole.

the threefold account of the nature of empirical knowledge is at once the account of its limitations. It is finite in that it always occupies a particular point of view that enables the subject to see some things while being blind to others. It can never grasp the whole, not because there are many particulars, like Herr Krug's pen, of which it is unaware, but because the horizon within which it interprets those particulars it does encounter is itself a particular perspective and not a universal, all-inclusive horizon. So meaning remains indeterminate and truth remains penultimate.[16]

This means that it would not be helpful to apply the terms 'fallibilism' or 'critical realism' to Climacus's view. These terms usually suggest a quantitative analysis. Sometimes we get it right, and sometimes we get it wrong. But when we get it right, our beliefs fulfill the classical definition of truth as adequation or correspondence between the intellect and its "objects." We know things as they really are; we apprehend what Kant calls the thing in itself *(Ding an sich)*. But on Climacus's view, this is never the case. At the most basic level, he sides with Kant against Hegel, who finds it necessary to deny Kant's claim that we cannot know things as they really are.[17] Climacus is a Hegelian holist for whom to know things as they really are is to know them in their ultimate context. But he draws a "Kantian" conclusion from Hegel's historicism. Since spirit, the subject of all our knowledge and the object of our highest knowledge, is historical and thoroughly immersed in time, there is always something unfinished, finite, and perspectively limited about our knowledge.

We might call such a view 'qualitative fallibilism,' since it suggests that always and not just sometimes our knowledge falls short of the ideal that common sense takes for granted and that "modern" philosophy (going back to Plato) tries to establish. But the quantitative connotations of the term 'fallibilism' are so strong that using the term 'qualitative' may not overcome them. We might do better with 'approximation.' It allows us to hold two

16. But, of course, not entirely indeterminate. Hans-Georg Gadamer expresses this by saying that our "fore-projections" (presuppositions, a priori anticipations) are always open to either "revision" or "replacement." *Truth and Method,* 2nd rev. ed., trans. Joel Weinsheimer and Donald G. Marshall (New York: Crossroad, 1989 and 2004), pp. 267 (1989) and 269-70 (2004). This, I believe, is the sense in which Climacus says our knowledge is "unfinished."

17. For Hegel's attempt to refute Kant on this point, see *The Encyclopedia Logic,* §§40-52. Kant's claim is not just that metaphysics in its traditional sense is not possible, but that the "objective knowledge" we have in common sense and science fails to pass the adequation-correspondence test. This is what it means to say that his empirical realism is qualified by or *aufgehoben* in his transcendental idealism.

views that Climacus has no desire to refute, namely (1) that not all beliefs are equally warranted, since some perspectives are more illuminating than others,[18] and (2) that, for all practical purposes, we can treat the results of our best approximations as knowledge, even if strictly speaking they fall short of meeting the criterion. Just as some curves approach the x and/or y axis asymptotically but are never fully tangent with either, so our quest for knowledge is the quest for beliefs that come closer than others to the truth in the fullest sense.

Thomas Anderson offers an analysis of Climacus on approximation that I find misleading by being only partially true. He sets out to refute interpretations of "Kierkegaard," usually meaning Climacus, that see him as a skeptic. Surely Anderson is right if by skepticism is meant the view that we can know "nothing," that "every belief and every truth claim about reality have no cognitive warrant."[19] But he sets up a false either/or between skepticism and "classical" or "empirical" realism. Since we are talking epistemology here, we need to note that realism is not merely the claim that the real is and is what it is independently of what we may think about it, but the further claim that we can know it as it really is. At least some of our beliefs correspond to or perfectly mirror the real.[20]

The problem with this either/or is that it fails to take into account a third, more complex possibility. It begins by conceding that there are domains of belief for which such an empirical realism is an appropriate analysis, at least for practical purposes. 'The earth is round' and 'Copenhagen is in Denmark' would be good examples. But this view goes on to insist that this "knowledge" and this "truth" must be qualified by and subordinated to (*aufgehoben* in) a transcendental idealism that shows how, strictly speaking, they fail to correspond to the real. Kant and Hegel and Climacus (as I see him) hold to such a third, dialectical view. 'Transcendental' here signi-

---

18. Hans-Georg Gadamer is thinking along these lines when, in his hermeneutical version of a perspectival theory of knowledge, he speaks of "legitimate" or "enabling" prejudices and especially when he speaks of "true" and "false" prejudices. *Truth and Method,* pp. 277, 295, and 298-99 (1989) or 278, 295, and 298 (2004). We are never so "objective" as to be free from perspectival pre-judice (prejudgment, a priori assumptions), but some prejudices help us to understand, while others lead to misunderstanding.

19. Anderson, "Kierkegaard and Approximate Knowledge," p. 187.

20. The central argument of Richard Rorty in *Philosophy and the Mirror of Nature* (Princeton: Princeton University Press, 1979) is that analytic philosophy in the twentieth century ended up undermining this kind of realism. He opts for a hermeneutical view that echoes, as it were, Climacus's "response" to Nagel. See note 15 above.

fies a reference to the a priori conditions for our judgments or beliefs, what hermeneutical theory refers to as presuppositions or prejudices ("true" or "false").[21] The 'idealism' signifies the decisive role played by "subjective" elements in our knowledge, the way in which the presuppositions that are brought to any encounter with the real co-determine, with the real, the beliefs or judgments that result.[22] For Climacus these a priori elements are what are always vulnerable to "revision" or "replacement" and are thus, in his language, "unfinished."[23]

Anderson denies that for Climacus approximation means that we can, "at best, approach but never achieve truth about empirical reality"; he affirms that the perspectival character of knowledge "does not render it unable to truly grasp reality"; and he denies that the falsifiable character of empirical knowledge means that it "cannot be true."[24] Climacus has no problem granting that approximation, perspective, and falsifiability are compatible with a certain empirical realism that attributes "truth" and "knowledge" to our beliefs about the shape of the earth and the location of Copenhagen.

What Anderson fails to note is that, like Kant and Hegel before him, Climacus raises the question of the status, the alleged ultimacy of this realism. Kant and Hegel agree that metaphysics does not fit into this scheme and that either it is impossible (Kant) or we need, and can have, a very different kind of knowing, along with a very different account of knowing (Hegel). In other words, the knowledge analyzed by empirical realism is not knowledge in the deepest sense, nor does it give us truth in its highest form. Climacus makes two rather different points, one of which qualifies the sense in which empirically realistic knowledge gives us knowledge, while the other qualifies the sense in which it gives us truth.

The first of these comes in the discussion of "objective uncertainty" that is our current theme. Climacus wants to argue that the historical knowledge

21. See note 18 above.

22. Kant develops the dialectic of empirical realism and transcendental idealism in the Transcendental Aesthetic of the *Critique of Pure Reason*. See A 26-28, 35-36 = B 42-44, 51-52. But of course it applies just as much to the categories of understanding (Transcendental Analytic) as it does to space and time as the forms of intuition.

23. This is why he is closer to Gadamer and contemporary hermeneutical theory than to either Kant or Hegel. See note 15 above. Kant and Hegel think that philosophy can articulate categories or a priori forms of thought that are not, in this sense, unfinished, though Hegel thinks they only become fully manifest through historical development. See the text at note 12 above.

24. Anderson, "Kierkegaard and Approximate Knowledge," pp. 188, 193. This last point expresses what I have called "quantitative fallibilism."

that is the propositional content of Christian faith is objectively uncertain in a more radical sense than the fallibilism of Anderson's realism allows. It is not merely falsifiable in terms of possible new data; it is permanently and essentially uncertain because of the way Hegelian holism qualifies the realism of 'Napoleon lost the battle of Waterloo' and 'Jesus of Nazareth suffered under Pontius Pilate.' Because of the penultimate character of the paradigms within which we seek to discover the "facts" about Napoleon or Jesus, the meaning and thus the truth about them remains unfinished. Historical knowledge does not consist in sentences like those just given, but in interpretations about the causes, the consequences, and the importance of the events in question. These require a full context that is never available to us.

Climacus's second qualification concerns the other half of his definition of faith, passionate appropriation. He calls attention to the existential tension that arises between a subjective appropriation in terms of which I define my identity, agenda, and destiny, and the objective uncertainty (holistically understood) of the beliefs presupposed by my decision. As we have seen, this is true not only for Christian subjectivity but already for Socratic subjectivity.

There is a sense in which Kant and Hegel and Climacus are empirical realists.[25] But it is misleading to leave it at that. For each of them empirical realism is *aufgehoben* in their own versions of transcendental idealism and thus demoted from being either the paradigm of our knowledge or the highest goal of our cognitive efforts.

Climacus's second heading in his analysis of objectivity is "the speculative point of view." He does not speak of approximation, and he does not throw any new light on what we are to understand by "objective uncertainty." He does poke fun at the system, which is supposed to be without presuppositions, for assuming "that we are all Christians." In other words, the "point of view" (read: perspective) of speculative thought is not the "view from nowhere" but a very particular historical-cultural location, whose ultimacy it simply presupposes. But instead of getting into an abstract debate over the starting point of the system,[26] he satirizes the poor fellow who begins to doubt whether he really is a Christian. He is berated by his wife.

---

25. They are also in certain senses skeptics insofar as each denies various knowledge claims in various domains. But none is simply a skeptic just as none is simply an empirical realist.

26. The importance of this question for Hegel is expressed in "With What Must the Science Begin," with which he begins the first part of his Logic, the Doctrine of Being. *Hegel's Science of Logic,* pp. 67-78.

Hubby, darling where did you ever pick up such a notion? How can you not be a Christian? You are Danish, aren't you? Doesn't the geography book say that the predominant religion in Denmark is Lutheran-Christian? You aren't a Jew, are you, or a Mohammedan? What else would you be, then? It is a thousand years since paganism was superseded; so I know you aren't a pagan. Don't you tend to your work in the office as a good civil servant; aren't you a good subject in a Christian nation, in a Lutheran-Christian state? So of course you are a Christian. (*CUP* 1:50-51)

Here as throughout this section, Climacus's focus is on the need for objectivity to be taken up into subjectivity and on the way this kind of Christianity does not do so. I call it census bureau Christianity, for surely the census will list this man as a Christian. Kierkegaard calls it Christendom. Climacus immediately points to the link between this kind of religion and speculative philosophy. "The speculative thinker . . . has become too objective to talk about himself. . . . Now, should we not agree to be human beings!" (*CUP* 1:51). Climacus agrees with Macbeth, when he says,

I dare do all that may become a man;
Who dares do more is none.

On Cavell's reading, Macbeth is saying "that to strike beyond certain limits is to be a beast," to sink below the level of the truly human.[27]

We can read Climacus's "should we not agree to be human beings!" as the segue to his long discussion of generic subjectivity, at the heart of which lies his discussion of truth as subjectivity, which he equates with faith. He begins by devoting about sixty pages to Lessing. At first this may seem surprising, but it should not be. He sees Lessing as an ally in relation to his motto: "Better well hanged than ill wed," and precisely because of the way he raises the question of faith and history. Climacus's view is that Christian faith includes historical beliefs, since the story of the incarnation, of the

---

27. *Macbeth,* I.vii.46-47. See Stanley Cavell, *Disowning Knowledge in Seven Plays of Shakespeare,* updated ed. (New York: Cambridge University Press, 2003), p. 229. Cavell identifies the sub-human as the beastly in light of Lady Macbeth's response to Macbeth, to the effect that it was when Macbeth was a beast and initially joined her in their crime without qualm that he was a real man. For Climacus, of course, "who dares do more" is the would-be speculative philosopher who would become so totally objective as to render all concerns about subjectivity unmanly, not as beastly, perhaps, but as puerile.

god in time, is a cluster of historical events. But he holds that all historical knowledge is objectively uncertain (the opening of *Postscript*) and that historical knowledge, even that of an eyewitness, is one thing, faith another (concluding chapters, IV and V, of *Fragments*).

Lessing makes the same separation. He asks, "who will deny (not I) that the reports of these miracles and prophecies are as reliable as historical truths ever can be?" The "not I" is almost certainly ironic, but Lessing wants to concede the point for the sake of his argument, which follows immediately. His claim is that *"accidental truths of history can never become the proof of necessary truths of reason."*[28]

Lessing is a rationalist whose theology, famously said by Jacobi to be a form of Spinoza's pantheism,[29] does indeed consist in necessary truths of reason. As such it differs decisively from the Christian theology that is of interest to Climacus. Necessary truths of reason would be derived by means of some version of the recollection theory, while Christian theology presents itself as a response to divine revelation. But the two are similar in that each makes metaphysical claims. So Lessing and Climacus are speaking the same language when the former asks,

> If on historical grounds I have no objection to the statement that Christ raised to life a dead man; must I therefore accept it as true that God has a Son who is of the same essence as himself? . . . If on historical grounds I have no objection to the statement that this Christ himself rose from the dead, must I therefore accept it as true that this risen Christ was the Son of God?[30]

Quite apart from the need for subjectivity, and quite apart from the problem of objective uncertainty, Lessing insists that there is a logical gap between historical premises and metaphysical conclusions. So he writes,

28. Gotthold Ephraim Lessing, "On the Proof of the Spirit and of Power," in *Lessing's Theological Writings,* trans. Henry Chadwick, Library of Modern Religious Thought (Stanford: Stanford University Press, 1957), p. 53.

29. For a helpful account of the *Pantheismusstreit* (pantheism controversy) raised by Jacobi's announcement, see Frederick C. Beiser, *The Fate of Reason: German Philosophy from Kant to Fichte* (Cambridge, MA: Harvard University Press, 1987), pp. 44-91. For the primary text, see *Concerning the Doctrine of Spinoza in Letters to Herr Moses Mendelssohn* in Friedrich Heinrich Jacobi, *The Main Philosophical Writings and the Novel "Allwill,"* trans. George di Giovanni (Montreal: McGill-Queens University Press, 1994), pp. 173-251 and 339-78.

30. Lessing, "On the Proof," p. 54.

But to jump with that historical truth to a quite different class of truths, and to demand of me that I should form all my metaphysical and moral ideas accordingly; to expect me to alter my fundamental ideas of the nature of the Godhead because I cannot set any credible testimony against the resurrection of Christ: if that is not a μετάβασις εἰς ἄλλο γένος [transition or crossing over to another genus], then I do not know what Aristotle meant by this phrase.[31]

The logical fallacy, whose Aristotelian name Lessing gives, is to switch from one genus to another in the movement from premises to conclusion in a syllogism, as if the premises were about dogs and the conclusion were about cats.

So far Lessing is a friend to the Climacus of *Fragments*. But he is about to introduce a theme that Climacus will take up in *Postscript*. He writes, "That, then, is the ugly, broad ditch which I cannot get across, however often and however earnestly I have tried to make the leap. If anyone can help me over it, let him do it, I beg him, I adjure him. He will deserve a divine reward from me."[32]

Doubtless Lessing's profession of earnest efforts and his asking for assistance are ironical. He tells us that this leap is one "against which my reason rebels."[33] But Climacus doubly welcomes his point. It has a weak and a strong sense. The weak sense is at once logical and existential. It rejects an apologetics for Christian faith grounded on historical knowledge, in particular miracles and fulfilled prophecies. The logical point concerns the fallacious inference of metaphysical conclusions from historical premises. The existential point concerns the necessity of a leap if one is to get over the gap, the "ugly, broad ditch," that separates the two. Cognition provides no bridge; a decision to act is needed.

But especially if Lessing is a Spinozist, there is a stronger sense to the rebellion of his reason (a combination of words that Climacus would find significant). It is at once epistemological and metaphysical. As a rationalist Lessing rejects the idea that one's religious and moral beliefs should depend on divine revelation rather than on human reason as recollection.[34] As a

31. Lessing, "On the Proof," p. 54.
32. Lessing, "On the Proof," p. 55.
33. Lessing, "On the Proof," p. 54.
34. Alastair Hannay writes, "Lessing's attitude appears consistently to have reflected the kind of trust in human self-sufficiency, in the long run, that forms the deep basis of all Enlightenment thought." Hannay, "Having Lessing on One's Side," in Perkins, ed., *International*

pantheist he opposes the theism presupposed by the claim that Christ is divine. It is the substantive conclusion (strong version) and not only the formal inference (weak version) that he finds to be against reason.

So we should not be surprised that Climacus takes Lessing seriously. Whether we attribute to Lessing the weak or the strong sense of his reason's rebellion — or, more likely, both — he supports Climacus's "better well hanged than ill wed" argument in *Fragments*. Christianity is better off to have the Lessings of the world reject it outright than to have the Hegels of the world (and the Kants, for that matter) put it through the filter of (some version of) reason as recollection and give it back to us as the new, improved, reasonable version of Christianity. Lessing is also friendly to the Climacus of *Postscript* insofar as he employs two notions that Climacus will develop there: the leap, and the notion that Christian faith goes against, not merely beyond, reason.

Climacus presents four "possible and actual theses by Lessing" (*CUP* 1:72). He "first of all attributes to Lessing two theses which are clearly his own rather than positions textually attributable to the historical Lessing himself."[35] Only the first of these concerns us here. It reads, "*The subjective thinker is aware of the dialectic of communication*" (*CUP* 1:72). We expect an introduction to the famous theme of indirect communication. We are right, but perhaps misled. For what really concerns Climacus here is double reflection as the task of any thought that will combine objectivity and subjectivity.

> Whereas objective thinking is indifferent to the thinking subject and his existence, the subjective thinker as existing is essentially interested in his own thinking. . . . Therefore, his thinking has another kind of reflection, specifically, that of inwardness, of possession, whereby it belongs to the subject and to no one else . . . he thinks the universal, but, as existing in this thinking, as acquiring this in his inwardness, he becomes more and more subjectively isolated. (*CUP* 1:72-73)

Kierkegaard Commentary, vol. 12: *Concluding Unscientific Postscript to "Philosophical Fragments*," p. 209. Hannay sees the Enlightenment as "a basic trust in the human being's capacity to secure its own basis for the traditional supports of human life (morality, religion, and the state)." This general view is not tied to any particular view of reason. In fact, Romanticism can be seen as a reformulation of this project rather than its rejection. See Hannay, pp. 211-12. In the language of Climacus, just as Spinoza, Kant, and Hegel are three versions of the Enlightenment project, so the Enlightenment and the Romantic reaction are two versions of the recollection project.

35. Hannay, "Having Lessing on One's Side," p. 207.

It's all about appropriation (*CUP* 1:75, 78-79), and appropriation is about action. David Gouwens describes double reflection this way: "One not only reflects upon, say, a theological doctrine or teaching *qua* teaching, but one then also reflects that category of thought back upon oneself, or better, reflects one's own life into the category."[36] The second degree of reflection, like Aristotle's practical syllogism, is a thought process that culminates in action, not merely in belief. But the connection between inwardness and isolation is important here. Double reflection is about the inner face rather than the outer face of action. It is about the heart rather than conformity with the crowd, whether that be a religious, cultural, or political public.

The notion of indirect communication is merely a corollary to this notion of double reflection. To explain and establish some propositional truth is not to lead one's hearer or reader — or, for that matter, oneself — to personal appropriation. Getting all caught up in propounding and proving some propositional content can actually be a distraction from the task of bringing one's attitudes and actions into conformity with it.

If the aim of one's communication is to inspire double reflection, culminating in inward, personal appropriation, the communication will have to be indirect. One will have to do something more than and different from teaching and arguing for some ethical, religious, or philosophical doctrine. One will have to stage a kind of sneak attack, like the Trojan horse, in which the message gets inside the defenses of the self before the self realizes what is happening. If the result is a surprise awareness of a need and a motivation to change, the communication is just to that degree successful.[37] It is authentically human speech because it serves authentic human existence.

Nathan the prophet must have been reading Climacus. After King David committed adultery with Bathsheba and had her husband killed, Nathan told him about a rich man who had many flocks but stole the only lamb of a poor man. David was incensed and called for the death of the villain, to which Nathan replied, "You are the man!" David saw the point and repented (2 Sam. 11–12). Psalm 51, the most powerful of the penitential psalms, bears the heading, "A Psalm of David, when the prophet Nathan came to him, after he had gone in to Bathsheba."

David didn't need to be taught that adultery and murder are forbidden

---

36. David J. Gouwens, *Kierkegaard as Religious Thinker* (New York: Cambridge University Press, 1996), p. 43.

37. This may be what Kierkegaard is getting at when he gives the third part of *Christian Discourses* the title, "Thoughts That Wound from Behind — for Upbuilding."

by God. He already knew that, but his knowledge was impotent. So Nathan didn't try to prove to him that the Ten Commandments come from God. David already believed that. Instead, Nathan found a way to jolt David out of the complacency of his first reflection into a second reflection that motivated change.

The next thesis for our consideration clearly comes from Lessing himself. Climacus cites and paraphrases the passages cited above in which Lessing points to (1) the logical gap between historical and metaphysical or moral beliefs and (2) the need for a leap to bridge that gap (*CUP* 1:93).[38] We might say that there are three gaps and three leaps: the cognitive leap involved in coming to hold historical beliefs about what is objectively uncertain; the cognitive leap involved in moving from historical beliefs to metaphysical and moral beliefs; and the existential leap involved in the personal appropriation of one's metaphysical and moral beliefs. Climacus is interested in all three, and thus in the logic of the leap. Lessing more or less neutralizes the first leap by conceding, for the sake of argument, a closer approximation to objective certainty than Climacus (or we) are likely to suppose. But he does so in order to focus our attention on the second and third leaps; so Climacus welcomes him to the discussion.[39]

With Lessing's help, Climacus makes three points about the leap. First, it involves a decision, since thought by itself does not carry us over the gap to which it calls our attention. In the case of Christianity (and for Socrates, too, as a matter of fact), this is a decision in time on which we base our eternal happiness (*CUP* 1:95-102). Since, as we have seen, the juxtaposition of time and eternity generates paradox for both Socratic and Christian subjectivity, to leap is to dwell within the horizon of paradox.

There is nothing particularly puzzling about the idea that the existential leap involves a decision. But what about the cognitive leaps? Is there a will to believe thesis in Climacus? If so, what sort? Does he hold to a direct volitionalism, according to which we can directly and consciously will to believe some statements to be true? Or does he imply an indirect volitionalism, according to which a variety of choices we make play a role in what beliefs we end up with? If, for example, I decide either to stop or to start regular church attendance, Bible reading, and prayer, and if I carry out such

38. There are earlier references, but only in passing, to the leap. See *FT*, 42n. and *PF*, 43.

39. As a matter of fact, Kierkegaard does not use the term 'leap of faith,' but there is no point in insisting on this since he links his discussion of the leap so closely to his analysis of faith.

a decision, this is very likely to have an effect on my theological and quite possibly my moral beliefs.

Steve Evans gives a helpful overview of the debate about these issues. I think his conclusions in the direction of seeing Climacus as an indirect volitionalist are the most charitable and have the best textual support. He writes,

> Climacus by no means necessarily implies that beliefs are consciously chosen. If anything is evident about Kierkegaard as a psychologist, it is that he is a depth psychologist . . . he thinks that human beings hardly ever make choices with full consciousness of what they are doing. . . . Climacus nowhere says that beliefs can be controlled by the will *directly*. . . . Climacus may or may not think that particular beliefs are sometimes under the direct control of the will, but he certainly does not believe that this is always or even generally the case. What he does affirm is that what we want to believe ultimately plays a decisive role in what we do believe.[40]

The second point Climacus finds in Lessing on the leap is that it is risky. Earlier we encountered this risk under the image of being "out on 70,000 fathoms of water" (*CUP* 1:204).[41] Here the image is of the leap across a gorge, and the absence of *terra firma* under our feet is even more dramatic and distressing. This risk is both cognitive and existential. It endangers both "the *acceptance* of a doctrine that is the condition for an eternal happiness" and the decision "to *base* an eternal happiness on [the historical reports ingredient in that doctrine]" (*CUP* 1:96; emphasis added).

The third Lessing lemma about the leap is that the individual makes it in isolation. Jacobi might be the originator of the leap, but he does not understand it, "precisely because the leap is an act of isolation, since it is left to the single individual to decide whether he will by virtue of the absurd accept in faith that which cannot be thought. With the aid of eloquence, Jacobi wants to help one make the leap" (*CUP* 1:100). Here Climacus obviously refers to the specifically Christian leap; but the logic or structure of

---

40. See "Does Kierkegaard Think Beliefs Can Be Directly Willed?" in C. Stephen Evans, *Kierkegaard on Faith and the Self: Collected Essays* (Waco, TX: Baylor University Press, 2006), pp. 304, 306. Michelle Kosch also rejects the view that Climacus is a direct voluntarist with reference to belief. See her *Freedom and Reason in Kant, Schelling, and Kierkegaard* (Oxford: Clarendon, 2006), pp. 187-99.

41. See chapter 9 above.

individual responsibility and "isolation" applies just as much to Abraham (and thus to biblical religion in its Jewish form) and to Socrates (and thus to pagan, but human subjectivity).

Climacus fears that his contemporaries (and himself as well?) have lost the courage to leap as single individuals. "Just as in the desert individuals must travel in large caravans out of fear of robbers and wild animals, so individuals today have a horror of existence because it is godforsaken; they dare to live only in great herds and cling together *en masse* in order to be at least something" (*CUP* 1:355-56).[42] N.B. Climacus does not deny that belonging (for example, the ethical in *Fear and Trembling*) is a way to be; he only insists that when we reduce our being to belonging we fall below the religious (as in *Fear and Trembling*) or even below the truly human (*Postscript*).

Kierkegaard allows both Silentio and Climacus to be quite radically individualistic in their view of the spiritual life. But this does not mean that social relations are without value. Everything depends on the relation of the individual to his or her community or society. In his own name, Kierkegaard writes,

> When individuals (each one individually) are essentially and passionately related to an idea and together are essentially related to the same idea, the relation is optimal and normative. Individually the relation separates them (each one has himself for himself), and ideally it unites them. (*TA*, 62)

By an "idea" Kierkegaard seems to mean something rather Platonic, a moral or religious ideal that transcends individuals' social bond as their guide and judge. Ontogenetically, it can be argued that society is prior to the individual; but spiritually, for Kierkegaard, being individually and passionately committed in faith to "an idea" must be prior. This is his version of the idea of "civic virtue." When this order is reversed and the ethical (in the Hegelian sense, as presented in *Fear and Trembling*) merely recapitulates ontogeny, society becomes an idol. "And what is the basis of this other than a disregard for the separation of the religious individual before God in the responsibility of eternity. When dismay commences at this point, one seeks

---

42. Climacus's description of modern society as having a herd mentality puts him into an interesting conversation with Nietzsche. Cf. Kierkegaard's analysis of "the present age" in *TA*, 68-112.

comfort in company" (*TA*, 86). Seen in context, the radical individualism of the pseudonyms need not be taken to be the whole truth but rather an emphasis on that dimension of the truth whose neglect Kierkegaard sees as disastrous.

We come to the final Lessing thesis. Like the previous one, this one can be actually attributed to him, for it is a direct quotation.

> *If God held all truth enclosed in his right hand, and in his left hand the one and only ever-striving drive for truth, even with the corollary of erring forever and ever, and if he were to say to me: Choose! — I would humbly fall down to him at his left hand and say: Father, give! Pure truth is indeed only for you alone.* (*CUP* 1:106)

Climacus did not speak of approximation in his analysis of "the speculative point of view" under the heading of "objectivity." But his critique of the system in his commentary on this thesis could be summarized in the statement, "the system can never be more than an approximation to the truth."

The analysis comes in two parts. The first concerns the unfinished condition of the system, at least in the versions presented in Denmark by the likes of Heiberg and Nielsen.[43] Climacus unsurprisingly turns to satire. When Lessing wrote the words above, the system was obviously not finished. "If he were living now, now when the system has been completed for the most part or is at least in the works and will be finished by next Sunday, believe me, Lessing would have clutched it with both hands" (*CUP* 1:106). Climacus adds that he himself was prepared to fall down and worship the system, but "at the very moment I had already spread my handkerchief on the ground, so as to avoid dirtying my trousers by kneeling," he thought to ask whether the system was finished, promising " 'I will prostrate myself, even if I should ruin a pair of trousers' (on account of the heavy traffic to and from the system, the road was rather muddy)" — only to be told, " 'No, it is not entirely finished yet.' . . . But if the system is not finished, there is not any system" (*CUP* 1:107). Why, Climacus asks, call a fragment a system (*CUP* 1:108)?

This is the point at which he makes his claim that *"(a) a logical system*

---

43. Jon Stewart suggests that these two, rather than Hegel himself, are the targets of this critique. *Kierkegaard's Relations*, pp. 261-62. In this case Stewart's "the Danish Hegelians, but not Hegel himself" thesis seems on target. (See note 14 above and my critique of this thesis in chapter 1.) Although Hegel published two somewhat different versions of his Logic and was in the midst of revising his *Science of Logic* at the time of his death, he does not seem to think of his system as unfinished.

can be given; (b) but a system of existence [Tilværelsens System] *cannot be given"* (*CUP* 1:109).[44] Actuality is temporal at both the personal and the world historical levels. The system (whose?) is thus doubly partial and perspectival, written from the limited standpoint of a particular individual at a particular point in historical time. As such it is essentially unfinished, vulnerable to supplementation and even subversion,[45] as the subsequent history of Hegel's system would show. Only by a leap of faith, whose warrant it would be hard to produce, could the system be considered finished and thus in fact a system.

The second way in which Lessing's thesis suggests that the system is an approximation at best concerns its beginning. Here Hegel himself is clearly at issue, for he makes a big point of having an absolute beginning.[46] He begins his *Phenomenology* with Sense Certainty and his Logic with Being because both are taken to be in some sense immediate. That is to say, they are what they are all by themselves without reference to anything else.[47] But the system does not generate itself spontaneously. It stands in an essential relation to its author, more specifically to the author's decision to become a speculative philosopher and write a system. "The beginning of the system that begins with the immediate *is then itself achieved through reflection*" (*CUP* 1:112).

'Reflection' has a double sense here. In one sense, it refers to an actual discursive thought process, one that leads the thinker to adopt "the speculative point of view." But such a process does not stop on its own. It reaches its conclusion (its termination and its determinate content) only by a decision, a resolution (*CUP* 1:112-13, 116), or, we might say, a leap. One may conclude that a system is both possible and desirable, but one risks the discovery that this expresses one's blind spot rather than one's insight.

The other sense of 'reflection' is as a logical category in which it serves as the general form for thinking beings that cannot be or be understood apart from their other. In this sense parents are reflected in their children and vice versa. Causes are reflected in their effects and vice versa. Or, more to the point, the system is reflected in its author and its author's personal and historical location (read: perspective) — and vice versa.

---

44. See the discussion of this text in chapter 9.

45. In Gadamer's language, revision or replacement. See note 16 above.

46. See note 26 above.

47. Hegel writes, "For mediation is a beginning and a having advanced to a second," but "at the beginning we have as yet no other." *The Encyclopedia Logic,* Remark to §12 and Addition to §86.

This is the point at which Climacus makes his claim that "Existence itself is a system — for God, but it cannot be a system for any existing [*existerende*] spirit. System and conclusiveness correspond to each other, but existence is the very opposite" (*CUP* 1:118).[48] If the starting point of the system is, if not arbitrary, nevertheless accidental by depending on a contingent decision, and if the system cannot bring itself to a conclusion apart from just such a decision, then the system is no system and its disciples are deeply deceived. Only by abstracting from the conditions of human existence could the system project seem plausible. This is why Climacus reiterates his plea, "should we not agree to be human beings!" (*CUP* 1:51) no fewer than three times in his discussion of this Lessing thesis (*CUP* 1:109, 114, 117).

Faith is a leap, whether the form of its subjectivity is pagan (Socrates) or biblical (Abraham, the one becoming a Christian). But speculative philosophy is also a leap of faith. It is not, of course, the religious faith that gives primacy to subjectivity over objectivity. But it is the faith that believes what it cannot know to be true with any objective certainty. It is the risky decision that flees from the finitude of human existence in order to attain, *per impossible,* what is only possible for God. With more than a little irony, Climacus concludes his Lessing meditations by suggesting that we not denounce the "objective tendency" by calling it "impious, pantheistic self-worship" but rather call it "comic" or "ludicrous" (*CUP* 1:124-25).

But faith is also a striving, and this in two senses. Epistemically, in the light of objective uncertainty and approximation, faith is neither the abandonment of the ideal of truth as correspondence (adequation) nor the complacent (arrogant?) claim to be able to achieve it, even with the qualification "at least in principle." It is the perpetual striving for a closer approximation in the awareness that not only the conclusions we have reached at any given time but also the criteria by which we seek to ground and establish them are open to revision or replacement, vulnerable to supplementation or even subversion. This is the legitimate requirement of objectivity.

Existentially or subjectively speaking, the striving is of another kind. Not waiting until the objective task is completed, the task is to bring one's existence into conformity with whatever essential "truth" one currently has available. This, too, is the task of a lifetime; for, like the epistemic task, the existential task is never completed in our present lives. It is to a further analysis of this striving that we now turn.

48. See the discussion of this text in chapter 9.

CHAPTER 11

Faith as a Striving Pathos That Goes Against Reason

A large portion of Climacus's very long postscript is given over to the comparison of Religiousness A with Religiousness B. It is another of those wonderful asymmetries that gives to *Postscript* its charm. The discussion of A is almost seven times as long as the discussion of B.

Before looking at the specifics, we can note three things about Religiousness A.

First, like the discussion of truth as subjectivity and the reflections on Lessing, it belongs to Climacus's analysis of generic or merely "human" subjectivity. There is nothing specifically Christian or even biblical about it.[1] The specifically Christian is left for Religiousness B.

Second, accordingly, it is described as a religion of immanence over against the transcendence ingredient in Religiousness B. This is an epistemological point. It means that Religiousness A is grounded in recollection rather than in revelation. The truth we need is already within us and needs but to be discovered, although Climacus treats this discovery as anything but inevitable. But it is also an ontological point, for it means that the God of Abraham, the personal God who makes promises and gives commands, is not needed and, accordingly, makes no appearance.

Third, this is a religion of striving, perpetual striving as a matter of fact. Climacus's account picks up and develops this theme from the final thesis attributed to Lessing. Striving can be a matter of ideals and aspiration, but Climacus speaks the language of 'task' instead (*CUP* 1:407, 414, 431, 525-27).

---

1. Abraham's faith in *Fear and Trembling* is biblical without being Christian. Its kinship is with Religiousness B.

The norm by which this faith is guided and the very call to live up to this norm are discovered rather than chosen, though we can choose to submit to it or to ignore it. It does not come to us from beyond us; but it comes to us as an assignment, not an extra-credit option. So this faith, like Abraham's in *Fear and Trembling,* in spite of important differences, is the task of a life-time, a striving that never reaches its goal.

In the light of these three characteristics, we can say that Religiousness A is the religion of Socrates — not the Socrates who is merged with Plato as a speculative thinker *(Fragments, Phaedo)* but the Socrates who is sharply distinguished from him *(Postscript, Apology).* This is the Socrates of Socratic ignorance (objective uncertainty), of Socratic irony (indirect communication), and of Socratic uncertainty "if there is an immortality" (objective uncertainty again). Alluding to Socrates as an example of Religiousness A, Climacus writes, "A pagan can also . . . venture everything on the 'if' of immortality" *(CUP* 1:429). He also explicitly adds, "Religiousness A can be present in paganism" *(CUP* 1:557).[2]

This is a good place to repeat a sentence from chapter 9: "Just as infinite resignation is the necessary condition for biblical, Abrahamic faith for Silentio, so for Climacus this generic, human subjectivity is the *sine qua non* for Christian faith." Climacus writes,

> Religiousness A must first be present in the individual before there can be any consideration of becoming aware of the dialectical B. . . . [H]ow foolish it is if a person without pathos wants to relate himself to the essentially Christian, because before there can be any question at all of simply being in the situation of becoming aware of it one must first of all exist in Religiousness A. *(CUP* 1:556-57)

In other words, Religiousness A is not another religion at the level of Religiousness B, with its own particular "church," scriptures, and traditions. It is rather the genus of which Christianity is a species. When Climacus says that one must first be in Religiousness A in order actually to be in Religious-

---

2. Here Climacus gives a satirical reprise of the parable of the Christian who prays to the true God in untruth and the pagan who prays to a false god in truth (see chapter 9 above). He contrasts the cheap, comfortable, easy Christianity — "after all, he is baptized, has received a copy of the Bible and a hymnbook as a gift; is he not, then, a Christian, an Evangelical Lutheran Christian?" — with Religiousness A, which is "so strenuous for a human being that there is always a sufficient task in it" *(CUP* 1:557). On the importance of Socrates for Kierkegaard, see chapter 9, note 16, above.

ness B, he is not doing developmental psychology. The meaning is the same as when we say that an animal must first be a dog in order to be a collie. The priority is logical or conceptual, not temporal.

Climacus spells out Religiousness A in terms of three expressions of "existential pathos": the "initial," the "essential," and the "decisive" expressions. 'Pathos' signifies the affective dimension of the self. In chapter 6 above, passions were distinguished from emotions in terms of the dispositions to have various emotions and the emotions themselves that arise out of those passions under particular circumstances. The dispositions were understood as the concerns of the self, what we deeply care about. Thus, if I have a passion for fly-fishing, I will be angry if I think you have stolen my equipment. Climacus makes the same distinction, but not linguistically. He uses both *Pathos* and *Lidenskab* to move back and forth between the dispositions and the emotions.[3] But if we see the self in terms of intellect, will, and affections, Climacus is clearly directing our attention to our affective side.[4] We might say that he is writing his own *Treatise Concerning Religious Affections.*[5]

To qualify 'pathos' as 'existential' is to distinguish it from merely aesthetic pathos, which expresses different emotions grounded in different cares or concerns.

> In relation to an eternal happiness as the absolute good, pathos does not mean words but that this idea transforms the whole existence of the existing person. Aesthetic pathos expresses itself in words . . . whereas exis-

---

3. See the helpful discussion in Robert C. Roberts, "Dialectical Emotions and the Virtue of Faith," in *International Kierkegaard Commentary,* vol. 12: *Concluding Unscientific Postscript to "Philosophical Fragments,"* ed. Robert L. Perkins (Macon, GA: Mercer University Press, 1997), pp. 76-82. He suggests that the initial expression of existential pathos, resignation, falls on the dispositional side as expressing a fundamental concern or mode of caring, while the essential and decisive expressions, suffering and guilt, signify emotions grounded in that disposition; see p. 84.

4. Roberts suggests that *Postscript* is more psychological than *Fragments,* and he suggests as evidence the centrality "of such concepts as *subjectivity, inwardness, existence, eternal happiness, existential pathos, and dialectical pathos.*" "Dialectical Emotions," p. 73. In this sense *Postscript* can be read as a commentary on the concept of faith as a passion in *Fragments.*

5. A major work of Jonathan Edwards (1746). In the context of the Great Awakening, Edwards was trying to sort out good from bad emotions in a context where there was fear of excessive emotion. Kierkegaard writes, here and elsewhere, in critique of a present age that "has crossed out passion in order to serve science [objectivity]" (*FT,* 7). His critique of "the present age" in *Two Ages* is that it has allowed reflection to usurp the proper place of passion.

tential pathos results from the transforming relation of the idea to the individual's existence. If the absolute τέλος [end, goal] does not absolutely transform the individual's existence by relating to it, then the individual does not relate himself with existential pathos but with aesthetic pathos. (*CUP* 1:387; spelling changed)[6]

Roberts nicely suggests that aesthetic pathos is shallow rather than deep because its concerns, along with the associated emotions, do not get to the heart of who we are.[7] My (entirely fictitious) passion for fly-fishing would be a good example. Even if that passion were so all-consuming as to be a crucial part of my identity, it would remain shallow, as we shall see. Strong concerns do not mean deeply human caring, as the various modes of addiction show us. In accord with the fourfold theory of stages found in *Postscript*,[8] Climacus links speculative objectivity with such aesthetic pathos when he gives as an example of the latter the passion for "having a correct idea" (*CUP* 1:387). The passion does not generate personal transformation.

We have just seen Climacus present existential pathos in its religious mode[9] as a "relation to an eternal happiness as the absolute good." God and immortality are often linked as two major religious concerns, and we can ask why Climacus chooses the latter rather than the former for defining Religiousness A. Of course, he does not isolate them from each other, but writes, "The absolutely differentiating one relates himself to his absolute τέλος, but *eo ipso* also to God" (*CUP* 1:413). But his emphasis is on eternal happiness. Why?

Three possible replies come to mind. First, Climacus speaks a bit carelessly when he speaks of "an eternal happiness as the absolute good." For a theist, at any rate, God is the highest good in the sense of being good

---

6. Cf. *CUP* 1:389-90: "The pathos that corresponds to and is adequate to an eternal happiness is the transformation by which the existing person in existing changes everything in his existence in relation to that highest good." In this sense, "The pathos of the ethical is to act."

7. Roberts, "Dialectical Emotions," p. 83.

8. See chapter 9 above.

9. We have seen Climacus speak of "the ethical and the ethical-religious." The latter would seem to suggest that there is an ethics that has the religious as its ground, as Kierkegaard will argue in *Works of Love*. Perhaps the former term suggests an ethics that does not have any overtly religious ground but that is linked to the eternal in two ways: (1) the hope of eternal happiness and (2) the authority of norms not reducible to the laws and customs of any particular society and culture (Hegel's *Sittlichkeit*). The ethics of Socrates and Kant could serve as examples.

(or goodness itself) in a way in which nothing other than God is good. As a Platonic-Thomistic tradition puts it, every created good (including my eternal happiness) is good by participation in the divine goodness and as such is less perfectly good than divine goodness itself. As St. John of the Cross puts it, "souls possess the same goods by participation that the Son possesses by nature."[10]

Moreover, especially in this tradition, it is often said that "God is the highest good for the human person." But this is like a Zen koan; it brings thought to a screeching halt. How could anything other than some condition, event, or relation that is mine be *my* highest good or goal? It makes sense to say that the right relation to God is *my* highest good and should be my absolute goal. But unless it is shorthand for such a statement, to say that God is *my* highest good or absolute goal is perplexing and misleading. And it is surely *my* highest good of which Climacus wants to speak, not God's eternal perfection but the eternal happiness for which I, as an existing individual, may hope. By focusing on this, Climacus tells us that he doesn't really mean to say that eternal happiness is *the* highest good but rather *my* highest good. This theme fits well with the analysis of subjectivity as existential striving.

Second, *Postscript* is a postscript to *Fragments,* and the discussion of existential pathos comes in chapter four, entitled "The Issue in *Fragments:* How Can an Eternal Happiness Be Built on Historical Knowledge?" Climacus's problematic is and has been from the outset about eternal happiness rather than directly about God.

Finally, Climacus has already defined Socrates' religion in terms of his "if there is an immortality." Belief in personal life after death is something shared by Socrates and Christianity; so it makes sense to make it the focus of the comparison of Religiousness A, Socratic religion, and Religiousness B, Christianity.

The "initial" expression of existential pathos is resignation. I have spoken of the norm that governs Religiousness A in the singular. Here it is: *"Simultaneously to Relate Oneself Absolutely to One's Absolute τέλος and Relatively to Relative Ends"* (*CUP* 1:387). Here the task is to resign, in infinite resignation, we might say,[11] all finite goods as goals. "Now if to [the

---

10. St. John of the Cross, "The Spiritual Canticle," in *The Collected Works of St. John of the Cross,* trans. Kieran Kavanaugh, O.C.D., and Otilio Rodriguez, O.C.D. (Washington, DC: ICS Publications, 1991), p. 624. John emphasizes that such participation involves a transformation of the soul, though not substantially; see pp. 164-65, 560.

11. Climacus reviews the earlier pseudonymous works by Kierkegaard in "A Glance at a

existing person] an eternal happiness is his highest good, this means that in his acting the finite elements are once and for all reduced to what must be surrendered in relation to the eternal happiness" (*CUP* 1:391). This is what it means for this hope to "absolutely transform the individual's existence" (*CUP* 1:387).

Since the existing person is both infinite and finite, this means that the highest good must be an infinite good, an absolute τέλος, and not just another finite good more important than the others. As usual, Climacus turns to satire and gives us a picture of what resignation is not.

> I do not know whether one should laugh or weep on hearing the enumeration: a good job, a beautiful wife, health, the rank of a councilor of justice — and in addition an eternal happiness, which is the same as assuming that the kingdom of *heaven* is a kingdom along with the other kingdoms on *earth* and that one would look for information about it in a geography book. (*CUP* 1:391)[12]

Resignation can also be positively expressed this way: "If [the goal of eternal happiness] does not *absolutely* transform his existence for him, then he is not relating himself to an eternal happiness; if there is something he is not willing to give up for its sake, then he is not relating himself to an eternal happiness" (*CUP* 1:393).

For Climacus, being willing to give up finite goods (which remain goods!) does not mean abandoning the concrete life in the world of finite goods for "the abstract attire of the monastery."[13] Immediate life is "firmly rooted in the finite." But "when resignation is convinced that the individ-

---

Contemporary Effort in Danish Literature" (*CUP* 1:251-300); so we know he is familiar with the analysis of infinite resignation in *Fear and Trembling*.

12. Metropolitan Anthony (Anthony Bloom) puts this point in terms of prayer. "Too often prayer has no such importance in our lives that everything else fades away to give it room. Prayer is additional to a great many things; we wish God to be present, not because there is no life without him, not because he is the supreme value, but because it would be so nice, in addition to all the great benefits of God, to have also his presence. He is additional to our needs, and when we seek him in that spirit we do not meet him." *Living Prayer* (Springfield, IL: Templegate, 1966), p. 13.

13. Climacus is sharply critical of the monastic ideal for (1) thinking that resignation could be adequately expressed through outward behavior and (2) thinking that there was special merit in that outwardness (*CUP* 1:405). But the monastics weren't all wrong. "In the monastic movement there was at least passion and respect for the absolute τέλος" (*CUP* 1:414; cf. 419).

ual has the absolute orientation toward the absolute τέλος, everything is changed, the roots are cut. . . . He is a stranger in the world of finitude. . . . Just as the dentist loosens the gum tissue and cuts the nerve and lets the tooth remain, so also is his life in finitude loosened" (*CUP* 1:410).

In spite of this strong language, Climacus insists that resignation "does not necessarily mean that the existing person becomes indifferent to the finite" (*CUP* 1:413). We recall the knight of faith in *Fear and Trembling*, who is already the knight of infinite resignation. "He finds pleasure in everything . . . one would take him for a mercantile soul enjoying himself . . . the finite tastes just as good to him as to one who never knew anything higher" (*FT*, 39-40).[14] Being finite, one can pursue finite goods and enjoy success in gaining them. But as infinite, one must never treat as absolute any of these goals or even the collective totality of them. "It is true that the individual oriented toward the absolute τέλος is in the relative ends, but he is not in them in such a way that the absolute τέλος is exhausted in them" (*CUP* 1:400). Because of the absolute τέλος one's bond to them has been "loosened"; one must always be willing to "give them up" whenever they conflict with pursuit of the infinite good; and in this sense they are always already "surrendered."

Whenever one takes seriously the task of being absolutely related to one's absolute goal and only relatively committed to relative ends, "existence becomes exceedingly strenuous" (*CUP* 1:409; cf. 422). This is how Climacus understands his task of making things more difficult rather than less.

That brings us to the "essential" expression of existential pathos: suffering. Here the task is *"Dying to Immediacy and Yet Remaining in the Finite"* (*CUP* 1:431). It requires "taking power away from immediacy. . . . The actual individual is, after all, in immediacy and to that extent is actually in the relative ends absolutely" (*CUP* 1:431; cf. 460-61).

But isn't this the task already set forth under the heading of resignation? Is not the task still defined as "simultaneously to relate oneself absolutely to one's absolute τέλος [end, goal] and relatively to relative ends" (*CUP* 1:431)? What is new here? How do we have a second stage of existential pathos?

I like to think of it this way. The simplest state of what is here called immediacy is the life of infants. They are absolutely committed to two finite ends, a full tummy and a dry bottom. Lacking either, their world falls apart and they howl in discomfort, frustration, and even, it would seem, in anger. As they grow older their "needs" become more complex; they learn

14. See chapter 2 above.

to subordinate less important desires to more important ones; and in the process they learn at least a little about delayed gratification. In the process desires lose their sheer immediacy insofar as they are subjected to norms. But these more or less automatic developments, which may be slow and very incomplete, never constitute adopting an infinite and absolute goal and transforming one's existence by subordinating all other ends to it. So in relation to the norm in terms of which resignation is defined, the self remains in a complex immediacy in which desire is not subordinated to and in that sense mediated by *that* norm.[15]

If and when such a task is undertaken, it turns out to be very difficult, partly because we are so deeply immersed from birth in immediacy and partly because, no matter what degree of success we achieve in carrying out this task, it is always unfinished, requiring renewed, strenuous effort. To experience this distinctive difficulty is to suffer in a distinctive way.[16] The second dimension of existential pathos comes from expecting and accepting this suffering.[17] The new element here is the discovery of a suffering that is essential to religious existence and is not a contingent matter of fortune or misfortune. Climacus emphasizes the importance of the "essential continuance" of this suffering (*CUP* 1:443, 445, 447, 451, 499). This suffering is the pathos that accompanies the perpetual dying to immediacy. So we might say that the task of resigning all finite goods becomes the task of becoming

15. For both Hegel and Kierkegaard 'immediacy' is a relative term. The immediate can contain a network of complex mediations while remaining immediate in relation to some other by which it is not mediated, not affected, not teleologically suspended *(aufgehoben)*.

16. Sylvia Walsh puts it this way with reference to religious suffering in Religiousness A. It arises in "the attempt of religious individuals to transform their inner existence so as to sustain an absolute relation to the absolute. Suffering becomes the expression for this attempt because they are continually prevented from actualizing such a relationship by the fact that they remain in existence and are constantly faced with the task of bringing their immediacy into subjection." "Standing at the Crossroads," in *International Kierkegaard Commentary*, vol. 20: *Practice in Christianity*, ed. Robert L. Perkins (Macon, GA: Mercer University Press, 2004), p. 127.

17. Perhaps this is the truth of Kant's perverse notion that anything done out of inclination is without moral worth. Surely the goal of the moral and religious life is to learn to love the right and the good. As David R. Law puts it, the problem with the analysis of resignation is that "it does not stress clearly enough that the absolute relation to the absolute telos must be *sustained through time* in all the concrete experiences of human existence." "Resignation, Suffering, and Guilt in Kierkegaard's *Concluding Unscientific Postscript to 'Philosophical Fragments*,'" in Perkins, ed., *International Kierkegaard Commentary*, vol. 12: *Concluding Unscientific Postscript to "Philosophical Fragments*," p. 269; emphasis added.

resigned to the suffering this involves, accepting it without anger, bitterness, and resentment.

Climacus again emphasizes the inwardness of the self's transformation here. But beyond this he tells us what he means by the term, namely "that inwardness is the individual's relation to himself before God" (*CUP* 1:436-37).[18] By speaking of God, Climacus reminds us that he is concerned with what it might mean to become a Christian. But in this context, where no theism is presupposed, he might better have spoken of the eternal. He often does this when he wants to discuss a spirituality that goes beyond the Hegelian ethical *(Sittlichkeit)* but does not presuppose a biblical monotheism. For example, he writes, "poetry is youth [the aesthetic], and worldly wisdom comes with the years [socialization and the Hegelian ethical], and religiousness is the relation to the eternal; but the years make a person only more and more obtuse if he has lost his youth and has not won the relation to the eternal" (*CUP* 1:458). In other words, there is a tragic blindness in the person whose aesthetic pathos is not *aufgehoben* in existential pathos.

To undertake this task and to accept the suffering it entails is to experience a certain "self-annihilation" (*CUP* 1:461). The immediate self that we are, "proximally and for the most part" (as Heidegger would put it), takes itself and its immediate desires, those not relativized by subordination to the eternal, to be absolute. Perpetual dying to immediacy is the perpetual, painful dismantling of that self and, in that sense, a self-annihilation.

Michelle Kosch badly misreads Climacus here: "What is demanded is a strenuous effort to overcome one's individuality."[19] But the self that is to be annihilated is not the self as individual but the self as immediate, the self as absolutely committed to relative, finite ends. We have just seen that for Climacus "inwardness is the individual's relation to himself before God" (*CUP* 1:436-37). This is an intensification of individuality, not its annihilation. Climacus says that Religiousness B, that is, Christianity, "makes the inwardness the greatest possible" (*CUP* 1:572). Since Religiousness B includes Religiousness A as its presupposition, the two represent different intensities of individuality. Neither is the annihilation of the individual as such; both are the strenuous attempt to abolish the insistence of the immediate self that it and its finite goals should be absolute, the true meaning of selfhood. One undertakes this project within the immanent horizons of recollection; the

---

18. This structure will be developed more fully in *Sickness unto Death*.

19. Michelle Kosch, *Freedom and Reason in Kant, Schelling, and Kierkegaard* (Oxford: Clarendon, 2006), p. 167.

other within the transcendent horizons of divine revelation, or, as Silentio would put it, in response to the promises and commands of a personal God.

The task of this self-annihilation is the bad news that Climacus does not, like the preachers he regularly ridicules, try to hide. But he also insists that this bad news is not the whole story. As with Rudolf Otto,[20] there is a *tremendum* about the eternal, that which frightens and repels. But in dialectical tension with this there is also the *fascinans,* that which comforts and attracts. So Climacus also writes, "We left the religious person in the crisis of sickness; but this sickness is not unto death. We shall now let him be strengthened by the very same conception that destroyed him, by the conception of God" (*CUP* 1:488).

Wherein lies this strengthening? We might expect a reference to hope, but instead Climacus speaks of joy. Those who express their relation to an eternal happiness as the absolute τέλος can "at the same time, by knowing about the relation, be beyond suffering, since in that case the expression for the essential relation to an eternal happiness is not suffering but joy . . . joy in the consciousness that the suffering signifies the relation" (*CUP* 1:452). This is not pure joy, for "the existing person cannot make the dialectical transaction by which suffering is converted into joy" (*CUP* 1:452). Since the joy of knowing that one is related to an eternal happiness is dialectically inseparable from the suffering entailed in that relation, "the perfection of joy is frustrated, as it always must be when it must be possessed in an imperfect form" (*CUP* 1:452). Faith is lived on earth, not in heaven, and Copenhagen is not the New Jerusalem, where death is no more and happiness is eternal and unalloyed (Revelation 21).[21]

Kierkegaard will write fourteen discourses in his own name on joy in the midst of suffering.[22] In these, without ignoring the suffering side of the equation, he emphasizes the joy. But for Climacus the emphasis is one-sidedly on the suffering. We can understand this if we remember that his intention "is to make it difficult to become a Christian, yet not more difficult than it is" (*CUP* 1:557). He is protesting against a cheap and easy religion that consists in little more than being a respectable citizen in a so-

20. See the discussion of Otto in chapter 5 above.

21. Might the religious persons "transcend suffering through joy over the fact that they are related to eternal happiness, in which there is no suffering"? Climacus "denies this possibility, since it would mean they have become eternal rather than existing individuals." Walsh, "Standing at the Crossroads," p. 128.

22. Seven of these are in *UDVS* and seven in *CD*. For illuminating commentary on both groups, see Walsh, "Standing at the Crossroads," pp. 129-45.

ciety where almost everyone goes to church; and he is protesting against a cultural elitism for which the age's advances in knowledge are more important than the difficult and painful existential tasks that remain for each individual, whether intellectually gifted or not.[23]

Looking back later over his authorship, Kierkegaard suggests that critique needs to be one-sided if it is to have any bite.

> The person who is to provide the "corrective" must study the weak sides of the established order scrupulously and penetratingly and then one-sidedly present the opposite — with expert one-sidedness. . . . If this is done properly, then a presumably sharp head will come along and object that "the corrective" is one-sided. . . . Ye gods! Nothing is easier for the one providing the corrective than to add the other side: but then it ceases to be precisely the corrective and itself becomes an established order. (*PV,* 205)[24]

One of the advantages of pseudonymous writing is that Kierkegaard can allow his pseudonyms to be as one-sided as the situation seems to require. He practices a hermeneutics in which the "solution" to the problem of perspectivism is not to flee perspectives but to multiply them, remembering that it is the nature of a perspective to enable us to see some things while hiding others from our view.[25] If in *Fragments,* faith is a "happy passion" (*PF,* 49, 54), in *Postscript* the subjectivity presupposed by faith is a painful passion, both as suffering and, finally, as guilt.

For the decisive expression of existential pathos is guilt. In one sense we don't move on to new territory, for the task remains the same: "simultaneously to relate oneself absolutely to the absolute τέλος [end, goal] and rela-

---

23. In our context, advances in science and technology play the role that advances in speculative philosophy played for Kierkegaard and his contemporaries.

24. Walter Lowrie writes, "The only title he appropriated to himself was 'the Corrective' — and this, as he understood it, was far from being a proud title. For he recognized, as we have seen, that the corrective as such was obliged to insist upon a 'vigorously one-sided' aspect of the truth, and therefore was himself in need of correction and never should be treated as a norm. 'The next generation will always need an opposition to the corrective.'" *Kierkegaard* (New York: Harper & Brothers, 1962), 2:556. The interior quotation is from *JP* 1:332, entry 710; cf. *PV,* 18 and 205.

25. Here Kierkegaard and Nietzsche agree. The latter defines objectivity "not as 'contemplation without interest' (which is a nonsensical absurdity), but as the ability . . . to employ a *variety* of perspectives and affective interpretations in the service of knowledge." *On the Genealogy of Morals,* trans. Walter Kaufmann (New York: Vintage Books, 1967), Third Essay, Section 12.

tively to relative ends" (*CUP* 1:525). But as with suffering, a new dimension comes into focus. The perpetual need to die to immediacy generates suffering, since the task is existentially difficult. The perennial failure to have achieved this goal generates guilt.

Climacus tells us that this guilt is total and essential (*CUP* 1:526, 528-29). I have a single task to perform. No doubt it is complex and is constituted by a variety of sub-tasks. Since at any given time I have failed to fulfill this task, I am guilty and liable to feel guilty. Whether I have fulfilled quite a few of the sub-tasks or not very many, I am quite simply guilty. If I am told to clean up my room and I pick up my clothes and make my bed but leave a pile of dirty dishes under the bed, I have simply not fulfilled the task assigned to me. This is the meaning of total guilt. But in the example it is total only in relation to one task among many. To be total without qualification, to be essential guilt, I would have to have failed to fulfill the one task that is infinite or absolute, which is just the picture Climacus is painting. This is essential guilt because it is not some partial and accidental part of my existence but the very nature of my identity as an existing person (subjectivity, inwardness). This is Religiousness A's version of original sin (though Climacus leaves the language of sin for a different use, as we shall see).

One way Climacus expresses this notion of total/essential guilt in distinction from partial/accidental guilt is to say that the former is a matter of recollection, the latter a matter of memory (*CUP* 1:530, 540). 'Recollection' here, in contrast to memory, does not have exactly the same sense as it does in *Fragments*, where the contrast is with divine revelation. But they are at least cousins. In *Fragments* (and *Postscript* for that matter) Platonic recollection takes me out of time and into eternity. What I recollect is the eternal truth, the same at all times because conditioned by no time. Ideally, the knower as well as the object known has been purified of any temporal contamination (especially the body and the senses for Plato, history and tradition for moderns). Memory, by contrast, enables me to recall events that have taken place in time.[26]

Where guilt is a matter of memory, it relates to specific things I have done or failed to do at some moment in time. "I hid cigarettes under my mattress so that my parents wouldn't find them," or "I failed to take the dirty

---

26. We have noted that Climacus expands the notion of recollection to include even temporal knowledge insofar as, like recollection in the strictest, Platonic sense, no divine revelation is needed and we are able to be self-sufficient in our knowing. In Climacus's language, we already have the "condition." See chapter 5 above.

dishes from my room back to the kitchen." So I feel guilty. Where guilt is a matter of recollection, by contrast, it is not a matter of any particular acts of commission or omission, but of the failure at any time and thus at every time to have fulfilled *the* task of relating myself, in resignation and suffering, absolutely to my absolute end and only relatively to my relative ends. When theologians say that our deepest problem is not sins but sin, they are making the same sort of distinction.[27]

We might describe the guilt that comes from memory finite or quantitative. Climacus calls it comparative and childish (*CUP* 1:530-31, 533, 536, 540, 542). A child, he writes, "has much memory . . . but no recollection" (*CUP* 1:540). The child might say, "I am a good boy because, although I left the dirty dishes under my bed, sister left her whole room a mess."

This shows up in the way in which guilt is linked to the concepts of punishment and satisfaction. "To every lower conception of guilt there corresponds a satisfaction that is lower than that highest conception, which is eternal recollecting, which therefore accepts no satisfaction" from the guilty one (*CUP* 1:541). Climacus gives as examples the notion of civil punishment, such as a fine or imprisonment, the concept of Nemesis, and the idea of penance, which "makes guilt finite by making it commensurable" (*CUP* 1:541-42).[28]

But it is the child's understanding of punishment that Climacus develops most fully, and that is why I have been using children's examples up to this point. All his examples arise because "it is deeply rooted in human nature that guilt requires punishment" (*CUP* 1:549). The problem with self-inflicted penance, however, is that "however well intentioned it is, it still makes guilt finite. There is in it a childlike hope and a childlike wish that everything could be right again" without having to endure "the eternal recollecting of guilt in hidden inwardness. . . . No, the most rigorous punishment is the recollecting itself" (*CUP* 1:550).

How is this childlike? "What is it that makes the child's life so easy? It is that so often 'quits' can be called and a new beginning is so frequently made" (*CUP* 1:550). Of course, the price for this fresh start or renewed in-

---

27. Kosch suggests five indications, at least implicit in *Postscript*, in support of the claim that past infancy we are always, already guilty. *Freedom and Reason*, pp. 162-63.

28. As with monasticism, Climacus tries to balance his account. "If the penance of the Middle Ages was untrue, then it was a stirring and enthusiastic untruth." If it is false to think that God "would take pleasure in a person's scourging himself, it is surely an even more dreadful untruth to leave God, if I dare to put it this way, continually out of the picture" (*CUP* 1:542).

nocence is the punishment that makes it possible by cleaning the slate. So Climacus recalls the person he once heard speak of "the happiness of childhood to be spanked" (*CUP* 1:551). People laughed, thinking the comment was ironic, but Climacus insists on taking it at face value. The point, of course, is not that children enjoy being punished, but rather that, at least when seen from an adult point of view, there is something liberating about a situation in which at that price "'quits' can be called and a new beginning is so frequently made" and "the most rigorous punishment" avoided. So he writes, "But the greatest contrast is the eternal recollecting of guilt, and the saddest longing is quite properly expressed by the longing to be spanked. . . . To long for the happiness of childhood away from all the stuff and nonsense in life . . . is still not nearly as sad as to long for it away from the eternal recollection of guilt" (*CUP* 1:551-52n.).

If the doctrine of knowledge as recollection is the desire to be the ground of our own knowledge, flight from the idea of recollecting the truth about our guilt to various finite, quantitative, comparative, childish notions expresses the desire to be the ground of our own goodness. If we can make sufficient satisfaction for our own faults, we will not need to depend on divine forgiveness. Platonism in epistemology is indeed a cousin of Pelagianism in religion.

The discussion of Religiousness A has been under the heading of pathos. As Climacus turns to Religiousness B the label becomes the dialectical. That signifies a structure of opposition in which divergent elements are in unresolved tension with each other. This does not mean that the passionate, emotional dimension of the religious life is left behind; rather, it is intensified by the dialectical tension. That tension is the one between faith and reason or understanding.

As in *Fragments*, the decisive feature of the Christian alternative to the religion of recollection is the incarnation, the God in time. As in *Fragments*, the question can be posed, "How Can an Eternal Happiness Be Built on Historical Knowledge?" (*CUP* 1:361). As in *Fragments*, the answer is that the immanence of recollection must be superseded by the transcendence of revelation. And as in *Fragments*, this involves "the absolute paradox, the absurd, the incomprehensible" (*CUP* 1:561). In other words, faith will understand itself in terms of mystery, that which exceeds the capacities of reason as recollection, the unaided, inherent powers of human understanding.

But there are two ways to say this. One can be called the Thomistic way because of the powerful way it is developed by Aquinas. Faith grounded in revelation goes beyond reason; but just as, on a larger scale, grace is the perfecting of nature rather than its abolition or annihilation, so here faith goes beyond reason but not against it. Reason is not a sufficient ground of faith, but faith is not unreasonable, and reason, properly employed, can be a handmaid or servant of faith.

Like Luther before him, Climacus explicitly rejects this scholastic synthesis and insists that faith goes *against* the understanding (*CUP* 1:565-66). This involves "faith's crucifixion of the understanding" (*CUP* 1:564). This is not to be understood in terms of the difference between those who are intellectually brilliant and those who are not. "The misunderstanding consists in the delusion that the incomprehensibility of the paradox is supposed to be connected with the difference of greater and lesser understanding, with the comparison between good and poor minds. The paradox is connected essentially with being a human being" (*CUP* 1:566; cf. 564).[29] When it comes to essential knowing, Climacus is ever the epistemic egalitarian.

The merely human ground of the problem is why Socratic ignorance can be presented as an analogy to Christian faith (*CUP* 1:566). This "doctrine of analogy" (quite different from that on which Aquinas bases his harmony of faith and reason) is important here. Climacus refers the reader back to the passages in which Socrates is presented as a commentary on truth as subjectivity. "Socratic ignorance is an analogue to the category of the absurd. . . . The Socratic inwardness in existing is an analogue to faith" (*CUP* 1:205). Here Socrates is to be distinguished sharply from Plato. The doctrine of knowledge as recollection to which Socrates appeals contains "an intimation of the beginning of speculative thought, but for that very reason Socrates did not pursue it; essentially it became Platonic . . . and Socrates essentially emphasizes existing, whereas Plato, forgetting this, loses himself in speculative thought" (*CUP* 1:205; cf. 206n.). Because he is "beyond speculative thought," Socrates "acquires, when rightly depicted, a certain analogous likeness to what the imaginary construction set forth [in *Fragments*] as that which truly goes beyond the Socratic: the truth as paradox is an analog to the paradox *sensu eminentiori* [in the more eminent sense]; the passion of inwardness in existing is then an analog to faith *sensu eminentiori*" (*CUP* 1:206n.)

What, then, might "the truth as paradox" mean in a Socratic context?

29. The view rejected here is that of Hegel, who writes, "Religion is for everyone. It is not philosophy, which is not for everyone," and then, in that context, explains that religion is a matter of mystery only for those who have not risen to the level of speculative thought. *Hegel's Lectures on the Philosophy of Religion: One-Volume Edition — The Lectures of 1827*, ed. Peter C. Hodgson (New York: Oxford University Press, 2006), pp. 106, 422-25.

"Viewed Socratically, the eternal essential truth is not at all paradoxical in itself, but only by being related to an existing person" (*CUP* 1:205). The "contradiction" that makes Socrates a dialectical thinker is the tension between the temporal and the eternal. The fully temporal individual nevertheless has an essential relation to the eternal, to norms that are not reducible to the laws and customs of one's quite temporal society and culture. The only available link for Socrates is recollection, but since this provides no adequate access to the eternal, as if one could reflect oneself out of time and into eternity,[30] the existing individual is left with a learned ignorance. This is not sheer blindness or mindlessness but a certain complex insight, and this insight is an analog to Christian faith.

A few pages later Climacus states that Christianity presents itself as "*the paradox.* . . . An offense to the Jews, foolishness to the Greeks [1 Cor. 1:23] — and an absurdity to the understanding." Then he reiterates the comparison on which his "doctrine of analogy" is based.

> Suppose that Christianity was and wants to be a mystery, an utter mystery, not a theatrical mystery that is revealed in the fifth act. . . .[31] Suppose that a revelation *sensu strictissimo* [in the strictest sense] must be a mystery and be recognizable just by its being a mystery, whereas a revelation *sensu laxiori* [in the broader sense], the withdrawing into the eternal through recollection, is a revelation in the direct sense. (*CUP* 1:213)

Here the contrast seems to be between Christianity as mystery and Platonic/Hegelian speculation, which, by allegedly "withdrawing into the eternal through recollection," purports to have a direct revelation, a vision in which mystery is replaced by pure insight.[32] But if we read the passage in the context of those just cited above, we can fill in a contrast with Socrates as well, for whose ignorance truth remains a mystery *sensu laxiori*. This would be another way of seeing Socratic ignorance as an analog to Christian faith, for which terms such as 'paradox,' 'absurd,' and 'mystery' are to be understood *sensu eminentiori* or *strictissimo*.

Climacus describes three dimensions of the dialectical tension between

---

30. We can recall Plato's account of pure knowledge in the *Phaedo* as getting rid of the body in order to "contemplate things by themselves with the soul by itself" (66d-e).

31. This evokes the third problem in *FT* where Silentio contrasts the role of secrets in aesthetic contexts, where surprise endings give a certain kind of pleasure, with the "secret" in Abraham's faith such that he was not able to tell his family what he was doing.

32. See note 26 above.

the individual's immersion in time and the essential link to the eternal. First, there is the paradox that "the eternal, essential truth is itself not at all a paradox, but it is a paradox by being related to an existing person" (*CUP* 1:205). This formulation, like the almost identical one cited above, belongs to the analysis of Socratic ignorance. But it also belongs to Religiousness A, which I've been equating with Socratic "faith." For Religiousness A "only the actuality of existence is, and yet the eternal is continually hidden by it and in hiddenness is present" (*CUP* 1:571).[33] This is the paradox of Religiousness A.

By contrast, the second and third "dialectical contradictions" (*CUP* 1:570, 574, 578) belong to Christianity as Religiousness B, where one gets the paradox, the absurd, and the mystery *sensu eminentiori* and *strictissimo*. In spite of the element of paradox in Religiousness A that we have just noticed, Climacus uses the term 'paradoxical-religious' for Religiousness B. He describes the second contradiction this way:

> *The paradoxical-religious* establishes absolutely the contradiction between existence and the eternal, because this, that the eternal is present at a specific moment of time, expresses that existence is abandoned by the hidden immanence of the eternal. In Religiousness A, the eternal is *ubique et nusquam* [everywhere and nowhere] but hidden by the actuality of existence; in the paradoxical-religious, the eternal is present at a specific point, and this is the break with immanence. (*CUP* 1:571)[34]

This is clearly a reference to the doctrine of the incarnation, the claim that Jesus of Nazareth was and is the eternal Son of God.

The third contradiction makes Religiousness B even more distinctive.

The Dialectical Contradiction That the Historical under Consideration Here Is Not Something Historical in the Ordinary Sense but Consists of

---

33. Nietzsche gives a very different account of Socrates. He is "the type of the *theoretical man*. . . . Whenever the truth is uncovered, the artist will always cling with rapt gaze to what still remains covering even after such uncovering; but the theoretical man enjoys and finds satisfaction in the discarded covering and finds the highest object of his pleasure in the process of an ever happy uncovering that succeeds through his own efforts." *The Birth of Tragedy* (New York: Penguin Classics, 1994), §15. We might call this the abolition of mystery through recollection.

34. *CUP* §1 (1:570) and §2 (1:574) give two similar definitions of this second contradiction between the temporal and the eternal, basing one's eternal happiness on something in time or in history.

That Which Can Become Historical Only against Its Nature, Consequently by Virtue of the Absurd. (CUP 1:578)

Since we normally take the human and the divine to be mutually exclusive, the claim that Jesus is "truly God and truly man" and that in him the human and divine natures are united "inconfusedly, unchangeably, indivisibly, inseparably" is deeply problematic, to say the least.[35] Climacus has been telling us that the first "dialectical contradiction," the first degree of paradoxicality that is found in Socratic ignorance (= Religiousness A), is an analog of the contradiction and paradox found in Christianity (= Religiousness B), the paradox just described in the second and third dialectical contradictions. Now we can see the point of this "doctrine of analogy." Christianity requires that the individual "venture everything" in faith. "A pagan can also do that, for example, venture everything upon the 'if' of immortality. But then it requires that the individual also risk his thought, venture to believe *against understanding (the dialectical)*" (*CUP* 1:429; emphasis added). In other words, Socrates is not a proto-Thomist who says that faith goes beyond but not against reason; he is rather an analog of the Christian faith that goes not merely beyond but against reason.

Climacus will say that Christian faith goes "against" the understanding, that it embodies a "crucifixion" of the understanding (*CUP* 1:564-65). But when he does so he refers to something that has been, can, and should be present outside the horizons of Christianity, if in a less intense sense. We must keep this in mind as an important clue when asking about the meaning of his "against reason" thesis.

Another important clue is found in our earlier discussion of the "annihilation" involved in the suffering that is the essential expression of existential pathos in Religiousness A. Some have mistakenly taken this to mean the abolition of individuality as such. But a closer look reveals that it signifies the *annihilation* of immediate individuality only insofar as it takes itself to be absolute and ultimate and the *teleological suspension* of immediate individuality in the individuality that is mediated (yes — we can use the Hegelian term here) by its relation to the eternal and the task it sets. The lesson, of course, is that we should not latch onto just any possible meaning of the phrase "against reason" and attribute it to Climacus. We must look carefully to see what fits in the context of all he has been saying.

The most obvious sense in which Religiousness B, like the construction

35. The language is taken from the Chalcedonian Creed of A.D. 451.

224

or thought-project of *Fragments,* is "against" reason or the understanding is that it rejects the claims of recollection in any of its various modes to be either (1) the only form of genuine knowledge or (2) the highest form of genuine knowledge with normative hegemony over what any purported divine revelation will be permitted to mean. If that is what is meant by reason, biblical faith will be against it. Some Platonisms and post-Kierkegaardian positivisms would be examples of the first case, while Spinoza, Kant, and Hegel would be good examples of the second.[36]

In these examples, the modes of "reason" to which faith cannot submit without losing its own soul are forms of speculative philosophy. In our own time, the natural sciences are more likely to play this role. But Climacus's argument remains the same: to declare or to presuppose the hegemony of either speculative philosophy or natural science over all other claims to knowledge is simply to beg the question against biblical faith. Of course such faith is unreasonable on that assumption and must either be (1) abandoned altogether or (2) brought into conformity with the latest version of "reason." Climacus might well repeat an earlier response: "It is just as you say and the amazing thing is that you think that it is an objection" (*PF,* 52). Faith has long since insisted that, in its claim to be grounded in the wisdom of God, it is bound to seem foolishness from the perspective of human wisdom, which remains just that — merely human wisdom, which in its plurality and changeableness is anything but self-evidently absolute in its autonomy.

The view that Christianity must, in order to be itself, reject the claims of unaided human cognition to autonomous hegemony is surely part of Climacus's "against reason" thesis. But in these terms biblical faith goes beyond Socrates, as in *Fragments,* without finding in him any analogy to itself. He merely represents the recollection mode of learning, in its proper humility (according to Climacus), that is purportedly surpassed in Christian faith.

---

36. The second is also the position of Heidegger. He repeatedly says that it is the task of phenomenology to "correct" theology, since theological concepts are to be "*ontically* sublated," that is to say they are "*ontologically* determined by a content that is pre-Christian and that can thus be grasped purely rationally." Thus the theological concept of sin is to be corrected by the phenomenological concept of guilt as developed, for example, in *Being and Time.* "Phenomenology and Theology," in Martin Heidegger, *Pathmarks,* ed. William McNeill (New York: Cambridge University Press, 1998), p. 51. In *Being and Time,* trans. John Macquarrie and Edward Robinson (New York: Harper & Row, 1962), §§57-58, the call of conscience from which guilt emerges comes "*from* me [*aus mir*] and yet *from beyond* me [*über mich*]." This suggests the same kind of autonomy, and thus recollection *(aus mir),* combined with moral realism *(über mich),* that one finds in Plato and Kant.

The analogy is perhaps ontological rather than merely epistemic. The Socrates whom Climacus admires is not two different entities somehow glued Platonically together, a sensate body whose natural habitat is the cave of temporality and a soul whose true home is the eternal sunshine of pure intellect.[37] In his bodily mortality he is fully of the earth; for life in the cave there is no flight to the empyrean. There is only the actuality of existence, "and yet the eternal is continually hidden by it and in hiddenness is present" (*CUP* 1:571). In his temporal, bodily, mortal life, Socrates is the paradoxical unity of the temporal and the eternal in the mode of an unresolved dialectical tension. It is precisely this tension that gives rise to Socratic ignorance and irony.

We might say that Climacus understands Socrates as "truly temporal and truly eternal" and that the temporal and eternal dimensions of his human personhood are united "inconfusedly, unchangeably, indivisibly, inseparably." This is paradoxical, at least in relation to all "Platonic" thought, according to which opposites must be mutually exclusive. If the self is to be both temporal (mortal) and eternal (immortal), it must be by virtue of a *changeable* togetherness of a temporal body that is *separable* from an eternal soul. Insofar as Socrates understands himself over against this Platonic dualism, he thinks *against* reason or understanding insofar as they are Platonically defined, not only in terms of recollection but also in terms of the ontology of the self that Plato joins to it. At the same time Socrates becomes a double analog. He is an analog of the Jewish and Christian view that the human self is an integral, if paradoxical, unity of the temporal and the eternal such that immortality would have to take the form of bodily resurrection, not the permanent separation of two independent substances, a corruptible body and an incorruptible soul. Even more strangely, he is an analog of the Jesus of orthodox Christology in whom the human and divine natures reside in dialectical tension just as the temporal and eternal dimensions of the human self do in Socrates.[38]

It is this second analogy that is of interest to Climacus. We have seen that the Christian affirmation is paradoxical *sensu eminentiori* or *strictissimo* for two reasons: it affirms the presence of the eternal not just in time but at a particular time and place (*CUP* 1:574), and it affirms that the eternal

37. For Plato's allegory of the cave and analogy of the sun, see *Republic*, Books VI and VII.

38. On the contrast between Jesus and the Platonic, dualistic Socrates of the *Phaedo*, see the famous essay by Oscar Cullmann, "Immortality of the Soul or Resurrection of the Dead?" in *Immortality and Resurrection,* ed. Krister Stendahl (New York: Macmillan, 1965), pp. 9-53.

becomes historical only "against its nature" (*CUP* 1:578). To see such an affirmation as "against reason" is not merely to go beyond and against an epistemology of recollection; it is to go beyond and against a certain ontology, a dualistic, atomistic ontology according to which opposing natures cannot be united but only juxtaposed. When reason is defined in terms of this ontology, both the paradoxical-dialectical union of temporal and eternal that Socrates understands himself to be and the paradoxical-dialectical union that Christians understand Jesus to be are against nature and thus unreasonable. But this reason turns out to be a particular, substantive, metaphysical worldview whose ultimacy can be presupposed only by begging the question against orthodox Christology.

For Silentio in *Fear and Trembling,* faith went beyond infinite resignation by virtue of the belief that for God all things are possible, even the resurrection of the dead. For Climacus in *Fragments* and *Postscript,* faith goes beyond speculative philosophy and scientific naturalism (and any version of "reason" defined in terms of either) by affirming that a historically particular human person can simultaneously be the eternal Son of God.

The views of reason that are gone "beyond" in faith are quite natural and not at all bizarre. They are present in each of us, just as the ethical (in its Hegelian definition as the laws and customs of one's people) is present in each of us. So there are two things to notice. First, if in faith one goes beyond these modes of reason, it will not be to abandon or abolish them but to suspend them teleologically in something taken to be higher and more inclusive. One will feel the tension between the relative and the absolute in a passion born of paradox. Second, this going "beyond" will be a turning "against" only insofar as the modes of thought relativized in the process insist on being absolute. It is in their alleged absoluteness that they must be repudiated, just as it is only in its immediacy that individuality must be annihilated.

The analysis of Religiousness A and B has moved from pathos to the dialectical, from the passions of subjectivity to the question of faith and reason. According to well-established traditions, Platonic, Stoic, and often Christian, the term 'passions' is inherently pejorative and the life of virtue is a life of reason governing, even extirpating the passions. Climacus seems almost perversely to turn this schema upside-down. He writes in praise of the passions of subjectivity and at least with respect for a faith that turns against reason. This expresses his double argument. First, there are passions without which we cannot be fully human, and any intellectualism that ignores or belittles these is dehumanizing. These passions arise not only in the process of trying to determine what to believe, but especially in the process of converting ourselves by converting our beliefs into practices. Second, 'reason' comes in a variety of modes, none of which can preclude faith (response to divine revelation) as a source of knowledge without begging the question. Especially when reason is defined in relation to a substantive, metaphysical worldview, it represents not so much an alternative to faith but an alternative faith whose grounds are themselves open to debate. It is not the neutral tribunal whose *imprimatur* faith must attain but a finite partner in the conversation that is human reason.

PART THREE

Anti-Climacus

CHAPTER 12

Faith as Willing to Be Oneself — Before God

We come now to our third and final pseudonym, Anti-Climacus, the author of *Sickness unto Death* and *Practice in Christianity*. Kierkegaard originally intended to publish *Sickness unto Death* under his own name, but at the last minute he attributed it to Anti-Climacus, explaining in his journals,

> It is absolutely right — a pseudonym had to be used.
>
> When the demands of ideality are to be presented at their maximum, then one must take extreme care not to be confused with them himself, as if he himself were the ideal. . . .
>
> The difference from the earlier pseudonyms is simply but essentially this, that I do not retract the whole thing humorously but identify myself as one who is striving. (*JP* 6:181, entry 6446)

As pseudonyms, Johannes de Silentio and Johannes Climacus served two important functions. They distanced what they had to say from Kierke-gaard himself, leaving the reader alone with their ideas, and they allowed Kierkegaard to talk about faith from the standpoint of someone outside of faith. In *Sickness* pseudonymity serves a different function. Kierkegaard "felt unable to present himself in his own person as someone able to exem-plify [the high spiritual standards which religious faith and observance re-quired] and to judge others. He must not appear to presume to have become a Christian of the kind he was now describing."[1] So he found it necessary

---

1. Alastair Hannay, *Kierkegaard: A Biography* (New York: Cambridge University Press, 2001), p. 374.

to keep the reader from assuming that in describing faith he is describing himself and to remind all his readers, including himself, that faith is a task word and not an achievement word. As Climacus puts it, faith is a perpetual striving, a matter of *becoming* a Christian.

In their Historical Introduction to *Sickness*, the Hongs suggest that the "Anti-" in Anti-Climacus "may be misleading. It does not mean 'against.' It is an old form of 'ante' (before), as in 'anticipate,' and 'before' also denotes a relation of rank, as in 'before me' in the First Commandment" (*SUD*, xxii). But if Anti-Climacus is "before" Climacus in the sense of a higher rank, it would be because he is "against" Climacus in the sense of being simply serious and direct rather than dialectically humorous/serious and indirect. We have seen, in chapter 7, that jest and seriousness are not mutually exclusive for Climacus; but Anti-Climacus is not a humorist in the way Climacus is. He is more straightforwardly serious. If, indeed, "Anti" signifies higher rank or greater importance, it means that Kierkegaard has come to privilege direct over indirect communication.

But it is always a mistake to become so caught up in reflection on the significance of pseudonymity as to neglect the substance of what each pseudonym presents for our consideration.

Two other preliminary comments. The Preface opens with a worry. "Many may find the form of this 'exposition' strange; it may seem to them too rigorous to be upbuilding and too upbuilding to be rigorously scholarly." Anti-Climacus wants it to be both rigorously scholarly and upbuilding, but he is more concerned with the latter, and he does not wish to purchase the former by means of a "scholarly distance from life" or "the kind of scienticity and scholarliness that is 'indifferent,'" and as such "a kind of inhuman curiosity." So his account of what is "essentially Christian must have in its presentation a resemblance to the way a physician speaks at the sickbed" (*SUD*, 5). For the work of the physician properly rests on the best scientific knowledge available, but its purpose and thus its essence are to heal.

As the doctor is to the scientist, so the preacher is to the scholar. The good theologian, we might say, combines the roles of preacher and scholar, and in this sense Anti-Climacus aspires to be a good theologian. Accordingly, the subtitle of *Sickness* is *A Christian Psychological Exposition for Upbuilding and Awakening*. The exposition must be theoretically sound (rigorous) both theologically and psychologically, but the goal goes beyond theory to the practice of upbuilding and awakening.

Second, were he writing today Anti-Climacus would probably say 'phenomenological' rather than 'psychological.' For he certainly does not mean psychology in the empirical, experimental sense that dominates that discipline today. He means a non-theological, non-experimental account of what it is to be a human person in terms of which health and malfunction can be identified.[2] Such a project would typically be called phenomenology today, even if phenomenology sometimes values scientific rigor over upbuilding and awakening.[3]

In *Sickness* despair is the sickness unto death, and, surprisingly, it is faith rather than hope that is the opposite and the overcoming of despair. "The opposite to being in despair is to have faith" (*SUD,* 49). Anti-Climacus gives five formulations of his definition of faith. Three of them have the following form:

> Therefore, the formula set forth above, which describes a state in which there is no despair at all, is entirely correct, and this formula is also the formula for faith: in relating to itself and in willing to be itself, the self rests transparently in the power that established it. (*SUD,* 49)

Virtually identical formulas are found at *SUD,* 14 and 131.

There are four aspects of faith in these definitions.

(1) The self is completely free from despair. This is strong language, suggestive, perhaps, of an always unfinished task of a lifetime.
(2) The self relates to itself.
(3) In doing so, the self wills to be itself.
(4) In doing both (2) and (3), the self relates to another, namely the power that has established it.

Sprinkled in among these three formulations are two others in which the power that has established the self is explicitly identified as God, as one would expect in an exposition of Christian faith.

---

2. For suggestions on how to read Kierkegaard as a phenomenologist, see *Kierkegaard as Phenomenologist: An Experiment,* ed. Jeffrey Hanson (Evanston, IL: Northwestern University Press, 2010).

3. See, for example, Edmund Husserl, "Philosophy as Rigorous Science," in *Husserl: Shorter Works,* ed. Peter McCormick and Frederick Elliston (Notre Dame: University of Notre Dame Press, 1981), pp. 161-97. By contrast, Emmanuel Lévinas calls himself a phenomenologist and is very much concerned with awakening. See, for example, his "From Consciousness to Wakefulness: Starting from Husserl," in *Of God Who Comes to Mind,* trans. Bettina Bergo (Stanford: Stanford University Press, 1998), pp. 15-32, and "Philosophy and Awakening," in *Entre Nous: Thinking-of-the-Other,* trans. Michael B. Smith and Barbara Harshav (New York: Columbia University Press, 1998), pp. 77-90.

. . . for the self is healthy and free from despair only when, precisely by having despaired, it rests transparently in God. (*SUD*, 30)

Faith is: that the self in being itself and in willing to be itself rests transparently in God. (*SUD*, 82)

Three differences emerge immediately. First, there is the notion of coming to faith from having already despaired. Second, the notion of the self relating to itself is replaced in one formula by the notion of the self being itself. Third, the ground that has established the self is specifically identified as God.

We need not be too puzzled by these differences. First, since despair will eventually be identified as sin (*SUD*, Part Two), the notion that we come to faith having already despaired simply means that we come to faith as sinners and not from innocence. Just as we have no need for doctors if we are not sick, so the need for faith emerges only east of Eden. Just as in *Postscript* the immediate self is always already absolutely committed to relative ends, here the immediate self is always already in despair. In a section devoted to the universality of despair, Anti-Climacus rejects as "superficial," as "a very poor understanding," and as "totally false" the view that we are in despair only if we think we are (*SUD*, 22-23, 26). Despair is a certain kind of anxiety, and "all immediacy is [this] anxiety" (*SUD*, 25). Faith requires the conversion that in *Postscript* is called transformation.

Second, we can guess that for Anti-Climacus the being of the self is a relational being (triply so, as we shall see) so that only when its relations are right is the self really itself. Despair is an ontological defect, which is why we can feel happy and be in despair at the same time (*SUD*, 25). Just as Augustine sees evil as a privation of being, so Anti-Climacus sees despair (sin) as a failure to be oneself. Descartes' "I think, therefore I am" becomes "I have faith, and just to that degree I am." Zarathustra's "Become who you are!"[4] becomes "Become yourself by overcoming despair in faith."

Third, we should not be surprised to find a Kierkegaardian pseudonym using the term 'God' interchangeably with some more abstract, generic term such as 'the eternal,' or in this case 'the power that has established the self.' Often this signifies the attempt to leave open the space for something like Socratic religion (Religiousness A in *Postscript*), a mode of existing that

4. Friedrich Nietzsche, *Thus Spoke Zarathustra*, trans. Walter Kaufmann (Princeton: Princeton University Press, 1966), p. 239 (Fourth Part, The Honey Sacrifice).

is genuinely religious without being theistic in the mode of the Abrahamic monotheisms.

Here, perhaps, the significance is different. If we ask who or what, other than a personal God who is an agent and a speaker, might be seen as the ground that has established the self, two fairly obvious candidates come to mind: nature (Spinoza and various scientific naturalisms) and society (Hegel and various socio-psychological ontologies of selfhood).[5] While Anti-Climacus does not explore these possibilities in *Sickness,* they are worth thinking through in connection with *Sickness* for at least two reasons: their current power and popularity, and the way they map onto Kierkegaard's theory of the stages.

Scientific naturalism maps onto the aesthetic stage insofar as the moral categories of good and evil, right and wrong are not fundamental to being; whatever reality they have is derivative from some amoral value such as survival. Sociological theories of selfhood, including various historicisms, map onto the ethical stage insofar as the highest normative criterion for the self is some particular socio-historical "universal," some (one or more) state, nation, society, church, or sect to which the self belongs and by which it has been formed.[6] To see God as the power that has established the self is not to deny the naturalistic and the sociological perspectives, but to subordinate them to a theological perspective in a double *Aufhebung* or teleological suspension.

So we need not be puzzled by the differences among the various formulations or definitions of faith. But we are bound to remain puzzled by another feature of their account of faith — its remoteness from ordinary ways of thinking. The definitions of faith offered so far by our two previous pseudonyms may be controversial in one way or another. But they do not stray very far from relatively familiar ways of thinking about faith, whether positively or negatively. One might say that there is something of the ordinary language philosopher in Silentio and Climacus. This remains true of

---

5. Freud might be read as an attempt to combine the two. The same with Wilfrid Sellars, who seeks to place a theory of normativity (ethical and epistemic) in terms of community intentions or "we" intentions in the context of an overall scientific naturalism. See Sellars, "Philosophy and the Scientific Image of Man," in *Frontiers of Science and Philosophy,* ed. Robert G. Colodny (Pittsburgh: University of Pittsburgh Press, 1962), especially pp. 75-78.

6. See chapter 3 above. This is the ethical of *Fear and Trembling* and of Judge William in *Either/Or* 2. While the judge often speaks of the "eternal" validity of the self, suggesting a source of normativity higher than the laws and customs of one's people, he effectively deprives this notion of its force by his inability to conceive that *we* could be wrong in relation to God.

Anti-Climacus insofar as he presents faith as existence "before God" (*SUD*, 5, 27, 33-35, 46, 77-79, 85). But the notion that faith is a mode of relating to oneself and, more particularly, of willing to be oneself takes us beyond familiar usage. How does Anti-Climacus get from there to here, where 'there' signifies his point of departure and 'here' signifies these definitions of faith with "willing to be oneself" playing such a prominent role.

The answer is simple enough. He begins with a definition of the self. However, it is anything but a simple definition. I remember vividly the first time I read it. Nothing I have ever read — not even the passages where Hegel says "The True is thus the Bacchanalian revel in which no member is not drunk," or "*Essence* is the *supersession* of all distinctions, the pure movement of axial rotation, its self-repose being an absolutely restless infinity"[7] — has brought me to such a screeching halt. My students have had a similar experience. Here is the definition that is the starting point for Anti-Climacus:

> A human being is spirit. But what is spirit?[8] Spirit is the self. But what is the self? The self is a relation that relates itself to itself or is the relation's relating itself to itself in the relation; the self is not the relation but is the relation's relating itself to itself. A human being is a synthesis of the infinite and finite, of the temporal and the eternal, of freedom and necessity, in short, a synthesis. A synthesis is a relation between two. Considered in this way, a human being is still not a self.

After adding a fourth dyad, "the psychical and the physical," Anti-Climacus adds that only when the relation relates to itself is it a self and that it has either established itself or been established by another. Then he completes his definition:

> The human self is such a derived, established relation, a relation that relates itself to itself and in relating itself to itself relates itself to another. (*SUD*, 13-14)

The self is thoroughly relational; indeed, it is triply so, as promised above. So the short formula is this: the self is (A) a relation that (B) relates

---

7. G. W. F. Hegel, *Phenomenology of Spirit*, trans. A. V. Miller (Oxford: Clarendon Press, 1977), pp. 27, 106. The older, Baillie translation speaks of life, or essence, or infinitude as "the pure rotation on its own axis."

8. Hegel had defined spirit socio-psychologically as " 'I' that is 'We' and 'We' that is 'I.' " *Phenomenology of Spirit*, p. 110.

itself to itself and (C) in so doing relates itself to another. A, B, and C represent three dimensions of the self, and if we take them one at a time, Anti-Climacus's rather turgid definition becomes less perplexing. We might say it is as simple as A, B, C.

According to A, the self is a relation, a.k.a. a synthesis of the finite and the infinite, of the temporal and the eternal, of necessity and freedom, and of the physical and the psychical. Anti-Climacus might better have spoken of a dialectical tension than of a synthesis; for the unity of the elements is paradoxical and unresolved.[9] They do not dissolve into some third thing that is neither. The model would be more like oil and water than like the union of hydrogen and oxygen in a molecule of water. The self is an "object" that can be studied by psychology and sociology; but at the same time it is a "subject" that is capable of art and philosophy, morality and religion in ways that are irreducible to these sciences. Both perspectives are true, but neither is the whole truth.

If we ask why Anti-Climacus nevertheless speaks of syntheses, the best answer might well be that he wants to avoid any hint of a substance dualism à la Plato or Descartes. It is not that the self is a perishable substance to which one set of predicates applies and an imperishable substance to which the opposing predicates apply. The self is a single individual to which both sets of predicates apply, however different they may be from each other.[10] For Anti-Climacus the so-called "mind-body problem" is not a puzzle or a problem to be solved so much as a mystery to remind us that we are "fearfully and wonderfully made" (Ps. 139:14).

Anti-Climacus is emphatic. Simply as such a synthesis "a human being is still not a self. . . . If, however, the relation relates itself to itself, this relation is the positive third, and this is the self" (*SUD*, 13). It is with B, the self's relation to itself, that we first come upon an actual self. We might think that

---

9. For Hegel, the dialectical is the realm of opposition, and speculative thought moves beyond this to grasp as Reason the unity in opposition of what the mere Understanding can only grasp as separate and opposed. Understanding is the realm of antinomies, while "everything rational can equally be called 'mystical.'" Hegel, *The Encyclopedia Logic,* trans. T. F. Geraets, W. A. Suchting, and H. S. Harris (Indianapolis: Hackett, 1991), §§79-82. Strange as this may sound, it is Kierkegaard rather than Hegel who is the dialectical philosopher, the thinker of unresolved paradoxes.

10. Cf. P. F. Strawson, who argues that persons are a peculiar kind of individual to whom both M-predicates, those properly applied to material bodies, and P-predicates, those distinctively applied to persons, are appropriate. *Individuals: An Essay in Descriptive Metaphysics* (London: Methuen & Co., 1959), pp. 103-10.

this self-relation is self-consciousness. The transition from consciousness to self-consciousness is of central importance to such modern thinkers as Descartes, Kant, and Hegel — and, later on, in very different ways, to Husserl and Freud. Anti-Climacus's own concern for transparency seems to point in the same direction.

But he rather identifies the self's relation to itself with freedom. The synthesis that is not quite the self yet, "even though it is derived, relates itself to itself, which is freedom" (*SUD*, 29).[11] The self is a self only insofar as it presides over itself.[12] Now we can see why the concept of will is so central to Anti-Climacus's account of faith. The self is *a self* only insofar as it is an agent in relation to itself, and it is *itself* only when it exercises this agency properly.

With this freedom comes responsibility. Having read Silentio and Climacus, we suspect that we are about to hear about the self's task, and we are not disappointed. Anti-Climacus speaks of the self, "whose task is to become itself" (*SUD*, 29).

The concept of 'task' is utterly fundamental to Kierkegaard's writings. It plays a crucial role in all three pseudonyms under consideration here. Even before Silentio, it is important to Judge William's exposition of the ethical stage (see especially *EO* 2:251-70). The judge recalls that as a five-year-old schoolboy he was given his assignment for the next day, "the first ten lines in Balle's catechism, which I was to learn by heart. Every other impression was now erased from my soul; only my task stood vividly before it." He tells how he learned it, had his sister test him on it several times, and recited it to himself as he fell asleep, planning to review it in the morning.

> It seemed to me that heaven and earth would tumble down if I did not do my homework, and on the other hand it seemed to me that if heaven and earth did tumble down this upheaval would in no way excuse me from

11. In a fascinating journal entry, Kierkegaard argues, paradoxically, that only an omnipotent God could create a finite but free person. "The greatest good, after all, which can be done for a being, greater than anything else that one can do for it, is to make it free. In order to do just that, omnipotence is required," since only omnipotence is "able to withdraw itself again . . . in such a way that . . . that which has been originated through omnipotence can be independent" (*JP* 2:62, entry 1251). The implication is that neither nature nor society could withdraw its impact in this way.

12. M. Merleau-Ponty similarly writes that "our existence" needs phenomenological reflection "in order to become acquainted with and to prevail over its facticity." *The Phenomenology of Perception*, trans. Colin Smith (London: Routledge & Kegan Paul, 1962), p. xv. As I read it, to prevail over one's facticity is to preside over the fourfold synthesis of Anti-Climacus in all its concrete specificity.

doing what had once been set before me — doing my homework. . . . I had but one duty, to do my homework, and yet I can derive my whole ethical view of life from this impression.

I can smile at such a little fellow of five years who approaches a matter that passionately, and yet I assure you that I have no higher wish than that at any period of my life I may approach my work with the energy, with the ethical earnestness, I did then. It is true that later on in life one gets a better idea of what one's work is, but the energy is still the main thing. (*EO* 2:267)

This passage is almost surely autobiographical, and it is definitive not only for Judge William's view of the ethical but also for Kierkegaard's own view of the ethical-religious. Kierkegaard now has "a better idea of what one's work is." As we have just seen, for Anti-Climacus the task is to become oneself. This means to become concrete in relation to the polar elements while keeping them in dialectical tension. For example:

But to become concrete is neither to become finite nor to become infinite, for that which is to become concrete is indeed a synthesis. Consequently, the progress of the becoming must be an infinite moving away from itself in the infinitizing of the self, and an infinite coming back to itself in the finitizing process. But if the self does not become itself, it is in despair, whether it knows that or not. (*SUD*, 30)[13]

In other words, in our freedom we are responsible for being in despair. "And because the relation [of the self to itself] is spirit, is the self, upon it rests the responsibility for all despair at every moment of existence, however much the despairing person speaks of his despair as a misfortune and however ingeniously he deceives himself and others" (*SUD*, 16). In the case of ordinary illness the individual might be "responsible for catching the sickness," but it cannot be said "that he *is bringing* it upon himself. To despair, however, is a different matter. Every actual moment of despair is traceable to possibility; every moment he is in despair he *is bringing* it upon himself. It is always the present tense" (*SUD*, 16-17).

13. On Kierkegaard's "psychology" as a psychoanalytic or "depth" psychology of the unconscious, see my essay, "Kierkegaard's Psychology and Unconscious Despair," in *International Kierkegaard Commentary*, vol. 19: *The Sickness unto Death,* ed. Robert L. Perkins (Macon, GA: Mercer University Press, 1987), pp. 39-66.

Like the Sartrean self, I am who I choose to be; but unlike the Sartrean self, I am given a right way (faith) and a variety of wrong ways (despair) to choose.[14]

The third dimension of the triply relational self, what is here called C, is the relation of the self to "another," namely "the power that has established it." When this power is identified as God, the self is understood to be created. But this is not just a causal fact about the self's origin. Here, too, "it is always the present tense," for, as we have seen, the self that has been established by God lives at every moment "before God." For Anti-Climacus, just as everyone is always already in despair whether they know it or not, so everyone exists "before God" whether they know it or not. The tri-relational structure being described is ontological before it becomes psychological (phenomenological) and religious.

Despair as an illness is a triple misrelation on the part of the self. As John Glenn puts it, "It is a failure to *will* to be the self one truly is — in other words, a deficient self-relation — which involves also an imbalance among the components of the self as synthesis and a deficient God-relation."[15] Faith, as the total overcoming of despair, will require the conversion or transformation in which misrelation becomes right relation in all three dimensions of the self.

Glenn suggests that the threefold definition of the self is the key to the structure of *Sickness*. In doing so he makes that structure more transparent than Kierkegaard's own table of contents does. After some preliminary discussion (*SUD*, 5-28), Glenn's first part (*SUD*, 29-47) analyzes the forms of despair with reference to the self as the synthesis (or dialectical tension) of opposing elements but without reference to whether the self is conscious of despair or not. Glenn's second part (*SUD*, 47-74) discusses forms of despair that are modes of the self's self-relation as willing and thus forms of consciousness. Glenn's third part (*SUD*, 77-131), entitled "Despair Is Sin," describes despair in terms of the self's relation to God.[16]

---

14. See Jean-Paul Sartre, "Existentialism Is a Humanism," in *Existentialism from Dostoevsky to Sartre*, rev. ed., ed. Walter Kaufmann (New York: New American Library, 1975), pp. 345-69. Or *Existentialism Is a Humanism*, trans. Carol Macomber (New Haven: Yale University Press, 2007).

15. John D. Glenn Jr., "The Definition of the Self and the Structure of Kierkegaard's Work," in Perkins, ed., *International Kierkegaard Commentary*, vol. 19: *The Sickness unto Death*, pp. 5-21.

16. Glenn, "Definition of the Self," pp. 6-18. The first and second part of Glenn's analysis occur within Anti-Climacus's Part One, while Glenn's third part is identical with Anti-

The first part, à la Glenn, is a phenomenological description of quasi-selves whose misrelation consists in privileging one side of the polar tensions at the expense of the other. Read in the light of what follows, this involves both not willing to be oneself, for the synthesis is what the self is, and not resting transparently in God, for it is God who has established the self as that (complex) synthesis. Thus we get the despair that lacks finitude, the despair that lacks infinitude, the despair that lacks necessity, and the despair that lacks possibility.

These phenomenological analyses are very rich and invite illustration in terms of various literary figures and philosophical theories. The details are not as crucial to Anti-Climacus's account of faith as the following general claim. As these misrelations are constitutive of despair and thus antitheses to faith, faith will require a certain psychic health that is not directly spiritual in terms of the God relation. From reading *Sickness unto Death*, psychotherapists might well learn that there are spiritual as well as psychological dimensions of psychic health; and pastoral counselors might well learn that there are psychological as well as spiritual dimensions to a healthy faith. The self is not just a synthesis of the physical and the psychical but also of the psychical and the spiritual. In other words, it can be described in terms of P-predicates (those of the psychotherapist) and S-predicates (those of the pastoral counselor), neither being reducible to the other. Faith, as the deepest health of the self, will require P-health and S-health, and willing to be oneself will involve one's relation both to the synthesis one is and to the God before whom one exists.[17] Perhaps physical health could provide an analogy, since it requires both a good diet and proper exercise, neither of which can render the other irrelevant.

The person who lives in the despair that fails to keep the polar elements in a balanced tension is very likely in *"Despairing Ignorance of Having a Self and an Eternal Self"* (SUD, 42). Such a person "is presumably happy, imagines himself to be happy, although considered in the light of [ontological] truth he is unhappy." This is because "he is completely dominated by the sensate and sensate-psychical, because he lives in sensate categories, the pleasant and the unpleasant . . . because he is too sensate to venture out and to endure being spirit" (SUD, 43). This would be the aesthete, although if

---

Climacus's Part Two. Glenn also argues that these three parts of *Sickness* map onto the three stages or spheres of existence, a suggestion I find less compelling or helpful than his analysis of *SUD* itself. Cf. my suggestion above that the threefold definition of the self maps nicely onto the three stages.

17. See the discussion at note 10 above.

we are thinking of the young man of *Either/Or* 1, the balance would have to be shifted toward the sensate-psychical; for he is not the hedonist for whom the pleasant is primarily physical.

Perhaps Anti-Climacus has been reading Climacus, for he lumps the speculative together with the aesthetic and takes a shot at Hegel and his ilk.

> A thinker erects a huge building, a system, a system embracing the whole of existence, world history, etc., and if his personal life is considered, to our amazement the appalling and ludicrous discovery is made that he himself does not live in this huge, domed palace, but in a shed alongside it, or in a doghouse, or at best in the janitor's quarters. (*SUD*, 43-44)

This is not because the fundamental categories for the speculative thinker are the pleasant and the unpleasant. They are rather absolute knowing (Reason, the Concept) and merely relative knowing (Understanding, Representations). Within this horizon the task of becoming oneself as presented by Anti-Climacus does not even arise. This is the ironical ignorance of the speculative thinker.

Nor does it necessarily help to be religious in the sense of a baptized, catechized, regular church-attending "Christian." Such a person is not immune to the same ignorance found in the aesthete and the speculative thinker. To be sure, Christianity seeks to distinguish itself from the "world," from "the natural man," from "paganism." The despair that is ignorant of being in despair is "the most common in the world." We can and should call it paganism, but then we should recognize that "paganism in Christendom is precisely this kind of despair" (*SUD*, 45; cf. 46-47). We should not take this to mean that in the countries that make up Christendom there are aesthetes and speculative thinkers (who probably don't go to church except to be married and buried, or perhaps at Christmas and Easter). The term "paganism in Christendom" is important to Anti-Climacus, and it points to a third site of the unconscious despair of ignorance: the all too typical churchgoer for whom the life of faith is a matter of externals and social conformity. Successful socialization is all the conversion or transformation that is required of the immediate self.[18]

---

18. For the way this theme is developed in *Christian Discourses*, see my essay, "Paganism in Christendom: Kierkegaard's Critique of Religion," in *International Kierkegaard Commentary*, vol. 17: *"Christian Discourses" and "The Crisis and a Crisis in the Life of an Actress,"* ed. Robert L. Perkins (Macon, GA: Mercer University Press, 2007), pp. 13-33.

If the surprise of the first part of our text is that faith has a psychological as well as a spiritual dimension, the second part (*SUD*, 47-74) takes us to the even more surprising claim that faith is not merely a relation to oneself but even a willing to be oneself. That suggests that despair is a kind of refusal to be oneself. That is already implicit in the despair that flees from one dialectical pole to its opposite, refusing to be the dialectical tension between them. But Anti-Climacus makes it explicit early on. The despairing individual "wants to be rid of himself . . . he now cannot bear to be himself . . . this self is now utterly intolerable to him . . . he cannot get rid of himself . . . he despairs over not being able to get rid of himself. . . . To despair over oneself, in despair to will to be rid of oneself — this is the formula for all despair" (*SUD*, 19-20).

Anti-Climacus takes willing to be an exercise of free agency and, as such, a form of consciousness. So now he is dealing with conscious rather than unconscious despair (*SUD*, 47). But we should notice two things. First, he does not consider conscious/unconscious to be a simple either/or. "Actual life is too complex merely to point out abstract contrasts such as that between a despair that is completely unaware of being so and a despair that is completely aware of being so. Very often the person in despair probably has a dim idea of his own state, although here again the nuances are myriad" (*SUD*, 48). In other words, it is a matter of degree, and in speaking simply of conscious or unconscious despair we are dealing with ideal types. An individual "may try to keep himself in the dark about his state through diversions and in other ways . . . yet in such a way that he does not entirely realize why he is doing it, that is to keep himself in the dark" (*SUD*, 48). If it makes sense to say that I am trying to achieve some goal, there must be some element of consciousness at work, but I may at the same time be trying not to notice what I am doing or why.[19] In any case, the shift is from despair as an objective imbalance between opposing aspects to a subject's act that can be described as wanting or willing.[20]

19. This account is much closer to Sartre's concept of bad faith than to Freud's rather mechanistic concept of the unconscious. See Jean-Paul Sartre, *Being and Nothingness,* trans. Hazel Barnes (New York: Philosophical Library, 1956) or (New York: Washington Square Press, 1992), part 1, ch. 2. Cf. C. Stephen Evans, "Kierkegaard's View of the Unconscious," in *Kierkegaard in Post/Modernity,* ed. Martin J. Matustik and Merold Westphal (Bloomington: Indiana University Press, 1995), pp. 76-97.

20. With reference to despair as an act, Michelle Kosch places too strong an emphasis on agency to do justice to *Sickness*. She writes that for Judge William, in *Either/Or*, despair is "a passive or fatalistic attitude towards one's existence, motivated by a misconstrual of the

Second, there are two basic forms of despair under analysis here: "α. In Despair Not to Will to Be Oneself: Despair in Weakness" and, paradoxically, "β. *In Despair to Will to Be Oneself: Defiance*" (*SUD*, 49, 67). But once again Anti-Climacus insists, "the opposites are only relative. No despair is entirely free of defiance; indeed, the very phrase 'not to will to be' implies defiance. On the other hand, even despair's most extreme defiance is never free of some weakness. So the distinction is only relative" (*SUD*, 49). Once again we are dealing with ideal types, just as one never meets in empirical reality with anything that strictly corresponds to the definition of a circle.

Anti-Climacus distinguishes two modes of the despair of weakness: (1) "Despair over the Earthly or over Something Earthly" (*SUD*, 50) and (2) "Despair of the Eternal or over Oneself" (*SUD*, 60). The former is *"despair in weakness,"* while the latter is *"despair over [one's] weakness"* (*SUD*, 61). Both involve misfortune. In the first case one wills to be rid of oneself because things have gone badly, in the other case because one has handled the situation badly. In the one case I wish to be "someone else" who was spared my misfortune; in the other case, "Like a father who disinherits a son, the self does not want to acknowledge itself after having been so weak" (*SUD*, 53, 62). A reversal of fortune does not, as such, change anything. "If help arrives from the outside, the person in despair comes alive again, he begins where he left off." Instead of feeling depressed, he may be happy. But "a self he was not, and a self he did not become" (*SUD*, 52).

In this context, faith as willing to be oneself does not signify wishing to be the self in misfortune or the self who has handled misfortune badly. The notion of self-acceptance comes closer to what Anti-Climacus means. To will to be oneself, concretely, means to accept rather than disown or flee from oneself in one's weakness, both as vulnerability and as failure.

---

nature of one's agency." This is true as far as it goes, though it doesn't make explicit the judge's concern for *responsible* agency. But then she writes, with respect to *Sickness,* that "the person in despair has the wrong conception of himself as agent. . . . Despair is described as in the first instance an act, not a psychological state. . . . Despair in the most general sense will turn out to be the unwillingness to accept human agency with all of its particular conditions." Michelle Kosch, *Freedom and Reason in Kant, Schelling, and Kierkegaard* (Oxford: Clarendon, 2006), pp. 143, 154. This fits the middle third of *Sickness* quite well, but it fails to recognize the third part as the capstone of an analysis that is not merely psychological but also Christian. For Anti-Climacus is not primarily concerned about agency such that God is merely one of its "particular conditions." As a resting striving, there is a dialectical structure to faith that Kosch's legitimate but one-sided preoccupation with agency obscures.

Three brief points about despair in weakness, each of which tells us something about faith. First, despair as the unwillingness to be oneself is an expression of pride. This means that, like Silentio (*FT,* 34, 49, 73), Anti-Climacus links faith inextricably to humility (*SUD,* 61, 65).[21]

Second, despair as the unwillingness to be oneself involves a pathological form of individualism. The self erects a door, "a real door, but a carefully closed door, and behind it sits the self, so to speak, watching itself, preoccupied with or filling up time with not willing to be itself and yet being self enough to love itself. This is called inclosing reserve [*Indesluttethed*]" (*SUD,* 63; cf. 64-67).[22] Anti-Climacus calls this a form of pride, though this will be denied by the despairing self, "as if it were not because he wants to be proud of his self that he cannot bear this consciousness of weakness" (*SUD,* 65).

Kierkegaard's writings are often seen as an extreme form of individualism. But he presents an essentially relational self. To be sure, here in *Sickness* the self is related (or misrelated) to itself; but it is also essentially related (or misrelated) to God. And in *Works of Love* the self is essentially related to the neighbor, the human other.[23] The individualism that can rightly be attributed to Kierkegaard's various voices is a protest against a social ontology (theory) and a social conformism (practice) in which the individual is dissolved into some collective or other (Silentio's universal) and in the process the self ceases to be responsible for the task of becoming itself. From that standpoint it makes perfectly good sense to criticize inclosing reserve as a pathological attempt to embody an absolute individualism. It is, we might say, the aesthetic self on its way to becoming the demonic self. Faith will

21. Silentio often links this humility with courage, as if to indicate that this humility is not itself a form of weakness, as Nietzsche would suggest. Anti-Climacus also links faith to courage (*SUD,* 8-9, 43, 85, 95), but only once as "humble courage" (*SUD,* 85).

22. This concept of a practically solipsistic, spectator self plays an important role in both *Stages on Life's Way* and *The Concept of Anxiety,* where it is linked with the demonic. It is no surprise that R. D. Laing often refers to Kierkegaard in his account of the schizoid self in *The Divided Self* (Baltimore: Penguin, 1965).

23. For the suggestion that there is a social dimension in *Sickness* itself, see Stephen Crites, "*The Sickness unto Death:* A Social Interpretation," in *Foundations of Kierkegaard's Vision of Community: Religion, Ethics, and Politics in Kierkegaard,* ed. George B. Connell and C. Stephen Evans (Atlantic Highlands, NJ: Humanities, 1992), pp. 144-60; John W. Elrod, "The Social Dimension of Despair," in Perkins, ed., *International Kierkegaard Commentary,* vol. 19: *The Sickness unto Death,* pp. 107-19; and Robert L. Perkins, "Kierkegaard's Anti-Climacus in His Social and Political Environment," in *International Kierkegaard Commentary,* vol. 20: *Practice in Christianity,* ed. Robert L. Perkins (Macon, GA: Mercer University Press, 2004), pp. 275-302.

involve the essentially relational self being properly related to itself, which it can be only as properly related to God and neighbor.

Third, three times in the discussion of the despair of weakness, Anti-Climacus tells us that it can be found in the Christian in Christendom (*SUD*, 52, 56-57, 63-64). This means that faith, which has been defined ideally as the complete overcoming of despair, cannot be reduced to the outward signs by which one is recognized as a good Christian in Christendom, for that self may well be deeply in despair.[24]

Like despair in weakness, despair as defiance is another mode of willing, defined as *"In Despair to Will to Be Oneself: Defiance"* (*SUD*, 67). It involves "a rise in the consciousness of the self . . . the despair is conscious of itself as an act: it does not come from the outside as a suffering under the pressure of externalities but comes directly from the self" (*SUD*, 67). It is a willing to be oneself that is unwilling to be itself. But this is not as paradoxical as it seems. It only signifies a self that wills to be the self it chooses while refusing to accept the self it actually is and the task of becoming that self. The defiant self is conscious of itself as "an infinite self," and this is the self it wants to be,

> severing the self from any relation to a power that has established it, or severing it from the idea that there is such a power. With the help of this infinite form, the self in despair wants to be master of itself or to create itself, to make his self into the self he wants to be, to determine what he will have or not have in his concrete self . . . he does not want to put on his own self, does not want to see his given self as his task. (*SUD*, 67-68)

Anti-Climacus identifies three versions of defiant despair: the stoic self, the Promethean self, and the demonic self that is "rarely seen in the world" (*SUD*, 68-74). We might add a fourth: the Sartrean self. For in "Existentialism Is a Humanism"[25] the slogan "existence precedes essence" means that the only norms to which the self is responsible are those it chooses for itself; there is no essence prior to the individual's choices in and through which norms are given to the self. It is free to become whatever self it chooses to become, not in the sense that there are no constraints at all on this freedom, but in the sense that there are no normative constraints on this freedom.

---

24. Each of the three passages just referred to contains a satirical account of what it takes to be a "Christian" in Christendom.

25. See note 14 above.

There is nothing that I ought to become, no task given to me by what I always already am.

This is an autonomy more radical than Kant's; for not even my own reason has any right to constrain my will by prescribing any duties, obligations, or tasks. It is an atheism more radical than Nietzsche's; for his "become who you are" means "become the will to power that you always already are." This is a normative essence that precedes existence.[26]

It is not only as a source of normativity that transcends the self's own choices that defiant despair is "offended" at the idea of God. That would entail a willingness to be comforted or consoled by another when one experiences misfortune and suffering. Beyond that, it would entail hope that there could be help from the God for whom everything is possible. But that would mean

> being helped by a superior, or by the supreme one, [and] there is the humiliation of being obliged to accept any kind of help unconditionally, of becoming a nothing in the hand of the "Helper" for whom all things are possible, or the humiliation of simply having to yield to another person, of giving up being himself as long as he is seeking help. (*SUD*, 70-71)

Here, as with Silentio, faith is linked with hope in the God for whom all things are possible; and here again, faith means overcoming the pride whose most extreme form is open defiance. And once again, it means humility, this time the humility not to be humiliated by one's (normative and causal) dependence on God.

Now that we have looked, however briefly, at the two types of despair as failures to will to be oneself, we can take up a comment Anti-Climacus makes at the outset. He calls despair in weakness "feminine despair" and despair in defiance "masculine despair" (*SUD*, 49).[27] In several ways he qualifies this linkage, suggesting that he does not mean it in a fully literal sense. He says, for example, that the one form is "so to speak, feminine despair, the other masculine despair" (*SUD*, 49). He says that the one form "could be called feminine," while the other "may be called masculine" (*SUD*, 67). He explicitly states, "I am far from denying that women may have forms

26. See note 4 above. Nietzsche has not overcome metaphysics; he has only presented an alternative to Platonic and Christian metaphysics.

27. Cf. *PC*, 77, where Anti-Climacus writes, "One can be cruel in several ways. The powerful can cruelly have a person be tortured — but the weak can cruelly make it impossible for love to help him [her?]."

of masculine despair and, conversely, that men may have forms of feminine despair, but these are exceptions." Then he repeats his claim that weakness and defiance are always mixed in various proportions. "And of course the ideal is also a rarity, and only ideally is this distinction between masculine and feminine despair altogether true" (*SUD*, 49n.).

It seems clear that Anti-Climacus is working with ideal types based on all too common stereotypes. Sylvia Walsh puts it nicely. While this linkage "is drawn in terms of traditional Western stereotyped views of masculine and feminine genders that are themselves highly questionable from a modern psychological point of view, it reflects the historical situation of women in his time as well as patterns of personal and social development many men and women are still encouraged and trained to follow."[28]

Here again we find the suggestion that faith, as an ideal type that is the task of a lifetime, will require psychological as well as spiritual health. In other words, it will require a healthy relation to my gender as well as to God. Certain modes of femininity and certain modes of masculinity predispose one to despair and express themselves in despair. Faith, as the total overcoming of despair, will require a transformation in the theory and practice of gender. Since the traditional, patriarchal stereotypes are linked to despair, it will be a theological as well as a psychological task to develop healthy alternatives. Anti-Climacus does not tell us what these are, but in setting the task he tells us something important about his understanding of faith.

The third and final part of *Sickness* (à la Glenn; *SUD*, 77-131) corresponds to the third part of the definition of the self, its relation to "another" (*SUD*, 14), and of the definition of faith, "resting transparently in the power that established it," namely God (*SUD*, 14, 30, 49, 82, 131). According to Anti-Climacus's table of contents, however, it is Part Two. As divided into two rather than three parts, the structure of the text mirrors the distinction between Religiousness A and Religiousness B in *Postscript*. *Sickness* is presented as a "Christian, psychological exposition" (the title). Although there is reference to God from time to time in the first two parts (Anti-Climacus's

---

28. Sylvia Walsh, *Living Poetically: Kierkegaard's Existential Aesthetics* (University Park: Pennsylvania State University Press, 1994), p. 260. See also Walsh, "On 'Feminine' and 'Masculine' Forms of Despair," in Perkins, ed., *International Kierkegaard Commentary*, vol. 19: *The Sickness unto Death*, pp. 121-34. Without exactly calling Kierkegaard a feminist, Wanda Warren Berry finds in his reflections on forgiveness a "springboard" for feminist theology. See "Finally Forgiveness: Kierkegaard as a 'Springboard' for a Feminist Theology of Reform," in Connell and Evans, eds., *Foundations of Kierkegaard's Vision of Community*, pp. 196-217.

Part One), the analysis is more nearly psychological or phenomenological than theological. The therapist with no Christian commitments or concerns might find the descriptions of various forms of despair quite helpful, especially since, as we have seen, it is quite possible to understand "the power that has established the self" as nature or as society rather than as God.

But now, corresponding to Religiousness B, we get an explicitly theological analysis. One indication of this is that the official Part Two is entitled "Despair Is Sin" (*SUD*, 75, 77). Another indication is that the phrase "Christianly understood" or "from the Christian point of view," along with explicit appeals to Scripture, defines the context of this portion of the text (*SUD*, 77, 81, 96, 101). More specifically, a third indication is the explicit inclusion of the incarnation and the atonement (*SUD*, 85, 89, 100, 113), along with the forgiveness of sins (*SUD*, 109-15), in the analysis of despair and faith.

Not surprisingly, once again we find the suggestion that Christendom is nevertheless more a matter of despair than of faith (*SUD*, 117). One can affirm the Lutheran doctrine of *sola scriptura* (Scripture alone) and confess the doctrines of the faith as expressed in Luther's catechisms or other writings and still be in despair.

The analysis has moved from milder to more serious or more intense forms of the sickness that is despair. Conscious despair as the unwillingness to become oneself is a more intense form than mindlessly allowing the polar elements of the self to be out of proper balance. Within that second degree of despair, defiance is a more intense form than weakness. And now we read,

> Sin is *before God, or with the conception of God, in despair not to will to be oneself, or in despair to will to be oneself*. Thus sin is intensified weakness or intensified defiance: sin is the intensification of despair. The emphasis is on *before God*, or with a conception of God; it is the conception of God that makes sin dialectically, ethically, and religiously what lawyers call "aggravated" despair. (*SUD*, 77)

These three sentences constitute the "topic sentence" for the entire essay that is Part Two. It is developed in five paragraphs that I shall call (a) through (e).

(a) That the "theological self" exists "directly before God" means that God, as the power that has established the self, is not just a causal part of the self's emergence but a normative part of the self's existence. Before God one becomes a human self whose criterion is God. A cattleman who (if this were possible) is a self directly before his cattle is a very low self, and similarly, a master who is a self directly before his slaves is actually no self — for in both cases a criterion is lacking.

Kierkegaard would have loved the Garfield cartoon I keep in my copy of *Sickness.* Jon asks Garfield, "I am not pathetic! . . . Am I?" To which Garfield replies, "Jon, you're asking a cat's opinion."

Anti-Climacus immediately continues, "The child who previously has had only his parents as a criterion becomes a self as an adult by getting the state as a criterion, but what an infinite accent falls on the self by having God as the criterion!" (*SUD,* 79). The "infinite accent" that arises when the self moves beyond society (parents, the state) to God as the criterion means that the teaching about sin, "a teaching that unconditionally splits up 'the crowd,' confirms the qualitative difference between God and man" (*SUD,* 121; cf. 99, 117, 122, 127).[29] We recall that in *Fragments* Climacus writes, "But if the god is to be absolutely different from a human being, this can have its basis not in that which man owes to the god (for to that extent they are akin) but in that which he owes to himself or in that which he committed. What, then, is the difference? Indeed, what else but sin" (*PF,* 46-47).

(b) The sin that is in question here is not the breaking of one or another of the commandments but the more basic posture or fundamental project out of which such actions arise: despair as the unwillingness to be oneself before God in some mixture of weakness and defiance. Accordingly, Anti-Climacus speaks of sin rather than of sins. "The state of sin is a worse sin than the particular sins; it is the sin" (*SUD,* 106; cf. 81-82). If my besetting sins have been cheating on my wife and on my income tax, and if I have cleaned up my act in both respects, I am no less a sinner insofar as I still refuse to take on the task of becoming the self I am before God. The issue is qualitative, not quantitative.[30]

(c) To speak of refusing is appropriate here. Because despair is a mode of willing that is unwilling to be itself before God, it can be described as

29. These passages are a primary source for Karl Barth's early emphasis on the "infinite, qualitative difference" between God and the human person. See chapter 7, note 27, above, and *PC,* 28, 63, 128, 131, where Anti-Climacus returns to this theme.

30. This echoes Climacus's analysis of guilt in Religiousness A. When guilt is merely the memory of particular actions rather than the recollection of a basic condition, it is merely quantitative and not the total, essential guilt that partially defines Religiousness A. See the discussion in chapter 11 above.

"disobedience," "defiance," and "self-will" (*SUD*, 80-82, 90, 93). To emphasize this, Anti-Climacus devotes an entire section to refuting the Socratic
definition of sin as ignorance (*SUD*, 87-96) and follows this up with a section entitled "Sin Is Not a Negation but a Position" (*SUD*, 96-100). Orthodox theology has gotten it right when it has "rejected as pantheistic any
definition of sin that made it out to be something merely negative — weakness, sensuousness, finitude, ignorance, etc." (*SUD*, 96).[31]

(d) In keeping with his earlier analyses of despair, Anti-Climacus finds
the root of despair in sin as pride (*SUD*, 111-12). Correspondingly, faith will
have to be a matter of "humble courage" (*SUD*, 85-86). To speak of sin as
disobedience is to speak the language of deontological ethics, the language
of duty and obligation. To speak of sin as pride and of faith as humble courage is to speak the language of virtue ethics. Kierkegaard moves easily back
and forth between these two approaches to the moral and religious life.[32]

(e) We have seen above that despair is the pride that finds it humiliating
to need to be "helped by a superior, or by the supreme one" or to be "obliged
to accept any kind of help unconditionally" (*SUD*, 71). Insofar as one is a
sinner, that help would have to be forgiveness, and insofar as faith is the
only full overcoming of despair, it would have to be divine forgiveness. So
we come to what functions as the eleventh commandment in *Sickness*, or
rather the first, the *telos* toward which the analysis of sin has been headed,
"Thou shalt believe in the forgiveness of sins" (*SUD*, 115). It is clear that
in this context "believe" does not signify a mere theological affirmation. It
involves a double willingness to be oneself: the humble courage to accept
oneself as a sinner and to accept the help that comes in the form of God's
forgiveness.

In stressing that faith is obedience to an imperative and as such is an act
of willing, Anti-Climacus echoes Climacus's emphasis on faith as a striving. So why does Anti-Climacus describe faith as "rest[ing] transparently

---

31. Cf. *SUD*, 82, where "sin is not the turbulence of flesh and blood but is the spirit's
consent to it." Judge William assures his young aesthetic friend that "the Christian God is
spirit and Christianity is spirit, and there is discord between the flesh [*Kjød*] and the spirit
[*Aand*], but the flesh is not the sensuous [*sandselig*] — it is the selfish" (*EO* 2:49; cf. 91). The
non-identity of the sinful and the sensuous is a recurring theme in *The Concept of Anxiety*
(*CA*, 49, 58, 63, 68, 70, 73, 76, 80).

32. I say Kierkegaard rather than just Anti-Climacus because, as I read the text, the First
Series of *Works of Love* is a deontological ethics, while the Second Series is a virtue ethics.
C. Stephen Evans makes a strong argument for the union of these two perspectives in ethics
in *God and Moral Obligation* (New York: Oxford University Press, 2013).

in God" (*SUD*, 82)? We have seen that he is a dialectical thinker. There is the dialectical tension between the polar elements of the self, such as finitude and infinity, possibility and necessity. And there is a dialectical tension between weakness and defiance in the despair that always wants in some way to be rid of oneself. So we might expect there to be a dialectical tension between gift and task, resting and striving in the life of faith. We have seen that Anti-Climacus sees the self as the task of becoming itself (*SUD*, 29, 35, 68). So he is not abandoning the emphasis on striving. At the same time, there is a resting in faith insofar as the believing soul accepts both the fact of being a sinner and the gift of divine forgiveness. To the degree that pride finds such acceptance humiliating, the journey to faith is a striving; and to the degree that humble courage prevails over that pride, it is a resting.

I like to think of it by analogy with swimming. Swimming is a striving; it takes effort to get from here to there in the water, or even just to stay afloat. But unless it is also a resting, a letting go and letting the water hold one up, it doesn't happen. I remember trying to learn to swim as a boy. I thought I had to use my arms and legs to stay effectively on top of the water. Naturally, I made no progress until I learned to trust that the water would hold me up and, with that support, to move about.

If this analogy captures something of the dialectic of striving and resting in Anti-Climacus's account of faith, it puts him in close contact with Luther's famous formula: *simul justus et peccator*. The believing soul is simultaneously justified, rightly related to God as forgiven, and a sinner, still in need of conversion and transformation. Forgiveness is a gift in which one can rest, free of fear, anxiety, and despair; but it does not eradicate the sin that calls for a lifelong striving in grateful obedience.[33]

So the formula for faith as the overcoming of despair is this: "in relating itself to itself and in willing to be itself, the self rests transparently in the power that established it," namely God (*SUD*, 131). Finally, then, what are we to make of this transparency? Surely it is not the self-consciousness of transcendental philosophy as developed by the likes of Descartes, Kant, and Husserl, for it is not in the service of modern philosophy's self-imposed requirement of certain, objective knowledge.

With that hypothesis as a clue, we might find some help in *Works of Love* to compensate for the reticence of Anti-Climacus to tell us what he means by transparency. Kierkegaard there speaks of the thinking that is

---

33. Cf. the title of M. Jamie Ferreira's commentary on *Works of Love*, namely *Love's Grateful Striving* (New York: Oxford University Press, 2001).

directed toward an external object of some sort. By contrast, "it is something else to be so turned in thought that continually, every moment, one is conscious, conscious of one's own state during the thinking or of what is happening in oneself during the thinking. But only the latter is essential thinking — it is, namely, transparency." In the former case "a thinker explains something else by his thinking and, behold, he does not understand himself . . . therefore all his thinking, however penetrating it seems, is still basically superficial. . . . At the bottom of all the clarity there lies an unclarity, but true clarity can be only in transparency." By contrast, when "one does not have an external object, then one has an inward direction in self-deepening, then he must make a discovery concerning his own inner state, and this discovery is first very humbling" (*WL,* 361).[34] To put it in the language of Climacus, transparency is the self-understanding that is made possible by the switch from objectivity to subjectivity.

Paul Cruysberghs makes the illuminating suggestion that transparency is the opposite of inclosing reserve.[35] Just as inclosing reserve is the cutting off of the self from others, both human *(Works of Love)* and divine *(Sickness unto Death),* so transparency is an essential openness to the other, an awareness of oneself as essentially related to others so that the health of the self depends on healthy relations with God and neighbor. To emphasize the difference between this transparency and that of the transcendental project, Cruysberghs adds, "Being transparent to God is identical with purity of heart, with willing just one thing, the good. But, taking into consideration that we are double-minded, transparency before God means as well to understand ourselves in our unclarity. Transparency indeed is a question of self-knowledge, which includes knowing that we are unclear about ourselves."[36]

As willing to be oneself before God, faith includes the understanding of ourselves as in need of help and the willing acceptance of the help offered to us by God. That leads us to the second book by Anti-Climacus, *Practice in Christianity.*

---

34. See Jamie Ferreira's "Love's Transparency," ch. 16 of *Love's Grateful Striving.*

35. Paul Cruysberghs, "Transparency to Oneself and to God," in the *Festschrift* for Niels Jørgen Cappelørn, *At være sig self nærværende,* ed. Joakim Garff, Ettore Rocca, and Pia Søltoft (Copenhagen: Kristeligt Dagblads Forlag, 2010), p. 127.

36. Cruysberghs, "Transparency," p. 139.

CHAPTER 13

Faith as Contemporaneity
with Christ — Without Offense

Practice in Christianity is the second work by Anti-Climacus. Its three parts take the form of reflections on three biblical texts. The first part takes its title from Matthew 11:28, "Come Here, All You Who Labor and Are Burdened, and I Will Give You Rest." It bears the subtitle, "For Awakening and Inward Deepening" (*PC*, 5). Anti-Climacus calls these words of Jesus "the invitation" (*PC*, 56-57).[1] This picks up from *Sickness unto Death* the theme of faith as resting, but only to put it immediately in dialectical tension with striving. The editor, Kierkegaard himself, tells us that in this book "the requirement for being a Christian is forced up by the pseudonymous author to a supreme ideality. . . . From the Christian point of view, there ought to be no scaling down of the requirement nor suppression of it." It must be said "as spoken to me alone — so that I might learn . . . to resort to *grace*" (*PC*, 7). The requirement must be intensified to emphasize that faith is an always unfinished task. But the point is not to reduce faith to striving; it is rather to locate that striving in the place of rest, namely grace.[2]

This opening dialectic reappears at the end of the first part (*PC*, 5-68), providing bookends or a front and back cover for the analysis in between. The moral of the story is that the individual must "accept the grace that is offered to every imperfect person," not in the language of Law, "as if it were the individual himself who by his own power is to hold to Christ," but in

---

1. In Handel's *Messiah* the invitation is preceded, in a single aria, by the words of Isaiah 40:11: "He shall feed His flock like a shepherd, and He shall gather the lambs with His arm, and carry them in His bosom, and gently lead those that are with young."

2. This is the very Lutheran dialectic of Law and Gospel.

the language of love, "that it is Christ who holds on to him." But just to this end the individual "shall humble himself under the requirements of ideality . . . in their entire infinitude." They constitute a "horror" into which "only the consciousness of sin can force one." But "at that very same moment the essentially Christian transforms itself into and is sheer lenience, grace, love, mercy" (*PC*, 67).

This dialectic of striving and rest, of sin and grace is why Christianity is betrayed when it is reduced to "a showpiece of gentle comfort" (*PC*, 62) and why Christ is regularly depicted as "the sign of offense and the object of faith" (*PC*, 9, 23-24, 35, 39). It is interesting that Anti-Climacus says "and" here rather than "or." Just as in *Sickness* faith is, ideally speaking, the total elimination of despair but in actuality the always unfinished task of such a victory, so here faith is, ideally speaking, the total triumph over offense but in actuality the always unfinished task of overcoming offense.

Anti-Climacus begins his meditation on his chosen text with a lyrical outburst whose key word, regularly repeated, is "Amazing!" (*PC*, 12-22). We know that

> ordinarily it is the case that the person who is able to help must be searched for, and once he is found it may be hard to gain access to him, and when one has gained access one perhaps must still plead with him for a long time, and when one has pleaded with him for a long time, he perhaps at long last lets himself be prevailed upon — that is, he sets a high price on himself. (*PC*, 11-12)

What is amazing here is that the helper goes in search of those who need help, pleading, as it were, "Now remain with me, for to remain with me is rest. The helper is the help. Amazing!" (*PC*, 12-15).

Before we get too carried away with this triumphal march in D major, sometimes seen as the key of glory and of gold, Anti-Climacus modulates to B minor, a key of sadness and suffering. The shift is signified by two words, "The Halt" (*PC*, 23). The text for the second part of Anti-Climacus's text will be Matthew 11:6, "blessed is he who is not offended at me" (*PC*, 71). So a more detailed analysis is forthcoming. But already here in the first part the barrier between the helper and those who need help is the possibility of being offended at the inviter and his invitation.[3] "The possibility of offense

---

3. The concept of offense plays an important role in *Sickness*. See especially *SUD*, 83-87 and 125-31. But it is even more central in *Practice*. It is also crucial for Climacus. See especially

is the crossroad. . . . From the possibility of offense, one turns either to offense or to faith, but one never comes to faith except from the possibility of offense" (PC, 81). Faith occurs just to the degree that offense is the road not taken.

Anti-Climacus has a lot to say about the possibility of offense; but offense is only possible, not necessary. The beauty of the invitation need not disappear. To see only the command and not also the promise, to see only the striving and not also the resting, to see only sin as the absolute difference and not also the forgiveness of sin is to have "a perception that only sees half the face, as it were, of one of modern theology and philosophy's most insightful exponents of the *triumph of faith over despair* [in *SUD* and *over offense* in *PF, SUD,* and *PC*]." Kierkegaard is "'the great and melancholy Dane in whom Hamlet was mastered by Christ.' Unfortunately . . . the darker aspect has prevailed and the second part of Forsyth's 'dialectic,' which redeems Kierkegaard from the melancholy of the first, fades, unheeded, into obscurity."[4]

The first reason for this is that Jesus speaks his invitation not from glory "at the Father's right hand" but from abasement. "From glory he has not spoken a word. So, then, it is Jesus Christ in his abasement who has spoken these words [of invitation] . . . the Jesus Christ who abased himself and took the form of a servant."[5] To be sure, Jesus has said that he would come again in glory, "but this has not happened as yet. . . . Is he, then, not in glory now? Yes, of course, this the Christian *believes.* But it was in the condition of abasement that he spoke those words" (PC, 24).

> So [it is] the lowly, destitute man with twelve poor disciples from the commonest class of people, for a long time an object of curiosity but later in the company only of sinners, tax collectors, lepers, and madmen,

chapter 8 above. For a helpful analysis of offense in both texts by Anti-Climacus, see Niels Jørgen Cappelørn, "The Movements of Offense Toward, Away From, and Within Faith: 'Blessed is he who is not offended at me,'" in *International Kierkegaard Commentary,* vol. 20: *Practice in Christianity,* ed. Robert L. Perkins (Macon, GA: Mercer University Press, 2004), pp. 95-124.

4. Simon D. Podmore, *Kierkegaard and the Self Before God: Anatomy of the Abyss* (Bloomington: Indiana University Press, 2011), p. xi. The interior quote is from P. T. Forsyth, *The Work of Christ* (Blackwood, Australia: New Creation Publications, 1994), p. xxxii. See also note 30 below on not letting the darker side obscure the brighter.

5. Here Anti-Climacus evokes the "kenosis" hymn of Philippians 2:6-11 that describes Jesus as emptying himself of his divinity so as to take on the form of a servant. See my essay, "Kenosis and Offense: A Kierkegaardian Look at Divine Transcendence," in Perkins, ed., *International Kierkegaard Commentary,* vol. 20: *Practice in Christianity,* pp. 19-46.

because merely to let oneself be helped by him meant to risk one's honor, life, and goods, in any case exclusion from the synagogue . . . [who says], "*Now* come here all you who labor and are burdened"! (*PC,* 37)

Faith is acknowledging this one as the Helper, as the Expected One, as the God-man. But this one, who speaks from abasement, the humble form of a servant, seems a paradoxical candidate for such roles. His invitation seems to presuppose claims that don't fit easily with appearances; so we may be offended by the invitation and the claims as most of the Inviter's contemporaries eventually were. But we are "just like his contemporaries" (*PC,* 37); our decision whether to come to him for help or to turn away in offense is made in response to Jesus Christ in his abasement, not in his glory. "If the glory had been directly perceptible so that everyone could see it as a matter of course, then it is surely an untruth that Christ abased himself and took the form of a servant; it is superfluous to warn against offense, for how in all the world could anyone be offended by glory attired in glory!" (*PC,* 65).

It would be a mistake to think that when Anti-Climacus speaks of faith as a mode of contemporaneity with Christ he has something mystical in mind. It is rather an epistemic contemporaneity of which he speaks. As Climacus argued in *Fragments,* our historical distance from Jesus puts us neither at an advantage nor at a disadvantage in relation to those who lived in Jesus' time and place and witnessed his life. This is because (a) what faith affirms to have happened is not simply a historical event, but the incursion of eternity into time, of the divine into the human; and (b) for just this reason faith at any historical moment depends on being given the condition to see with the eyes of faith.[6] So here in *Practice,* the one who stands at the crossroad, choosing between faith and offense, is in the same epistemic situation as those who were eyewitness contemporaries of the Inviter and the invitation. What faith affirms about Jesus was not "directly perceptible" then, nor is it now.

One way to put the first of these two points, namely (a), is to say that what faith affirms about Jesus if it is to be Christian faith is that Jesus is something "absolute" and thus "incommensurable" with anything finite and thus relative.[7] Because he represents the bridging of the "infinite chas-

6. See chapter 7 above.

7. This is the logic not only of the incarnation but of any divine agency in history. Thus, for example, when Deutero-Isaiah speaks in Isaiah 41 of the new act of salvation that God is

mic difference between God and man," Jesus is not "a merely historical person, since as the paradox he is an extremely unhistorical person. . . . For Christ's life upon earth, the sacred history, stands alone by itself, outside history." In relation to the absolute "there is only one time, the present; for the person who is not contemporary with the absolute, it does not exist at all. And since Christ is the absolute it is easy to see that in relation to him there is only one situation, the situation of contemporaneity" (*PC*, 62-64). Of course, this does not mean that the narratives about Jesus are myths rather than history, for then there would be no paradox. It rather means that Jesus is not "a merely historical person."

The immediate corollary to this analysis is that historical distance and the historical knowledge it makes possible cannot be the sufficient ground for faith, which in that case wouldn't be faith anyway. As Climacus has put it, faith affirms an "objective uncertainty" in a "leap." Christian apologetics has often argued that historical evidence for the resurrection of Jesus (in which glory wins out over abasement), while not providing demonstrative, knock-down proof, can provide compelling support for faith — at least if one does not make question-begging assumptions that exclude any genuinely supernatural agency.[8]

Anti-Climacus turns our attention to another kind of "historical argument." It is perhaps more subtle and therefore more dangerous to faith from his perspective; it is less theoretical and therefore more easily embedded in the consciousness of Christendom without critical reflection. It is the argument from results, and it goes something like this: "Do not the results of Jesus' life prove that he is truly the Helper, the Expected One, the God-Man of the creeds? Has not Christianity, which makes these affirmations, become the overwhelming, official religion of Denmark, and, for that matter, of all of Europe?"[9]

To which Anti-Climacus responds: "*Is the Result of Christ's Life More Important Than His Life?* . . . No, by no means, just the opposite; if this

about to perform, "In vv. 12-17, the attention of [his] hearers was drawn to the divine immeasurability. In vv. 18ff. the subject is the divine incomparability." Claus Westermann, *Isaiah 40–66: A Commentary*, trans. David M. G. Stalker (Philadelphia: Westminster, 1969), p. 53.

8. Two sophisticated versions can be found in N. T. Wright, *The Resurrection of the Son of God* (Minneapolis: Fortress, 2003), and C. Stephen Evans, *The Historical Christ and the Jesus of Faith: The Incarnational Narrative as History* (Oxford: Clarendon, 1996). Lessing's argument in "On the Proof of the Spirit and of Power" (see the discussion in chapter 10 above) is against any apologetic appeal to miracles and thus, *a fortiori*, to the resurrection.

9. Perhaps post-colonial thought had not yet arrived in Golden Age Denmark.

were the case, then Christ was only a human being. . . . But that God has lived here on earth as an individual human being is infinitely extraordinary. Even if it had had no results whatever, it makes no difference; it remains just as extraordinary" (*PC*, 31). In Anti-Climacus's eyes, *"The Calamity of Christendom"* is that Christ is "neither the person he was when he lived on earth [abasement] nor the one he will be at his second coming [glory] (which must be believed),[10] but is someone about whom we have learned something in an inadmissible way from history." As a result, "we are completely secure and, in reliance on the fact that history makes it absolutely certain that he was the great one, conclude: Ergo this is the right thing" (*PC*, 35-36).[11]

Over against this complacent certainty, Anti-Climacus suggests that, "humanly speaking" (*PC*, 39, 60, 63, 78, 82), the claim that "an individual human being is God" is "madness," "insane," and "crazy" (*PC*, 62-63, 78, 82).[12] It "conflicts with all (human) reason" (*PC*, 26). Epistemic contemporaneity generates the possibility of epistemic offense. But here, as in our earlier pseudonyms, this possible offense is relative to a particular point of view whose absolute authority cannot simply be presupposed: "humanly

---

10. Anti-Climacus might have said the same thing about the resurrected Christ. As Jesus put it to Thomas, "Blessed are those who have not seen and yet have come to believe" (John 20:29). Some Eucharistic liturgies include the words

We remember his death,
We proclaim his resurrection,
We await his coming in glory.

Anti-Climacus can allow that historical knowledge can tell us a lot about Jesus' death, its nature and its causes; but he will have to insist that Jesus' resurrection and his coming in glory are matters of faith that go beyond, even against the canons of the historian's craft. For an argument to the latter conclusion see Van A. Harvey, *The Historian and the Believer: The Morality of Historical Knowledge and Christian Belief* (New York: Macmillan, 1966).

11. Cf. *PC*, 27, "But what does [the fact that Christianity has changed the shape of the world] demonstrate? At most it can demonstrate that Jesus Christ was a great man, perhaps the greatest of all. But that he was — God — no, stop." Like Climacus, Anti-Climacus seems to have read Lessing, for he calls such an attempted argument a μετάβασις εἰς ἄλλο γένος, a logical fallacy. See the discussion in chapter 10 above.

12. The madness motif runs throughout *Practice*, relative, of course, to "humanly speaking." As Sylvia Walsh puts it, offense has to do with "the incongruous qualitative makeup of Christ's being that contradicts our natural or normal understanding and expectations of what it means to be an individual being, on the one hand, and to be divine, on the other." "Standing at the Crossroads: The Invitation of Christ to a Life of Suffering," in Perkins, ed., *International Kierkegaard Commentary*, vol. 20: *Practice in Christianity*, p. 147.

speaking" or "(human) reason." Over against the various forms this hermeneutical horizon can take there is "faith's understanding" (*PC*, 78). Faith may indeed be a leap, but it is not a blind leap. It is an interpretation, a mode of understanding, and it has its own interior rationale. There is a "logic of insanity."[13]

The logic of insanity is nicely illustrated by a member of the Anti-Terrorism Task Force in a Nelson DeMille novel. After a short stay in Yemen, it feels as if "I'd stepped through the looking glass and everyone on this side was crazy, and they'd been crazy for so long that they made sense to one another, but not to anyone who just arrived from Earth."[14] To those offended by biblical faith, Earth represents the life-world that is either godless or presided over by a very tame, humanly constructed "God." But to those who get past offense to faith, it is precisely that life-world that is crazy, though it somehow makes sense to its inhabitants.

In the language of Climacus and Silentio, the issue is whether recollection has hegemony or needs to be teleologically suspended (relativized) in divine revelation.[15] In the former world, Jesus might be, as his Roman and Jewish enemies thought, a dangerous threat to peace and tranquility (not to mention their own power); or he might be a great prophet, that is, a religious leader.[16] There is room for this latter view in Islam, in Gandhi's Hinduism, and perhaps in Trungpa's Buddhism.[17] But to claim that Jesus

13. I take this wording from the earlier translation by Walter Lowrie: *Training in Christianity* (Princeton: Princeton University Press, 1944), p. 58. At *PC*, 54 in the Hongs' translation we read only "as they say in the context of madness." I think the bolder translation captures the point Anti-Climacus is making. The context of this "madness" called Christian faith is a life-world, in this case the mega-narrative that is the biblical story from Genesis to Revelation, within which the "madness" makes sense. See my essay, "Kierkegaard and the Logic of Insanity," in *Kierkegaard's Critique of Reason and Society* (Macon, GA: Mercer University Press, 1987), pp. 85-103.

14. Nelson DeMille, *The Panther* (New York: Grand Central Publishing, 2012), p. 165.

15. Luther has just such a teleological suspension in mind when he writes that it is the nature of the soul, as distinct from the spirit, "to comprehend not incomprehensible things but such things as the reason can know and understand. Indeed, reason is the light in this dwelling; and unless the spirit, which is lighted with the brighter light of faith, controls this light of reason, it cannot but be in error. For it is too feeble to deal with things divine." "The Magnificat," in *Luther's Works*, vol. 21, ed. Jaroslav Pelikan (St. Louis: Concordia, 1956), p. 363.

16. The historical account of Jesus given in N. T. Wright, *Jesus and the Victory of God* (Minneapolis: Fortress, 1996), devotes far more attention to Jesus as a prophet than to Jesus as the Son of God in either sense, though he addresses both. Perhaps Wright agrees with Kierkegaard that that is as far as the historian, as such, can go.

17. With reference to Christ chasing the money lenders out of the temple, Chögyam

is the Son of God, either in the Jewish sense of Messiah (Expected One in the diction of Anti-Climacus) or in the Christian sense of God incarnate, or both, requires taking the biblical narrative and the story it relates as a special revelation of realities within history but beyond the ken of the historian's knowledge ("human understanding"). This world is on the other side of the looking glass from the world where human understanding has hegemony. Where recollection is made absolute, Jesus becomes relative, a merely historical phenomenon, however interesting and important. From that standpoint, whose legitimacy is open to debate, it is madness (irrationality) to claim that Jesus is the Absolute that renders everything else historical (including Christendom) relative (*PC*, 62-63).

It is not just at the epistemic/metaphysical level that Jesus' divinity is at odds with "humanly understood" or "(human) reason." There is also social/political/economic tension. Jesus embodies a "*divine* compassion" that is in conflict with "*human* compassion." At the level of the latter,

> Sausage peddlers will consider that in being compassionate it is descending too far down to go to paupers in the poorhouse and express equality with them; the compassion of sausage peddlers is trapped in one consideration [*Hensyn*], consideration for the other sausage peddlers and then for saloon keepers. Thus their compassion is not totally reckless [*hensynløs*]. . . . To make oneself quite *literally one with the most wretched* (and this, this alone is *divine* compassion), this is "too much" for people, something they can shed a few emotional tears over during a quiet Sunday hour and involuntarily burst out laughing over when they see it *in actuality*. (*PC*, 59)

With reference to both the metaphysical problem and the social problem, the critique of Christendom that runs through Anti-Climacus's account is rendered most explicit in a jury trial that he stages. Following the Gospel narratives, he distinguishes two periods in Jesus' life: the first, in which he was "idolized" by the people (the *hoi polloi*) but not by the cultural elite; and the second, in which the people "turned away" from him as well (*PC*, 40-56). The trial takes place during the first period, and the ten

---

Trungpa writes, "I would not say that was aggressive action; that was truthful action, which is very beautiful. It occurred because he saw the precision of the situation without watching himself or trying to be heroic. We need action like that." *Cutting through Spiritual Materialism* (Berkeley: Shambhala, 1973), p. 182.

jurors are taken from among the best and the brightest of the Established Order. Schleiermacher had written a famous treatise entitled *On Religion: Speeches to the Cultured among Its Despisers*. In response, Anti-Climacus writes, as it were, *On Christianity: Speeches to the Cultured among Its Complacent Professors*.[18] It takes place when Jesus is "the hero of the moment . . . the sensation he creates is enormous . . . [and] the crowd is enraptured with him" (*PC*, 41). The question is whether he should be acknowledged as the Expected One.[19]

Each of the first five jurors to speak is designated only as a "sagacious and sensible person" (as distinct from "the crowd," whose piety they obviously look down on). One juror objects, "Instead of haughtily and domineeringly keeping the people from himself at the distance of profoundest servility," he makes himself "accessible to all . . . as if being the extraordinary meant to be the servant of all" (*PC*, 42). Another complains about "this sheer madness that he considers himself to be God. . . . But he is already past thirty. And he is literally a nobody" (*PC*, 43). Another wishes, "if only one could trick his wisdom out of him — without becoming his follower! . . . for I am quite capable of editing and publishing it . . . the wisdom he obviously possesses, by being entrusted to him, has been entrusted to a fool" (*PC*, 44). A fourth wonders why Jesus is willing "to be at everybody's beck and call every hour of the day, more zealous than the busiest practicing physician — and why?" If it were for money or honor or political prestige, it might be understandable. But as it is, it can only be judged "stupid" (*PC*, 45). The fifth "sagacious and sensible" person insists on staying "perfectly cool and calm" and suspending judgment indefinitely. "I do not mean about his claim to be God, for in all eternity I shall never be able to have any opinion about that; no, I mean about him as a human being. Only the outcome of his life will be able to decide whether he actually was the extraordinary" (*PC*, 46).

No doubt the most interesting verdict comes from Juror No. 6, a clergyman.

---

18. 'Professors' retains its semantic ambiguity here, signifying both university academicians and, more broadly, those who profess or confess the Christian faith, meaning virtually everyone in Denmark.

19. Here and in subsequent quotations, I alter the Hongs' translation by using uppercase E and O here because Anti-Climacus uses the term as equivalent to Christ or Messiah. It functions as a possible title and not merely as a description. Similarly, I use uppercase E and O for the Established Order to emphasize the possible relations between the Expected One and the Established Order.

The honesty is this claiming to be the Expected One and then to resemble him as little as he does — this is honest, just as when someone planning to pass counterfeit paper money makes it so crudely that anyone with any knowledge promptly can detect it. — It is true that we all look forward to an Expected One, but that it is God in person who is to come is not the expectation of any *rational person,* and every religious person shudders at the blasphemy of which this person is guilty. (*PC,* 47; emphasis added)

In other words, in order to have a "religion within the boundaries of mere reason,"[20] Jesus must be reduced to the merely human. After assuring everyone that "we are all agreed" in looking forward to an Expected One, our pious clergyman draws a procedural conclusion from his analysis.

Therefore the authentic Expected One will look entirely different, will come as the most glorious flowering and the highest unfolding of the Established Order . . . he will recognize the Established Order as the authority, will summon all the clergy to a convention, present to it his achievements, together with his credentials — and then if in balloting he has the majority he will be accepted and hailed as the extraordinary that he is: the Expected One. (*PC,* 47)

Even if Anti-Climacus does not present himself as the humorist Clima-cus professes himself to be, it is clear that Kierkegaard has not abandoned satire as a trope in philosophical theology! While chuckling, we should not miss the point, namely that this is what happens to Jesus when reason becomes the ideological mirror and legitimation of any Established Order and in that capacity the "only infallible rule for faith and practice."[21] This reconstruction of Jesus into a justification of the Established Order (but not its judge) is perhaps most obvious in "liberal" Christendom that disavows orthodoxy's claim that Jesus is God incarnate; it is perhaps less obvious, but even more insidious from the perspective of Anti-Climacus, in "conser-vative" versions of Christendom that loudly proclaim Jesus' divinity while making him the absolute, divine legitimation of the Established Order.[22]

The next juror is a philosopher, who finds it "so dreadful, or rather so

20. See the discussion of Spinoza, Kant, and Hegel in chapter 1 above.
21. The phrase comes from the ordination vows sometimes used in Presbyterian churches based on the Westminster Confession of Faith and the Westminster Shorter Cate-chism. In that context it applies to Scripture.
22. As Joan Baez used to sing, "If God is on our side, we'll start the next war."

insane, that an individual human being presumes to be God . . . such an extreme form of pure subjectivity and sheer negativity has never been seen. He has no doctrine, no system." It "betrays little philosophic training, to think that God could reveal himself at all in the form of an individual human being. The human race, the universal, the totality, is God" (*PC*, 48-49).

We come then to a "sagacious statesman," whose judgment is in terms of power. "A statesman looks only at what power a person has, and that [Jesus] at this moment is a power cannot . . . be denied. . . . He has considerable powers, but he seems to destroy them, instead of using them; he expends them, but *he* receives nothing in return" (*PC*, 49). The statesman's advice is to stay away from Jesus.

The next to last juror is a "solid citizen" who recommends "moderation." We hear that "they are all running after him. Well, who are these 'all'? Idle and unemployed people, street loafers and tramps. . . . But not many of the property owners and well-to-do and not a one of the sagacious and reputable people by whom I always set my watch." After naming several, our "solid citizen" also names a pastor who "said last evening at the club: 'That life will have a horrible ending'" (*PC*, 50-51).

Finally comes the scoffer who is admired for his wit. He finds it comical that "an individual human being just like the rest of us says that he is God. . . . Assuming that the distinctive mark of being God is . . . to look exactly like everybody else, neither more nor less: then we are all gods." Of course there is this comical contradiction: "that a human being just like the rest of us, but not as well-dressed as the average person, therefore that a poorly dressed person who most likely belongs . . . under the welfare department — that he is God" (*PC*, 51-52).

The jurors frequently refer to the claim that this individual, Jesus of Nazareth, is divine, is God incarnate. I have referred to this as the epistemic/metaphysical issue (metaphysical, for short). But they also make frequent mention of aspects of Jesus' life that I have labeled the social/political/economic issue (social, for short). We could add the objection cited earlier, contrasting Jesus' understanding of compassion with that of the sausage peddlers, to this latter category, since Anti-Climacus might easily have put it in the mouth of one of his jurors.[23] So there are two quite distinct types

---

23. It is this social dimension of the first part of *Practice* that leads Robert Perkins to speak of "A Worldly Reading of Jesus' Invitation to the Wretched." See "Kierkegaard's Anti-Climacus in His Social and Political Environment," in Perkins, ed., *International Kierkegaard Commentary*, vol. 20: *Practice in Christianity*, pp. 284-90. See also chapter 12, note 23, above.

of objection, opening the possibility of two different types of offense that must be overcome if faith is to occur. As Anti-Climacus turns to the second part of his treatise, his more systematic analysis of offense will take this difference into account.

As already noted, this second part (*PC*, 71-144) takes the form of a reflection on Matthew 11:6, "Blessed Is He Who Is Not Offended at Me" (*PC*, 71).[24] It subdivides into three sections: three preliminary theses about offense, a classification of three types of offense (incorporating the two types already distinguished), and a corollary about indirect communication.

The first thesis affirms that faith always stands in tension with the possibility of offense. It verbally evokes Silentio and his notion of faith as the always unfinished task of a lifetime. Faith "conquers the world by conquering at every moment the enemy within one's own inner being, the possibility of offense." We should not fear the world, that is, the misfortunes that belong to worldly existence, "but fear yourself, fear what can kill the faith and in that way kill Jesus Christ for you — the offense. . . . Fear and tremble, for faith is carried in a fragile earthen vessel, in the possibility of offense" (*PC*, 76). Just as belief is never completely immune to despair, so it is never completely safe from the possibility of offense. Although it comes from revelation and not from recollection, the requirement of faith is a kind of Platonic ideality that is never perfectly embodied in merely human actuality.

Second, in an important footnote, Anti-Climacus takes a swipe at "modern philosophy" and its preoccupation with doubt. Reminding us of his first work, Anti-Climacus tells us that "in modern philosophy there is a confused discussion of doubt where the discussion should have been about despair. . . . 'Despair,' however, promptly points in the right direction by placing the relation under the rubric of personality (the single individual) and the ethical." By the same token, "the practice has been to use the category 'doubt' where the discussion ought to be about 'offense' . . . the relation, the relation of personality to Christianity, is not to doubt or to believe, but to be offended or to believe." Modern philosophy should have pointed the individual to "the ethical, the religious, the existential" (*PC*, 81n.).[25]

---

24. And of seven other New Testament passages that speak of offense. The third part of *Practice* is entitled "From on High He Will Draw All to Himself" and is a meditation on John 12:32, "And I, when I am lifted up from the earth, will draw all people to myself." Though it does not add significantly to Anti-Climacus's concept of faith, it can be fruitfully read in conjunction with Climacus, in *Fragments,* on the teacher giving the condition for recognizing the truth. See chapter 7 above.

25. The most obvious example of "modern philosophy" here would be Descartes, and

The third thesis is that speculative thinking destroys Christianity by going further than faith to "'comprehend' the God-man," thereby eliminating the possibility of offense. "The God-man is not the union of God and man — such terminology is a profound optical illusion. The God-man is the unity of God and an individual human being. That the human race is or is supposed to be in kinship with God is ancient paganism; but *that* an individual human being is God is Christianity" (*PC*, 81-82).

It is clearly Hegelian thought to which Anti-Climacus refers as speculation. In his exposition of Christianity as "the revealed religion" in the *Phenomenology of Spirit*, Hegel writes, "The divine nature is the same as the human, and it is this unity that is beheld" in Christian faith. But to think of this as occurring uniquely in an individual is an immediacy that must be transcended. In such a belief "Spirit as an individual Self is not yet equally the universal Self, the Self of everyone. In other words, the shape has not yet the form of the Concept, i.e. of the universal Self." It remains in the "defective" form of picture thinking or representation *(Vorstellung)* and needs to be "advanced" to the form of the Concept *(Begriff)*. When this happens the resurrection will signify that "Spirit remains the immediate Self of actuality but as the *universal self-consciousness* of the [religious] community." When the immediacy of the individual is replaced by the mediated universality of the community, "This death is, therefore, its resurrection as Spirit."[26]

Anti-Climacus attributes this attempt to avoid the possibility of offense by turning the doctrine of the incarnation into a form of collective self-congratulation (by the Established Order) to "the entire modern age" (*PC*, 123) rather than merely to modern philosophy. Although he points us to a very explicit theoretical self-deification of the human community in speculative philosophy, he apparently thinks that the voice of the philosophers is the voice of the people, that outside the academy Christendom manages not to notice how profoundly its unspoken thoughts are spoken by speculative philosophy. The human spirit becomes the Absolute Spirit, while the God of

---

then, perhaps, Kant and Fichte, with their attempts to steer between the Scylla of dogmatism and the Charybdis of skepticism. But Hegel comes into view as well. He tells us that the road on which he will be our guide "can therefore be regarded as the pathway of *doubt* [*Zweifel*] or more precisely as the way of despair [*Verzweifeln*]." G. W. F. Hegel, *Phenomenology of Spirit*, trans. A. V. Miller (Oxford: Clarendon, 1977), p. 49. But this doubting despair is not the despair of *Sickness;* it is rather the failure to find in any horizon of understanding short of idealism's speculative system a sufficient home for absolute knowing.

26. Hegel, *Phenomenology of Spirit*, pp. 460-71. I have replaced Miller's unfortunate translation of *Begriff* as 'Notion' with 'Concept.'

the churches becomes its Most Significant Cheerleader, or perhaps its Predecessor, as in John the Baptist. As Silentio has put it, when the communal universal is the highest, "the ethical is the divine" (*FT,* 60). But for him as for Anti-Climacus, this is paganism and not biblical faith, even if it occurs in Christendom.

The central part of this second part of *Practice* distinguishes three types of offense: A, B, and C. A is about the offense "that is not related to Christ as Christ (the God-man) but to him simply as an individual human being who comes into collision with an Established Order" (*PC,* 85). With the metaphysical issue bracketed, the social issue takes center stage. To be contemporary with Jesus in his abasement is surely to encounter just such a disturber of the Established Order's complacency.

Anti-Climacus makes the same reference to Hegel's *Philosophy of Right* that Silentio cited as an expression of the absolutizing of the ethical, the laws and customs of the Established Order. When Hegel called individual conscience "'a form of evil' . . . he deified the Established Order. But the more one deifies the Established Order, the more natural is the conclusion: ergo, the one who disapproves of or rebels against this divinity, the Established Order — ergo, he must be rather close to imagining that he is God" (*PC,* 87).[27] Nothing is "more natural" to one who thinks this way than offense.

Anti-Climacus finds just such an attitude in Judaism at the time of Christ. It "became, through the scribes and Pharisees,[28] a complacent, self-deifying Established Order. . . . This commensurability and congruity are sure indications that an established order is in the process of deifying itself" (*PC,* 89). This "commensurability and congruity" are the perfect fit of inner and outer, of individual conscience and the laws and customs of one's society; in that context "custom and usage become articles of faith" (*PC,* 92). It is nicely expressed in the verdict of the clergyman cited above, for whom the Expected One "will come as the most glorious flowering and the highest unfolding of the Established Order" (*PC,* 47).

There is nothing anti-Semitic in this reference. Some passages in Nietzsche seem to be such but turn out not to be, since he immediately and gleefully reminds the (presumably "Christian") reader just who it is that purports to be the heir and fulfillment of Judaism. In the same way, Anti-Climacus's target is not ancient Judaism but contemporary Christendom.

---

27. See *FT,* 54. The passage from Hegel is in the Remark to §140 of the *Philosophy of Right.*

28. Anti-Climacus might well have added the Sadducees, who dominated the Sanhedrin.

His jurors all reside in Copenhagen, and the epitome of his critique is the slogan, "paganism in Christendom" (see *SUD*, 45-47, 56).[29]

It is in this context that Anti-Climacus gives us what we can take as the most powerful summary of the philosophy of religion offered by our three pseudonyms.[30]

> Every human being is to live in fear and trembling, and likewise no Established Order is to be exempted from fear and trembling. Fear and trembling signify that we are in the process of becoming; and every single individual, likewise the generation, is and should be aware of being in the process of becoming. And fear and trembling signify that there is a God — something every human being and every Established Order ought not to forget for a moment. (*PC*, 88)

Because the metaphysical issue has been bracketed in A, it does not represent offense "κατ᾽ ἐξοχὴν [in an eminent sense]" or "*sensu strictissimo* [in the strictest sense]" (*PC*, 82, 87). The "essential offense" (*PC*, 94, 102) is strictly Christian and involves the paradoxical claim that Jesus is God incarnate. It comes in two forms, B and C. B brings the metaphysical issue back into view. It is "the possibility of offense in relation to loftiness, that an individual human being speaks or acts as if he were God, declares himself to be God, therefore in relation to the qualification 'God' in the composition God-man" (*PC*, 94).

The passages cited in which Jesus "speaks or acts as if he were God" include accounts of miracles, promises of eternal life, and acts of forgiving sins. Unlike many subsequent apologists, Christ does not say "Ergo," as if

---

29. I have used this phrase in my interpretation of *Christian Discourses*. See "Paganism in Christendom: On Kierkegaard's Critique of Religion," in *International Kierkegaard Commentary*, vol. 17: *"Christian Discourses" and "The Crisis and a Crisis in the Life of an Actress,"* ed. Robert L. Perkins (Macon, GA: Mercer University Press, 2007), pp. 13-33.

30. One might also read it as the most succinct summary of the prophetic dimension in Kierkegaard's philosophy of religion. There is a softer, gentler side, perhaps best found in his communion discourses. See Kierkegaard, *Discourses at the Communion on Fridays*, trans. Sylvia Walsh (Bloomington: Indiana University Press, 2011). See also George Pattison's discussion of the Christian experience of being "ransomed, healed, restored, forgiven," especially in relation to the two discourses on the woman who was a sinner (Luke 7:36-50). Pattison, *Kierkegaard's Upbuilding Discourses* (New York: Routledge, 2002), pp. 205-10. The quoted phrase is from the hymn version of Psalm 103 by Henry F. Lyte, "Praise, My Soul, the King of Heaven." The discourses are the tenth and twelfth communion discourses in Walsh's translation.

he had proved that he was divine. Rather, he says, "blessed is he who is not *offended* at me." Which leads to the question, "if the delusion under which Christendom has labored these many years were indeed true, that it was in fact *directly* visible that Christ was the one he claimed to be, then why such a strange response?" (*PC*, 94-96). Anti-Climacus concludes that

> there can be no question of any demonstrating . . . there is no *direct* transition to becoming a Christian. . . . The miracle can demonstrate nothing, for if you do not believe him to be who he says he is, then you deny the miracle. The miracle can make aware - - now you are in the tension, and it depends upon what you choose, offense or faith; it is your heart that must be disclosed. (*PC*, 96-97)

Taken at face value, Shakespeare's *Henry the Fifth* is a piece of shameless, militaristic nationalism, nowhere more than in Henry's locker-room pep talk just before the battle of Agincourt. It concludes

> We few, we happy few, we band of brothers;
> For he to-day that sheds his blood with me
> Shall be my brother; be he ne'er so vile,
> This day shall gentle his condition.
> And gentlemen in England now abed
> Shall think themselves accurs'd they were not here,
> And hold their manhoods cheap while any speaks
> That fought with us upon Saint Crispin's day. (IV.iii)

But, referring to the film versions by Laurence Olivier and Kenneth Branagh, Harold Bloom isn't moved. He writes, "Both movies are lively, patriotic romps, replete with exuberant bombast, provided by Shakespeare himself, with what degree of irony we cannot quite tell but are free to surmise." After quoting the passage above, Bloom continues, "That is the King, just before the battle of Agincourt. He is very stirred; so are we; but neither we nor he believes a word he says." And who are "we"? "We" are those who read a possibly ambiguous text "which allows you to achieve your own perspective [on *Henry the Fifth*]" as highly ironical.[31] The dramatically divergent readings reveal the reader more certainly than they reveal Shakespeare.

31. Harold Bloom, *Shakespeare: The Invention of the Human* (New York: Penguin Putnam, 1998), pp. 319-21.

So it is with Jesus, as Anti-Climacus sees him. The phenomena, the data, are open to two diametrically different interpretations: offense or faith. At the crossroad, where the roads divide, what can be seen does not dictate the decision. It is not "*directly* visible that Christ was the one he claimed to be." This is the sense in which Climacus (and Silentio) refer to faith as a leap, a decision without the security and support of an adequate ground.

C signifies the possibility of "essential offense in relation to lowliness, that the one who passes himself off as God proves to be the lowly, poor, suffering, and finally powerless human being" (*PC*, 102). This brings us back to the social issue. But the possibility of offense lies not only in the discrepancy between the metaphysical loftiness and the social lowliness. There is the added, crucial fact that Jesus in his lowliness and abasement is the "paradigm" or "prototype" for the believer (*PC*, 107-9, 115; cf. 238-41).

Here we encounter what I call Religiousness C.[32] In *Concluding Unscientific Postscript* there is nothing specifically Christian about Religiousness A. Religiousness B is specifically Christian because of its affirmation of the incarnation, the claim that an individual person is God come in the flesh. There, and in *Fragments,* Jesus is the paradox to be believed. Here he is not only that but also the "paradigm" or "prototype" to be imitated by the believer. This is a central theme not only in *Practice,* but also in such texts as *Works of Love, For Self-Examination,* and *Judge for Yourselves!* Here we find what I take to be the telos of Kierkegaard's philosophy of religion, presented both pseudonymously and in his own name: a life of self-sacrificial love.

I call Religiousness C the teleological suspension of Religiousness B. Notice the "not only . . . but also" of the previous paragraph. There is no attempt to replace a "cold" and "exclusive" metaphysics with a "warm" and "inclusive" ethics. The metaphysical paradox is retained in all of its paradoxicality as a source of possible offense. But it is placed in a larger context in which it is not important for its own sake alone. Over against the speculative instincts of the Hegelians and of Lutheran scholasticism,[33] Religiousness C represents something analogous to the primacy of practical reason in Kant, though it is a primacy of the practical that rests on faith as the

32. See my "Kierkegaard's Teleological Suspension of Religiousness B," in *Foundations of Kierkegaard's Vision of Community: Religion, Ethics, and Politics in Kierkegaard,* ed. George B. Connell and C. Stephen Evans (Atlantic Highlands, NJ: Humanities, 1992), pp. 110-29, and "Kierkegaard's Religiousness C: A Defense," *International Philosophical Quarterly* 44, no. 4, issue 176 (December 2004): 535-48.

33. See chapter 2, note 7, above.

reception of divine revelation rather than on reason as recollection. It is the primacy of the pietist traditions.

In the definition of the offense of lowliness, Jesus is seen as a "poor, suffering, and finally powerless human being." Anti-Climacus chooses to focus on suffering.[34] When Jesus is the "paradigm" or "prototype," to become a follower (disciple) is to expose oneself to suffering. Anti-Climacus says two things about this suffering. First, specifically or authentically Christian suffering is voluntary. As such it needs to be sharply distinguished from the sufferings that fall under the concept of misfortune or belong to the all too normal vicissitudes of life. Second, this is not merely the inward suffering that already belongs to Religiousness A, but the outward suffering of which Jesus' life and death are the model.

This does not mean that one should seek to be a martyr.[35] "I never asserted that every Christian is a martyr, or that no one was a true Christian who did not become a martyr, even though I think that every true Christian should — and here I include myself — in order to be a true Christian, make a humble admission that he has been let off far more easily than true Christians in the strictest sense" (*PC*, 227). But martyrs do have a special rank, and it is not an accident that the *Te Deum* lists "the white-robed army of martyrs" along with "the noble fellowship of prophets" and "the glorious company of apostles."

What I have called the social issue, the conflict between faith and the tendency of every Established Order to deify itself, is a prominent part of both offense A and C. Faith as the contemporaneity with Jesus that overcomes the possibility of offense requires voluntarily expressing that conflict in one's life, both in attitude (inwardly) and in action (outwardly). If one pledges allegiance to the flag, one does so with fingers crossed, to remind oneself of a higher allegiance. What the consequences of such a posture will be is up to God. If, in Constantinian Christendom, the Christian faces

---

34. For a brilliant analysis of the development of Kierkegaard's thinking about suffering from *Postscript* to *Practice,* including the essays on joy in suffering (see chapter 11, note 22, above), see Sylvia Walsh, "Standing at the Crossroads: The Invitation of Christ to a Life of Suffering," in Perkins, ed., *International Kierkegaard Commentary,* vol. 20: *Practice in Christianity,* pp. 125-60. She writes, "Suffering constitutes the crowning mark of Christian existence in Kierkegaard's thought. It is integrally related to the determination of every aspect of becoming a Christian, whether that be acquiring a consciousness of sin, facing the possibility of offense, dying to the world, or expressing Christian love through self-denial" (p. 125).

35. For a powerful treatment of the temptation to seek martyrdom, see T. S. Eliot, *Murder in the Cathedral.*

little or no significant opposition, that may well be not so much because Christianity has triumphed as because it has been abolished through its assimilation into the Established Order.

Finally, Anti-Climacus returns to a by now familiar theme. This kind of faith is "madness," but not intrinsically. It is madness relative to the "natural man," "what is secular," and "the understanding" that is the criterion for the natural man and the secular (*PC*, 111-17). Once again our author is a sociologist of knowledge, reminding us of the deep intertwining of the social and the epistemic. The implicit flip side of Kierkegaard's critique of the church, its pastors, and its bishops is a positive ecclesiology: the church should be the community that provides the believer with "the logic of insanity."[36] Theology and preaching should be the ideology of faith, the mirror and legitimation of authentic faith. Just to the degree that they fall prey to the "natural man," "the secular," and the understanding that is their ideology, the church fails to be the church.

The third and final section of this second part of *Practice* gives us Anti-Climacus's version of what is meant by indirect communication. In chapter 10 we saw that for Climacus it was a corollary of the notion that faith is appropriation and not merely assent. Direct communication appeals only to the intellect and aims at getting the listener or reader to understand certain statements and to assent to their truth. But the discourse of faith seeks to go beyond this in an appeal to the will and the affections. It seeks to evoke personal appropriation that brings the individual's life into conformity with that truth. In terms of the classical trivium, direct communication relies on logic and grammar, while indirect communication is a matter of rhetoric. Short of brainwashing, direct communication falls short of the goal of faith; or perhaps we should say that brainwashing is a pathetic alternative to the difficult task of indirectly communicating the essential truth of ethics and religion, of evoking conversion of the mind and the heart.

For Anti-Climacus the notion of indirect communication is perhaps more narrowly epistemic. In the first place, Jesus is a sign. This means that communication is not a matter of intuition (direct seeing) but rather of interpretation (active construal). In the language of Anti-Climacus it is a matter of reflection (this in relation to that) rather than of immediacy (this in relation only to itself). "The striking thing is the immediate, but my regarding it as a sign (which is a reflection, something I in a certain sense take from myself) indeed expresses that I think that it is supposed to mean

36. See note 13 above.

something . . . something different from what it immediately is." The point of communicating something as a sign "lies in making the recipient self-active" (*PC*, 124-25). That is why we can and must speak of interpretation. There is what is given and also what is taken, where the latter is not reducible to the former, as in the famous duck-rabbit gestalt figure that Wittgenstein reproduces.[37]

N.B. In neither Climacus's version nor Anti-Climacus's does indirect communication undermine the possibility that discourse seeks to present a specific claim to the mind (affirmation) and appeal to the heart (appropriation).

But Jesus is not merely a sign; he is a *"sign of contradiction,"* a paradoxical sign that contradicts normal expectations. Anti-Climacus gives us three examples.

The first is a text that combines jest with earnestness (such as Climacus gives us in *Postscript*). Shall we interpret it as nothing more than playful frivolity or perhaps playful skepticism? Or shall we construe it as having a serious purpose? And if the latter, shall we see that purpose as persuading us that this is the best philosophy of religion we can hope to find? Or shall we see that purpose as awakening and inviting us to the difficult task of becoming a Christian? All these readings are easy enough to find, which suggests that the text is inherently ambiguous, requiring active interpretation.

The second example comes from the notion that the (alleged) God-man appears in the form of a servant. This means "not to be in the character of what one essentially is" (*PC*, 132). This incognito calls for interpretation. We can construe Jesus to be a great religious teacher; or a tragic, misguided religious enthusiast; or an imposter; or God incarnate. Once again, the actuality of these interpretations suggests that as a sign he is inherently ambiguous (*PC*, 127-31).

The third example is once again a discourse, one that brings "attack and defense into a unity in such a way that no one can directly say whether one is attacking or defending. . . . One presents faith in the eminent sense and represents it in such a way that the most orthodox sees it as a defense of the faith and the atheist sees it as an attack" (*PC*, 133). Perhaps Anti-Climacus is thinking of Silentio and Climacus. Is their insistence that biblical faith goes against reason a defense or an attack?

37. Ludwig Wittgenstein, *Philosophical Investigations,* trans. G. E. M. Anscombe (Oxford: Basil Blackwell, 1958), p. 194. "But we can also *see* the illustration now as one thing now as another. — So we interpret it, and *see* it as we *interpret* it" (p. 193).

What Anti-Climacus says about the first of these examples fits all three. They all involve putting opposites "together in such a way that the composite is a dialectical knot. . . . If anyone wants to have anything to do with this kind of communication, he will have to untie the knot himself" (*PC*, 133). Indirect communication is unlike brainwashing or indoctrination. It recognizes the essential role of listeners or readers as active interpreters and respects their freedom enough to leave it to them whether, in the case of Jesus as a sign of contradiction, to be offended or to embark on the path of faith.

Doubtless there is more about the nature of faith in the writings of these three pseudonyms, to say nothing of the rest of the massive Kierkegaardian corpus. I have presented what I take to be the major points in three authors and five of the most widely read and discussed Kierkegaardian texts. In thirteen chapters I have presented a dozen accounts of faith. If I call them definitions it is not because I think any one of them — or all of them taken together, for that matter — gives us *the* definition of faith. I think of them as aspects or facets, each of which provides us with a distinctive perspective on the nature of faith, sometimes generically religious, sometimes generically biblical, often specifically Christian.[38]

There are three claims about these facets, taken together, that are at least implicit in the preceding chapters. In conclusion I want to make them explicit. In doing so I pose the same question to my readers in relation to each of the three claims: Do you see it this way too, and if not, why not?

The first claim is that these facets or *Abschattungen*[39] fit together coherently. This is not to say that they form a system insofar as that connotes completeness and totality. The pseudonyms' satires on the system give us an authorship of openness rather than closure, and this ineluctable incompleteness is an essential element in the objective uncertainty that is at the heart of Climacus's analysis of faith. But this negative point is fully compatible with the positive point which I am here affirming, namely that the facets

38. Phenomenologists may want to think of them in Husserlian terms as *Abschattungen* (adumbrations). The analogy is with perceptual objects, which "are given *abschattungsweise,* which means that they are never given completely. *More* is always appresented than can be grasped in any actual and present presentation. That is to say, in good English, that a perceptual object is both given and not given in the same perceptual presentation. It is given as having many aspects that are not now presented but which *could* be." James M. Edie, *Edmund Husserl's Phenomenology: A Critical Commentary* (Bloomington: Indiana University Press, 1987), pp. 115-16.

39. See previous note.

or *Abschattungen,* rather than canceling each other, supplement and complement one another. What emerges is something analogous to Gadamer's fusion of horizons in which different perspectives blend together, without losing their difference, to present a fuller, richer, multidimensional picture of the subject matter *(Sache)* under discussion.

Second, it seems to me that the ground of this coherence is the theistic conception of God that is everywhere presupposed, whether it be the God of Abraham or the God who becomes incarnate in Jesus of Nazareth. By 'theism' I do not mean what Heidegger calls onto-theology, a theoretical, metaphysical account in terms of abstract, impersonal categories such as First Cause.[40] I use the term rather to signify a biblical conception of God as personal, and I take it that in order to be personal God must be both a purposive agent (not merely a cause) and a speaker, one who can and does make promises to be trusted and commands to be obeyed. While the term 'theism' sometimes signifies a variety of onto-theological theories, my usage of it to signify biblical conceptions of a personal God is justified by the fact that it serves to distinguish such views from pantheism. For in the variety of pantheisms, such as those of Spinoza and Hegel, "God" is neither an agent nor a speaker.

Third, the coherence of the facets is best seen, I think, by viewing their accounts of faith as signifying aspects of what it means to live "before God" — this God, who is not merely the maker of heaven and earth, and thus the First Cause, but also the personal, covenantal God who enters into transcausal relations with humans by making promises and giving commands and who, as such an Other, always exceeds our grasp.

Ah, but a man's reach should exceed his grasp,
Or what's a heaven for?[41]

There is a simple reason why coherence theories of truth do not have the prima facie plausibility of correspondence theories. There is the lurking worry that a theory might be coherent without fitting very well with what is objectively real. In our case there is a double hermeneutical question of fit or faithfulness. How well does the interpretation I have given fit the texts under consideration? How faithful is it to the texts whose meaning it pur-

40. See my account in the title essay of *Overcoming Ontotheology: Toward a Postmodern Christian Faith* (New York: Fordham University Press, 2001).
41. Robert Browning in "Andrea Del Sarto," an eloquent statement of temporal, earthly finitude.

ports to give? It is obvious that by presenting my interpretations to my readers I am making the claim that they fit well, that they are faithful to a high degree (if somewhat less than that than which a more faithful interpretation cannot be conceived). This is the task of this book.

But there is a further question. The interpretation of texts is rarely, if ever, an end in itself. We interpret these texts (and every reading is an interpretation) because we want to understand what they are about, in this case faith (among other things). This is what Ricoeur calls the hermeneutical detour. Rather than waging a direct assault on "the things themselves," the hermeneutical approach takes "the detour through the contingency of cultures, through an incurably equivocal language, and through the conflict of interpretations."[42] It takes "the long detour of the signs of humanity deposited in cultural works" and "the detour of understanding the cultural signs in which the self documents and forms itself . . . [so that] reflection is nothing without the mediation of signs and works."[43] These all too contingent, all too particular cultural signs and works are, in the first instance, texts. Thus we interpret *Fear and Trembling*, for example, because we want to understand Abraham, and faith, and reason, and their relation to each other.

So the second question of fit and faithfulness arises. How well do the accounts that emerge in my interpretation of these texts fit what the texts are about? Are these good accounts of the nature of faith and reason and their relation to each other? Are they faithful to the realities of God and the human self "before God"? The atheist and the pantheist will doubtless find more misfit than fit, though a Marxian atheist might see a somewhat kindred spirit insofar as these texts include a sustained ideology critique. For the atheist and the pantheist anything of value will be available only after the texts have been in some substantive way "demythologized," that is, purged of their theism. Theists are more likely to respond more positively; but just to the degree that their theism has an onto-theological bent, and just to the degree that it belongs to some version of what Kierkegaard calls "Christendom," a self-absolutizing established order, these readers will have serious reservations about the fit and faithfulness to God and the self, to faith and reason. Even if we get Kierkegaard right, we won't have a very good philosophy of religion.

42. Paul Ricoeur, *Freud and Philosophy,* trans. Denis Savage (New Haven: Yale University Press, 1970), p. 42.

43. Paul Ricoeur, *Hermeneutics and the Human Sciences,* ed. and trans. John B. Thompson (New York: Cambridge University Press, 1981), pp. 143, 158-59.

When I write about such thinkers as Hegel, Levinas, and Derrida, I do so ambivalently. I find important insights in their work that I want to appropriate, and have appropriated, into my own thinking. But at the same time, there are deep and fundamental differences between their overall worldviews and my own. So my exegesis of their texts expresses a highly qualified agreement with the claims found in their texts. I do not write about Kierkegaard with the same ambivalence and qualification. This is not to say that I swallow him hook, line, and sinker without any disagreement at all. It is rather to say that I find in Kierkegaard a kindred spirit to a far greater degree than in any of the other thinkers to which I devote my scholarly attention. In other words, I find the textual interpretations I offer here to fit with a high degree of faithfulness not only the texts — it goes without saying that I think this — but also the various subject matters *(Sachen)* of those texts: God and the self, faith and reason.

Of course, that is a confession and not an argument. Like Kierkegaard, I am without authority. But I am not without hope. So I hope not only that these reflections will find readers but also that the readers will hear in them the voice of an other, or even the voice of an Other, calling them to consider not only whether these readings of Kierkegaard's texts fit them faithfully, but also whether their ontology, their epistemology, and their ethics[44] faithfully fit the realities within which we become whoever we are.

---

44. For me ethics is Janus faced, opening out into politics on the one hand and into spirituality on the other.

Index of Names and Subjects

Index of Scripture References